DISCARDED

What Is
Non-Fiction Cinema?

Thinking Through Cinema

Thomas E. Wartenberg, Series Editor

What Is Non-Fiction Cinema? On the Very Idea of Motion Picture Communication, Trevor Ponech

FORTHCOMING

Unlikely Couples: Movie Romance As Social Criticism,
Thomas E. Wartenberg

Visions of Virtue in Popular Film,
Joseph Kupfer

The Naked and the Undead: Feminism, Philosophy, and the Appeal of Horror, Cynthia Freeland

Reel Racism: Confronting Hollywood's Construction of Afro-American Culture, Vincent Rocchio

What Is Non-Fiction Cinema?

On the Very Idea of Motion Picture Communication

Trevor Ponech

Westview Press
A Member of the Perseus Books Group

Thinking Through Cinema

All rights reserved. Printed in the United States of America. No part of this publication may be reproduced or transmitted in any form or by any means, electronic or mechanical, including photocopy, recording, or any information storage and retrieval system, without permission in writing from the publisher.

Copyright © 1999 by Westview Press, A Member of the Perseus Books Group

Published in 1999 in the United States of America by Westview Press, 5500 Central Avenue, Boulder, Colorado 80301-2877, and in the United Kingdom by Westview Press, 12 Hid's Copse Road, Cumnor Hill, Oxford OX2 9JJ

Library of Congress Cataloging-in-Publication Data
Ponech, Trevor.
  What is non-fiction cinema? : on the very idea of motion picture communication / Trevor Ponech.
    p. cm.
  Includes bibliographical references and index.
  ISBN 0-8133-6703-4
  1. Documentary films—History and criticism. I. Title.
PN1995.9.D6P683   1999
070.1'8—dc21   98-55484
                                                                                                CIP

The paper used in this publication meets the requirements of the American National Standard for Permanence of Paper for Printed Library Materials Z39.48-1984.

10   9   8   7   6   5   4   3   2   1

Contents

Acknowledgments — vii

Introduction — 1
Notes, 7

1 What Is Non-Fiction Cinema? — 8
The Meaning of Non-Fiction, 8
Language, Cinema, and Assertion, 20
Essentialism in Context, 23
Skepticism About Intentions, 34
Notes, 36

2 Representation and Depiction — 40
Representational Systems, 42
Cinematic Representation, 51
Misrepresentation, 63
Notes, 69

3 What About Reality? — 73
In Search of Sasquatch, 74
Situations and Interpretations, 80
Notes, 95

4 Plans for Non-Fiction — 98
Intention, 99
Moderate Intentionalism, 104
Notes, 114

5	**Planning for Content**	116

Explaining Content with Intentions, 116
Nanook of the North, 124
Notes, 140

6	**Planning for Force**	143

Fiction, 144
Fixed Boundaries, Mixed Intentions, 150
Complex Illocutionary Plans, 158
Notes, 171

7	**Perceptual Access to Cinematic Meaning**	175

Visual Perception, 176
Perceptual Access to Cinematic Meaning, 180
Projective Illusion, 186
Imagined Seeing, 191
Transparency, 197
The Representation Thesis, 201
Notes, 206

8	**Aspects of Interpretation**	213

First Principles of Documentary Interpretation, 217
Illocutionary Uptake, 227
Truth in Non-Fiction, 233
Notes, 242

9	**The Truth of Non-Fiction**	246

Truth As Correspondence, 247
Non-Fiction Cinema and Justification, 251
Symbolic Meaning, Narrative, and Epistemic Access, 260
Notes, 276

Works Cited	281
Index	293

Acknowledgments

It was Peter Ohlin who introduced me to non-fiction cinema as both an art form and a vital area of scholarship; for all his guidance, insight, and support my thanks to Peter are long overdue. The chairman of McGill University's Department of English, Gary Wihl, also deserves acknowledgment for his commitment to my development as a scholar and colleague. I am especially grateful to my mentor and friend, Paisley Livingston. I cannot even imagine an intellectual life without this generous tutelary soul, who has for fifteen years shared with me his unique vision of philosophy's relation to humanistic inquiry. In recent years, Mette Hjort has been another special source of inspiration and support. At a turning point, this book and my prospects were much improved because she gave me a little writing table, and a real home, on Hollændervej. I am indebted to Thomas E. Wartenberg, whose "Thinking Through Cinema" series could not be a more appropriately named venue for my study. I would also like to thank the editors at Westview Press, including David Toole, whose intelligent copyediting made this book better. And thanks again to Paisley, for the unintended push to broaden the project's scope by asking me the musical question: "Is that all there is?"

The person who taught me that there is much more, that there is perceptible beauty in the world and irreducible love, and wished so hard for us to share these, died as I was writing this book. I finished the work as best I could—knowing there would be no evidence of love or beauty in it unless it bore her name. That is why I dedicate *What is Non-Fiction Cinema?* to Julie Rolston.

Trevor Ponech

Introduction

Why do some motion pictures count as **non**-fictions? A few moments' reflection will, I think, lead most of us to realize that we are often ready, willing, and able to say that this or that film, television program, cinematic artwork, and so on isn't fiction, or is a documentary.[1] Audiences, as well as filmmakers and the people who fund, market, and exhibit movies, do not sound to one another as if they are talking gibberish when they assert that a given work is different from others because it is non-fictional. Granted, for what now seems like a long time, it has been fashionable to demur at the suggestion that the line between fiction and non-fiction can ultimately be anything but blurry. Indeed, the term "non-fiction" seems to whisper that representation is pre-eminently fictional—that fiction is always already there and must with effort be negated. Many scholars and cineastes think that the pull of fantasy and illusion on the cinema is too strong for any of its genres to exist beyond fiction's rings. Hence there are those who doubt that an exact fiction/non-fiction distinction, if any at all, can be traced. Such people undertake exercises in filmmaking, interpretation, and critique geared toward revealing, or instating, the two modes' fusion. Academic cinema scholars, especially, have put a lot of energy into getting us to appreciate how incomplete the split is. Yet those who would collapse a distinction, or set out to show the underlying undifferentiation, must first be able to hold in mind a working concept of that distinction. Before one discounts the existence of something that is uniquely and finally non-fiction, one must think through the distinction in the first place.

The present study is an attempt to define non-fiction's special difference, if only to give other scholars a more substantial, thickly etched boundary to try to erase. To date, there has been a lot of confusion about the terms in which to define non-fiction, which has lead to faulty constructions as well as "deconstructions" of the genre. I hope my own formulation is at once precise and commonsensical. In any case, it is doubly set off from other research into the topic: first, by its argument that authorial intentions and actions fully determine whether a cinematic representation will be a non-fictional work; and second, by its position that the fiction/non-fiction conceptual fission is unequivocal, essential, and ineliminable. From the vantage of communicative pragmatics—which gives priority to the examination of how human symbolic action is rooted in beliefs, desires, and intentions—there will never be a time or place at which it is not simply wrong to interpret *Nanook of the North*, *JFK*, or CNN's coverage of the bombing of Baghdad as anything but non-fictions. The makers of these productions intend for them to be so received by spectators skilled at picking up on authors' more or less rationally held, openly expressed goals with respect to meaning. Generally speaking, then, a filmmaker instrumentally adapts a certain material artifact— images and sounds borne by whatever medium—to the task of indicating his or her non-fictional attitude toward some representational content. *What Is Non-Fiction Cinema?* details how such communicative feats are possible.

The first six chapters of this book explain what non-fiction is, what conditions a motion picture must fulfill before it can be a non-fiction film, and how an agent's means-ends reasoning, extensive planning, and purposive action can generate such a work. Because my analysis of audiovisual communication is more in debt to speech act theory and the philosophy of action than to cinema studies, I also try to justify my inevitable offenses against the taboo of publicly committing the so-called "intentional fallacy."

Chapter 1 sketches an analysis of the constative nature of documentary movies, derived from theoretical resources located at the crossroads of linguistics, analytic philosophy, and philosophy of mind—an intersection to which this book will return time and again.

The second chapter elaborates on a claim central to the project as a whole, namely, that cinematic non-fictions are perforce representations. The theses developed here pertain to the necessary representational component of communicative action, while pointing out the pragmatic dimension of representation. At the same time, Chapter 2 lays the grounds for subsequent arguments that fully natural representations (like sense perceptions) and artificial representations (like documentaries) can give us epistemic access to the world. Any representation per se has the function of indicating the condition of something else other than or external to itself. Braided into this idea is the premise that representational artifacts can and must convey some facts about their makers' mental states and how things stand in external reality. Fulfillment of the indicator function, and the resultant meaning, are explained largely in terms of constraints and dependencies bearing on the representational system's condition. Chapter 2 also introduces the thesis that motion picture representations have various kinds of meaning: natural and intentional, pictorial and non-pictorial, mental significance and external significance.

Introduction 3

Chapter 3 then goes on to examine the range of topics that are proper candidates for non-fictional representation. It rejects orthodox film theory's unreasonable requirement that documentaries must be about actual, objectively existing states of affairs; non-fictions can be about reality, but they might also normally describe imaginary and abstract-typical individuals, situations, and events.

Chapters 4 through 6, taken as a unity, present a brief for moderate intentionalism in the study of the documentary. In Chapter 4, I characterize moderate intentionalism as the claim that **one** vital determinant of cinematic meaning consists of a certain class of authorial psychological states. Some authorial intentions, it seems, do guarantee meaning. Skepticism about the effectiveness of these and other psychological attitudes—desires, beliefs, expectations, and the like—is not a viable option for those who are serious about accounting for the nature and origin of documentary meaning. Chapters 5 and 6 identify the mechanics of authorship with practical reasoning about goals, effects on a target audience, and representational strategies. One source of a work's significance thus consists of multiple, instrumentally and hierarchically linked complexes of intentions—plans—constraining the movie's content and illocutionary force.

Chapter 7 initiates a shift in perspective embodied by the last three chapters. The inquiry's final stage concentrates on how perception and reasoning can be reliable if not infallible guides to the spectator's comprehension of the documentary's objective meanings. The acts of watching and interpreting movies, I contend, typically lead to insights into their mental and external significance. Chapter 7 argues that visual perceptions provide information about the world and that our various kinds of perceptual experiences of motion pictures are typically acute and good sources of knowledge of the artifact itself, as well as of extra-cinematic states of affairs to which the movie is systematically related. In this chapter, I offer one plausible hypothesis about how visual sensation and higher order cognitive processes could intermesh so as to make spectatorship an epistemically positive engagement.

Chapter 8 situates visual perception and reasoning about real authors' intentions along side one another as inputs to full-blown, successful interpretive acts. I regard interpretation as the generation of beliefs and conjectures about the movie's force and content, and about the condition of some portion of the extra-cinematic world, in light of what we learn about the condition of the non-fictional representation. A successful interpretation is one, the constituent beliefs of which are (mostly) true.

The final chapter makes a concerted defense of the claim that our beliefs about cinematic constatives, and our beliefs about extra-cinematic situations, can be true and justified. I do not try to show that all beliefs expressed in or derived from non-fiction films could survive as knowledge; nor do I try to show that such movies are transparent windows onto the truth; nor do I prove that we can ever be totally secure in thinking that our cinematically-mediated beliefs are wholly true or furnish comprehensive, unimpeachable knowledge of the world. In opposition to much contemporary film theory, what I do maintain is that non-fictions may contribute evidence toward the justification of certain of our beliefs.

Operating within a realist framework inspired by recent work in epistemology, I take a fallibilist approach to the problem. On this conception, justification is neither absolute, mind-independent, nor ahistorical. Instead, it is gradational, that is, one is justified to a degree in believing something to be the case; it is also personal, insofar as the justifiability of one's belief in a proposition's truth may reasonably differ from that of someone else and depends upon the information and evidence available to them at a given moment. And how justified one is in believing that such and such is the case in reality may change with the addition of new evidence. Here, justification is understood to have both internalist and coherentist aspects: internalist, because it supports the notion that perceptual experience provides a partial foundation for empirical justification unanchored in any further beliefs; coherentist, in that it holds that beliefs sometimes receive pervasive, non-circular mutual support from one another. I propose that cinematic non-fictions, including those with substantial narrative and figurative components, sometimes contribute decisively to internalist and coherentist aspects of justification, thereby helping to make the belief that reality is as described the most intelligent and epistemically secure option.

I am eager to overturn a piece of received wisdom still held fast by many film theorists, namely, that non-fiction filmmaking and viewing do not lend themselves to knowledge acquisition. But I also want to put as much distance as possible between my investigations and the idea that the nature of non-fictional cinematic representation is necessarily or especially intimately related to the goal of telling, or purporting to tell, the truth. The great American documentarian Frederick Wiseman has often proclaimed that he is not in the business of making objectively accurate records of reality and prefers to regard his production practices and their results as closer to those of a novelist than a maker of factual films. His occasionally occlusive disavowals of seeking and claiming truth themselves beg the most basic questions about the nature of fiction and non-fiction and the possibility of attaining veridical, warranted beliefs by cinematic means. For instance, Wiseman likes to call his films "reality fictions."[2] He has also remarked that he regards "this objective-subjective stuff as a lot of bullshit. I don't see how a film can be anything but sub-

Introduction 5

jective."³ Whether or not he thinks his works truthfully represent reality, and whether or not he sincerely wants and expects his audience to arrive at any particular true beliefs about the pre-filmic situations his movies describe, Wiseman nonetheless appears to me to do everything as a filmmaker that he needs to do in order for his films to fit the overall pattern of non-fiction. He signals his intention that the viewer take certain non-fictional attitudes toward his films' contents. It is because he openly signals these intentions that his works are non-fictions.

At this preliminary stage of orientation and emphasis, it is only fair to warn readers of some of the present inquiry's shortcomings, not least of which is its neglect of the historical development of the non-fiction film. One will also search in vain for anything resembling an examination of the various kinds of documentary film styles and structures, their myriad rhetorical strategies, and the diverse social, poetic, economic, and other functions to which non-fiction films can be applied. With respect to these topics, I must defer to a body of literature to which I can add little, and from which I have learned much: Erik Barnouw's *Documentary: A History of the Non-Fiction Film;* Richard Barsam's *Nonfiction Film: A Critical History;* Bill Nichols's *Representing Reality;* and, most recently, Carl Plantinga's excellent *Rhetoric and Representation in Nonfiction Film.* Lacking depth, scope, and sophistication with respect to history and formalism, my study compensates with the analysis of a handful of basic questions bearing on the problem of how non-fiction films acquire their meanings and how spectators make inroads toward retrieving those meanings.

The word "analysis" here has a distinctive ring to it, since it refers to a philosophical preoccupation with conceptual clarification and puzzle-solving; an interest in rigorous argumentation and definition; and a high tolerance of schematizing definitions and of working out problems in abstraction rather than through close hermeneutical engagements with individual films. In the current academic context, interlocutors are not always clear about what they mean by certain key terms and have yet to explore many weaknesses of, and alternatives to, their own conceptions of certain cinematic phenomena. One needn't embrace or give absolute priority to the perspective of analytic philosophy in order to be a good cinema researcher. But I take it as a more or less truistic principle of scholarship that in the current context, logic and analytical philosophical methods, arguments, and reconceptualizations can only be welcome contributions to the research effort in general.

I will also be eschewing ideological, ethical-political critiques of documentaries and documentarians—such evaluations being the province of many theorists eager to make worldly pronouncements in the service of progressive politics. Here I emphasize that I do not believe film aesthetics to be radically autonomous from political, ideological, moral, and economic concerns; what is more, I do feel that critical and empirical inquiry into film's many conceivable links to these spheres is imperative. But I also think we ought to be careful not to conflate two separate research projects. There is, on the one hand, the explanation of why a documentary was made or has just the form, content, properties, and effects that it has—a task that may advert to social-historical, cultural factors. On the other hand, there is the explanation of what makes a given movie a documentary. The latter is my sole task.

Nor does my discussion extend to the effects on viewers downstream of their encounters with motion picture non-fictions. I seriously doubt that all (non-fictional) movies have ideological messages and/or any automatic ideological consequences, like "subject positioning" and the stultification of the masses by the illusion of presence. One may glean from my discussions of perception and interpretation reasons for expressing such doubts. In any case, practical, emotional, ethical-political, ideological, and other perlocutionary effects on viewers, if and when they occur, are not mechanically or hypodermically triggered by film viewing. Rather, they are conditional upon basic levels of comprehension and interpretive accomplishments.

As much as possible, I prefer to stay away from rehearsing and battling with previous work on non-fiction, especially contemporary film theoretical approaches to this topic. I hope readers will see my study as an escape from the bafflegab, gnosticism, and redundancy of some popular film theory. I have avoided historical overviews and close critiques of the existing literature for the more future-directed task of hypothesis building. Hence I have taken to heart one of Noël Carroll's conclusions about the prospects for film studies: "New modes of theorizing are necessary. We must start again."[4] This is exactly what I intend to do.

My study's title obviously alludes to André Bazin's venerable essays, collected for posterity as *What Is Cinema?* The allusion is deliberate, not least of all because I want to put readers in mind of my break from a certain tradition. I wish, that is, to reject emphatically the thought that the non-fiction film is, by definition, one that must achieve or purport to achieve an utterly realist mode of representation. Making non-fictions need not entail imitating one or another so-called realist style, nor does it require filmmakers to adopt representational strategies aimed at convincing viewers of the image's ontological identity with its object, the transparency of the depiction, or the movie picture's self-evident truth. Nor need the non-fiction film convey only facts or refer to and describe only that which really exists.

However, I also mean to suggest that my own modest volume is on a continuum with the works of scholars, like Bazin, who have challenged themselves with the task of describing the specificity of cinematic representation and communication. We already have a fair knowledge of how people communicate non-fictionally using language. So how is it that motion pictures can be used constatively by people to pass on ideas and (mis)information to one another? What follows is a model for one possible response to this question. It is essentially tentative and ultimately only partial. It promises not so much to resolve the puzzles at hand as to announce a new topic of research: the role of agency, rationality, and practical reasoning in non-fictional cinematic communication.

Notes

1. The sorts of motion pictures I have in mind may be live transmissions as well as works recorded on film, video, CD-ROM, or some other medium. They can be of any appreciable length, on any topic. As far as I am presently concerned, unedited and unviewed convenience store surveillance camera footage, an animated TV commercial for allergy medication, and some of the poetic works of Chris Marker can all have one thing in common: their status as non-fiction. Notice that I am not at all fussy about whether or not the motion picture in question consists entirely or mostly of photographically produced, instead of digital or hand drawn, images. I should also note that from time to time I will use the term "documentary" as a substitute for "non-fiction motion picture." I am aware that documentary can be, and in some discursive contexts should be, reserved to refer to a specific sub-category of non-fiction. But here I wish to take advantage of its popular use as a synonym for non-fictional cinematic representation in general.

2. See John Graham, "'There Are No Simple Solutions': Wiseman on Filmmaking and Viewing," in *Frederick Wiseman*, ed. Thomas Atkins (New York: Simon and Schuster, 1976), 36.

3. Quoted in G. Roy Levin, "Wiseman," in *Documentary Explorations: 15 Interviews with Filmmakers*, ed. G. Roy Levin (New York: Doubleday, 1971), 318.

4. Noël Carroll, *Mystifying Movies: Fads and Fallacies in Contemporary Film Theory* (New York: Columbia University Press, 1988), 234.

1

What Is Non-Fiction Cinema?

Some of the most cognitively and practically important questions we can ask of a motion picture concern whether it is a work of fiction or non-fiction, and why it is one rather than the other. These questions pertain to the kinds of effects that filmmakers seek to have on us, and to the sorts of assumptions they wish us to make about the relation between their movies and parts of extra-cinematic reality, including their own states of mind. Yet in place of cogent insights into the documentary's difference, scholarship for the most part has sown conceptual confusion. Although it could never banish all ambiguity and error from our thinking about this topic, a pragmatic account of what it is that causes a movie to be non-fiction is the best available theoretical option for anyone committed to reducing the confusion.

A wholly non-fictional motion picture need not be wholly factual. It need not contain a single, purely objective, unmanipulated representation or statement. It need not be on any particular kind of subject matter; nor need that which it depicts really exist, more or less as depicted, "out there" in off-screen reality. Nor is documentary, in my account, defined by the particular conventions or norms—pertaining to form, style, content, truth, or objectivity—according to which it is produced, classified, and/or interpreted. All of these paths to understanding the nature of non-fiction film, crisscrossing their way through the literature, lead to dead ends. A cinematic work is non-fiction if and only if its maker so makes it. A documentary motion picture, then, is simply one that results from the filmmaker having been directly guided by a particular purpose, namely, an intention to produce non-fiction.

The Meaning of Non-Fiction

I begin by lifting what I take to be one of the biggest barriers to a sensible, sound definition of the standard work of non-fiction cinema. This obstacle is the aboutness condition, be it an implicit or explicit component of one's understanding of the nature of this cinematic mega-genre.

The specificity of cinematic non-fiction is often sought at least partly in terms of its being, or trying to be, about actual or factual objects in extra-cinematic reality. John Grierson, a founder and proponent of the documentary film movement, characterized non-fiction movies in general as "plain (or fancy) descriptions of natural material" and the sub-genre of documentary as "creative shapings" of subjects drawn from life.[1] A standard film studies textbook definition maintains that "unlike most fiction films, documentaries deal with facts—real people, places, and events rather than invented ones."[2] Richard Meran Barsam defines non-fiction film as "the art of *re*-presentation, the act of presenting actual physical reality in a form that strives creatively to record and interpret the world and be faithful to actuality."[3] Even those who dismiss the very idea of a resolutely non-fictional motion picture do so with the ontological criterion in mind. Jean-Louis Comolli holds that as an "automatic consequence of all the manipulations which would mould the film-document" a sort of "fictional aura attaches itself to the filmed events and facts," thereby adding to or subtracting from their "initial reality."[4] One could also refer to Bill Nichols's influential work on non-fiction, which is predicated on the thesis that such representations "aim at" actual historical realities irreducible to discursive constructs, although they nonetheless bear the stamp of fiction. Rather than portraying the world as it truly is, they only present "a view of the world," the content of which is not a felicitous copy of reality but, to a significant degree, the reflection of the ideological imperatives and gender- (or race-, or class-) specific desires animating the filmmaker.[5]

Although it seems safe to say that cinematic non-fictions must be about something, and that they are either more or less true when understood to be about a given referent, reference to reality is the wrong filter on admissibility to this genre. In fact, it is no filter at all, unless one is willing to countenance confused, impoverished, or unrepresentative samples of truly non-fictional works. No doubt, documentarians typically attempt to record situations and events within actual historical reality. Yet while filming *Jurassic Park* (Steven Spielberg, 1993), everything that Spielberg and his colleagues deliberately aimed their recording devices at—latex dinosaurs, sets, scenery, excessively paid actors uttering bad dialogue while pretending to be chased by T-Rex—belonged within the actual historical world, too. If one supposes (correctly, I reckon) that Roger Patterson's 16-millimetre footage of Bigfoot is a hoax, then this film would fall well short of the standard, despite its maker's fervent desire that it not be regarded as fiction. George Holliday's famous video-tape of the Rodney King incident might also be filtered out, since it is not immediately obvious from the video itself what reality it shows—savage mob aggression or police officers lawfully subduing a threatening suspect? And insofar as a movie can be erroneous or only partially accurate, misleading or downright deceptive, making non-fictional status contingent on a positive epistemic relation between the image and the actual world merely facilitates the skeptic's hasty rejection of the possibility of an unequivocal, distinctly non-fictional class of movies.

In rejecting the aboutness condition, and the epistemic constraints often allied with it, I also want to make a clear distinction between non-fictional communication and the phenomenon of natural meaning. The thermometer's mercury level means that it is –21°C. That man's rolling gait means that he is a sailor.[6] These photos mean that there are glaciers in Antarctica. In each case, one object or situation is factually indicative of the condition of some other part of reality by virtue of how it is objectively related to that other state of affairs, due to the nomic and necessary constraints on their relationship.[7] If the man's rolling gait naturally indicates that he is a seaman, his gait depends on his being a seaman, but not on his or anyone else's belief that he is a sailor or on an intention to show that he has this occupation. Moreover, a natural sign's meaning or, if you prefer, the natural meaning of an item or state of affairs, is purely factual. For **X** to be a natural sign of **Y**, **Y** must really be the case. The mercury does not mean that it is –21°C if a demon makes the thermometer read ten degrees colder than the actual ambient temperature. And the photographs do not naturally mean that antarctic glaciers look just so if, lacking snapshots, I show you ones of Swiss glaciers instead, expecting you to be oblivious to the difference.

Natural meaning, being objective and informational, is untrammeled by intention, imagination, make-believe, connotation, fantasy, subjectivity, expressivity, figuration, infelicity, insincerity, and all that might lead to or converge with fiction. Since movies, unlike drawings or paintings, have this property, why not make it the grounds for identifying non-fiction cinema? We could, for instance, say that a documentary is any unit of photographically produced movie imagery having only or preponderantly natural meaning, leaving it to documentarians and theorists to devise norms of proportionality. We might even want to claim that every movie is, under one description, literally not fictional, insofar as its pictures are naturally meaningful with respect to how things stand in extra-cinematic reality.

To be sure, there is no trace of fiction in natural meaning. But defining cinematic non-fiction or stipulating its prototype on the basis of a-rational, mind-independent indicator relations does not really capture the actual conditions under which even surveillance camera footage becomes a work of non-fiction, versus a natural sign the function of which is more like a thermometer than a documentary. Nor does it explain why there is a description under which *Jurassic Park* is not a documentary. By the same token, it would exclude legions from the realm of genuine non-fiction, due to interpretive, rhetorical, figurative, and sometimes misrepresentative properties that result from their having been molded by an organizing consciousness. If film theory has taught us one lesson, it is that documentary is no more mind-independent a mode of representation than linguistic discourse.

I argue that the core of non-fiction consists not of an objective indicator relation, but of an **action** of indication, that is, somebody deliberately and openly indicating something to somebody else. Here the definition of non-fiction makes decisive reference to the nature of filmmakers' intentions. Documentaries acquire their status as such because they are conceived, created, shown, and used with certain definitive communicative purposes in mind. They are cinematic assertions; and naturally meaningful images are among the elements frequently employed by the communicator toward assertive ends.

From now on, I will say that in producing non-fiction, a communicator uses some unit of motion picture footage in an effort to assert that something is (or was, or will be, or could be) the case. Hence:

> To perform a cinematic assertion is to employ a motion picture medium, typically consisting of both visual and audio tracks, with the expressed intention that the viewer form or continue to hold the attitude of belief toward certain states of affairs, objects, situations, events, propositions, and so forth, where the relevant states of affairs and so on need not actually exist.

This definition fits a large number of ordinary non-fictions. However, I do not think that it covers every possible instance of the genre.

Let's look at *Trance and Dance in Bali* (1952), produced as part of Gregory Bateson and Margaret Mead's classic anthropological study of character formation in Balinese culture.[8] This short film, silent except for a non-synchronous music track, depicts the *Tjalonarang* (witch) play and consists of footage shot between 1936 and 1939 at numerous village dance club performances. The movie begins with a series of titles noting the time and place of the recordings, identifying the makers and their scholarly affiliations, and giving a synopsis of the theatrical's action. As the depiction unfolds, we observe a masked witch ward off the attacks of the dragon's followers, each armed with a long, sinuous dagger or *kris*. Sent into a trance by the witch, the attackers' ballet maneuvers give way to violent posturing: Bending backward, throwing their hips forward, and holding their arms straight out and above their chests, the dancers repeatedly mimic the action of thrusting their krisses into their own chests.

In offering these images, it seems appropriate to say that the authors' objective is to assert that this ritual performance has the aforementioned features. In other words, they would have us recognize their intention that we adopt certain beliefs concerning the *Tjalonarang* and how it is enacted. This attribution of assertive intent makes sense, insofar as it is consistent with what we know about their anthropological interests in culture, the circumstances under which the film was made, and their efforts to make it available as an empirical research tool. The attribution of assertive intent coheres better with what we know than, say, the assumption that the authors wish us to imagine that the movie depicts a ritual, or to make-believe that a given ritual occurred as portrayed. And it makes more sense to attribute to the authors an assertive intent than to assume their goal was to retell the *Tjalonarang* fiction primarily for the sake of encouraging their viewers to enjoy imagining the events of that narrative.

Many considerations have no direct, proximal bearing on whether or not *Trance and Dance in Bali* is non-fiction. Two among these are its accuracy and its objectivity. Seized by the imp of the perverse, Bateson and Mead could have somehow indicated that the *Tjalonarang* commemorates the arrival of extra-terrestrial astronauts—a ludicrous falsehood, but not the kind of thing that could cause the film to be fictional. It just so happens that the ethnographers, lacking a record of women dancing with krisses, once asked a troupe to break with their customary performance of this play by including female *kris* dancers, an innovation that became the norm by 1939![9] Having altered their subject matter, their work's objectivity is likely to be questioned; maybe its content has more to do with the filmmakers' ethically questionable, lifeworld-distorting desires than with the facts about Balinese culture. But from the perspective of communicative pragmatics, the act of cinematic assertion need not by definition be innocent of either bias or hegemony.

My general point is that the yoking of non-fiction status to idealized standards of objectivity and accuracy should be avoided. The sorts of agents who we can expect to find behind the camera have but limited rationality, their capacities for veridical beliefs and effective communication being facilitated as well as restricted by their finite cognitive abilities, powerful non-epistemic motivations, and the structures of the physical and social environments in which they are located. Theorists who demand that genuine non-fictions exhibit total accuracy of representation, or absence of mediation, manipulation, and artifice, are understanding the documentary in such a way that none could possibly exist. In virtue of being a highly selective perspective on some segment of physical space, and a two-dimensional rendering of three-dimensional objects, the normal photographic movie cannot aspire to being a literal re-presentation of the world. Why demand the impossible of non-fictions when their difference from fiction need only require they serve entirely feasible assertive ends?

We could note that *Trance and Dance in Bali* seems to have been made according to a crusty old ethnographic norm against self-referential depictions of the depictors. Perhaps a work's embodiment of, or classification by, some representational convention is one, if not the only, determinant of its non-fictional status. It's important to bear in mind that a convention is not an autonomous, self-generating property or regularity immanent to the work itself. Rather, it contributes to the effective realization of a goal, such as making a movie, only insofar as it coheres with the reasons guiding some person's relevant actions. A convention plays a mediating role: The agent adapts her work to a convention when she expects that doing so will help to bring about her aesthetic, professional, or communicative ends, like guiding her audience toward a certain conclusion. An author's selective adherence to the standards, rules, or "codes" associated with this or that variety of documentary—black-and-white photography, jerky camera movements, voice of God narration, and so on—would thus be one subordinate element in a more basic and decisive plan, namely, fulfilling her assertive intention.

Cinematically asserting that something or other is the case is akin to a constative speech act, such as a speaker performs in making an announcement, uttering a conclusion, recounting an event, describing an object, or predicting an outcome. These acts each exhibit the pattern exemplified by simple linguistic assertives: A belief is verbally expressed, along with a certain kind of "illocutionary force," namely, the intention that the hearer acquire or maintain a like belief. In writing or saying the sentence, "My students all dig Tarantino," I assert the content of that proposition (that my students all dig Tarantino) if I thereby express my (putative) belief that my students all dig Tarantino and my intention that you, the reader or listener, hold a corresponding belief.

According to Kent Bach and Robert Harnish, whose model of constatives I adopt, my utterance is an assertion provided that I make it in such a way that I try to signal to the receiver that I wish to elicit his or her credence in what I've said.[10] To assert is to attempt to give receivers reasons to think that one seeks to produce a certain effect on them, that effect being their recognition of one's intention that they form a given belief. This assertion's content is either true or false of the state of affairs to which it refers. Provided that the receiver enjoys a basic linguistic competence and grasps that my making marks or sounds are in fact communicative action, and barring uncertainty as to my sincerity or the operative meanings of certain words (dig, Tarantino), the receiver is likely to infer that I believe that my groovy young students admire Tarantino, and that I want him or her to have the same belief. This inference is simply the one that best accounts for my linguistic output, in light of the semantic meaning of the utterance, the way in which it is expressed, and the context in which it arises.

In representing the *Tjalonarang*, Bateson and Mead use cinematic techniques to achieve the same definitive goal associated with linguistic constatives. They intend for spectators to take the attitude of belief toward their representation's content. By content I mean the extra-cinematic objects, individuals, states of affairs, situations, and events indicated and described by the movie depiction. These items need not be actual or real. Just as one can make verbal assertions about extra-terrestrial beings, one can produce filmic assertions about them, even going so far as to use special effects to show what they allegedly look like. Nor, as I said earlier, need a film's description of its depicta be veridical. What is important is that, in steering the spectator's attention toward an audiovisual field, and at least some of the observable items in that field, the filmmaker takes steps (to try) to bring about on the viewer's part certain determinate perceptions and realizations regarding what objects and so forth are depicted.

In asserting that something or other is the case, cinematic agents typically expect audiences—employing a combination of perceptually derived beliefs about the depiction, non-perceptual beliefs and background knowledge, and inferences—to arrive at particular cognitions regarding not only what is shown on the screen but also how things stand in the world. By choosing to document a given ritual, by making preparations to record instances of it, selectively shooting these events, choosing some of this footage, editing these shots into a sequence, and taking steps to distribute this work, one of the effects intended by Bateson and Mead is to get whoever views the film to notice, for instance, that the *Tjalonarang* ends in convulsive, putative trance states. This is a non-fictional work because its makers openly signal their intention that viewers take the attitude of belief toward this situation.

There are no logical or metaphysical assurances that every cognition arising from non-fiction viewing will always be perfectly accurate. Owing to misperception, inattentiveness, and so on, one could come away with numerous flawed beliefs about what the filmmakers wished to show; such spectator errors also could be traced to the unclear or imprecise nature of the representation itself. Likewise, due to their own cognitive limitations, the depiction's ambiguity, or the filmmaker's errors or even malfeasance, spectators might form mistaken or unclear ideas about the extra-cinematic world. (Due to my own limitations, I still can not see whether one of the trancers really bites the head off a live chick.) But often observers do acquire true and justified beliefs in the wake of viewing documentaries. If you notice that the witch wears an *anteng*—a cloth sling in which a mother carries her baby—then you've exploited this motion picture to learn a fact about the traditional *Tjalongarang* play.

Much of what I've said hints at a basic agreement with Carl Plantinga, whose intelligent work on the nature of non-fiction merits critical commentary.[11] In a nutshell, he contends that such a movie is one that is more or less publicly labeled as asserting a belief that given objects, entities, states of affairs, events, or situations actually occur(red) or exist(ed) in the actual world as portrayed. By using the term "assertion"—which he understands to include non-linguistic assertions with pictures and sounds—Plantinga suggests that cinematic non-fictions are those toward which viewers can or should adopt the mental stance of belief.

I have a number of reservations regarding Plantinga's conception of the documentary's relation to assertion and shall spell these out as I proceed with my own thesis. One of the first problems that I perceive is that ︙ ︙ tion includes a questionable clause identifying non-fiction ︙ pression of truth claims. Rather than just identifying non-fiction producers' assertive intentions, Plantinga goes on to stipulate ︙ eral terms the content of the typical filmic assertion, namely, a belief the depicted items actually exist(ed) as portrayed. This added ︙ is confusing because it makes it sound as if the expressed belief's content helps make communication, be it linguistic or cinematic, non-fictional. But that job is in fact done by the author's expression of illocutionary force, and the work's status is secured by the communication's recognizable indication of an intention that the receiver adopt the attitude of belief.

Doubtless, there is a close connection between non-fiction and truth. Part of what it means to understand an assertion is to realize what the world would be like for it to be true, since an assertion is either true or false of the state of affairs to which it refers. Moreover, we usually assume that people believe what they assert. For this reason, we normally regard **S**'s assertion that **P** as manifesting her commitment to that proposition's truth, in as much as belief is a mental state consisting of a disposition to assent to some unit of content that may be expressed in the form of a proposition. Yet the association between non-fiction and the expression of truth claims is a defeasible one.

A second objection to Plantinga, then, is that the non-fiction maker need not be unequivocally committed to proclaiming the truth of her depictions. In *Reassemblage* and *Surname Viet Given Name Nam*, Trinh T. Minh-ha uses complicated stylistic gestures, as well as explicit verbal statements regarding her anti-realist film aesthetics, in an effort to undercut viewer assumptions about the veridical nature of ethnographic films. Even if she is implicitly making a second-order claim for the truth—or, given her entrenched skepticism, "truth"—of a postmodern account of cinematic representation, it still behooves us to provide a more fitting description of her actual communicative goals. One alternative is to say that her movies fall into the class of "suggestives": Rather than asserting the outright truth of beliefs $B \ldots B_n$ about certain indigenous African peoples or the postwar lot of Vietnamese woman in Asia and North America, the filmmaker expresses the belief that there may be reason, but not sufficient reason, to assent to $B \ldots B_n$.

Truth claims neither define non-fiction, nor exhaust membership in this category. Think of such speech acts as prohibitives, which consist of the speaker's expression of (i) his belief that his utterance, in virtue of his authority over the hearer, constitutes reason for the hearer not to engage in a certain conduct and (ii) the speaker's desire that because of his utterance the hearer not perform that conduct.[12] A motion picture analogue of a prohibitive could consist of an animated "No Smoking" graphic—an encircled cigarette figure with transverse bar suddenly superimposed across it, maybe to the accompaniment of a resonant sonic thud. Although this symbolic act implies the fact that some authority does not allow smoking in a given location, to subordinate it to the conceptual category of truth claims obscures the specific communicative function which it's designed to serve. This case leads me to note that the class of cinematic artifacts that are literally not fiction is larger than the class of cinematic constatives. So my own model of motion picture non-fictions has its limitations, since it is only meant to describe, as broadly as possible, the essential, irreducible pattern—the expression of constative illocutionary force—embodied by a single, albeit major group of non-fictions. It also follows that I concur with Plantinga's observation that we need a category of poetic non-fictions, not concerned primarily with assertion or argumentation, but with a primarily aesthetic function as their "organizational principle."[13]

There is a third degree of confusion triggered by Plantinga's characterization of paradigmatic non-fictions. We might ask, **How** do non-fictions assert beliefs that the depicted items actually exist(ed) as portrayed? What is a filmmaker doing when he or she asserts the truth of these beliefs? I am not sure how Plantinga would detail the pragmatics of this activity. But I suspect that claiming truth frequently involves something along the lines of confirmative communicative acts. In Bach and Harnish's taxonomy, these illocutionary acts, like assertions, consist of a speaker's expression of a belief as well as a desire that the hearer form a like belief. Differentiating it from an assertion is the speaker's expression that he has formed (and the hearer should form) the belief as a result of a truth-seeking procedure, such as observation, investigation, or argument.[14] A filmmaker, too, might intend viewers to acquire the belief that such and such is the case, for reasons above and beyond the viewers' recognition of the intention that they take that attitude.

Often the cineaste expresses the intention that we believe object, event, or situation O actually exists (as shown) in reality because, in portraying O, the maker thereby offers some probative support for belief in its existence. Television news programs and documentary reports usually exemplify the confirmative schema; not only do producers signal their wish that we take the attitude of belief toward the show's content, they also indicate that this attitude is warranted in light of evidence amassed through inquiry and documentation.

It is useful at this stage to make a distinction between primary and secondary motion picture confirmatives. A hard core of the former would be composed of works in which overall priority is given to the articulation of various focal claims that result from the makers ostensibly having undertaken truth-seeking procedures. Such a film is in a strong sense about the substantiation of these claims. Think of the PBS *Frontline* documentary *Innocence Lost* (1994), director Ofra Bikel's probe into the conviction of seven day care workers on sexual abuse charges. She and her colleagues are at pains to show that these accusations are the upshot not of careful investigation but of rumor, psychological testing biased toward confirmation, and a general failure to challenge distorted statements coaxed from pre-school age witnesses by police officers and negligent therapists. The filmmakers use the cinematic medium to present the results of their background research—the alleged victims' testimony is, for instance, illustrated by actors reading from official transcripts, their voices dubbed over courtroom sketches. Moreover, the medium is itself used to gather evidence, in the form of recorded interviews with parents, jurors, lawyers, therapists, and experts.

Many ordinary non-fictions are not principally devised to verify claims about the world. Yet it is still appropriate to regard them as confirmatives, only in a weaker mode, secondary in importance to other values and functions. Television talk shows are full of information about people's appearances, actions, and utterances. Are we therefore to assume that their main objective is to furnish proof of people's appearances and so forth? On the contrary, it seems to me that these programs are subordinated to the overriding goal of entertaining spectators with non-fictional images of individuals more or less spontaneously engaging in interactions like gossiping, quarreling, and confessing. But these and other non-fictions normally embody a standard, naturalistic use of the medium. In executing their specific purposes, they present recognizable, approximately accurate audiovisual images of actual, independently existing objects. Without belonging to the hard core of motion picture confirmatives, they nonetheless fit within a category of secondary confirmatives because, in achieving their particular ends, they satisfy a key presumption pertaining to content: By using the medium in a standard fashion, the producers endeavor to fulfill the audience's expectation that they will be able to see by the depiction what really occurred and how various objects and events actually looked or sounded.

Before moving on to an examination of some of the possible challenges to the sufficiency of my analysis, let me take a moment to summarize and refine some previous points.

The action definitive of much non-fictional cinematic communication is assertion. To make assertions cinematically, agents use motion picture technologies and representational strategies in order to indicate to viewers that they are supposed to take the attitude of belief toward that which is represented. The producers at CNN do not want us to imagine that Christiane Anampour is a correspondent reporting the day's events in some war-torn region; nor do they, or Anampour, wish us to make-believe that a mortar attack on an apartment building happened roughly as shown; nor do they wish us to make-believe that the footage records the attack in question. Instead, they anticipate that we'll pick up on a variety of cues that should help us to become attuned to their desire that we adopt an attitude of belief vis-à-vis objects, states of affairs, situations, and events either explicitly portrayed or implied by the motion picture.

To say of a filmmaker that he or she presents the film with a genuine, successful assertive intention is to say that that person must satisfy the same moderate, subjectively appropriate conditions that I think anyone must meet before we can say of them that they have openly communicated, and not merely covertly or privately expressed, a certain thought or message. A paradigmatic constative act occurs when the communicator signals his or her constative intention in a way that he or she has some good reason to suppose will be open and recognizable to a given target audience. In other words, this illocutionary intention must be among the maker's effective communicative intentions—that is, it has to be something that this person has indeed taken steps to try to signal to others, and the person must have some intelligent grounds for hoping that these steps will achieve their desired effect. The audience, however, need not actually grasp the nature of the communicator's intention, nor need they end up adopting the attitude in question toward the work's content.

Notice that my conditions for assertive success are more moderate than those advocated by Noël Carroll, who also supports an intentionalist definition of documentary. He requires of a "non-defective" assertive intention that the filmmaker be "committed to the truth or plausibility of the propositional content of the film and to being responsible to the standards of evidence and reason required to ground the truth or plausibility of the propositional content the film-maker presents."[15] Assertions may be wanting in the aforementioned respects, but they are no less assertive for it. The potential defects to which Carroll adverts strike me as extraneous to the decisive issue of whether or not a constative illocutionary force has been effectively signaled. Also, they lead our avowedly intentionalist definition back into the arbitrarily restrictive camp of irrelevant epistemic and methodological norms. What's more, Carroll asks of the genuine assertion that it be purebred in a way that seems unrealistic for ordinary communicators. One might, for example, adamantly, and without intent to lie, assert that **P**, while being conscious of one's growing doubts as to whether **P** is as true or plausible as one would like it to be. As I will show later, there are also non-fiction filmmaking strategies that allow for the possibility that the communicator is largely unaware of what, exactly, he would have the audience believe.

To make non-fiction, filmmakers follow what amounts to a rationality heuristic. Motion pictures are composed on the largely tacit but nonetheless operative assumption that audience members—by mobilizing a combination of visual and aural perceptions, background knowledge, and non-perceptual beliefs and inferences—will be more or less able to grasp the movie's content and intended force. When news broadcasters show scenes of apartment blocks under mortar fire, they exploit their viewers' capacity to recognize pictures and sounds of bombardment, as well as their ability to surmise that these recordings are the results of a certain type of causal relationship between the recording equipment and a prefilmic event not caused by the recording process itself. Of course, there's plenty of room for deception here, since perfidious filmmakers using special effects or stock footage could take advantage of the fallibility of perceptually-derived beliefs pertaining to cinematic representations. Yet a bogus depiction of warfare—made on a Hollywood back lot and passed off as authentic by gun-shy reporters—is for all its falseness no less a work of non-fiction.

A film's content is not always fully manifested in what is explicitly displayed on the screen. Often spectators must ascertain implicit content by making inferences, including inferences about authorial plans and preferences. Consider *The Thin Blue Line* (1988), Errol Morris's brilliant documentary about a man wrongly convicted of murdering a Dallas policeman. Arguably, Morris wants us to apprehend something to the effect that wishes and prejudices can all too easily undermine the pursuit of truth. At no time is this statement flashed on the screen or uttered by a speaker in so many words. Instead, we are warranted in inferring from the movie's other properties that the director would have viewers form this belief. Given the information related by the interviews and stylized reconstructions of witnesses' testimony—sequences in which the frailty of the charges against Randall Adams is juxtaposed with revelations about the reasons why various people were strongly inclined to assist in Adams's conviction rather than test the evidence—a suitable explanation of the movie's rationale would point to the author's interest in exposing the distortion of truth-seeking procedures by self-serving desires.[16]

Filmmakers usually expect audiences to marshal perceptions and background knowledge so as to decide whether a work is non-fiction. Now I suspect that at some initial moment—often prior to watching the film itself, given expectations arising from advertising, reviews, programming notes printed in television time tables, and so on—people settle on adopting a global attitude of belief toward many movies and broadcasts. Reconsideration occurs only if this judgment seems to be counter-indicated by some feature of the movie.

In any case, documentarians can guide viewers toward an understanding of a work's intentional status by exploiting their audience's attunement to various cues. One cue would be the absence of stereotypical traits of motion picture narrative fictions, for instance, the showing of actors performing apparently scripted roles, or the breaking down of scenes into sequences of carefully composed and blocked camera angles and shots. On the positive side, non-fictioneers also avail themselves of their public's familiarity with orthodox formats and styles associated with non-fiction, as well as with the public's ability to recognize some films as non-accidentally accurate depictions of actual historical, as opposed to imaginary, events. The inclusion of linguistic cues, like the utterance of assertions by on- or off-screen speakers, is another normal means of expressing the movie's main communicative intent.

These markers don't themselves make a work non-fictional; nor are they unequivocal, nomic indicators of authorial intentions. But they do provide evidence that will figure in spectators' reasoning about the author's likely goals. It is in light of our reasoning about why the maker would show us such and such, in this way, that we hypothesize that she must want us to treat the work as non-fiction. This assumption is sometimes the one that makes the communicator's behavior seem rational and appropriate. Spectators and filmmakers are frequently able to achieve a measure of this sort of coordination because of the mutual communicative assumptions that structure and constrain their rapport. For example, viewers tacitly assume that a cinematic artifact is produced with recognizable illocutionary intent, just as its makers tacitly assume that viewers will assume it is made with a recognizable intent.

Language, Cinema, and Assertion

In speech act theory, to which my analysis is heavily indebted, the constative communication involves the use, in writing and speech, of linguistic items. Given my reliance on this theory, a reader might wonder whether I am insinuating that films are themselves fundamentally linguistic or language-like structures that may be used to serve various illocutionary ends, like issuing assertions. In opposition to a great many film theorists, I do not think that the cinema is a linguistic mode of representation.[17]

Linguistic communication consists specifically of operations upon words and sentences according to semantic and syntactic conventions. The motion picture medium, however, is not obviously a form of, or an analogue to, a natural language or a system of signs governed by syntactico-semantic rules cum codes.[18] Aside from the fact that critics have yet to decide precisely which cinematic units of analysis are the constituent elements of this putative language, there is a dearth of probative support for the assumption that recording and comprehending motion pictures perforce entails the command of language-like tokens according to a quasi-linguistic grammar. Surely none of the rules upon which the combination and interpretation of filmic images is supposed to rest have been described with anything like the empirical rigor attained by contemporary linguistics' investigations of its object domain.

I think that Gregory Currie correctly identifies the nature of the disanalogy between language and cinema when he argues that the meanings of images, either individually or in their connectedness, are not determined by convention.[19] Following David Lewis, Currie understands conventions to be uniformities of coordinated practice based on the mutual expectations of members of some community.[20] Such regularities contribute enormously to verbal communication: Linguistic agents use words as they do because they intend certain meanings and know that others intending likewise would do the same; and all concerned want to continue these regularities because they coordinate what speakers mean by words and sentences and what hearers will take them to mean.

The gist of Currie's argument is as follows. Language is meaningful insofar as it is conventional, molecular, and recursive. Words, its basic units or "atoms," are individually meaningful owing to semantic conventions; in turn, the sentential meaning is a function of the meanings of individual words, plus commonly known rules of composition.[21] Cinematic meaning itself is non-conventional and non-molecular, because comprehension does not involve identifying individually meaningful atoms and building them up into significant wholes according to compositional rules. Rather, to the limits of visual discriminability every part of the photographically derived image is meaningful by virtue of its looking like some other, real thing.[22] In motion picture comprehension, visually detectable similarity plays convention's role in linguistic systems. Furthermore, deriving meaning from combinations of images is not a matter of exploiting a-contextual rules of grammar. That a standard piece of shot-reverse shot editing—in which the second shot is understood to represent the view of the individual shown in the first—has the meaning it does is not determined by convention, since there are far too many cases in which the second shot of such a construction is not subjective. Establishing the import of the shot-reverse shot, like that of other combinations, instead requires various inferences and assumptions about the context in which these shots occur, the course of the narrative so far, the location of the depicted character, and the likely narrative goals of a moderately rational filmmaker who apparently wishes to aid viewer comprehension by linking successive images in a non-arbitrary fashion.[23]

There is a fundamental distinction to be made between linguistic and cinematic assertions, since the conditions and practices that govern linguistic meaning from the bottom up—following and recognizing conventions—are all but absent from cinematic comprehension.[24] The essential disanalogy between them is also manifested in the behaviors causally related to non-fictional cinematic communication. An account of the actions productive of a cinematic non-fiction cannot be reduced to a description of those productive of assertions in a natural language, that is, to the manipulation of such natural language tokens as phonemes, marks, and sentences according to semantic and syntactic conventions.

Cinematic assertion consists of the determination of content and the expression of force by cinematic means. Here I have in mind the gamut of resources and methods that movie makers have at their disposal for establishing content and for indicating the appropriate intentional attitudes to take toward it. Generally speaking, then, cinematic communication consists of recording images and sounds, with the further intention of exhibiting this audiovisual package to somebody in the hopes that they will subsequently arrive at certain determinate realizations.

This broad description of the process hardly does justice to the variety of technologies and elements potentially at play. The tools of contemporary motion picture production include not only photographic, naturally meaningful pictures but also computer generated imagery. Graphics, animation, intertitles, and subtitles may be used. Cinematic communicators could establish the content of their works by way of mise-en-scène; by camera set-ups, movements, and effects; and by the selection and organization of images and sounds. They might also employ sound recordings of people, present on- or off-screen, communicating linguistically. To be sure, motion picture non-fictions usually contain spoken or written assertions. But that fact does not evince the essentially linguistic character of cinema any more than carrying water in a bucket evinces the liquid nature of the container. Rather, the motion picture medium is a distinct, non-conventional audiovisual representational system that can be used to embed tokens of other representational systems, such as linguistic items.

As I understand it, "assertion" refers to the functional adaptation of any representational system, linguistic or otherwise, to the same communicative goal. Hence we should not lose sight of the fact that linguistic and cinematic assertions do share an important feature. In discussing the pragmatics of communication, I have stressed that both result from a communicator's intention that others recognize her intention that they should adopt the attitude of belief toward some particular content or message. Filmmakers put pictures and sounds together so as to signal this reflexive intention, whereas speakers and writers use words and sentences. Comprehending assertions made in either representational system is not just a matter of knowing a-contextual semantic and compositional rules governing how the indicator elements are arranged. Instead, comprehension compels the interpreter to make judgments about non-conventional factors, namely, the rationality of the communicator and the illocutionary force she meant to express by producing a given artifact at a certain time and place.

Essentialism in Context

For various reasons, contemporary film scholars seem eager to historicize their definitions of documentary, which is to say that they are unwilling to subscribe to a hard and fast account of what non-fiction is, always and forever. Many would rather construe the nature of such works as subject to change over time and between social-cultural contexts and instances of reception. Generally speaking the desire to historicize is sparked by recognition that cinematic texts have no inherently non-fictional properties. These days, hand-held camera work crops up in television crime fictions at least as often as it does in documentaries; likewise, some documentaries contain scenes as carefully staged and dramatized as those in theatrical release fictions. Thus scholars seek extrinsic factors upon which to base the fiction/non-fiction demarcation. Owing to skepticism about intention's determinant status, along with a distaste for the bourgeois category of the individual author who exerts lucid, unfettered control over his work, film theorists do not often seek the relevant factors solely or principally in the purposive actions of filmmakers. Instead, the extrinsic determinants are identified as social-historical items, such as institutionalized norms that specify what constitutes a genuine documentary (and an authorized documentarian), viewers' interpretive activities, or revisable norms or conventions that coordinate filmmaking practices with audience expectations and interpretive strategies.

In the spirit of anti-essentialism, Bill Nichols writes that "documentary as a concept or practice occupies no fixed territory. It mobilizes no finite inventory of techniques, addresses no set number of issues, and adopts no completely known taxonomy of forms, styles, or modes."[25] He then proposes to define documentary from three perspectives, so as best to bring out the sets of concerns that must be examined in order to grasp the ways in which the object domain has been historically and variously constituted by filmmakers, spectators, and scholars.[26]

From the point of view of the filmmaker, the documentary can be identified with numerous socially, institutionally, and economically given mandates, practices, professional and ethical dicta, and so forth—all which are provisional and contestable by the transformative practices of individual filmmakers. Apropos of films themselves, documentary can be considered as a corpus of texts displaying shared styles, editing patterns, representational codes and conventions, national origin, period, and movement. Although there would not be a single inherently documentary trait shared by all, it is within the corpus that we can recognize various commonalities between certain texts. However, Nichols warns that the paradigmatic non-fictional forms and modes can "all be simulated within a narrative/fictional framework."[27] Hence membership in the corpus is arbitrated by the institutions of production and the conditions of reception.

From the viewer's perspective, there are sets of assumptions and "procedural skills of comprehension and interpretation" that stand out as documentary modes of engagement.[28] For instance, it is characteristic that spectators make sense of the cinematic non-fiction by inferring that the representation pertains to the actual world rather than an imaginary one, their expectation being that the sounds and images bear an indexical relation to reality.

It is interesting that Nichols ultimately settles on a description of the nature of non-fiction that is much less holistic and open-ended than the foregoing would have us expect from him: "At the heart of the documentary is less a *story* and its imaginary world than an *argument* about the actual historical world."[29] Implicitly, Nichols's most general definition of documentary is located in a framework of intentionalist, ahistorical background assumptions. Independent of who makes it, when and where it is made, and how it is interpreted, a non-fiction movie is one that issues from an individual's or group's attempts to express propositions about reality. For if filmmakers are not the ones doing the arguing and the aiming, who is?

Nichols might object to being called an intentionalist, but I see no way for him to shake the epithet. To make an earnest attempt to do so, he would have to demonstrate commitment to one or both of two quirky beliefs: namely, (i) cinematic and linguistic texts or artifacts possess significant autonomous causal powers such that **they** have the capacity to make arguments, and (ii) people acting individually and in concert lack the capacity to design and produce artifacts, be they linguistic or cinematic, with the expressed intention of making arguments. Neither belief is easy to sustain. Experience tells us that a film reel or video cassette can not even direct itself to function as a door stop, let alone as a discourse. The charge of ahistoricism is similarly hard to meet. Nowhere does Nichols suggest that there has been a time in cinema history during which documentary production was not a matter of making arguments about reality. Nor does he consider the problem of whether and how a work could depart from this teleological constraint yet remain a documentary. Not even the reflexive film, which Nichols favors as the most politically progressive and least illusory mode of documentary address, escapes this constraint since it too makes arguments and propositions about historical reality—its special ambit being the socially and historically conditioned processes and ideologies according to which the world is represented.[30]

For his part, Dirk Eitzen insists that "there is no such thing as a text that is intrinsically and necessarily a documentary."[31] Instead of being a kind of thing, a documentary is an occurrence, because such a work is only actualized at the moment when a viewer erects a particular type of "reading frame" around any given film. He identifies this frame as the spectator's presumption that the film, video, or television program is making truth claims.[32] Although it would be "unusual and unconventional" to regard *School Daze* (Spike Lee, 1988) as a documentary of a stage of Larry Fishburne's development as an actor and *High School* (Frederick Wiseman, 1968) as a "quasi-fictional commentary on high schools," neither interpretation would be wrong.[33]

There are, however, a number of things wrong with this reception-oriented account. Note first that all photographically produced motion pictures do have intrinsically and necessarily documentary properties, those being the natural meanings conveyed by their indexical, mechanically recorded image (and sound) tracks. The material artifact's natural indicator property is one constraint on viewers' interpretive activities; it is due to this condition that they may learn facts about either the actual historical Fishburne or the fictional character he plays in the film story. Note as well that natural meaning, although genuinely non-fictional, ought not be conflated with the action of non-fictional communication. The ontological distinction between these two categories is one that Eitzen effaces in order to help push *School Daze*, made with preponderantly fictional intent, into the nameless abyss.

Eitzen also errs by supposing that a movie's non-fictional status must reside either in the text or in the viewer's response. The excluded third alternative is to regard it as a relational property. Unlike shape or weight, the property of being a documentary is not objective. There is nothing about the cinematic text or material artifact by itself that makes it an instance of non-fictional communication. Documentaries are works—means by which authors try to achieve certain goals. It is therefore only with reference to its relation to a maker's purposes that we can decide whether a movie is non-fictional, fictional, or some combination of the two. Ignoring this relation, whereby a movie is functionally adapted to serving possibly multiple, hierarchized communicative ends, is another way in which Eitzen tries to get us to accept that *School Daze* is as reasonably treated as non-fiction as *High School* (and the converse).

Finally, the claim that a documentary is not realized until a receiver applies the specified interpretive frame to a text is self-defeating. Assume for a moment that there is, at a particular time and place, a publicly available, genre-specifying conceptual framework, like the presumption that non-fictions make assertions; and assume that it is by applying this frame that people within that social-historical context determine that a movie is a documentary. If viewers within a given community have the cognitive and actional capacities to use this frame, then filmmakers within the same population are also cognizant of it, and would sometimes allow their filmmaking activities to be guided by it, and seek, by way of such "situational cues" as verbal labels and textual or stylistic features, to trigger the audience's own application of this concept.[34] Assuming a filmmaker moderately reasonable and competent, and committed to creating a documentary readily identified as such, he or she could simply follow the framework. In cases in which this occurs, a work of non-fiction would result. Moreover, viewers who fail to apply the documentary frame to this movie would be just plain mistaken about a key fact concerning this work's provenance.

Eitzen is surely right to assume that viewers are free to treat anything as non-fiction, if they so desire.[35] But that truism, along with a description of the perceptual and cognitive conditions under which people usually come to regard movies as non-fictional, in no way rules out the possibility that a work's genre membership is fixed upstream of its reception.

Plantinga, whose initial turn to communicative pragmatics I applaud, contends that in the final analysis a movie is non-fiction because it's "indexed" that way.[36] Roughly stated, indexing consists of the public identification of a film as (non-)fiction, on the basis of how well it fits a current concept of what constitutes such a category of film.[37] Hence he maintains that a film's index is "a property or element of the text within its historical context."[38] At the outset, filmmakers and others involved in the production make their contribution to indexing by intending that the film take an assertive stance toward some state of affairs, by adopting certain prototypical styles, and by attaching various credits and titles to the work. Distributors, exhibitors, and advertisers make further contributions by overtly labeling the work as one that takes an assertive stance. Spectators play their part by attending to these cues, evaluating the film's consistency with their expectations about the currently standard characteristics of non-fictions, and by subsequently applying or withholding the documentary label.

Plantinga emphasizes that indexing, being a social phenomenon, depends as much on the audience taking up the index as it does on the producers' intentions. Even if *Eraserhead*'s (David Lynch, 1978) makers and distributors did intend the public to label their film a documentary, it could not be successfully indexed as such because its characteristics are too far beyond the currently recognized norms that audiences associate with that index.[39] On the other hand, viewers who identify *The Battle of San Pietro* (John Huston, 1945) as fiction are mistaken, for this movie does not violate the social conventions currently associated with documentary membership, and thus resists idiosyncratic attempts to index it otherwise.[40] "Like all linguistic categories, 'nonfiction' and 'fiction' are social in nature. They are named and defined within a culture, such that you or I can be mistaken about what a culture has paradigmatically named 'nonfiction' or 'fiction.'"[41] Thus Plantinga ultimately treats non-fiction as a social concept and defers to the group, rather than the individual, in matters of deciding what is and is not a documentary. A work is non-fiction if it satisfies to a greater rather than lesser extent those criteria that members of a certain group, at a given period in the group's history, agree constitute a work of non-fiction.

The foregoing invites comment with respect to several basic problems. First, by suggesting that it is culture that designates non-fictional status, Plantinga risks falling into the trap of reifying the social. Evidently, he sees peril in attributing too much responsibility to individual subjects for deciding what is and is not a documentary, and would rather vest authority in a social unit than in the agent. But culture cannot be made to do that job for us. As implied by other of Plantinga's remarks, culture has no causal autonomy from the people who make it up. Indeed it has no existence independent of the beliefs and desires—including the shared or mutual beliefs and desires—along with the actions and interactions of individual agents. Hence any theory that ascribes a determinant role to culture in the production of this or that category of artifact contains an abstraction that can end up masking the contributions of agency.

I think that the ill effects of this masking can be seen reflected in indexing's lack of explanatory depth. Plantinga proposes that non-fictional status is a matter of social convention: If in a given sociocultural milieu properties f, f', f'', and so on are by convention regarded as constituting non-fiction, then a work displaying those features will be non-fiction, within that milieu. But if the nature of such a basic category of human thought and symbolic interaction as non-fiction is to be explained with reference to conventions, then the explanation must be clear about several matters. It owes us at least working hypotheses about what a convention is and how such entities emerge. Otherwise the nature and emergence of non-fiction is not really explained but, rather, merely described as belonging to another class of objects, the ontology of which itself awaits explanation.

How does the convention that **f, f', f"** identify a work of non-fiction arise within a group? What conditions must be satisfied for that convention to come into being and effectively govern the production and reception of movies? Furthermore, is the nature of non-fiction entirely conventional, or are there non-conventional determinants of a work being non-fiction? Is the ontology of non-fiction itself entirely conventional, or is it just the superficial properties of non-fictions—those features, like absence of staged scenes, that variably and contingently indicate that a work is a documentary—that are subject to convention?

These last two questions are far from trivial, for in its present formulation the theory of indexing itself implies that the nature of non-fiction can and must be explained with reference to an intentionalist level of analysis not identical to, and preceding, conventionality. Plantinga says that a film's index is secured when the relevant parties label the work as taking an assertive stance. He does not go on to demonstrate that assertive stance is a historical, social, conventional construct. He thereby leaves open the possibility that the more basic analysis of non-fiction is one that regards it as someone's act of asserting—an act the nature of which is already fully defined by the intentions of the asserter rather than by an interpersonal indexing process into which the vehicle of the assertion is released.

Plantinga's notion of indexing also invites us to conflate two different activities: classifying a movie as either fictional or non-fictional, and making a non-fictional movie. In classifying the work, a viewer, exhibitor, and even the filmmaker himself may be wrong, inaccurate, or (inadvertently or wantonly) misleading. Here rightness or wrongness is a matter of the degree to which the applied label truthfully reflects the proximal conditions of the work's emergence. The proximal conditions I have in mind are not, in the first instance, social. They are the purposes that guide the author in making the work just as he makes it. Chief among these is the open expression of illocutionary force. When a work's creation serves primarily, but not necessarily only, the author's goal of expressing constative force, then we are justified in labeling it non-fiction. It is non-fiction because it was made in order to express that force.

Now Plantinga would take exception to granting causal priority to authorial intentions, gesturing toward the unreliability of the maker's own contribution to the indexing process. I fail to see how the possibility, in principle, of an author indexing the self-same work as either fiction or non-fiction undermines the definitive role of authorial intentions. Suppose for a moment that a cinema studies professor spends a couple of years researching and writing a treatise on the nature of non-fiction. In it he argues, in a turgid and colorless manner, that authorial intentions establish whether or not something is a documentary. The manuscript finished, he and his publisher decide, for reasons best kept to themselves, to index the book as fiction. All advertising and publicly circulating descriptions of the work call it such. It is given an evocative title, *What Is Your Forbidden Desire, My Love?* A suggestive, romance novel cover is provided, featuring a smoldering, half draped, Fabio-type male model laying on a plush canopied bed. If quizzed on one or another part of his book, the author answers using phrases like, "In my new novel, it's true in the fiction that documentary status is associated with illocutionary force"; and whenever given the opportunity, he speaks of the "characters" who populate the "plot," including Carlos, the handsome and brilliant young scholar who vanishes mysteriously in chapter 1, only to return just as mysteriously in chapter 3.

But imagine that, despite the writer's own adamancy to the contrary, most readers do not hesitate to classify the book as non-fiction. In this example, have authorial intentions failed to establish the work's genre membership? No. The writer's public avowals, deliberate though they may be, are simply inconsistent with the plans that actually motivated and controlled his production of the work, namely his intentions to utter various well confirmed assertions on a certain topic. In asking if a book or movie is non-fiction, we are not asking how anyone, the author included, would at any stage of its making or reception describe the work. We are asking what plans really guided the agent in making that artifact.

Here is another difficulty arising from Plantinga's argument for indexing. Like any contemporary investigator, he takes for granted that there are many kinds of documentaries, and that the genre as a whole is subject to major transformations in response to technological advances, aesthetic innovations, shifts in practitioners' political sensibilities, changes to the audience's beliefs about worthy topics, and so on. That claim sounds about right, and rests on very good historical footing. But I am uneasy with the subsequent claim that the genre's dynamism implies that documentary is an open concept, one lacking a stable, transhistorical, defining basis.

There are a lot of highly contingent sociocultural factors that motivate and constrain documentarians to design movies that look, sound, and mean as they do. Filmmakers with access to generous arts grants handed out by largely non-doctrinal, laissez-faire organizations might have more latitude to experiment with new and eccentric approaches than those who, say, must produce in direct accordance with rigid policies, norms of professional conduct, and marketing dictates imposed by a profit-driven corporation. The degree of competition for advancement, kudos, and resources, and the criteria by which these are awarded—all of which vary over time and between economic and institutional environments—could have dramatic effects on the structure and content of works. Not least of all, filmmakers adapt their choices of subject matter and representational strategies in anticipation of what a particular audience will understand, appreciate, enjoy, or find relevant. Although influencing and often restricting how people elect to make their non-fictions, none of these sociocultural conditions, singularly or in combination, causes a work to be non-fiction. A film is non-fictional because it is made with a constative illocutionary intent. And the nature of the intention to assert that **P**, along with its causal efficacy as a generator of non-fictions, does not as far as we know change from time to time and place to place.

In a sense, mine is indeed an essentialist, ahistorical account of how a production can be non-fictional. I favor it because it avoids the inconsistencies and errors contained in the available alternatives. Unfortunately, essentialism has objectionable connotations. It invites ideas of determinism and destiny, of ethereal twilight zones of immaterial forms and concepts transcending all limitations of time and space, social structure and history, politics and power. However, what I am proposing is light essentialism. It is limited in its scope, appropriate to the explanation of human action, and sensitive to context. I mean to imply nothing about communication in all possible worlds, or how non-fictions would be made a million years from now by a super-intelligent race of neuronally interconnected brains in vats. I merely contend that, in the absence of psycholinguistic and anthropological evidence to the contrary, it is currently safe to argue that there are general patterns of reasoning and action productive of non-fictions, whether linguistic or cinematic; so far as we can tell, these patterns are unlikely to differ between populations of people possessing psychological features, cognitive abilities, and language skills similar to the reader's own.

It should be stressed that neither party involved in the communicative exchange is unbound by material limitations. To have an assertive intention, and to infer that someone has acted on that plan, is to be in a particular state of mind, presumably one with finite neurophysiological, "wetware" instantiations. If a communicative intention has etiological powers, it is in part because it has a material basis; what is more, the information contained by such states must be systematically related to sensory-motor centers, perceptual states, and other cognitive and motivational conditions before an intention can either arise or effect behavioral output.

What Is Non-Fiction Cinema?

The concept of assertive intention also presupposes this mental item's relation to time and location. An intention to assert is an intention either to (start to) do something at a given place right now, or to do something in the non-immediate future. Insofar as it is a communicative intention, its emergence and execution are also influenced by social setting, an influence mediated by the communicator's beliefs about who his audience is, how they are related to him, and what they are likely to recognize as non-fiction.

My project is to answer a specific sort of question about documentaries, a sort evoked by asking: What is the proximal cause of a work being non-fiction? What is the proximal cause of a documentary having this or that feature? These belong to the kind of question that can be adequately answered by referring to an author's intentions and plans. I argue that regardless of diversity in space-time location, cultural context, spectators' interpretations, medium and style of representation, and veracity of representation, a work is non-fiction if and only if its author produces it with the purpose of getting the audience to recognize that they are intended to believe that such and such is the case. The defining condition or essence, if you will, of documentary is this assertive illocutionary force. But there are crucial respects in which this causal schema is anything but ahistorical or asocial.

The communicative situation—one's openly and deliberately sending to a second party some message or information having determinate force and content—is by definition a social situation. The communicator seeks to have a particular effect on a receiver (recognition of illocutionary force, acquisition of a belief), should that party come into contact with the message. For this coordination to be feasible—indeed, for it to be conceivable by either participant—communicator and receiver must be systematically connected to one another. More precisely, there must be a number of beliefs and assumptions held by both parties. These are exploited by the sender in order to act in a manner that will be meaningful to the audience, and exploited by the receiver as a basis for inferring the meaning of the communicator's act.

According to Bach and Harnish, successful communication requires various mutual contextual beliefs (MCBs).[42] Regardless of their truth, MCBs figure in the communicator's reasoning about how to make his assertion and in the receiver's judgments about the communiqué's force and content. But in order for communication to occur, MCBs must be held in common by the parties in the exchange; Bach and Harnish describe them as mutual beliefs since both parties have them, both parties believe they both have them, and both parties believe the other party to believe they both have them. MCBs are contextual because which ones obtain will depend upon the particular circumstances in which an instance of communication takes place—who is communicating, where, when, to whom, using what means of expression.

Here is a simple linguistic example. Suppose I say to my domestic partner, "I guess the dog must be outside." The discourse situation is such that I assume that we share a certain resource, namely a set of beliefs relevant to our very own circumstances: that we have only one dog, that household discussions normally pertain to our dog and not the neighbor's, that I have an interest in keeping track of its whereabouts, that neither of us is in perceptual contact with our pet right now, and so on. Moreover, I expect my partner to expect me to have these beliefs and to make sense of what I have said by supposing that my utterance is designed to be understood in the context of our mutual beliefs. On this basis, I am able to get the hearer to realize that I am speculating about Rover's current location.[43]

Of cardinal importance are several rather more generalized mutual beliefs. Within any given community—defined by the users of a certain natural language, for instance—there are pervasive presumptions that serve all agents as reliable foundations for communication. One of these is the communicative presumption (CP), the user-community's mutual belief that whenever a speaker says something to a hearer in the common language, he is doing so with overt illocutionary intent.[44] Because of the CP, merely making an utterance gives the receiver reason to believe that the utterer is acting with some illocutionary goal in mind; likewise, it compels the speaker's expectation that the hearer will think that he has an identifiable illocutionary intention. Successful communication requires the CP's satisfaction. The speaker must utter a linguistic expression with an illocutionary intent; the hearer must expect some such force to be intended and recognize what this force is.

There is also an array of defeasible general presumptions, which may be suspended or violated without making communication impossible.[45] One of these so-called conversational presumptions pertains to sincerity and consists of the mutual belief that speakers in fact possess the attitudes they express. Should a communicator apparently not fulfill this MCB, receivers would tend to regard him as speaking inappropriately or deceptively, unless some other explanation to the contrary could be found. The sincerity presumption is one of the reasons why it is normally appropriate for us to be interested in the truth-value of people's assertions. We assume that in asserting that **P** a person is usually, but not necessarily, assuming that we will assume that they are speaking sincerely and that we will suppose that their utterance manifests their commitment to the truth or possible truth of **P**. If the speaker's sincerity is questionable, we might have reason to doubt the truth of his statement, or we may discover the insincerity by recognizing the proposition's falseness.

Even when sincerity is not at issue, we may cite disconfirming evidence and reasoning in an effort to point out the irrationality, for the speaker or the audience, of commitment to a given proposition's truth.

Cinematic communication is subject to, and facilitated by, the same kinds of contextual and interpersonal conditions as linguistic exchange. Makers and viewers alike presuppose a variety of contextual beliefs and background knowledge. The producers of nightly news broadcasts assume that you assume that their mandate is to attempt to report a selection of facts about current events and topics. Further MCBs will concern such things as locations (e.g., Washington is the capital of the United States), persons ("Bill Clinton" is co-referential with "the president of the United States"), and anterior events and conditions (Clinton became president in an election, as is the genial custom in the United States).

Still other MCBs concern relevance. A news item beginning with the question, "Why did Airline Flight 000 crash?" would typically be constructed to satisfy the general assumption that the rest of the report will furnish verbal utterances and audiovisual information germane to answering this question about this particular catastrophe. It would be further expected all around that this material is to be taken literally and sincerely.

The preponderance of cinematic works, and all motion picture constatives, also partake of the communicative presumption. The vast majority of publicly accessible motion picture artifacts result from extensive intentions, plans, and purposive action. Of course, this fact means neither that all movie works nor all cinematic non-fictions have a determinate illocutionary force. Take, for example, Peter Kubelka's *Arnulf Rainer*, composed entirely of successions of light and dark frames. It surely results from the concerted pursuit of various artistic effects, is literally not fictional, and is the outcome of no specific illocutionary intention, so far as I can tell. However, the fact that most of the movies confronting us are works—rather than accidental by-products of a-rational, wayward causal chains—does normally support a crucial expectation on the part of both producers and spectators.

This mutual expectation is that audiences will try to ascertain, and makers will try to signal, a certain illocutionary force. Because motion pictures, like linguistic utterances, are in a great many standard cases functionally adapted to the job of transmitting ideas, information, and messages between parties, it is generally assumed that they are made to convey a sense of what kind of attitude—belief, make-belief, directive, supposition, question, dissent, and so on—one should have toward their units of content. Hence the CP is ordinarily a factor in both filmmaking and viewing and is necessarily a condition for the achievement by cinematic means of genuinely communicative, including assertive, ends.

I say that the CP ordinarily figures in the making and reception of movie works because there can be contexts in which it is explicitly suspended. Agents of the artistic avant-garde, like Kubelka, might conceivably create films with neither the assumption nor intention that their target audience, an elite class of connoisseurs wise to the creator's non-communicative aesthetic agenda, shall look for illocutionary force. Correspondingly, this more or less ideal audience might readily and appropriately suspend their expectation that works such as Kubelka's have any specific communicative force behind them.

Skepticism About Intentions

Much of what now counts as cutting-edge documentary film theory is antipathetic to my emphasis on purposiveness and pragmatics.[46] Throughout this book, I take several stabs at convincing readers that this antipathy is a mistake. For now, I offer these stage-setting remarks. An approach such as mine is likely to be regarded by many theorists as a naive, even sinister commission of the intentional fallacy. After all, an author's communicative intentions are not always easily reconstructed. Moreover, an ideologically suspect filmmaker, such as Leni Riefenstahl, could take refuge in my ahistorical, decontextualized analysis of the nature of non-fiction film, saying that it was merely her intention to document the Nazi Nuremberg rally. But my analysis in no way precludes the coexistence of an intention to make non-fiction with other motivations, like intentions to deceive, deify, spread ethically-politically reprehensible doctrines, arouse emotions of fear and awe, and so on. Furthermore, I can think of no good reason why scholars should not investigate a wide range of agential plans and purposes, reference to which might help to explain why a given documentary was produced and why it has the properties that it has.

I add that two substantial philosophical tasks face those who might be tempted to express anti-realism about the causal role of intentions or skepticism about the definitive influence of intentions on cinematic assertion. They would be responsible for offering informed arguments supporting the conclusion that movies cannot be assumed to result from agents acting on stable, decisive purposes and plans—where an informed argument is one addressing contrary hypotheses and data emerging from within the best currently available work in such pertinent fields as linguistics, the philosophy of action, and philosophical psychology. Such theorists would also need to offer similar grounds for maintaining that it is always or often one reasonable option to doubt that competent spectators have the ability to detect the actual intentions of cinematic communicators. In formulating their arguments, they would want to take into consideration that proponents of an intentionalist approach to defining documentary, although being realists about the causal functions of intentions, need not be aiming for infallible attributions.

Moreover, there is one practical problem facing skeptics. To be consistently rather than merely academically anti-realist, they would need to find a new way of explaining and categorizing ordinary human behavior, including their own. Trivial matters like settling on a response to a phone message asking you to pick up bread on your way home are only complicated by suspending the assumption that your mate spoke as he did because he had a determinate purpose in mind. Likewise, your assumption that the promotion and tenure committee will recognize a number of articles as your achievements rather than just texts that your computer coughed up would be either disingenuous or inconsistent in the absence of your commitment to intentionality.

To wager that non-fictional motion pictures result from a particular kind of intention is not to hope that it will always be immediately clear what the filmmaker's aims were. Aside from paying close attention to the cinematic work, it is sometimes necessary to steady our inferences about authorial goals with extensive background research, marshaling whatever evidence (notes, production documents, letters, interviews, other works in the filmmaker's corpus) might be pertinent to reconstructing the proximal intentions giving rise to the movie in question. Even then there is no ultimate assurance that all of our judgments will always be correct. But again, we need not make a fetish of absolute certainty. For an attribution of non-fictional intent to be tenable, it need only be the case that, in light of argument and currently available evidence, it be more reasonable to believe than disbelieve that the filmmaker's activities really were subordinated to this end. It is this kind of reasoning about people's rationality and goals that film scholars routinely undertake when they anticipate their colleagues' attendance at scheduled meetings, decide if students' papers are plagiarized, or determine whether a PBS *Nova* episode on mummification has been misplaced in the horror section of the local video store.

Some theorists are bound to complain that by adopting the present approach, we obscure the social-historical determinants of non-fictional discourse. But there is no use crying about your hair once your head has been cut off. My argument is not that there are no significant social-historical and contextual conditions influencing and constraining documentary movie production. Nor do I suggest that such factors should not be the objects of critical and rational-empirical inquiry. All I insist is that somebody's illocutionary intentions are the sole determinants, in the etiological sense, of a work's non-fictional status. The film theorist's standard objections to this claim are not compelling. Thus I ask: Why should we not begin intentionality's principled, conscientious extension into the domain of non-fiction cinema studies?

Notes

1. John Grierson, "Documentary (1)," *Cinema Quarterly* (Winter 1932): 68.
2. Louis Giannetti, *Understanding Movies*, 7th ed. (Englewood Cliffs, N.J.: Prentice-Hall, 1996), 33.
3. Richard Meran Barsam, "American Direct Cinema: The Representation of Reality," *Persistence of Vision* 3/4 (1986): 131.
4. Jean-Louis Comolli, quoted in *Realism and Cinema*, ed. Christopher Williams (London: Routledge and Kegan Paul, 1980), 226.
5. Bill Nichols, *Representing Reality: Issues and Concepts in Documentary* (Bloomington: Indiana University Press, 1991), 115.
6. This example is one used by Charles Sanders Peirce in discussing what he calls indexical signs. See Charles Hartshorne, Paul Weiss, and A. W. Burks, eds., *Collected Papers of Charles Sanders Peirce*, 8 vols. (Cambridge, Mass: Harvard University Press, 1931–1958), 2:285.
7. My observations on natural indication derive from Fred Dretske's analysis in *Explaining Behavior: Reasons in a World of Causes* (Cambridge, Mass.: M.I.T. Press, 1988), 54–59.
8. A comprehensive discursive as well as photographic survey of Bateson and Mead's research is to be found in their *Balinese Character: A Photographic Analysis* (New York: New York Academy of Sciences, 1942). For a critical reevaluation of their work on Balinese culture, see Gorden D. Jensen and Luh Ketut Suryani, *The Balinese People: A Reinvestigation of Character* (Oxford: Oxford University Press, 1992).
9. Bateson and Mead, *Balinese Character*, 167.
10. Kent Bach and Robert Harnish, *Linguistic Communication and Speech Acts* (Cambridge, Mass.: M.I.T. Press, 1979), 39–46.
11. Carl Plantinga, "Defining Documentary: Fiction, Non-Fiction, and Projected Worlds," *Persistence of Vision* 5 (1987): 44–53; "The Mirror Framed: A Case for Expression in Documentary," *Wide Angle* 13 (1991): 41–53; "Moving Pictures and Nonfiction: Two Approaches," in *Post-Theory: Reconstructing Film Studies*, ed. David Bordwell and Noël Carroll (Madison: University of Wisconsin Press, 1996), 307–324; *Rhetoric and Representation in Nonfiction Film* (New York: Cambridge University Press, 1997).
12. Bach and Harnish, *Linguistic Communication*, 47.
13. Carl Plantinga, "Blurry Boundaries, Troubling Typologies, and the Unruly Nonfiction Film," review of *Representing Reality*, by Bill Nichols, *Semiotica* 98 (1994): 395.
14. A concise analysis of the confirmative is as follows. Where **e** is a sentence in some language, **S** is the speaker of that sentence, and **H** is the listener:

> In uttering **e**, **S** confirms (the claim) that **P** if **S** expresses:
> i. the belief that **P**, based on some truth-seeking procedure, and
> ii. the intention that **H** believes that **P** because **S** has support for **P**.

See Bach and Harnish, *Linguistic Communication*, 43.

15. Noël Carroll, "Fiction, Nonfiction, and the Film of Presumptive Assertion: Conceptual Analyses," in *Film Theory and Philosophy*, ed. Richard Allen and Murray Smith (Oxford: Oxford University Press, 1997), 187.

16. Here my remarks are meant to reflect Morris's own comments on his goals in making *The Thin Blue Line*. See Peter Bates, "Truth Not Guaranteed: An Interview with Errol Morris," *Cineaste* 17 (1989): 16–17; and "Bill Moyers Talks with Errol Morris," PBS broadcast, April 26, 1989.

17. Major and influential statements on the language of cinema, film semiotics—which regards the cinema as a system of conventional signs—and the determinant function of codes would include the following: André Bazin, "The Evolution of the Language of Cinema," in *What Is Cinema?* 2 vols., trans. Hugh Grey (Berkeley: University of California Press, 1967–1971), 1:23–40; Umberto Eco, "Articulations of the Cinematic Code," in *Movies and Methods*, ed. Bill Nichols (Berkeley: University of California Press, 1976), 590–607; Christian Metz, *Language and Cinema*, trans. Donna Jean Umiker-Sebeok (The Hague: Mouton, 1974). The influence of Roland Barthes on discussions of the semiology of the cinema would be difficult to overestimate. See his *Elements of Semiology*, trans. Annette Lavers and Colin Smith (London: Cape, 1967); and *S/Z*, trans. Richard Miller (New York: Hill and Wang, 1974). For an idea of how pervasive the idea of a language of cinema is, one might also look to Michael Renov's article, "Towards a Poetics of Documentary," in *Theorizing Documentary*, ed. Michael Renov (New York: Routledge, 1993), 12–36; and Bill Nichols's contention that, as far as representation is concerned, "everything is language" in "Getting To Know You," in Renov, *Theorizing Documentary*, 189.

18. Paisley Livingston, "Film and the New Psychology," *Poetics* 21(1992): 93–116.

19. Gregory Currie, "The Long Goodbye: The Imaginary Language of Film," *British Journal of Aesthetics* 33 (1993): 207–219. See also his *Image and Mind: Film, Philosophy, and Cognitive Science* (Cambridge: Cambridge University Press, 1996), 113–137. Stephen Prince, "The Discourse of Pictures: Iconicity and Film Studies," *Film Quarterly* 47 (1993): 16–28, also provides a useful critical perspective on this matter.

20. David K. Lewis, *Convention* (Cambridge, Mass.: Harvard University Press, 1968). This is the technical sense of "convention"—a word often associated with such potentially dissimilar conceptual objects as codes, norms, agreements, contracts, mutually binding obligations, social roles, traditions, rules, standards, accepted or acceptable practices, regularities, probabilities, artlessness, habits, stultifying reiterations of behaviors or routines, and so on—that I shall adopt throughout my study. I am therefore anxious to avoid the vagueness of many definitions of this term. For instance, Göran Hermerén, *Aspects of Aesthetics* (Lund: LiberVörlag, 1983), 83, says convention "refers to a set of assumptions, codes and traditions that are vital in the process of creating and understanding a work of art." Owing to its complexity, I am not eager to enter into a discussion of the nature of conventions. I choose Lewis's definition for its clarity, and for its capacity to pick out one typical feature of conventionality that necessarily figures in the operation of languages but that is evidently missing from other modes of com-

munication and social relation. Those wishing some background to the topic of conventionality might consult the essays collected in Mette Hjort, ed., *Rules and Conventions: Literature, Philosophy, Social Theory* (Baltimore: Johns Hopkins University Press, 1992).

21. Currie, "The Long Goodbye: The Imaginary Language of Film," 209–210.
22. Ibid., 214–215.
23. Ibid., 217.
24. Currie, "The Long Goodbye," 217–218, allows that there may be a number of genuine cinematic conventions, such as the slow fade out and fade in signifying a significant passage of time. But he adds that their existence at the most enriches cinematic meaning, rather than constituting it as in the case of natural language.
25. Nichols, *Representing Reality*, 12.
26. Ibid., 14–31.
27. Ibid., 24.
28. Ibid.
29. Ibid., 111 (emphasis in the original). Nichols immediately interjects that by "argument" he intends not only argumentation but also, very generally, representations and propositions, be they tacit or explicit, about this or that state of affairs in historical reality.
30. Ibid., 56–75.
31. Dirk Eitzen, "When Is a Documentary?: Documentary As a Mode of Reception," *Cinema Journal* 35 (1995): 98.
32. Ibid.
33. Ibid., 95.
34. Ibid.
35. Edward Branigan, in *Narrative Comprehension and Film* (New York, Routledge, 1992), 193, makes the same point. He goes on to discuss in detail some of the inferential procedures and reasoning heuristics that he believes spectators utilize in identifying and comprehending documentaries.
36. Plantinga, *Rhetoric and Representation in Nonfiction Film,* 15–24. For Plantinga, a film's index is ultimately one of a family of probable characteristics exhibited by prototypical exemplars of the non-fiction category. I criticize his Wittgenstein-inspired prototype theory in Chapter 5.
37. The term is first used in this application by Noël Carroll, "From Real to Reel: Entangled in the Nonfiction Film," *Philosophical Exchange* 14 (1983): 4–45.
38. Plantinga, *Rhetoric and Representation in Nonfiction Film,* 19.
39. Ibid., 21.
40. Ibid.
41. Plantinga, "Dialogue: Carl Plantinga Responds to Dirk Eitzen's 'When Is a Documentary?: Documentary As a Mode of Reception,'" *Cinema Journal* 36 (1996): 94.
42. Bach and Harnish, *Linguistic Communication,* 5–8.
43. These are mutual contextual beliefs, rather than knowledge, because they need not be true in order to facilitate communication: Rover could be long dead—yet owing to grief, we might have deceived ourselves into thinking that we still have a dog, that it goes outside, that we should let it in at night, and so

forth. While false, the relevant background beliefs are nonetheless exploited in the course of my assertion-making as well as the listener's correct uptake.

44. Bach and Harnish, *Linguistic Communication*, 7.

45. Ibid., 62–65.

46. For a representative sampling of some orthodox and influential modes of documentary film theory, readers could consult the essays collected in Michael Renov, ed., *Theorizing Documentary* (New York: Routledge, 1993).

2

Representation and Depiction

Whatever interests it serves and consequences its creation and distribution have, a photographically made cinematic constative is necessarily a representation. It is certainly common for us to think of documentaries in this way. We say, for instance, that they are about such and such; that they (mis)represent aspects of reality; that they show us how parts of the world look and sound or how someone supposes things to be; that they convey the attitudes and views of their makers and subjects, or of the groups and social formations with which these parties are affiliated. Indeed, to scoff at the very notion of documentaries conveying The Truth about Reality is still to assume that they exhibit a multitude of informative, non-accidental relations to many different sorts of extra-cinematic items. To assert that *Nanook of the North* (Robert Flaherty, 1922) gives a distorted picture of Inuit culture in the early twentieth century is to assume that the movie is systematically and objectively related to a given situation, the condition of which it nonetheless fails to indicate accurately. Moreover, if we really believed non-fictions to be unsuited to represent anything, we would have no reason to criticize their referential and epistemic failures—to do so would be like bemoaning a door knob's inability to record its handlers' thoughts. So the question arises: How do documentaries represent, and fail to represent, anything?

My answer to this question is based on the idea that a documentary is a kind of representational system. It is an artifact designed and used to indicate to us the states of other, extra-cinematic things. This claim does not, of course, describe what exactly it is that makes a work non-fictional. Nor does it imply either that all non-fictions are veridical when understood to be about this or that state of affairs or that all representation is truth-preserving. Nor does it commit us to the idea that non-fictional representations are only about actual or real objects. But this claim does suggest the nature and source of the motion picture non-fiction's objective meaning, namely, various kinds of systematic relations to and dependencies upon objects and situations beyond itself.

The notion that a documentary is a representational system should also help us to grasp that communicative action is at once productive of and contingent upon the act of making a representation. The meaning of this representation derives in part from its having (at least) one kind of "mental significance"; that is, it indicates someone's illocutionary intentions. Its meaning also derives from its having "external significance"—or truth-conditional content having to do with situations and events, other than the maker's states of mind—that it is the representation's job to describe.

Normally, cinematic non-fictions incorporate pictorial representations. Part of our understanding of a movie's meaning and content derives from what the movie looks like; and what it looks like depends, in part, on the visible condition of something external to itself. Owing to this dependence, the image may stand in an indicator relation to the extra-cinematic world. What is more, if and when a movie includes depictions—rather than, say, words scratched on raw film stock—many of its visible properties are significant to the extent that we experience a perceptual similarity between them and the visible features of a pre-photographic object. Thus explaining the workings of cinematic representation calls for an account of the essential features of cinematic depiction, as well.

Throughout the present study I take the position that cinematic non-fictions can and regularly do accurately represent reality. Below, I sketch what I have in mind by representation and explain the basics of how artifacts in general, and movies in particular, can be truth-conducive. This project entails two epistemological commitments. The first is the idea that facts (or information, as I shall use these words interchangeably) are in the world. According to the mainly pre-theoretical view that I adopt, it is a fact that **P** (microbes are smaller than pin heads) if and only if **P** is the case (microbes are smaller than pin heads) in reality. By definition there are no untrue facts, and, strictly speaking, there is no such thing as misinformation. When I say that a fact or information is "in the world," all I intend is that the fact that **P** cannot be produced by anyone thinking, knowing, communicating, or representing that **P** is the case—although the fact that so and so believes that **P** is, clearly, produced by that person believing that **P**. That **P** is a fact is caused not by who believes that **P**, how strongly they believe it, and how good they are at convincing others, but by **P** truly being the case; and to learn a piece of information is not to construct reality, but to learn how things stand in reality.

My second epistemic commitment is to the notion that certain relations between parts of the world can preserve facts. For example, a natural sign, like a pond's frozen state, conveys the information that the ambient air temperature must be below 0°C. And if I am a reliable narrator, I can, in the process of telling you that the pond is frozen, convey the same fact. In either case, one part of the world is informatively related to another part. A suitably equipped person—one who already knows a few facts about how parts of the world fit together—can use his visual experience of the water or his aural experience of my utterance to learn the condition of the air and hence acquire a true belief.

Finally, what lies ahead pertains generally to the issue of the determinacy of meaning. It helps establish my motives for supposing that the motion picture non-fiction's force and content are not essentially or significantly the product of interpretive activity. In the long run, I hope my line of argumentation will help establish in our minds the idea that cinematic meaning has an intrinsic stability and public accessibility. People sometimes suggest that works are typically polysemous, or that what they show or evince is decided by viewers' interpretive frameworks, or that the facts movies seem to make available are ultimately attached to them by audiences. The present discussion supplies some initial impetus to drop such claims. Were it not for the preponderance of viewer-independent, fact-preserving indicator relations, there would be no such things as cinematic depictions for theorists to label as meaning-indeterminate.

Representational Systems

I anticipate that many film scholars will be dissatisfied with my remarks on the nature of cinematic representation, finding them all too restricted to one aspect of representation, as well as neglectful of ideological and social-historical factors in the emergence and operation of cinematic meaning. One might well ask how an analysis that ignores most of the protean and nefarious ways in which the image structures our conscious and unconscious relations to the world—especially our so-called "imaginary," that is, ideologically and psychically inflected relations—could be at all interesting or relevant to the majority of contemporary scholars. I acknowledge my approach's limitations—and I do not suppose for a moment that it is the only or, for all intents and purposes, the best analysis of representation for cinema studies. But a detailed, explicitly argued, terribly flawed analysis of representation is more useful than none at all. In any case, it will have served its main purposes if it helps me to probe the nature of non-fiction and if its strengths and weaknesses inspire us to develop much better accounts of representation.

Nichols reminds his readers that there are several senses of the term "representation" pertinent to discussions of documentary.[1] One attaches to the sense of likeness, model, or depiction. Another has to do with political representation, that is, someone or thing standing for or acting on behalf of the interests and views of another individual or group. A third sense is allied with the rhetorical act of making a case or presenting an opinion in a convincing manner. Although I do not think that cinematic representation is ultimately defined in terms of likeness, it is, I suppose, this sense of Nichols's three applications of representation that concerns me. Moreover, the sense that I wish to specify is a necessary condition for people to perform the other two, political and persuasive, kinds of representational acts with movies.

My commentary's limited appeal derives from its contribution to the project of clarifying those conditions and relations to various externalities that must obtain before a unit of movie footage can be a representation. I need to make such a clarification because it is part of my thesis that motion pictures *tout court*, and cinematic non-fictions in particular, typically succeed in representing various things, including parts of reality. Insofar as other theorists are committed to or reliant upon the idea that cinematic meaning issues from the text's relations to things outside itself—authors, viewers, historical contexts, systems of gender, race, and class—they might seek in my discussion a basis for their own descriptions of the cinematic work's significance. Arguably, the model I adopt describes one thing that any human-made artifact must do if it is to be a representation. I do not suppose that this analysis captures many of the psychodynamic and social conditions animating the creation and reception of movies; nor does it pretend to reconnoiter the whole bewildering array of psychological and cultural consequences associated with human symbolic interaction. It just explains something elementary yet fundamental about what causes any item to be a representation.

The following can help us to avoid some of the problems arising from other statements about how it is that documentaries represent this or that. My approach does not violate semiology's received wisdom of the nonidentity of the sign and object, nor is it grounded in a metaphysics of presence. It does not require or imply anything along the lines of André Bazin's famous ontological thesis of the identity of the image with its prefilmic referent.[2] Despite the automatic conditions of its production, a face filmed is surely not the face itself, the two items displaying many patently obvious differences from one another.

Indeed, an account of any representational medium is an account not of identity but of how clearly different items or situations can be purposefully and systematically linked to one another. This stipulation rules out defining the nature of representation in terms of our possibly irrational or illusory substitutions of one object for another. Hence I deem unhelpful Trinh T. Minh-ha's impression of cinematic representation as the "artificial resurrection of the real" by "substituting the visual and verbal signs of the real for the real itself."[3] Momentarily setting aside the question of what might be buried in the quasi-mystical rhetoric of resurrection, the concept of substitution is a red herring because one thing substituting for another is not an inherently representational relation. If I replace rosemary with thyme in the risotto, I am not representing the former by means of the latter. Nor does the map's representational function derive from the fact that one looks at it instead of at the world. Rather, our interest in it as a representation issues from the way in which certain of its features are arranged and mobilized to indicate some of our planet's grosser features.

Of course, in cinema studies mention of signs substituting for reality is usually meant to raise the specter of the audience's confused fixation upon simulacra. But even if viewers were sometimes to mistake cinematic signs for reality itself—substituting the one for the other in their own minds—this fact would be unilluminating for an inquiry into what causes one thing to be a representation of another. The map elicits no such illusions, yet still serves as a representation. Likewise, the phenomenon I wish to clarify has nothing to do with making present something absent or non-existent. The coming of motion pictures may well have occasioned, as Edgar Morin argues it did, a renewal of supernatural thinking in modern, supposedly advanced societies.[4] His intriguing study finds amidst our emotional attachments to still and moving photographs a residue of magical reasoning and practices similar to those of so-called primitive people, who evoke and act upon dead or absent individuals, doubles, spirits, and occult forces by means of fetishes, amulets, and the like. The association of contemporary cinema with this mythic aura of "re-presentation" I leave to the inspection of anthropologists and psychologists of spectatorship.

What, then, of the old chestnut that cinematic representation—or at least some forms of it, privileged within certain traditions or historical moments—consists of mimesis, in the sense of copying or resemblance? To this day, one still sees references to the "mimetic powers of the camera," perhaps if only either to mock the idea of objectively true images of reality or to warn us of the danger of illusion.[5] Soon I will detail the nature and role of visible resemblance in motion picture representations. In advance of that discussion, I emphasize that cinematic representation is surely not essentially a matter of one thing being to some extent visibly symmetrical with another. One very obvious reason for rejecting this idea is that movies employ their sounds and images to indicate non-visible as well as visible states of affairs. But I also think it wrong to assume that the concept of resemblance is the key to defining any mode of representation, visual or not.

Using three differently sized coins, we could show the ranking of three job candidates; the more preferred the candidate, the smaller the coin's circumference. None of the indicator elements look like any of the candidates, and none bears any visible resemblance to the non-visible property of being more or less favored. Yet they do represent the candidates' ranking. On the other hand, I do not suppose it impossible that stones could wash up onto the shore in the likeness of Marcello Mastroianni's face. Although we are free to treat this apparition otherwise, and would probably be tempted to do so, my intuition is that it would neither genuinely picture nor represent the actor. By the same token, Marcello's face as reflected in the water as he lounged by his pool might aptly be described as his natural image, but it was not strictly speaking either a picture or a representation of him.

For one thing to be a pictorial representation or depiction of another, more than some kind of resemblance is needed. There must also be a certain type of systematic connection between the putative picture and the object. The former has to look as it does because it is its function to look that way. Along the same lines, the constraints on representation in general are stiffer than those on resemblance. For something to be a representation, it must have properties the existence of which is sustained or explained by their power to indicate what properties another object has or is supposed to have.

Here now is my proposal, based on Fred Dretske's discussion of representational systems, like sensory and cognitive ones, internal to living organisms and possessing an intrinsic capacity to inform these creatures about the world's structure, thereby helping to guide their movements through the environment. A representation may be defined as: "any system whose function it is to indicate how things stand with respect to some other object, condition, or magnitude."[6]

One of this definition's strengths is that it also applies to classes of systems the indicator capacities of which do not result from adaptive processes of natural evolution, namely, artifacts whose representational function depends on the way they are made and deployed by an agent. In the context of planning a dinner party, my partner and I could, by an act of explicit agreement, decide upon some rules to help us with the seating arrangements: For present purposes, this knight will indicate Adam's position at table, this bishop Martin's seat, this rook Matt's place, and Berne's spot will be signaled by the king. Using the chess pieces, we invent a representational system designed to indicate, roughly and schematically, the prospective structure of a very small segment of our world. None of its elements naturally or necessarily indicates who sits where; on previous occasions, we have used these same items to describe car crashes. So their indicator functions are strictly harnessed to our current beliefs about the relations between the tokens, certain of our friends, and their future positions relative to one another at our dining table.

To help explain the types of representational systems and their various features, consider this more elaborate example. It consists of a device physically linked to an object, **O**. Let's say that the object in question emits a mysterious glow, which oscillates randomly between two colors. The device is equipped with a pair of receptors, each made of material that is naturally sensitive to the radiation given off with one of the colorful glows; when stimulated, each sensor automatically undergoes a photochemical reaction that in turn triggers a switch connected to one of a pair of lamps. Thus the system is constructed so that one of a couple of lights, **AMBER** or **BLUE**, will illuminate, contingent on whether **O** is in one of two conditions, amber or blue. This representational system includes two expressive elements, the lights. It also has representational content, consisting of a topic and a comment. The topic is the system's referent, **O**. The comment is what it indicates about **O**, that it is amber or blue.

Our exemplary representational artifact—more precisely, its indicator elements and the states they can occupy—is not by itself meaningful. Essential to its capacity for meaning is its stable, non-accidental dependency on something outside itself. Otherwise the system would have no representational power; and were it not for our knowing or being able to figure out what its being amber or blue depends on, neither state would make much sense to us. Here my observations are intended to suggest a relational theory of meaning, to date developed furthest within the field of linguistics, according to which meaning resides in the systematic relations between different parts of the world, such that awareness of one object enables us to learn the condition of another.[7] Supporting these relations are various types of constraints on how parts of reality fit together. In the current example, some of these are nomic. Since the representational system is connected to its object by way of various photosensitive cells, certain physical laws play a role in the behavior of the system's indicator elements. Certain necessary constraints also apply. Just as a bachelor cannot be married, **AMBER** cannot at one and the same time be both on and off. Still other constraints pertain to the planning and practical reasoning of the device's makers and users. At some stage, certain agents had to have decided that they would hook up their machine to **O** (or to whatever **O**-type things that come along), and that they would fix it so that **AMBER** would go on when **O** is amber and **BLUE** would go on when **O** is blue. Anyone knowing of their intentions, or able to ascertain them, would thus have corresponding insights into the system's rationale.

Of course each of the cited constraints is to some extent conditional, insofar as none will hold if particular background conditions are not met. Not even the logical impossibility of the system's **AMBER** lamp being both on and not on, simultaneously and in the same sense, will obtain if the system's engineers change their minds and re-calibrate it so that a **GREEN** lamp lights up in the event of the object being amber. By the same token, saboteurs could snip some wires or stampeding elephants could trample the device. Now broken, none of the usual constraints on its relation to **O** would apply.

When the representational system is working, it does something special. By dint of the given constraints, one situation, the state of the system, conveys information about a different situation, the state of **O**. If you are cognizant of the device, and know of the regularities whereby it is connected to **O**, you will be able to learn a fact about **O** (that it is amber) by learning a fact about the system (that it is **AMBER**). Note that the information furnished by the representation has what Jon Barwise and John Perry call "priority" relative to the expressive medium itself.[8] The same fact, that **O** is amber, could be indicated in a variety of ways—with bells instead of lights, or in the form of a natural language proposition such as, "I have a feeling that **O** is amber." The existence of this fact does not depend on how it is represented, nor on its being represented. Hence the representational modality should not be confused with the information that it carries.

Moreover, the system cannot convey the information that **O** is blue unless the object actually is in that condition. Granted, the system could malfunction: The **BLUE** light could flash on pretty much at random due to an internal snafu. The system thus ceases to mediate information per se about **O**. Worse still, one of the operators, bent on world domination by control of the **O**-indicators, could fool with the system so as to cause it to register **AMBER** or **BLUE** according to his own megalomaniacal desires. Again, to the extent that the device's states no longer depend on **O**'s condition, it no longer carries information about that item. But insofar as the evil operator manipulates the representation with the goal of getting people to acquire certain thoughts or beliefs—which they might mistake as factual—regarding **O**, it is nonetheless still meaningful.

Not everything that a representation means will necessarily coincide with the information that it actually conveys. In our example, the evil operator gives the system the job of indicating that **O** is amber whether or not this is so. By surreptitiously suspending the nomic constraints, perhaps by disabling the receptors' sensitivity to **O**, and making the indicator elements' output strictly conditional upon his own intentions concerning which light should go on at any given moment, he sees to it that the system has meaning—it comments on the state of a certain topic—without necessarily carrying facts about that object. Yet it is not only in cases of misrepresentation that we discern the difference between intended meaning and meaning qua information. Somebody examining the representational device might be able to discover facts that it is not the system's purpose to convey. Inspecting its structure, one could recognize that the system's makers know how to design and build electrical circuitry. This is "collateral information"—the makers did not intend to represent or indicate this fact.[9] The system carries this information, without anybody meaning it to.

At this point, another interesting facet of the present example bears noticing. Like the chess pieces of the earlier model, the current system is a representation because somebody has given it a particular indicator function. Artificial representational systems are, after all, just those sorts of indicator ensembles that signify that **P** is the case if and only if another system, namely a human agent, has given it the job of indicating that **P**. But not all artificial representations are exactly the same. For instance, the coins used to denote the candidates' ranking constitute an entirely symbolic system of representation. The same is to be said of the chess pieces. Independent of our beliefs and intentions, these tokens and the relations between them have no inevitable connection to Adam, Martin, Matt, Berne, and their positions at table; if my partner and I forget which figure is assigned to indicate which guest, or if we decide to do our planning with colorful jelly beans, the figures will cease to mean anything about who shall sit where.

The **O**-representing device is somewhat different. It, too, has a symbolic component, since agents have to conceive of and implement a basically arbitrary connection between the state of the machine (i.e., this or that lamp flickering on) and the condition of a given object. Indeed, somebody has to decide in the first place that **O**'s condition is worth indicating and then construct an instrument to do the task. But this system is also designed to exploit the intrinsic indicator powers of certain of its components. Recall that its receptors are naturally sensitive to radiation emitted by **O**. Provided that no one tampers with them, and that the relevant laws of nature are not suspended, they will undergo an automatic change of state if and when **O** changes state; and these receptors, being wired to the machine's indicator lamps, mechanically activate corresponding changes in those lamps. Like thermometers and scales, our imaginary device is a hybrid. It is a representational system combining symbols with natural meaning.

The above example suggests that representational systems may possess one or both of two identifiable sources of meaning, natural and nonnatural. Which one(s) the system possesses will determine the kind of representation it is. Both types of meaning permit a representation to have significance with respect to how things stand in the world, as well as to how things stand with the user of the system. Both types of meaning can also convey information. However, in the pages below I underscore that it is only with the introduction of non-natural meaning that the possibility of misinformation or misrepresentation arises.

Symbols, I have implied, are creatures of non-natural meaning; indeed, henceforth I will use the terms "non-natural" and "symbolic" meaning interchangeably. What the chess pieces indicate, in the dinner planning scenario, depends on what the users want them to indicate. Having decided on a number of regularities according to which they are to be mobilized, the position of the knight relative to the king indicates for us Adam's prospective place relative to Berne. These tokens have symbolic meaning because they exhibit intentional counterfactual dependence. If we had assigned the indicator functions differently, the knight would have denoted Martin's place; and if we had wanted to show Matt sitting next to, instead of across from, Adam, the tokens would have been in an appropriately different spatial relation to one another. In other words, the condition of the representational system and the significance of its elements are predominately governed by a rationality constraint—our beliefs and attitudes about what the tokens mean and our skill and felicity in operating on them according to the rules that we have set for ourselves.

The rationality constraint is no less operative in cases in which the symbol system is used to recall a previous state of affairs. I could use the chess pieces to instruct you about where people sat at last night's dinner. Whether or not, and to what degree, I accurately reconstruct the seating plan will, again, depend upon my beliefs and desires. If my recollections are true, and if I am able to mobilize the tokens in a coherent manner (rather than, for example, making more than one of them stand for Matt), I will be able to use the system to represent the earlier situation. But in contradistinction to natural meaning, a symbolic representation can mean that **P** without **P** actually being the case. If my memory fails, or if I decide to scandalize you by indicating, contrary to what I know to have been the case, that the rivals Berne and Matt sat side by side, then the system will fail to represent how the world was. It all depends on me.

These tracks in the snow mean that a cat was here. The width of this tree ring indicates the amount of rainfall last year. That man's rolling gait means that he is a sailor.[10] The thermometer's mercury level shows that it is very cold, −21°C today. "The recent budget means that we shall have a hard year."[11] This photo means that there is at least one fountain in the *Place des Vosges*. Each of the foregoing depends for its meaning on a "natural sign." One object or situation is indicative of another's (past, present, or future) condition, not by virtue of how someone uses it or what someone wants it to signify, but by virtue of how it is objectively related to the other entity or state of affairs.[12]

If the man's rolling gait naturally indicates that he is a seaman, his gait depends on his being a seaman, but not on his or anyone else's belief that he is a sailor or on an intention to show that he has this occupation. Likewise, if the budget naturally means hardship, it is because tough times necessarily follow its policies' application. Moreover, a natural sign's meaning or, if you prefer, the natural meaning of any object or state of affairs, is purely factual. For **X** to be a natural sign of **Y**, **Y** must really be the case. Tracks do not naturally mean feline peregrinations if made by a robotic, ersatz cat's mechanical paws. The mercury does not mean that it is –21°C if a bored, prankish god sees to it that the thermometer reads ten degrees colder than the actual ambient temperature. And the photograph does not naturally mean that the *Place des Vosges* looks just so if, lacking a snapshot, I show you one of *Place St. Michel* instead, expecting you not to know the difference. An item's natural meaning is just that which it really indicates—independent of what anyone wants to indicate **by** it.

The term "natural," then, refers to a-rational indicator relations, where the indicator's state is not conditional on any agent having any particular attitudes or plans regarding the link between it and the indicated object. This kind of meaning, when it occurs, is supported by constraints other than an agent's beliefs and communicative intentions. However, we should be careful not to equate natural meaning with causal processes. Dretske's injunction against conflating informational with etiological relations motivates this caveat.[13] Ordinarily, and in all the cases that interest us as scholars of non-fiction cinema, there are determinant causal processes underlying the capacity for one item or state of affairs to signal how things stand with respect to another. But even when these processes do clearly account for the "flow of information," the meaning relation is not itself reducible to the causal one. One way of explaining this principle is with reference to the "ghost channel."[14] Say that you and I are at separate locations watching the same television broadcast. Although there is no determinant, signal-bearing physical link or channel between your TV set and mine, what I see on my monitor reliably indicates what you can see on yours; nothing happening at one of these sets causes the other to look as it does, yet each carries information about the other.

In warning against merging informational with causal relations, Dretske also notes that effects need not always embody information about their causes. For instance, if I show you only the back of a playing card, the cause of your visual sensation is decidedly one particular card, the two of clubs; but because what is visible is equally compatible with any one of fifty-one other conditions obtaining on the card's face, what you see does not mean that the two of clubs is on the reverse.[15]

I am not always sure what theorists mean to say when they refer to photographically made pictures as being indexical signs of real objects, but in my thesis I shall understand "indexical" as synonymous with natural signification. Hence I will be parting company with those who would be inclined to agree that indexical signs "bear a physical trace of what they refer to, such as the fingerprint, x ray, or photograph."[16] There need be no physical link between the natural indicator and its object. There need be only an information-preserving relation, which exists independently of anyone's intentions toward such a relation.

What, then, is the connection between natural meaning and representation? Do the tracks **represent** the cat's paws? One might be inclined to think so, especially when there is a vivid resemblance of the imprint to the original's contours. Our commonsense assumption that photographs are representations might also suggest that other natural signs are representations, too. It is imperative to avoid confusion over this matter. Something being a natural sign—even one that pre-theoretically strikes us as being visibly similar to its object—is not sufficient to make it a representation. Natural significance must therefore be distinguished from representation.

According to the definition that I support, **X** represents **Y** if **X** is supposed to indicate how things stand with respect to **Y**. Although the condition of tracks, tree rings, and mercury do reliably indicate certain other states of affairs, they do not have this capacity because they have somehow functionally adapted themselves to serve as indicators of those states. However, people can give such natural signs a representational function, or contrive to manufacture or use a natural indicator with a representational purpose in mind. Realizing their natural significance, botanists could routinely use tree rings as a kind of instrument for gathering information about rainfall. Police use fingerprints in a similar way. Thermometers, of course, are constructed in order to serve a particular end. In all three cases, natural signs are harnessed to adventitious interests and efforts to indicate one or another state of affairs. The photographic image is thus akin to the thermometer. It is an intentional artifact, the natural meaning of which someone employs for representational purposes.

Cinematic Representation

On the whole, a documentary, as well as many of its components—such as its image track and portions thereof—might be usefully characterized as a sort of representational system. More precisely, it is frequently constructed out of several parallel and embedded representational systems, notably: photographic imagery, sound tracks, non-photographically produced images (e.g., computer-generated pictures) and visual figures (e.g., graphs), and spoken and written natural language utterances. These components—which include sundry elements with natural meaning—are made, combined, and manipulated in order to indicate how things stand with respect to other objects, conditions, and states of affairs. All cinematic constatives can thus be assimilated into the same broad category to which the **O**-indicator and the thermometer belong. They are symbolic systems of representation that employ natural signs.

It is not my aim to demonstrate that all movies are necessarily representations. To make that claim, I would have to the show that none of the items that we might possibly want to call a movie fails to represent anything. Perhaps there are experimental works that are fully non-representational. I neither care nor need to make any effort to take a stand on that issue. All I wish to maintain is that a certain class of non-fictional works, those combining assertion and photographic depiction, are representations. Crucially, the kind of artifact I have in mind has visible features that stand in a relation of non-conventional dependence on the visible properties of other, extra-cinematic objects. This statement is not itself a definition of depiction. But it does begin to identify one aspect of those motion pictures that usually interest us when we study documentaries.

What is so important about whether or not a movie is a representational system? The central reason why the question merits attention is this: By definition, representational systems convey meaning. What they indicate, and what they "say" about that topic, are first and foremost decided by factors having independence from what interpreters happen to believe or desire them to mean. If cinematic constatives are fundamentally of this category, then their meaning is not especially contingent on how spectators experience and interpret them. The work's content and information await discovery rather than invention by us.

The idea that a cinematic constative is a representational system leads us to a budget of commitments regarding the nature of this type of artifact. Generally speaking, the documentary's meaning is a property of its relation to something external to itself. More precisely, it can have two kinds of meaning: natural and symbolic. The first, synonymous with factuality and information, arises when the work's state—how it looks, for instance—depends first and foremost on a-rational relations between this state and that of some other object or situation. Indicator relations of this kind are by definition information-preserving; for example, a photographic image cannot naturally mean that **P** unless **P** is (or was, or will be), in fact, the case.

On the other hand, symbolic, or non-natural, meaning denotes communicative situations in which agent rationality determines meaning. Here we shift our focus from what a cinematic segment naturally means to what a cinematic agent means—means to indicate, show, represent—by that segment. A work can non-naturally mean that **P** without **P** actually being or having been the case; and whether or not its symbolic meaning is factual depends proximally on the truth of the author's beliefs, and/or on whether his intent is non-deceptive. Recall that when the machine indicates **AMBER** regardless of whether **O** is an amber or a blue condition, but contingent on what the evil operator wants to signal, nonnatural meaning occurs.

Previously I observed that a representational system's content can be identified in terms of topics and comments. Now I want to elaborate on how to talk about content, while switching to a new terminology that will serve us well in the long run. Watching a daytime talk show, we can see that Oprah Winfrey and Elizabeth Taylor are seated in armchairs, facing each other, on a stage in a television studio before an audience. This image has "external significance."[17] Its crucial features and the constraints upon them—along with facts bearing on how, when, and where the motion picture was made—enable the depiction to describe a certain extra-cinematic situation involving Oprah, Liz, chairs, and so on. Should the situation that it is used to describe be a real world state of affairs, we would say that the image is accurate.

Construing content in terms of external significance has the advantage of capturing something of the complexity of the motion picture representation and the world to which it is connected. A movie's content is amenable to description in the same terms that we use to classify noncinematic states of affairs, that is, with reference to objects and individuals having certain properties and existing in various relations to one another at space-time locations. What until now I have been loosely calling a "situation" is itself a collection of these constituents. Some situations are more or less stable and protracted; others, such as those we call "events," are rather more dynamic and changeable. In any case, movie comprehension is like making sense of reality: It entails recognizing both actual and typical situations and individuating the elements out of which they are built.

Cinematic constatives, like their linguistic counterparts, also have "mental significance."[18] Imagine that you are watching an exposé of how garbage destined to be recycled is instead being dumped at a landfill by the waste disposal company contracted by the municipality to do the recycling. Watching this report, you learn of a scandal. You also learn of the reporters' state of mind, that is, that they know or think that this scam is taking place and wish you to adopt the attitude of belief toward a proposition to that effect. But what if their story were a hoax, the situation it describes being non-existent? In case of lying or insincerity, the program would still be mentally significant to the extent that it carries information about what someone wants you to believe.

Neither external nor mental significance has to be a by-product of the viewer's relation to the movie. To make this claim is not at all to deny that a non-fiction's content can be ambiguous or give rise to competing interpretations. Even less is it to declare that documentarians enjoy full command over cinematic meaning. Nor do I regard either the viewer as an infallible interpreter or meaning as transparently obvious. Indeed, throughout the remainder of this book I will be concerned to show that context, background knowledge, perception, and cognition are decisive factors in the work having meaning to some interpreter.

To return to our immediate concern, some of the cinematic representational system's indicator elements are significant to viewers for what they naturally signify. The sound track encompasses such elements, as does the image track. Because my study is mainly about cinematic constatives that are also photographic pictures, I place special emphasis on the photo-pictorial mode of representation and on the types of meaning that derive from such images. This phase of the discussion begins with an examination of two premises: The movie image has natural pictorial meaning; and it has natural non-pictorial meaning.

Standard, photographically generated non-fictions consist of many units having pictorial properties. Earlier I suggested that pictures involve resemblance. The time has come to clarify how this word is to be understood in discussing depiction. Like Christopher Peacocke and others, I favor a perceptual approach to the nature of depiction, the central ideas of which I shall now rehearse.[19]

When we observe a picture, some of the intrinsic properties of our visual sensation are analogous to those of the visual sensation that we would have were we to see the pictured object itself or a member of its kind from a given angle. In other words, a photographic picture of a horse and a horse have approximately similar appearances within our visual field. Of course, the two sensory experiences can not be identical. But they can be roughly congruent, with respect to such properties as visually experienced shape, proportion, line, pattern, position, color, gradients of brightness, contrasts of luminosity and color, and spatial relations between parts of the scene. From an empirical standpoint, this similarity of "visual-field properties" is explained by the optical array reaching the observer's eyes: The structure of light reaching someone looking at the picture is roughly analogous to that which reaches or would reach the observer of the actual scene.[20] Given the mechanics of vision, these arrays excite similar sensations of the figure of a horse. And by virtue of still poorly understood sub-intentional visual processes, both sensory experiences tend to result in the viewer coming to believe that he is seeing the figure of a horse. Hence the upshot of one's visual experience of either the picture or the object itself is its association with the concept "horse," and the subsequent recognition of a (picture of) a horse.

There are two further conditions on an artifact serving as a depiction, both of which can be satisfied by the movie image. Andrea, wanting to build a new dog house and needing to describe to the carpenter the desirable sorts of aesthetic and practical features, shows her my dog house. Temporarily, my dog house functions as a representation of what Andrea wants to erect. But it is not a depiction. Pictures and their objects, it is argued, occupy a similar "sensory space"—which is to say that they trigger the experience of similar shapes within one's visual field. However, depictions and their depicta, unlike my actual and Andrea's prospective dog house, are not visually experienced as occupying a similar three-dimensional region of physical space.[21] Here we have the basis for a distinction between pictures and sculptures; and in the current example, I would say that Andrea is presenting the carpenter with a three-dimensional model.

The second condition on depiction is intentionalist. **D** is not a picture unless someone creates or uses it as such. In other words, a picture arises from an agent's efforts to give viewers the above-mentioned sort of visual experience. Your reflection in the pond as you search for your golf ball does not satisfy this constraint. But a photographically made picture does pass this test, even when its causal history is unorthodox, as in cases in which the photo is an accidental by-product of a cat stepping on the shutter. Photographs have this strong association with depiction because a camera is designed to produce pictorial representations, which are the automatic result of the causal interactions of external objects with a machine calibrated to generate pictures, regardless of whether the operator knows or cares what is in front of the lens. This is not to say that everything issuing from the apparatus will be a depiction. An out of focus picture of a black horse taken on a dark night will be a natural, indexical sign of its referent, but the image's unrecognizability makes it a bad candidate for pictorial status.

A motion picture therefore represents by giving rise to a perceptual experience that is, in a strictly delimited way, with respect to how the picture's object appears to us in sensory space, similar to that which one would have were one looking at the object itself. This concept of perceptual similarity is not to be confused with a more problematic notion of resemblance, namely, the idea that pictures look like that which they represent or are in some respects structurally similar to or isomorphic with real-world referents.[22]

The world is full of things, the visible properties of which may be similar to one another. But unless one thing is designed to facilitate the experience of a certain kind of congruence between a visual experience of it and another item, no privileged combination or critical mass of visible properties that resemble one another will make the former a picture of the latter. In many ways, any real horse would look much more like the actual historical Trigger than would old film footage of Roy Roger's steed. A horse could even be bred to bear an uncanny resemblance to this head of celebrity livestock, such that a knowledgeable observer would immediately recognize the likeness. Moreover, there are many respects in which the photo's own properties, visible and other, are unlike those of the original. It is much flatter and smaller, does not smell, feel, or behave like Trigger, and has none of his biological functions, performing talents, self-control, and horse sense. Yet that which makes something a Trigger-picture is precisely that which makes it unlike Trigger or a Trigger-double: It is not visually experienced as occupying a similar three-dimensional region of physical space, and it is not intended to be so experienced. Without necessitating the ascription of identical visible properties to the picture and its object, we need say only that the depiction and its object give rise to similar shapes within one's visual field. Thus, resemblance *simpliciter* is not the conceptual key to depiction.

It is important to stress that photographic depictions, unlike other types of pictures, acquire their pictorial properties from the lawful physical constraints on their appearance. Hence it is often said that they display natural counterfactual dependence on that which they depict.[23] If the pre-filmic object were to have different visible properties, the image would be correspondingly different, due to the way the recording apparatus is devised to capitalize on certain material processes and natural regularities. Provided that we have in mind unedited, continuous shots, natural counterfactuality also extends to such properties as duration, direction of movement within the frame, speed of depicted events, and order of depicted events.

Unlike the relation of the painting to its object, natural counterfactuality is uncircumscribed by the depictor's state of mind. Projected onto a screen, the optical array reflected by the surface of a super-8mm movie of Emma is objectively contingent on the structure of part of an array reflected by a different surface, that of Emma. In this distinctive way, facts about how her image looks depend upon and preserve facts about how she looks, that is, her short hair, dark eyes, and high cheekbones. Once the lens, lighting, and camera angle are chosen, Emma appears taller in this footage than she does in real life not only because the filmmaker wants her to look that way, but because of how her actual visible dimensions are mechanically rendered by the photographic device under the prevailing conditions. Holding fixed all the other variables, a change in the subject's physique would produce a corresponding difference in the image. In contrast, how she is portrayed in a painting would depend on the artist's beliefs about her appearance and upon goals regarding how he will picture her. Without also altering the painter's intentions, a change in Emma's proportions would not automatically yield a change in the painted image's visible features.

It is in part because of their natural significance that motion pictures can give spectators access, by visual means, to facts about the visible properties of extra-cinematic objects. Now it strikes me that the sentence "Emma has short, black hair," written on a slip of paper, could also allow a person to become perceptually attuned to a visual state of affairs. The reader sees that the sentence looks a certain way, and thereby apprehends the condition of another scene. Its visible features are, to be sure, systematically related to how that external scene looks. But how the inscription looks is only superficially connected to its referent's visible condition, and the reader's discovery of Emma's appearance is only incidentally a matter of visual perception.

Here is what I mean. It is not one's visual experience of the observable properties of the sentence, its words, or the spatial relations between words or letters that makes it possible for one to realize that Emma's hair is short, for a sighted but illiterate person will not perceive that such is the case by looking at the sentence. Indeed with or without a working knowledge of English, nobody can get much of an appreciation for what Emma looks like by seeing the sentence. In contrast, the super-8 footage is meaningful even to the pre-linguistic; not only does it indicate that the subject has close cropped hair, it shows what her short hair looks likes, while also embedding information about the height of her forehead, the shape of her ears, the distance between her eyes, and so on. The phenomenological character of the visual experience of Emma's picture is closer to that of seeing Emma than is the experience of reading even the most elaborate description of her.

The movie picture in limited respects looks to us like its object. Moreover, its capacity to carry information about the depictum is conditioned by objective, a-rational constraints. No belief, convention, or any other intentional state intervenes in such a way as to relate systematically the movie picture to its natural significance. It is for this reason that we should reject Umberto Eco's assertion that the photographic image is "transcribed" in the photographic emulsion according to a "code of transmission," thereby ensuring that the relation between image and pre-filmic referent is "wholly arbitrary."[24] To accept his claim is to construe the term "code" so broadly as to conflate natural casual processes with genuine conventionality. On the other hand, the sentence "Emma has short, black hair" displays intentional counterfactual dependence on the scene's visible features. Were Emma's hair longer and blonde, the writer would have to have a correspondingly different belief about how things look and would have to follow appropriately different intentions in order to communicate this fact; successful linguistic expression of this information depends on the scribe knowing and adhering to those semantic, syntactic, and orthographic conventions that would permit him to publicize the content of his (not necessarily) visually derived beliefs.

Because films, videos, and the like are visual artifacts, the spectator's engagement with them is predicated upon actually seeing recognizable images of objects, people, events, and so on. In other words, the content of motion pictures is largely visually determined. Indeed, seeing is **essential** to gaining access to parts of the movie's meaning. For this reason, Currie contrasts filmic with literary works.[25] Grasping the content of the latter need not depend on seeing, for non-visual reading in Braille or Morse code will acquaint one with the work, too.

Here it is relevant to note that the nature of visual perception is currently the topic of intense research and debate within both empirical and philosophical circles. But I can conceive of no reason to mimic those film theorists who abolish a seeing/reading distinction by assuming visual perception to be first and foremost a linguistic or semiotic process of translating "unorganized sensory input" into signs upon which we perform further mental operations.[26]

A responsible sampling of the research into vision would encounter numerous competing hypotheses. Gibsonian direct theories of perceptual processing, for example, hold that stimuli reaching the observer are themselves so information-rich as to determine unambiguously the character of the corresponding entry-level internal representation. Rival computationalist theories contend that visual systems must actively extract and organize the information borne by the signal; instead of entailing the application of preexisting syntactico-semantic rules or codes, this process might be said to involve the system in problem-solving operations, like a detective who forms conclusions on the basis of memory, inference, prior learning, and available evidence.[27]

To say that distinctively visual cognition consists of perceptual achievements fundamentally different from the comprehension of linguistic constructs is surely not to deny that at a higher level of mental activity language still plays a key role in the acquisition of knowledge by visual means, that is, as an invaluable source of concepts for classifying and recognizing objects visually detected. But it is to say that motion picture comprehension is a basically visual, as opposed to linguistic, operation.

There is nothing essentially pictorial about natural meaning: The sailor's gait, the mercury's height, and the budget's policies do not furnish a visual experience similar to that which they indicate, any more than red spots picture the measles virus that causes them. Sometimes movie images also have important natural non-pictorial meanings. Even when an image does not literally picture a given state of affairs—does not give rise to a visual sensation of a given object—it could still be in an in-

Representation and Depiction

dicator relation to the object or situation in question, due to the natural constraints on the depiction's existence.

An inventory of George Holliday's amateur video of African-American motorist Rodney King's beating by white Los Angeles police officers could list the following natural meanings: It preserves information about visible states of affairs, like who performed what physical gestures for how long and in what sequence and what those behaviors looked like. For example, its natural pictorial external significance includes the fact that at around four minutes into the tape, King is on the ground and Officer Powell is hitting him with a baton, subsequent to which Officer Briseno steps on the back of King's neck. The video's non-pictorial external significance also would include facts pertaining to the camera operator's location: Given the nomic conditions on its existence and traits, the footage perforce signifies Holliday's spatial-temporal position relative to the recorded event.

In other respects, pinning down the imagery's natural meaning is more problematic. For instance, any attribution of natural non-pictorial mental significance is bound to be tenuous and ill-advised, not because we cannot make reasonable inferences about some of the videographer's thoughts but because the connection between those states of mind and the tape's observable properties is far too conditional. From the evidence of the tape, it seems safe to assume that Holliday had at least a belief to the effect that there was a photographable event occurring off in some direction. Similarly, the imagery strongly suggests that he was indeed trying to control his camera and not merely pointing it haphazardly. So it makes sense for us to regard the footage as evincing a state of mind appropriate to guiding and sustaining recording activity.

Our knowledge that one kind of psychological state, an intention to tape an observed event, regularly gives rise to recordings such as Holliday's makes this mental significance more than a outside possibility. However, it is far from obvious that the recording's condition **must** indicate the presence of any of the aforementioned mental constraints on its production. The artifact's form and content are not exclusively compatible with any one set of authorial states; Holliday might have been acting on much different motivations and cognitions, yet could have turned out a work narrowly identical to the now famous video. The chain that leads our interpretations back from the work to the maker's psychology thus lacks a natural counterfactual linkage between the two. Ultimately, we must make a corresponding leap, the justification for which will be the application of the rationality heuristic plus available evidence.

One aspect of the video tape's natural meaning qua external significance is also especially controversial. Here again, the significance in question has to do with psychological conditions. What, if anything, does the document naturally indicate about the law enforcers' intentions, as well as those of their victim? Judging by how it looks, does it mean that the police are trying to take lawful steps toward subduing a recalcitrant suspect, or that they are administering a racially motivated beating? Does the video indicate that King resists if not antagonizes his arrestors, or does it show that he is confused and self-protective under a hail of more than fifty undeserved baton blows? Lawyers, jurors, and an awful lot of television viewers dickered over this dimension of the tape's meaning, which raises the prospect of its interpretation ultimately having more to do with observers' attitudes and desires than with the laws of optics and light. Under what conditions could we truly assert that the video indicates that, say, these police want to act legally and professionally?

The grounds for including this external significance among the document's natural meanings would be the same as those for describing any meaning—pictorial or non-pictorial, external or mental—as natural. A cinematic depiction, **D**, naturally means that **P**—that, say, the police are trying to act prudently—only if **P** actually is (was) the case. What is more, the state of **D** or certain of its features must exhibit a natural, necessary counterfactual dependence on **P**: If it were not really the case that **P**, then the picture could not be just as it is or look just as it does. And now we can see at least one reason why Holliday's tape is potentially troublesome. Perhaps the image track or portions of it would look the same irrespective of whether the officers are acting on cautious professional judgments executed under stressful circumstances or on racial hatred. Were this so, **D** would at best be only an equivocal sign of how things stand with respect to the depicted agents' intentions; an enormous variety of psychological conditions could have constrained the agents' behaviors, and subsequently certain of the video's properties, to be just as we observe them to be.

True, **D**'s condition is distantly caused by whatever desires actually do motivate those agents, since it is these states that trigger their conduct as registered on tape. But **D**'s causal reliance on **P** being the case is no guarantee that it will unequivocally mean that **P**. Natural counterfactual dependence—being a relation by which one situation necessarily bears some information about another—is not identical to a cause-effect relation. The back of a playing card is no guide to its face value because neither's appearance is counterfactually dependent on the other's. Likewise, a photographic depiction, to the degree that the way it looks fails to depend naturally-counterfactually on whether it is **P** or one of **P**'s possible rivals, will not be naturally informative with respect to **P**, despite its causal history. In such cases, the depiction has **P** as its external significance conditionally, that is, only if the agents' actions that it records were motivated or produced in a certain way. By the same token, judging why the pictured agents act as shown would require going well beyond the imagery's natural meaning and involve such inquiry, evidence, and reasoning as necessary to justify a preference for one of the competing explanations. In a nutshell, it would require reasoning about intentional constraints on the agents' behavior rather than about natural counterfactualities bearing on the tape's visually observable condition.

A cinematic representational system, I have claimed, typically combines natural with symbolic meaning. Again, an indicator element, or an ensemble of them, has symbolic meaning to the extent that its significance depends on what the maker or user thinks it indicates or wishes to indicate by it. Linguistic tokens, embedded in the cinematic work in various ways, have symbolic meaning and may provide clues to the symbolic meaning of other features of the movie. Mise-en-scène; shot composition, angle, and framing; editing, special visual effects, and sound effects; and the juxtaposition of image with sound can all convey symbolic meaning.

Here is a fanciful but telling illustration. Fritz, a cineaste, is called as an eye witness in a murder trial. He is asked, "How was the victim, **M**, killed?" Having prepared his response in advance, Fritz shows a brief motion picture sequence produced, we shall say, long before the crime occurred. It depicts a person in shadows approaching another human figure from behind and apparently slipping a cord around his victim's neck. The witness thereby testifies that he thinks **M** was strangled, although he could not clearly see who did it. In taking stock of this scenario, it is important to note that the film's provenance rules out it naturally meaning that the victim died as shown. Its natural external significance concerns wholly different individuals, events, and locations, the footage being an out-take from a melodramatic fiction Fritz made years ago. By itself, the movie is not even about **M**, the assailant, his weapon, the crime scene, and so on. However, facts about the testifier, the discursive context, and the depiction make it possible for the footage to indicate that Fritz believes he saw such and such happen.[28]

That which I am calling the movie's symbolic meaning displays intentional counterfactual dependence. If the cineaste weren't under the impression that the killer struck as described, and were he not trying to express this same impression with the imagery in question, the movie would not mean that it seems to Fritz that **M** was strangled by a mystery man. In short, within the courtroom setting, the film indicates what it does because a communicator wants it to.

Naturally, certain aspects of how the film looks and what kind of situation it seems to show, deriving from its fixed natural pictorial meaning, allow for its functional adaptation to present purposes; a travelogue of Barcelona's architectural highlights would hardly work as well. Furthermore, the exhibition context enables Fritz's exploitation of the imagery to carry the designated meaning. Having been called to testify, and asked a direct question, he can be reasonably sure of people recognizing his constative intentions in showing the film and grasping his desire that its content be regarded as relevant to that of the question. He knows that his actions and the audience's interpretation of them take place in a framework of various mutual beliefs and presumptions.

Fritz believes, for example, that inquiry is focused on a certain past event, to which he bore a certain relation; and he knows that the audience, aware of these facts, expects his contributions to this stage of inquiry to pertain to his experience of that event. And by virtue of these background conditions, the court is able to infer the film's mental and external significance, to wit, that Fritz wants them to believe that he saw that the murder took place approximately as pictured. Finally, I add, facts about the witness (what he really saw, the accuracy of his beliefs, the sincerity of his assertions) and facts about the world (what really happened to **M**) determine the truth of his testimony.

As the foregoing suggests, symbolic meaning shares with natural meaning a number of familiar manifestations. The movie may have pictorial and non-pictorial non-natural meaning and may carry both external and mental significance.

D has symbolic pictorial meaning when it has an external pictorial significance different from that of **D**'s natural pictorial meaning. Early in Orson Welles's *F For Fake* (1973), there is a series of angles establishing that Welles is on a railway station platform; the final shot in this series, **F**, has him framed tightly against the backdrop of a white rectangular screen that we watch a pair of assistants move into place behind him. From this image we cut to a brief insert showing a bank of lighting equipment at some unspecified location. The next shot, **F'**, is again of the director in front of the white screen, his position and clothing graphically matching **F'** with **F**. "This is a film about trickery and fraud—about lies," says Welles to the camera, at which point he walks off in one direction as the screen is carried off in another, and we see that the current location is not a train station but a set decorated with a multitude of window frames. In this moment of self-reflection, Welles reminds us that one of the filmmaker's own tricks is to confuse the difference between an image's symbolic and natural pictorial significance. What **F'** really depicts is a man in front of a screen on a movie set at some unspecified time. But for a moment, we think that it shows quite another situation—one continuous with **F**. Framing, composition, and editing relate **F'** to an external visible situation other than that which the shot itself naturally indicates.

F for Fake is a virtuoso cinematic juggling act that puts in motion Welles's own personal anecdotes, self-reflexive strategies like the one noted above, interwoven stories about writer Clifford Irving and art forger Elmyr de Hory, the faked autobiography of Howard Hughes (the work of Irving, perhaps with de Hory's help), and an extraordinary tale of forged Picassos that Welles sets aloft only to knock down as a seductive but obvious deception for which more than one viewer has likely fallen. The point of all this chicanery is the exposition of a thesis. Filmmakers, it seems, aim at producing the same sorts of effects sought by counterfeiters, fakers, and magicians. Their mutual pleasure is to fool the expert guardians of authenticity and value, as well as audiences who themselves enjoy being shocked and gulled.

Now the situation that this analogy proposes is not the kind that can be literally pictured. Nonetheless, the movie's content and construction suggest this external significance. What's more, the documentary has a corresponding symbolic mental significance: Welles believes, or at least wants for us to believe, that the practices of filmmakers, fakers, and illusionists are akin.

Misrepresentation

Thus far I have argued that: cinematic constatives are meaningful because they are representational systems; they have natural as well as intentional meaning; to the extent that they are members of the class of photographic depictions, motion picture non-fictions also have natural pictorial meaning; and finally, non-fictional movie representations have meaning because they capture and convey facts about mental as well as external states of affairs. In preparation for later discussions, I conclude this chapter with a few brief observations concerning the sources and scope of misrepresentation and error. Historically, film scholarship seems almost irresistibly drawn to the opinion that the cinema, apparently the most realistic of representational systems, is overshadowed by the risk, even the necessity, of distortion, error, and illusion. However, it is imprudent to grant priority to the goal of theorizing the cinematic work's contributions to epistemic breakdown.

It is symbolic meaning that introduces a crucial semantic possibility to cinematic communication. Natural meaning, as I understand it, is a sort of relation that cannot fail to hold. In this sense, a thermometer means that it is −21°C just in the case it is −21°C. If the thermometer is somehow broken—maybe the applicable physical laws have been suspended, or else a wizard is exercising his occult powers—and registers an arctic air temperature when it is actually warmer, then it does not erroneously mean that it is −21°C, despite the mercury's level. Rather, it is a natural sign that the world has gone crazy, or that there is a wizard at work.

In the same sense, a photographically made picture naturally indicates only what there is to be indicated: that a particular scene photographed under specific conditions yields an image having these properties. Of course, viewers could mistake it for a natural sign of one state of affairs when it is actually indicative of quite another. But in that event, it is merely observers who get things wrong and not the image that misinforms. It is only when they are endowed with some amount of symbolic meaning that artifacts may be misrepresentations, where misrepresentation involves actually and determinately indicating that **P** when **P** is not the case. Like any such representational system, a movie's powers of misrepresentation depend on its maker's or user's goals and skills in manipulating its elements and assigning significance to them.

For argument's sake, suppose that *Alien Autopsy: Fact or Fiction?* (Tom McGough, 1995) contains only inauthentic film of a postmortem on a polydactylic, pot-bellied extra-terrestrial. Thus someone, adapting the image track's features to give the impression of photographic evidence that aliens have visited earth, that they have six fingers and toes, and that their cosmic viscera look just so, produced the autopsy footage with the plan that spectators would at least consider ascribing a certain natural external significance to it. If *Alien Autopsy* is as described, then it is an attempt to induce what Richard Allen calls "reproductive illusion."[29]

Allen applies this term to cases in which we are instructed that an image's content is or may be actual when in fact it is staged; one is under a reproductive illusion to the degree that one is correspondingly fooled or unsure. Cinematic prestidigitators try to achieve this in assorted ways: camera tricks, lighting, mise-en-scène, special effects, montage, digital imagery, misleading linguistic cues, and so on. Reproductive illusion arises from plans to lead spectators to misidentify the work's objective external significance; the success of this operation hangs on the extent to which viewers confuse natural meaning with a non-natural, non-factual meaning.

Not every misrepresentation is a reproductive illusion. Deception can occur in the absence of any attempt to jam the viewer's ability to recognize the depiction's natural external significance. While making it understood to the court that the footage bears absolutely no photographic relation to the real historical event of Pat's murder, Fritz could nonetheless employ it to misinform people, should he know that the crime did not happen as he asserts cinematically. Furthermore, misrepresentation is not synonymous with deception. Suppose that Fritz is sincere, that is, he does believe that the murder was committed approximately as shown, but that it was really a second assailant, unseen by Fritz, who delivered a lethal blow. The cineaste's beliefs are faulty, and the symbolic, intentional, counterfactual meaning of his model of the pre-filmic event reproduces this error; yet because he has the attitude expressed, he is nonetheless a cooperative participant in this communicative act.

Consider another example, designed to throw into relief how misrepresentation-resistant an indicator system can be when it employs natural signs. Unbeknownst to me, Emma has an identical twin, Etta. In fact, it is Etta who I have recorded on the super-8 footage. But throughout the planning, production, and exhibition phases I have labored under a misapprehension, intending and thinking myself to represent one person when I was portraying another. Thus I believe that I have wonderful footage of Emma and say so to all of my friends when I roll the film for them. In as much as I mean for the film to be taken a certain way by spectators, as caused by Emma having posed before the camera, I thereby unwittingly use it to misindicate how things stood with respect to some small portion of the pre-filmic world, and I in turn plant false beliefs in others.

Thus I mistakenly ascribe a certain natural meaning to the picture and in doing so unwittingly ascribe a symbolic meaning to this work. But there are two reasons to regard the above example as principally an instance of successful pictorial representation, in spite of the depictor's epistemic failure and the cascade of failures to which it might lead. The first step is to recognize the bootstrapping of my failed intention to depict Emma to a successful intention to depict Etta. My plan to represent Emma is a plan to represent that person in front of me. Indeed, the same would be said if I were drawing my subject from life instead of photographing her. As G. N. Kemp remarks, an artist's intention to make a picture **from** a given scene involves a demonstrative mode of presentation.[30] Hence the depictor's intention to make a picture of Emma, or Etta, or whoever, is subordinated to his intention to depict that which is now in front of him. Provided that it is an intention to picture the appearance of the actual prevailing scene that informs one's actions, and provided that one acts on no plan to confuse viewers about the work's actual content, the proper object of the resultant pictorial representation will be that scene, independent of one's false beliefs about who or what it is.[31]

The second reason to regard the current example as a representational success derives from the work's natural external significance, this being the pre-filmic state of affairs it objectively describes. Despite my error, the movie cannot but picture Etta posing before the camera, all the relevant background constraints being equal to this outcome.[32] Depicting the actual external situation is the camera's default mode of operation. In contrast, a painter, his perceptions and beliefs about the model's visible properties determining the picture's content and its rapport with the depictum, must intend to paint from the scene before him. So even in cases in which the depictor has false ideas about the appearance of the scene before him—say, for instance, that I hallucinate that the woman in front of the camera has three eyes—the photographic apparatus, in doing what it is designed to do, biases the depiction process toward representation rather than misrepresentation.

Film theories often propose that any attempt to represent reality inevitably leads instead to misrepresentation. Prima facie, this assertion looks authoritative because it rests squarely on a truism. Whenever one thing represents another, there is a loss of information and an attendant risk of people acquiring distorted notions about the referent. This loss of information happens in roughly two ways.

First, the loss is a consequence of the necessary and manifest differences and asymmetries between two structures: representational medium and represented object. The totality of the latter's being and properties are not magically reproduced or made immediately present by the former. Rather, some of the medium's own properties preserve a portion of facts about some of the object's own properties, by virtue of constraints that determine that the condition of the former shall depend upon the condition of the latter, but not necessarily the converse.[33] Plainly, the map is not the territory, although some of cinema studies' most field-defining debates—over Bazin's identity thesis, over the spectator's experience of perceptual illusion—are, respectively, over whether anyone should intelligently or could falsely ever believe otherwise.[34]

The rationality of representation accounts for another way in which information is lost and obscured. A commonsense assumption, shared by every practicing cinema scholar regardless of theoretical orientation, is that each movie is the result, to a greater or lesser degree, of agency and action. Hence every representation is the product of filtering operations, whereby the maker's or makers' beliefs, intentions, judgments, preferences, selections, points of view, desires, sensibilities, and perceptions— as these pertain to that which they wish to portray and to the effects they want to achieve—exert a decisive influence over the representation's form and content. In the process, some information about the object domain is discarded or left out. Meanwhile, regardless of whether the makers or the spectators know it, the process of representation makes it seem that the object has non-existent properties or properties that it in fact lacks. I take it that these are the sorts of processes that theorists have in mind when they say that every documentary is necessarily an interpretation of reality.

The claim that attempts to represent reality inevitably lead to misrepresentation is merely prima facie authoritative because citing the fact of lost information, and the various ways in which this loss happens, at most helps to explain how the failure occurs, if and when it does occur. Misrepresentation is a special case of information loss; not every instance of the latter is an instance of the former. The reasons why we need to make this distinction bring us back to our definition of a representation as a system whose function it is to indicate how things stand with respect to some other object, condition, or magnitude. An item is a misrepresentation, then, to the degree that it fails to indicate something that it is supposed to indicate.

Your mate asks you, "Where's my watch?" You reply, "On the coffee table." In fact, the watch is in the bathroom. Provided that it is your goal to give a true verbal description of where the watch is (or to have your utterance understood as serving this goal), you have misrepresented this object's condition. Because of a deficiency on your part—a false belief regarding the whereabouts of your mate's time piece—your utterance does not do what it is supposed to do: If the watch is in the bathroom, an utterance designed to indicate the current actual condition of the watch should mean it's in the bathroom. But "On the coffee table" means on the coffee table.

Say that **R** is a representation of any kind, whereas **O** is any object, situation, or event; let **C** denote some condition, feature, or causal power of **O**. With this notation in mind, I suggest the following as a heuristic description of the conditions under which **R** is a misrepresentation:

1. **O** is **C**;
2. **R**'s function is to indicate that **O** is **C**, if **O** is **C**;
3. **R** fails to indicate that **O** is **C**; or **R** indicates that **O** is -**C**; or **R** indicates that **O** is **C'**, when **O**'s being **C'** is logically or empirically incompatible with its being **C**.

Notice that no **R** is designed to signify all there is to know about **O**, under every condition, at all times, from every point of view, for every observer. Therefore, a black-and-white image's failure to register its referent's multi-chromatic appearance does not cause it to be a misrepresentation.

By the same token, the oblique angle shot that constitutes Auguste and Louis Lumière's *Le Train arrive à la gare de Ciotat* (1895) is, as far as it goes, an accurate portrayal of what that famous train looked like from a particular vantage point. This single, fixed perspective on its arrival affords little if any explicit information about how the locomotive actually looked from any other position at that moment, but it is not meant to do so and hence cannot be faulted for depriving us of fully objective, wholly transcendent or omniscient knowledge of the event. Likewise, a depiction made with a distorting lens is nonetheless a naturally meaningful sign that is not itself a misrepresentation.

In the most dramatic cases of distortion, the filmmaker or user is not employing the depiction as a reliable means of showing the object's natural appearance or proportions. Rather, the point is to elicit certain audience impressions of the relation between this picture and how the object is supposed to look to them: Spectators are intended to notice an abnormality in the object's appearance, relative to their expectations of how it should look to them or how it would look to them if viewed directly (or in a standard photograph, reproducing more closely the natural conditions of perception). One consequence of this abnormality is the viewer's increased vulnerability to mistakes about the actual information available from the picture. Gazing upon images made with wide-angle or long lenses, our judgments about the shape of depicta and the spatial relations between them can be uncertain or wrong. But again, to the extent that the image is not intended to ease its audience's access to information about how things really look, it is not strictly speaking a misrepresentation.

There are, however, other ways in which distorting lenses may be pressed into the service of misrepresentation. In more subtle instances of optical manipulation, a device might be chosen because it is unlikely that spectators will recognize that it causes an object or space to appear, say, larger than it would appear to them in actuality. Here misrepresentation consists of the maker taking advantage of an expected cognitive weakness of his viewers in order to lead them to think that the photograph indicates something other than what it naturally-counterfactually signifies.

When we reflect on motion picture misrepresentation, we often think of documentaries that get, or seem to get, facts about their object domain substantially wrong, and not merely because of a distorting lens or a limited perspective on the pre-filmic event. In *Roger and Me* (1989), director Michael Moore scrambles the chronology of various events, thereby giving the strong impression that a string of ludicrous commercial ventures in Flint, Michigan, were in reaction to a spate of General Motors lay-offs during the middle to late 1980s, although these municipal projects were in fact conceived and abandoned before these lay-offs were announced.

Not surprisingly, Moore has been accused of giving an erroneous, even deceitful account of the course of events.[35] One of his defenses against this charge has been that it was not his intention to describe the actual sequence of events, nor to offer evidence of direct causal links between any given economic relief project and any one round of plant closings in the history of General Motors' operations in Flint. What he contends is that his manipulations were designed to show better how the city "turned toward these goofy ideas as a means to divert public attention from the real issue," the "real issue" apparently being the corporate irresponsibility and greed that had jeopardized the local economy since the late 1970s.[36]

Judgment of whether *Roger and Me* misrepresents the course of events in question would turn on the outcome of an examination of Moore's effective communicative and truth-seeking intentions. A critique of this aspect of his movie requires more than deciding whether the relevant parts of this film are true or false when understood to be about a sequence of events in Flint during the middle to late 1980s. We also need to ascertain whether the director's purpose is to get viewers to believe that he is literally indicating a real course of events—plant closings triggering the aforementioned "goofy" recovery schemes—occurring in Flint during the middle to late 1980s.

Sometimes a work's status as a misrepresentation is easier to establish. *The Eternal Jew* (1940) is unambiguously identified by its makers, director Fritz Hippler and his colleagues at the Reich Propaganda Department, as a revealing examination of the inherent characteristics of all actual Jews and of their threat to European society over the ages, but with an emphasis on their presence in twentieth century Germany. Insofar as one of its functions is to indicate how things really stand with respect to the Jews throughout history and around the world, and insofar as it asserts literally and sincerely that this group is generally a rapacious, parasitical plague on humanity, we have enough reason to conclude that it misrepresents its intended referents. Of course, there are other ways in which *The Eternal Jew* is an entirely adequate representational system. As just implied, it fulfills the function of indicating which extra-cinematic state of affairs it is supposed to describe as well as the job of specifying the constative (as opposed, say, to make-believe or ironic) illocutionary force of this description.

Theorizing misrepresentation is important, but before we can begin that task in earnest, it is advisable to reflect a little on the nature and conditions of positive representational achievements. This task has logical and conceptual priority because understanding how and why cinematic works sometimes interrupt our epistemic access to reality presupposes that we know the norm from which the misrepresentation by definition deviates. The task also has empirical priority, since the symbolic practices from which genuine misrepresentations result necessarily have embedded within them modest representational success, whereby, owing to the filmmaker's communicative efforts, facts about illocutionary force and referential intentions are conveyed to the spectator. Critiques of cinematic representation that ignore these priorities undermine themselves by missing the very grounds for the emergence of the kinds of failures they seek to explain.

Notes

1. Bill Nichols, *Representing Reality: Issues and Concepts in Documentary* (Bloomington: Indiana University Press, 1991), 111.
2. André Bazin, "The Ontology of the Photographic Image," in *What Is Cinema?* 2 vols., trans. Hugh Grey (Berkeley: University of California Press, 1967–1971), 1:9–16.

3. Trinh T. Minh-ha, "The Totalizing Quest of Meaning," in *Theorizing Documentary*, ed. Michael Renov (New York: Routledge, 1993), 96.

4. Edgar Morin, *Le Cinéma ou l'homme imaginaire: essaie d'anthropologie sociologique* (Paris: Minuit, 1956).

5. Brian Winston, *Claiming the Real: The Documentary Film Revisited* (London: British Film Institute, 1995), 251.

6. Fred Dretske, *Explaining Behavior: Reasons in a World of Causes* (Cambridge, Mass.: M.I.T. Press, 1988), 52.

7. See Jon Barwise and John Perry, *Situations and Attitudes* (Cambridge, Mass.: M.I.T. Press, 1983), 10–14.

8. Ibid., 29–30.

9. Dretske, *Explaining Behavior*, 59.

10. Charles Sanders Peirce, *Collected Papers*, 8 vols., ed. Charles Hartshorne, Paul Weiss, and A. W. Burks (Cambridge, Mass.: Harvard University Press, 1931–58), 2:285.

11. H. P. Grice, "Meaning," *Philosophical Review* 66 (1957): 377.

12. Dretske, *Explaining Behavior*, 54–59.

13. Fred Dretske, *Knowledge and the Flow of Information* (Oxford: Basil Blackwell, 1981), 26–39.

14. Ibid., 38–39.

15. Ibid., 30.

16. Bill Nichols, *Blurred Boundaries: Questions of Meaning in Contemporary Culture* (Bloomington: Indiana University Press, 1994), ix.

17. Barwise and Perry, *Situations and Attitudes*, 28–31.

18. Ibid., 41–43. In conformity with Barwise and Perry's usage, I restrict the reference of "mental significance" to that which a work indicates or is supposed to indicate about its author's or authors' psychological states.

19. Christopher Peacocke, "Depiction," *Philosophical Review* 96 (1987): 383–410; G. N. Kemp, "Pictures and Depictions: A Consideration of Peacocke's Views," *British Journal of Aesthetics* 30 (1990): 332–341; Noël Carroll, "The Power of Movies," *Daedalus* 114 (1985): 79–104. See also Gregory Currie's discussion in *Image and Mind: Film, Philosophy, and Cognitive Science* (Cambridge: Cambridge University Press, 1995), 80–82. Currie's remarks on the perceptual nature of our experience of pictures is influenced both by Peacocke and Carroll, as well as by Flint Schier, *Deeper into Pictures: An Essay on Pictorial Representation* (Cambridge: Cambridge University Press, 1986).

20. Peacocke, "Depiction," 404. Julian Hochberg offers support for this claim in "The Perception of Pictorial Representations," *Social Research* 51 (1984): 841–862.

21. Peacocke, "Depiction," 386–387.

22. Stephen Prince, "The Discourse of Pictures: Iconicity and Film Studies," *Film Quarterly* 47 (1993): 25, construes the photographic image's pictorial properties in terms of select structural isomorphisms between it and its referent.

23. Kendall Walton, "Transparent Pictures: On the Nature of Photographic Realism," *Critical Inquiry* 11 (1984): 246–277; and Gregory Currie, "Photography, Painting, and Perception," *Journal of Aesthetics and Art Criticism* 49 (1991): 23–29.

24. Umberto Eco, "Articulations of the Cinematic Code," in *Movies and Methods*, ed. Bill Nichols (Berkeley: University of California Press, 1976), 594–596.

25. Gregory Currie, "Visual Fictions," *Philosophical Quarterly* 41 (1991): 140.

26. Bill Nichols, *Ideology and the Image* (Bloomington: University of Indiana Press, 1981), 24.

27. Shimon Ullman defends such a position in "Against Direct Perception," *Behavioral and Brain Sciences* 3 (1980): 373–415.

28. Here I gesture toward a distinction that Carroll has described in terms of the difference between physical and nominal portrayals; see *Philosophical Problems of Classical Film Theory* (Princeton: Princeton University Press, 1988), 149–151. Every image in a live-action movie depicts some definite, actual person, object, location, or event that caused the image to look just as it does. But such a movie can also depict a particular person, object, location, or event different from the one that gave rise to the image. Hence *Psycho* physically portrays Anthony Perkins, but nominally portrays Norman Bates. Nominal portrayals are, Carroll tells us, a function of such contextual factors as how the image is related to voice-over commentary, titles, editing, and the movie's narrative. In what follows, my objective is to unpack the notion of nominal portrayal in terms of the intentional constraints on the depiction's meaning—constraints that likewise govern the operation of the aforementioned contextual factors.

29. Richard Allen, *Projecting Illusion: Film Spectatorship and the Impression of Reality* (New York: Cambridge University Press, 1995), 90–97.

30. Kemp, "Pictures and Depictions: A Consideration of Peacocke's Views," 336–337.

31. Because I have a faulty belief about what I have successfully pictured, the film has the non-natural mental significance that I think that the depiction's model is Emma. Because I sincerely hold this belief, and am using the footage to express it, the film accurately indicates one of my mental attitudes. Note also that there is room here to "historicize" the work's meaning: In time I could learn of my mistake and begin to regard it as a picture of Emma, thereby changing its mental significance for me.

32. In an imperfect world such as ours, background conditions can, of course, fail or be suspended. The recording mechanism could break down, or I could tamper with it in such a way that it does not produce a visually recognizable image of anything in front of the lens.

33. The Gobi Desert's location north of the Ganges River does not depend on any map representing their relation as such; and an erroneous map would not move the Ganges' banks a micron nearer the Gobi. On the other hand, some representations, such as recipes, blueprints, plans, and intentions, effectively guide the realization of extra-representational states of affairs, the features of which depend upon the content of the relevant plans. Of course, this dependency is limited and characteristically asymmetrical: If one rips up the blueprints, one does not thereby destroy whatever exists of the corresponding edifice. I shall have much to say on the topic of the determinant role of internal representational states in the production of non-fictional movies in Chapter 4.

34. "The map is not the territory," a familiar phrase to readers of Gregory Bateson, derives from Alfred Korzybski, *Science and Sanity: An Introduction to Non-Aristotelean Systems and General Semantics* (Lakeville, Conn.: International Non-Aristotelean Library, 1933), 58. I owe my familiarity with this phrase and its

origins to Paisley Livingston; see his *Literary Knowledge: Humanistic Inquiry and the Philosophy of Science* (Ithaca: Cornell University Press, 1988), 207.

35. See, for example, Harlan Jacobson's discussion of *Roger and Me* and interview with Michael Moore, "Michael and Me," *Film Comment* 25 (1989): 16–26.

36. Moore, quoted in Jacobson, "Michael and Me," 22.

3

What About Reality?

From the outset, I have resisted the tendency to define non-fiction film in terms of an object domain, such as some privileged class of referents and subject matters called "reality," of which documentary (ostensibly) supplies objectively true representations. But I have also maintained that any artifact we would ordinarily want to label "non-fiction" would have to be a representation, that is, the kind of thing that can and does have some sort of semantic content because it has been designed to fulfill an indicator function. So the question arises, What **are** non-fictions about? In essence, my answer is as permissive as it is brief: whatever. Lest my latitudinarianism be mistaken for neglect of this important question, I shall try to offer what I take to be at once a precise, open-ended, and intuitively plausible way of characterizing the wide range of items to which cinematic non-fictions may be meaningfully related.

Outlined in its broad strokes, the objective of this chapter is threefold: First, instead of presuming, or stipulating, that non-fictions refer to or are supposed to refer to reality, I identify their content with situations. The situations to which a non-fiction pertains may be actual, concrete, and particular; but they may be typical and imaginary, too. A second objective is to refine my use of a previous distinction between natural and non-natural meaning. Hence I introduce the claim that non-fiction movies have interpretations, some of which are natural. Interpretation*, as I shall refer to it from now on, in order to distinguish it from the spectator's activity of comprehension, is a technical term. It denotes a situation, or kind of situation, described by the movie. Sometimes we can attribute a work's interpretation* to its natural indicator capacity. On other occasions, by presuming that certain express intentions effectively determine meaning, we individuate a work's representational content on the basis of much more than natural counterfactual dependencies. This observation leads to a third proposal.

A movie may possess a multiplicity of interpretations*, in the present technical sense of this word. Thus a work can describe a number of conceptually distinguishable situations. Which ones a viewer notices will be relative to his or her perceptiveness, background knowledge, preoccupations, and reasons for watching. Moreover, it frequently happens that an author means for his film to have an interpretation* quite different from any natural external significance it might have. Indeed, as is frequently the case, a work's natural interpretation* might be subordinated to a filmmaker's or user's plan to indicate quite another situation, not naturally signified by any of the representation's indicator elements.

The job at hand is to say what motion picture constatives can be "about." But it is not my intention to provide a means of generating sweeping descriptions of the totality of a work's significance. I do not, for instance, set out a system within which to account for all of the information carried by a cinematic representation. Mental significance, that which the movie indicates about its maker's psychological states—such as his beliefs, emotions, and illocutionary intentions—does not fall under the present analysis. Nor am I concerned with that which the work incidentally indicates about the proximal conditions of its own emergence. Watching movies normally introduces us to collateral facts pertaining to such things as socially-derived beliefs and attitudes held by members of the community with which the filmmaker is affiliated, the technological conditions facilitating the film's production, the practices of filmmaking, the institutional context in which the work was produced, and the movie's relation to others in its genre or its author's oeuvre. Although a movie can be exploited to learn about these domains, they are not what the movie is about—not unless it is made with the purpose of representing how things stand with respect to states of affairs, conditions, and events within said domains. Hence what I have to offer is a way of analyzing **one** aspect of the documentary's **external** significance. This aspect is to be identified with situations, both actual and abstract, that agents, by manipulating and relying on the medium, make an effort to describe.

In Search of Sasquatch

Here, listed in no special order, are a few fairly standard propositions regarding the nature of non-fictional cinematic representation:

1. "... a documentary has as its primary purpose the representation of the real ... "
2. "... it treats reality, past or present (or future?), either by direct recording or by some indirect means as compilation or reconstruction ... "

What About Reality?

3. "The documentary film came to be identifiable as a special kind of picture with a clear social purpose, dealing with real people and real events, as opposed to staged scenes of imaginary characters and fictional stories of the studio-made pictures."
4. "Instead of surrogates for life (theatrical performance, film drama, etc.) we bring to the workers' consciousness facts (large and small), carefully selected, recorded, and organized from both the life of the workers' themselves and from that of their class enemies."
5. "A nonfiction filmmaker is committed by the genre to conveying the literal facts . . . "
6. "Later he [John Grierson] defined it as 'the creative treatment of actuality.'"
7. "You photograph the natural life, but you also, by your juxtaposition of detail, create an interpretation of it."
8. ". . . the art of *re*-presentation, the act of presenting actual physical reality in a form that strives creatively to record and interpret the world and be faithful to actuality."
9. "The *projected world* of a [non-fiction] film is . . . a *model of the actual world*."
10. "Documentary has most often been motivated by the wish to exploit the camera's revelatory powers, an impulse only rarely coupled with an acknowledgment of the processes through which the real is transfigured."
11. ". . . a kind of fictional aura attaches itself to the filmed events and facts. From the moment they become film and are placed in a cinematic perspective, all film-documents and every recording of a raw event take on a filmic reality which either add to or subtract from their particular initial reality (i.e. their 'experienced value'), un-realising or sur-realising it, but in both cases slightly falsifying and drawing it to the side of fiction."
12. "The essential opposition between the documentary and the fiction film is part, I contend, of the convention that, since the emergence of modern historical consciousness, has posited an absolute distinction between the representation of 'fact' and the representation of the 'imaginable.'"
13. "Documentary directs us toward the world of brute reality even as it also seeks to interpret it, and the expectation that it will do so is one powerful difference from fiction."[1]

I do not suggest that this collection of quotations even begins to evoke the spectrum of critical opinion on the controversy over documentary's special difference; nor do these lines, ripped as they are from context, sum up the authors' many contributions to this debate. But the selection does have the virtue of assembling for comparison and contrast a number of ordinary claims about cinematic non-fictions. Although I think that some of them are wildly wrong, others are at least plausible and even truistic, as far as they go. However, all are symptomatic of the same shortcoming. Commentators have dug deeply into the question of whether it is reality or irreality that documentaries present to us. But as best as I can tell, their commentaries on what non-fictions are about lack the sort of clarity and detail found in discussions of meaning and reference inside contemporary linguistics, philosophy of language, and epistemology. Subsequently, they add up to a less than satisfactory reckoning of what non-fictions can and do represent.

So what do these samples from the literature have to say on the topic of documentary's object domain? Most of them associate the genre with some general kind of thing called "reality," although they diverge with respect to whether non-fiction ever accurately portrays this domain. Although I cannot say much more about the ontological assumptions of each of our authors, I wager that they would all roughly agree with a description of the real as a collection of phenomena existing, or supposed to exist, independently of their being represented, and without any given observer needing to believe, desire, think, or imagine that they exist. Hence the play *Hamlet*, the Great Barrier Reef, *e coli*, and black holes are all among the furnishings of reality. Traffic jams, the value of gold, the norm against demanding bigger servings at dinner parties, and folklore about ghosts, are also real; these are social facts, contingent for their existence on the relevant doings and attitudes of various groups of people—doings and attitudes that exist independently of the individual observer's cognition of them. Hamlet, unicorns, ghosts, and objects that travel forward in time so fast that they always get where they're going a couple of minutes before they've left are not part of reality, because they do not exist independently of anyone's thoughts of them. Of course, people's thoughts and concepts of Hamlet and so forth are entirely real.

There are obviously a number of differences between the assembled claims. Numbers 3, 4, and 7 emphasize the documentary's mission to portray natural, everyday scenes and individuals, as opposed to contrived, theatrical, imitative, and fictional scenes performed by actors. Numbers 4, 5, and 12 propose that the movie aspire, if not inevitably succeed, to communicate facts, that is, true beliefs. Number 5's "literal facts" could be read as explicitly restricting the information to that which concerns real phenomena, rather than "facts" about imaginary objects and states of affairs, like what gnomes eat and how Luke Skywalker acquires The Force. There are certainly literal facts regarding, say, what some population of people traditionally believes or pretends that gnomes eat; and there are true and justified propositions concerning occurrences in the fictional story of *Star Wars* (George Lucas, 1977). Although I cannot guess what the others would say, I expect that Carroll, author of claim 5, would also welcome the possibility of a documentary conveying information about popular beliefs and fantasies, as well as about fictional truths.

The sense of number 13's "brute reality" is obscure to me. Judging by his overall approach to documentary, I do not think Nichols wants to imply that its ambit is restricted to visible objects; on the other hand, if "brute reality" means things as they are independent of anyone's representation of them, then the modifier "brute" adds nothing new to the sense of the word "reality." And if his aim is to evoke the idea that reality can sometimes be brutal, this stirring sentiment gets us no closer to understanding what and how documentaries represent.

Two of the descriptions do seem relatively more restrictive of documentarians' activities. Number 8 stipulates their object domain as "actual physical reality." Taken at face value, this might exclude many if not all psychological and social phenomena, such as beliefs and desires, emotions, and the function of ritual in aboriginal cultures; depending on whether the claimant has a visual bias consonant with his Bazinian quest for "re-presentation," non-visible, theoretically postulated physical objects, like quarks, would also be ruled out of bounds. And the wording of number 10 connotes a foregrounding of film's portrayal of visually observable items.

Alternatively, the facts mentioned in numbers 4, 5, and 12 are not strictly identified with those pertaining to physical or visible entities; these propositions, like 3, are very accommodating of social and psychological realities. Number 2 is similarly open-ended in this respect. It refuses to reduce non-fictional representation to natural counterfactual relations between a visual recording and a pre-filmic object, thereby hinting at the possibility of depicting future states of affairs.

Finally, numbers 3, 4, 9, and 11 put a slightly finer gloss on the notion of reality by mentioning that it consists of things like people, lives, states of affairs, and events. Plantinga's number 9 indeed supports the most inclusive list of referents. A projected model of the world is any state of affairs—physical, psychological, or social—that is explicitly mentioned, implied, or otherwise represented by the documentary movie. Although indexed as making assertions about reality, these models need not be true or accurate.[2]

Once epistemological considerations are introduced, consensus that the idea of non-fiction is intimately tied to that of the real gives way to a fundamental opposition. The proponents of numbers 1 through 9 all suppose that documentaries can and frequently do contain knowledge of extra-cinematic reality. Following the Griersonian philosophy espoused in numbers 6 and 7, number 8 makes a point of noting that filmmakers do not merely produce mechanical records of actuality, they also interpret their objects. But Barsam stresses that the effect of the maker's subjectivity need not be a distorting image of the world. Dziga Vertov, in number 4, also points out that filmmaking entails acts of selection, organization, and manipulation. In fact, none of the first nine realist critics would assume other than that the documentary and its representations of the world bear some imprint of the organizing consciousness that produced them, and that this agent, being fallible, could proffer a flawed picture of reality.

The anti-realists of the last four citations agree that representation betokens interpretation. They go on to insist that this insight is significant because it means that, although many filmmakers and other interested parties go to lengths to convince us otherwise, the motion picture cannot be trusted as a source of knowledge. One way of reading this set of statements is as basically consistent with Nichols's contention that although non-fictional representations "aim at" actual historical realities, they nonetheless bear the stamp of fiction. Rather than portraying the world as it truly is, they only present "a view of the world," the content of which is not a felicitous copy of reality but to a significant degree the reflection of the ideologically determined objectives and gender- (or race-, or class-) specific desires animating the filmmaker.[3]

I sympathize with the anti-realist rhetoric insofar as I, too, think it is a good policy (a) not to assume that everything you see on television or in the movies is accurate, and (b) always to remember that documentaries are created by people whose many powerful desires and non-epistemic motivations can interfere with or preempt a commitment to truth-seeking. *The Eternal Jew* (Fritz Hippler, 1940), which compares Jews to vermin, is the product of a filmmaker whose self-interests and Nazi sympathies defeated any inclination toward verification activities. Number 10, however, appears to cross the threshold into radical constructivism. Take a blatant, but hypothetical, example of filmic interpretation: With some tricky editing, film footage is made to show the wrong man—the Kenyan instead of the South African—winning the 1996 Olympic marathon. No doubt viewing such imagery could help change or confuse some people's memories of what really happened. Yet there is no question here of "transfiguring" the actual Olympic event itself, since in the absence of backwards causation no amount of montage can alter the fact that the South African won.

Number 11, for its part, evinces a fundamental skepticism about the movie image's capacity to give us access to knowledge of the world. In a backlash against naive realism's fantasy of the photographic image's ontological identity with its referent, number 11 testifies that the depiction is not its object. Rather, the recording process cuts the image off from its referent, either by adding photographic properties to the representation or subtracting many of the object's properties from the photograph. The idea that there is something intrinsically false or fictional about the representation reverberates in the last two passages. Numbers 12 and 13 underscore that, contrary to standard conceptions of the documentary, what this genre shows us is not purely reality but rather a domain of imaginary or fictional objects, like Hippler's parasitic Jews—ideologically inflected mythopoeisis is the inevitable result of attempts to represent the world.

With the exception of Carl Plantinga, who has latitudinarian leanings similar to my own, the authors cited above seem a little uncharitable in their attitude toward the permissible content of the documentary. Let me explain myself by way of an anecdote. As a child, I went to a screening of Roger Patterson's 16-millimetre movie of a Sasquatch, the mythic quasi-hominid of the Pacific Northwest. I recall the exhibitor billing it as documentary footage; excluding television programs, it was probably the first non-fiction film I ever saw. Shot in 1967, the footage shows a gigantic, hair-covered, apparently female figure (also known as Bigfoot, for obvious reasons) ambling among trees and rocks near remote Bluff Creek, California. I was thrilled by the film, and had I not been only seven years old I would have lit out on my own expedition to Bigfoot territory the very next day. Having matured into a rational empiricist, I today dismiss the existence of "cryptids" and feel it safe to assume, in light of available evidence, that there are not and never have been Sasquatches and that the footage is a hoax.[4] Yet I am distressed to think that my fond memories of this cinematic experience, "indexed" in my mind as an example of non-fiction, now have to be subject to a major revision, namely, a relabeling of the movie as fiction or pseudo-non-fiction.

As a component of my pragmatic definition of non-fiction, I need a description of documentary's content that, unlike claims 1 through 8, will be Sasquatch-friendly. It should require no epistemological trade-offs, which is to say that accepting that non-fictions can refer to chimerical or non-existent entities ought not to entail thoroughgoing skepticism about either the existence of non-fiction or the genre's capacity to give viewers access to reality. This description of documentary's content must also have ecological validity, that is, it should be capable of covering the whole range of topics found in actual non-fictions. What is more, this description shall be non-normative. I am not such a control freak that I need to tell filmmakers which subject matters to pursue and which aesthetic properties, forms, structures, representational strategies, and filmmaking practices to adopt. I should like to be blunt about this point: I neither know nor care what the "proper" content and style of the non-fiction movie are.

Situations and Interpretations*

I prefer an approach in which content is identified with situations and events and their constitutive elements. Situations, readers will recall, consist of individuals having properties and standing in relations to one another at various space-time locations.[5] Although I plan to speak generally of situations, it is worth noting that a static situation, defined across a single location, is called a state of affairs; more dynamic ones, involving changes to constitutive elements or spatial-temporal coordinates, are, properly speaking, events.

A metaphysical assumption, one that coheres with our common sense notions of how the world around us is constructed, is that reality is itself made up of masses of situations, and that we as cognitive and communicative agents are adept at individuating and representing these items. So, for instance, you lying on your comfortable couch with this book in your hands is one such rudimentary situation. It contains some individuals, including a person, a couch, and a book; these items have sundry properties, like the couch's size and your literacy, as well as the book's linguistic signs; and various relational states obtain, such as the couch's comfort for you, your being on the couch, and you seeing the book which is in your hands. This scene's elements can be characterized as uniformities across situations. They pop up again and again in other situations, such as (a) you sprawled on the couch watching TV, (b) my book in the recycling bin, or (c) you exhibiting your literacy by reading *Hamlet*. Locations, too, are invariants, because different things can go on at the same time and/or place: As you lounge with my book (wondering what is on television), your friend could be seated next to you reading *Hamlet*.

Meaning, in contemporary linguistics, is sometimes characterized as the systematic relation of one situation, the linguistic utterance, to another, different situation. Whenever spoken or written, the sentence "The cat is on the mat" gets its content by virtue of (a) the speaker's adherence to the conventional constraints on linguistic meaning, plus (b) context-specific facts about who is making the utterance, when, where, and with what intentions. Spoken by Maya, the sentence is connected to how things actually stand, with respect to her cat, in some part of the world right in front of her, at present. Now take the same sentence as spoken by Jacqueline, who is watching an animated movie on video with her daughter. It too is connected to how things actually stand in some part of the world right in front of the speaker, right now. But in describing the state of the depiction appearing on the monitor, it describes a fictional state of affairs arising at a given point in the movie's narrative. Hence the same linguistic structure, owing to intricate facts concerning who the two respective speakers are, where they are located, and what external events they are aware of, winds up with two different meanings. In each case its external significance—the situation it describes—is established by conditions extrinsic to the conventional meanings of linguistic tokens themselves.

By identifying the documentary's content as I do, I wish to restrict discussion to a relatively narrow slice of that content: its content exclusive of its mental significance and constituting only a portion of its total external significance. Hence I identify interpretation* with that extra-cinematic situation or situation-type that it is the work's function to designate and describe. *Alien Autopsy: Fact or Fiction?* (Tom McGough, 1995) conveys a good deal about the cunning special effects wizards who made it, including information about their fanciful ideas of how extraterrestrials should look. But it is not the filmmakers' plan to assert that they imagine beings who look just so. The situation that they employ the footage to evoke is not the authors' thinking or making-believe, at a given time and place, that aliens have pot bellies. Nor is the movie supposed to indicate the sophisticated materials and technologies at its creators' disposal, although this, too, is part of the work's overall significance. Although the filmmakers may expect and even desire some audience members, like other special effects wizards, to recognize a variety of collateral facts, their representational plan does not grant priority to describing any situation but the postmortem examination of an alien—an imaginary scene that they assert could be real. In this case, intentions, plans, and practical reasoning play the determinate role in fixing this interpretation* as the principal one. But there are other instances in which facts about the camera's relation to an actual external scene overdetermine the artifact's interpretation.

In their theory of situation semantics, Barwise and Perry are careful to separate what they call a linguistic expression's "interpretation" (what I refer to as interpretation*) from the information provided by that expression.[6] One reason not to equate these two things is the priority of information, that is, the independence of information from structures used to carry it: I could inform you of my toothache in French, in Morse code, or by way of a dumb show. Another reason is the conditional nature of the relationship between utterances, their interpretations*, and the transmission of information.

To borrow an example, the sentence "She has a broken leg" only carries the datum that Jonny's dog has this injury if the vet uses it to convey this fact about that dog.[7] If he is joking or insincere, that datum is not made available. And a mistake by the doctor—maybe he thinks "broken" means "sprained," or perhaps he is wrong about the limb's condition—would yield a sentence describing a certain situation, this dog's leg being broken, but having negative value as information about the dog's leg.

The authors also point out that the information available from linguistic constructs is generally underdetermined by interpretation*: In addition to facts about the described state of affairs, the veterinarian's utterance conveys a welter of facts about his beliefs, the language he speaks, his profession, and so forth. Thus, although a sentence's interpretation* is one of the features permitting it to carry information about the world, it is not to be equated with the information carried by that sentence. Rather, it is equated with the semantic content that the agent effectively intends to communicate to somebody.

A motion picture's interpretation* is built up by cinematic rather than merely linguistic means. Of course, linguistic structures embedded within the cinematic representation help to describe situations and facilitate the viewer's access to them, but the strategies of cinematic representation extend well beyond the parameters of linguistic communication. Pictures and sounds, mise-en-scène, graphic designs, image and sound editing, theatrical acting, and other manipulations of both the prefilmic scene and the image and sound tracks themselves may all contribute to the instantiation of the movie's content, that is, establish the situation that the film describes.

For my present purposes, I shall divide situations into three general categories: real or actual, typical, and imaginary. Real situations, states of affairs, and events exist "out there" in the world. They consist of actual particular individuals, properties, and relations existing at actual particular locations. Real situations are the sorts of things we see, experience, participate in, and cause to occur; in turn, they stand in causally effective relationships to one another.

Situation types are more schematic, in as much as they are to be identified with certain more or less "disembodied" kinds of situations. Hence, instead of containing only particulars, they also include at least one variable. For example: Erika has on many actual occasions consumed particular portions of gelato and plans to do likewise well into the future. What is common to all of these specific gelato-eating events, abstracted from the specific and unique portions and locations, is a certain internal structure—Erika consuming some quantity of gelato at some time and place. This situation type is factual to the degree that it refers to and accurately describes the structure of one or more actual, realized situations. Thus, Erika eating gelato in Seattle during the summer of 1997 is a factual situation type because several particular instances of that event indeed transpired. On the other hand, her eating gelato in Rome that same summer is an unrealized kind of event, as there were no concrete tokens of that activity. Instead, we should say that the latter is an imaginary type of situation.

Imaginary situations and situation types have no existence or causal efficacy apart from somebody entertaining thoughts about them. The threat to fish from the Loch Ness Monster is entirely conditional upon, and is no greater than, people's beliefs or make-beliefs regarding Nessie's feeding habits. In short, the only limitation on the structure of imaginary situations, and the nature of imaginary individuals and their properties, is ultimately the inventiveness of one's imagination.

And yet, imaginary situations are somewhat more complicated items than the foregoing immediately suggests. Presumably, we can conceive of many objects, traits, states of affairs, and events that are entirely nonexistent or unrealized. These ideas issue from the mental act of imagining that such and such is the case, where the object of the imaginer's act is some thing or kind that he does not know to exist or knows not to exist, like the Loch Ness Monster and Santa Claus. Such concepts do not refer to or describe—are not themselves interpreted* by—an actual situation or situation type. Mental as well as artificial representations of strictly imaginary situations are therefore false, insofar as they do not refer to or veridically describe anything existing apart from someone's concept of that thing.

But there is a historically or contextually contingent feature of some representations of imaginary situations, namely, their eventual correlation, in our minds, with a real situation. Some portrayals of strictly imaginary items happen to acquire a degree of positive truth value. Hence the representation of the imaginary state of affairs accidentally turns out to be functionally adaptable to the job of describing, approximately accurately, some real world situation, if and when someone correlates it with that real situation. Without Georges Méliès trying to be prescient or a good aerospace engineer, *A Trip to the Moon* (1898) depicts an fictive situation bearing an uncanny resemblance, for those able to make the appropriate association, to what would become a familiar scene by the middle of the twentieth century, that is, the ocean splashdown of a returning space capsule.

We can also put representations of imaginary situations to special use as **models**. Here is how I understand this term. A model consists of an imaginary situation; it is a product of imaginings and has no existence independent of somebody's ideas about it; and from the perspective of the imaginer's own current knowledge, to represent this situation is to describe a currently unrealized, non-actual situation. However, this representation's content is one that is subordinated to a cognitive function. It is conceived or used with the intention of describing a second, possibly actual situation or situation type—one that the imaginer or user does know or reasonably believe to exist. Thus the agent represents an imaginary situation, S_i, in an effort to represent another actual (type of) situation, S.

A model, then, is an imaginary situation that plays a heuristic role relative to a certain practical or truth-seeking enterprise. This role can arise within contexts of creation and fabrication. Here, a concept of an unrealized situation or object serves as a design scheme guiding efforts to make a given item; attempts to realize the properties ascribed to the model are the cause of the actual item's structure. Models are also found within contexts of discovery, as when theoretical models of hypothesized objects, such as subatomic particles, guide the empirical research of investigators. Most important for my discussion, imaginary situations can also be put to modeling ends in various contexts of conceptual clarification, puzzle solving, and hypothesis revision. Rather than helping to direct an empirical search for a given item, the goal is to clarify our ideas about some actual or postulated state of affairs. As a source of illustrations of and perspectives on a given topic of inquiry, the imaginary situation is thus an input to hypothesis development and an aid to critical discussion.[8]

When does a documentary, or part thereof, represent a given situation? The general answer, of course, is that a movie represents such and such when its function is to describe that situation. Which situation a unit of film refers to, and what condition it indicates that referent to be in, depends on the constraints bearing upon the representation's condition. Grasping the film's content entails recognizing or learning which constraints relate the state of its explicit and implicit features to a given extra-cinematic situation. Some of these constraints are natural. Others pertain to the author's intentions and plans (the dependency of content on authorial intentions is the topic of Chapter 4).

For now, I underscore that cinematic content has an inescapable intentional basis. Upstream of representation are someone's intentions and plans to indicate something, no matter how loose or minimal, as when the filmmaker acts on a demonstrative intention to record whatever it is that passes before his lens. Even in cases of kinky wayward causation, in which, owing to a distinct absence of authorial control, the result is not necessarily the sort of thing we want to assume is a work (prior to its being used in some way by an agent)—for example, a video camera spontaneously turning on during an earthquake and recording the collapse of the bookshelves—there is an inevitable purposive basis to depiction. Photo-pictorial descriptions of situations issue from still and movie cameras because such machines are created to produce pictorial representations. They are the automatic result of the causal interactions of external objects with a machine calibrated to generate pictures, regardless of whether the operator knows or cares what is in front of the lens. The content of footage from surveillance cameras in banks is minimally to moderately reliant on agent intentions; the British social documentary of the 1930s is a lot more dependent.

In explaining the concept of the interpretation* it is important to acknowledge the fact, often cited by those denouncing claims on behalf of the photographic image's objective realism, that films are never merely the mechanical reproduction of unmediated reality. Even before the scene is chosen, the camera pointed, and the mechanism engaged, human attitudes, choices, desires, and goals factor into what the representation will be like.[9] Moreover, insofar as people usually make movies by executing more or less specific plans to represent this or that state of affairs, they **use** photographic media to represent particular things, setting into play, depending upon, and exploiting their capacity for producing naturally meaningful pictures.

Due to its nomic connection to the world, any photographic depiction naturally describes some actual extra-filmic situation. I do not wish to contest the distinction between interpretation* and information, but I do propose a special qualification of this distinction in the case of certain non-linguistic representational systems, like photographically produced imagery. By virtue of its natural indicator elements, the cinematic, audio-visual artifact is always related to some real situation, about which it preserves a selection of information. This information is necessarily about whatever is/was transpiring before the camera; which situation the cinematic artifact picks out depends upon which situation it naturally carries information about. A natural interpretation*, then, is a situation to which the representation is necessarily related and that it partially describes, owing to the condition of its natural indicator elements. Thus the content of a still or moving picture of Madonna consists in part of photographically mediated information about a particular state of affairs, namely, Madonna, some of her visible properties, and some of her visible relations to other objects at a certain place and time.

There are instances in which, despite being in a natural counterfactual relation to such and such an extra-cinematic situation, it hardly makes sense to say of a picture that it describes that situation's perceivable features. Madonna photographed out of focus and in the dark would be unrecognizable, hence this image cannot be said to have a natural interpretation* containing a description of a Madonna-related situation. Such a photo would describe no such thing, even if its actual (blurry and gray) appearance does somehow depend on this person having stood in front of the camera.

Thus the conditions for attributing a natural interpretation* **S** to a unit of motion picture footage must include: (1) an extra-cinematic situation **S** that actually exists; (2) a causal relation between the photographic (and usually sound) recording device and **S**'s observable features, such that some of the resultant audiovisual artifact's features display natural counterfactual dependence on some of **S**'s audible and visible features; (3) a recording that consists of one or more takes of no fewer than **n** recognizable images.[10]

To be sure, not all of the information naturally indicated by a picture is part of its natural interpretation*. There is also information about the sort of lens and film stock used and about the camera's spatial-temporal relation to the object. We should also bear in mind that the depiction might be naturally interpreted* by one state of affairs, whereas its interpretation* *simpliciter*—that which its maker or user intends for it to describe—is quite different.

If movies are fundamentally intentional artifacts, why claim, as I do, that it is sometimes appropriate to identify their content with a natural interpretation*? As I say, few films contain only this kind of interpretation*. But so long as it is photographically made, any motion picture will have natural meaning in relation to external objects. Provided that the image (and sound) is recognizable, part of this natural meaning will be a description of the visible (and aural) features of a real situation, in addition to whatever these visible features themselves happen to indicate about that situation. And often, either within a particular segment or on balance, throughout the artifact as a whole, a movie's interpretation*—what someone wants to represent cinematically—is overdetermined by this natural interpretation*.

Witness the case of three videographers. Suppose they descend on a scene of a tree in a park; they start shooting, but each from a very different angle. Eventually they dump all of that footage onto one tape, one segment after another, each a continuous take showing events involving dogs, birds, breezes, and what not. Rough though it is, they treat their compiled footage as a finished work, giving it a title *(Look, a Tree!)*, showing it to friends, entering it in a film festival. The videographers in this example do not carefully and creatively assemble the compilation in order to depict the course of events—they do not try to depict **S** by juxtaposing, intercutting, and otherwise whipping their respective footage into a sequence. With such minimal image manipulation, surely it makes sense to identify the collected footage's content in terms of its natural interpretation*. The work they put into making meaningful footage is subordinated to and reliant upon what it indicates about **S**, independent of what the trio thinks, wants, or is trying to indicate. Indeed, by minimizing their manipulation of the depiction's content and look, during both the pre- and post-recording phases, their overall representational strategy is to take advantage of the imagery's natural external significance.

It should be added that viewers are free to adopt a natural orientation toward images arising in even the most constructed films.[11] Watching Vertov's *The Man with a Movie Camera* (1929), one could examine a depiction of a Moscow street scene and thereby learn various historical details pertaining to that location, without relating this image to the shots before and after it, and without regard to the authorial intentions bearing on

What About Reality? 87

why this footage came to be photographed and then integrated with the rest of the movie. Relative to one perspective, most movies are simply accretions of images with natural interpretations*.

On the other hand, the hierarchical relation between natural interpretation* and interpretation* is frequently reversed. As a rule of thumb, the grounds for privileging the latter increase in proportion to the role agential factors play in determining what situation will be depicted and how that situation will look to viewers. For example, the tree videographers could have endeavored to describe the pre-videographic course of events by imposing somewhat more post-videographic order on their footage; they could have tried to describe the extra-cinematic situation by means of establishing relations between their stock of naturally meaningful images, using various editing techniques, adding dissolves, maybe employing a split screen, and so forth. In so doing, they would have wound up with a qualitatively different artifact, the content of which is more appropriately regarded as its interpretation*.

The interpretation's* precedence over the natural interpretation* also arises when there is a distinction to be made between the situation naturally depicted by the footage and that which the producer or user intends to depict by it. Reenactments put on for the sake of reality-based television programs are cases in point. Moreover, not all motion pictures, or parts thereof, have natural interpretations*. *Toy Story* (John Lasseter, 1996) employs computer-generated imagery to achieve depictions and visual effects without photographic means, like the comparatively low-tech animated movies of old. There are no situations that its makers are counting on some photographic technology to describe. Yet this pictorial work nonetheless represents situations. An additional implication of this sort of case is that a work's interpretation* can sometimes be associated with non-actual, imaginary objects and events that, due to the constraints on photographic representation, cannot be described by a movie's natural interpretation*.

At this stage, a selection of examples should serve to bring the discussion down to earth. Though not an exhaustive catalogue of documentary content, the following illustrations furnish an array of items falling within the ambit of non-fictional cinematic representation. I stress that my aim is not to list exhaustively the possible contents of cinematic non-fictions and related sub-genres but to provide a conceptual framework in which to analyze these contents.

I also think it wise to observe, before I turn to examples, that any movie will describe a great many situations; indeed content could be associated with congeries of these things. Neither the filmmaker nor the spectator is likely to be aware of all the possibilities. Which situations we can individuate and reasonably attribute to the work will be a function of the natural constraints on production, the author's intentions and plans, the movie's actual properties, and the viewer's orientation toward the film. Mention of the last determinant acknowledges background knowledge and research resources as potential inputs to reception. Drawing on their respective bodies of disciplinary knowledge, the horticulturist and the veterinarian are apt to notice or look for different situations and events while watching *Look, a Tree!*: The horticulturist will see that the tree is a willow and that it's suffering from some kind of infestation; the veterinarian will remark that the dog is a purebred Jack Russell Terrier and that its owners should stop feeding it table scraps.

Real Situations. During a brief, unedited segment of Terry Zwigoff's *Crumb* (1995), the camera follows as underground artist Robert Crumb hops on a female admirer's back for a ride through the recesses of an art gallery holding a retrospective of his works. Independent of this scene's relation to the movie as a whole, the present footage is interpreted*, naturally, by a real event occurring at an actual particular time and place. Had a different situation transpired before the camera, the resulting depiction would have been automatically and correspondingly different.

Notice that we must go well beyond natural meaning in order to individuate the real event in question. What the film records is not merely a sequence of physical objects, properties, and gestures. Such a rough-grained account of the depiction's content would miss the fact that the individuals depicted are agents; the situation in which they are involved is a product of their actions. So any moderately fine-grained account of the described scene will at least imply that the image is naturally interpreted* by a situation consisting not strictly of audible and visible a-rational motor behaviors but of intentional actions, such as horseplay.

Under this account of the movie scene's natural interpretation*, the agents' actions and interactions are presumably generated by personality traits, in addition to more punctual desires and beliefs, as well as a conceivable gender-inflected hierarchical relation between an art celebrity and his fan. However, although many of the depiction's properties naturally mean that the pre-filmic situation in fact had various properties, the recorded sounds and images are no more nomically indicative of the subjects' psychological states than are these people's overt behaviors themselves. Insofar as the audiovisual tracks naturally convey information about the look and sound of an actual pre-filmic situation, they preserve a selection of the same kind of evidence supporting inferences about the agents' psychological states that would be available to an observer of the event itself.

Since the foregoing account of the scene's content invokes non-visible, social-psychological properties, doubts could creep in as to its accuracy.

One could go as far as to insist that we should not take such accounts literally or invest too much faith in their accuracy, as there is no guarantee that we have not been set up—that the ride was not scripted and staged, and hence uninformative with respect to either person's actual dispositions and motivations beyond those having to do with their intention to perform the scene and participate in making the movie. In the face of doubt, determining what we are warranted to infer about this sequence's natural interpretation*—as opposed to any larger significance that it might have in the context of the film as a whole—may require a concerted effort of confirmation. We might need to mobilize our background knowledge and beliefs, as well as other textual and extra-textual evidence, information, and opinions. Alas, despite our best efforts, we could reach mistaken conclusions about some of the properties of the situation that naturally interprets the image. But it is unlikely that we could be wholly mistaken. After all, we would have recourse to a fairly uncontroversial account of the scene described, that is, two agents executing intentions, for whatever reasons, conducive to one carrying the other on her back.

Later in *Crumb* a montage of images recounts a photography session for *Leg Show* magazine. All things being equal, this sequence, too, describes a real event, one that includes Crumb posing next to, on top of, and under members of a group of female models; and yes, he is shown enjoying another piggyback ride on one of these women. The constraints on this segment's interpretation*—how it describes the photo shoot—are not primarily the natural constraints on cinematic image-making. Post-filmically, Zwigoff and his editor have functionally adapted the raw footage to the job of representing the photography session by means of juggling and juxtaposing the raw footage, thereby also achieving various aesthetic and expressive effects, like jaunty pacing and a comic mood. In the process, a highly selective depiction of the pre-filmic episode emerges, one in which the duration and order of many component events (How long was Crumb standing next to the model in the short skirt? Did he pose with her before or after he posed beneath the feet of a group of the women?) are obscured.

Typical Situations. In a series of sixteen shots, the makers of *Hoop Dreams* (Steve James, Fred Marx, Peter Gilbert, 1994) create a sequence describing a certain kind of situation in which the movie's young African-American subjects, William Gates and Arthur Agee, frequently find themselves as a result of their pursuit of basketball stardom. This sequence, which contains synchronous sound in addition to voice-over commentary by the teens as well as the narrator, includes: images of inner-city Chicago at dawn; a shot of Arthur leaving his bedroom, the title "5:30 AM" appearing at bottom of the screen; various angles of him walking in the early morning light near his home, riding the elevated train, and walking along a snowy street in suburban Westchester; an image of two figures in the distance, jogging across the white expanse of St. Joseph High's school yard, the sun still low in the sky. Over a pair of shots of Arthur sitting in a train, the narrator states that, "Like Isaiah Thomas before them, both Arthur and William make a three hour round trip each day between city and St. Joseph's."

Each of the above images obviously has a natural external significance, tied to whatever event was transpiring in extra-filmic reality at a given moment of recording. Apparently most of the sequence is fabricated out of recordings of the actual component situations and events of at least one particular episode of Arthur's travel to school. Recognition of this fact is a constraint on the sense we make of the depiction's natural as well as intended meanings, since lots of meanings—for instance, that the subjects are young, Asian-American women living in San Francisco and going to Berkeley each morning—are prima facie incompatible with the imagery's natural interpretation*.

But at present what interests us is an aspect of this movie segment's non-natural significance, that is, what the filmmakers mean, in part, by these pictures, treated and conjoined just as they are. All things considered, it seems sensible to resolve this issue with reference to a situation type. What the depiction is engineered to show, then, is a typical course of events in the lives of both Arthur and William, illustrative of their long daily treks to a suburban school renowned for its basketball program. That the governing intention is to construct a somewhat abstract model of their routine, rather than to represent one concrete instance of either or both youngsters' commute, is evinced by several of the depiction's features. Chief among these is the narrator's explicit labeling of the sequence as exemplifying both subjects' routines. And rather than labeling the footage as describing the trip to St. Joseph's on, say, December 3, 1987, the makers simply note, in a title occurring at the segment's onset, that the time is "freshman year."[12]

It also bears remarking that the segment is a composite of brief shots, considerable space and time having been compressed to avoid spending over half the movie describing one specific trip that is not itself the documentary's focus. The upshot of the ellipses is a filmic construct relevant not for its description of a single, unique course of events but for the relation of the events it records to other events, unrecorded, in the teenagers' lives during that year.

Unobservables. During *Obedience* (Stanley Milgram, 1965), we watch as the teacher, one of several test subjects in a legendary 1962 social-psychology experiment, presses the 180 volt switch on an electric shock generator in front of him, the learner in the other room having misremembered one entry on a list of paired words. Hearing shouts of "Ow ... I can't stand the pain! Let me out of here!" the teacher turns to the experimenter and says, "He can't stand it. I'm not gonna kill that man in there. Do you hear him hollerin'? He's hollerin'." Judging by this statement, as well as his facial and body expressions, we can discern that the subject is nervous and distraught; he seems to believe that what is happening is real and that the learner is experiencing genuine suffering.

Such psychological states are, in my exposition, to be counted as unobservable elements of situations. Unobservables are any items not detectable by the unaided senses of normal human beings.[13] In addition to the familiar entities of everyday folk psychology, these encompass such hypothetically or theoretically postulated items, including molecules, microbes, electrons, and other physical magnitudes and regularities, as those assumed to have causal efficacy, and therefore explanatory value, in both scientific and ordinary discourses.

Now in the above example, a verbal description of some of the film's content would have embedded within it a description of one particular pre-filmic situation—more accurately, a pre-filmic course of events, consisting of various individuals (teacher, learner, experimenter, furniture, equipment, etc.), their properties (length of the teacher's hair, tone of the learner's voice, relative size of the shock generator, etc.), the spatial relations between individuals (the experimenter is next to the teacher, the learner is hidden from the other two agents' sight in an adjacent room, the teacher's smoldering cigarette sits on the table in front of the generator, etc.), the temporal order of actions (the teacher delivers a 180 volt charge, then the learner yells), and so forth, as recorded on the image and audio tracks. If the test subject looked, acted, and spoke as he did because he actually had the mental states that I am tempted to impute to him, then these unobservable agential properties are also parts of that situation.

The above situation is, I think, reasonably identified as one of the natural interpretations* of the corresponding audiovisual sequence. There is the requisite natural counterfactual dependency between the sequence's visible and audible features and those of the pre-filmic events. Rather than representing those events by constructing a sequence of intercut images and sounds, the authors rely on the natural significance of a single, continuous take.[14] And there is no distinction to be made between the pre-filmic situation naturally indicated by the depiction and the situation that the authors intend to indicate by means of that depiction.[15] But here again, it is important to note that the cinematic properties—the condition of the representation—do not nomically or necessarily indicate the depicted agents' psychological states. Rather, by naturally preserving some information about the extra-cinematic scene, the movie presents us with a selection of evidence upon which to base our inferences about the cognitive and affective states constraining the agents' actions.

Imaginary Situations. In *The War Game* (1966), Peter Watkins uses fictional scenarios to predict the possible consequences, for the British people and their civil defense systems, of nuclear war.[16] In choosing this constative strategy, Watkins also presents viewers with a duplex of hierarchized, reciprocally related interpretations*, one an imaginary situation, the other typical. His film is thus interpreted* by a model. It is also worth remarking that this documentary departs from that which Plantinga considers the index of non-fictional status. Rather than merely asserting that the states of affairs it presents occur in the actual world as portrayed, it invites the audience to imagine certain non-actual situations.

The War Game's audiovisual tracks also have various natural interpretations*, namely, all of those actual situations the movie describes—locations, objects, people wandering around in costumes and make-up pretending to have been atomically attacked—as a result of the mechanical conditions of picture and sound recording. But relative to the author's overriding intentions, this filmic work is not about these situations. Rather, natural significance is a means to an end: The structure and content of the real pre-filmic events, along with the manner of their recording, are constrained by authorial plans bearing on the imaginary drama he wishes to stage and the claims regarding nuclear preparedness he thereby wants to make.

Watkins uses imagery and sound to relate a fictional story of the terrifying circumstances leading up to and following a nuclear strike on a civilian target in Kent. But this narrative is unanchored in any actual offensive against this locale. The director does not know or for that matter believe that this region has been attacked as shown; he possesses no information about any actual, particular catastrophe involving Kent's destruction by missiles carrying nuclear warheads. One facet of the film's duplex interpretation*, then, is the strictly imaginary course of events that it describes. More precisely, *The War Game* describes two imaginary situations. One of these is Kent's destruction. The other is the imaginary documentary movie *The War Game* describes, that is, the one that is the product of an intention to assert that an actual nuclear war proceeded as depicted and that contains footage naturally counterfactually connected to the look of Kent in ruins, its inhabitants dying in firestorms.[17]

The major reason why *The War Game*'s imaginary interpretation* is as specified has to do with the filmmaker's constative intentions. The film's fundamental goal is to assert that the consequences of nuclear attack are likely to conform to scenarios embodied by the depiction of the imaginary disaster in Kent. The fictional narrative's primary importance is not that it is imaginary that Kent is nuked and that then assorted imaginary predicaments ensue. Rather, the purpose of the fiction-making and the imaginary scenarios is to illustrate or schematize other, actual kinds of situations in the interests of criticizing the shortcomings of public policies concerning nuclear weapons and preparedness. Hence the other facet of the movie's duplex interpretation* consists of the description of actual types of events—structures common to certain actual, past events abstracted from the unique contexts in which they originally occurred. That there is this intention to typify certain kinds of situations, like the physical and mental health consequences of massive destruction by intensive bombing, is signaled by open references to how background research into the historical precedents of Dresden, Hiroshima, and Nagasaki guided the representation's construction.

Let us now revisit Roger Patterson's movie. Although the image is a little blurry, and the creature is off a ways in the distance, it is apparent to many that a Sasquatch has been caught on film—which is precisely what Patterson and many exhibitors have wanted people to believe. But what if this Bigfoot, and Bigfoot in general, is a strictly imaginary individual? What objective content, if any, are we to attribute to this footage?

Clearly that content which is said to make this document special is out of the running. Since the individual in question does not have an ontological niche within the world's causal order, events such as a Sasquatch stepping over rocks and logs at a given location cannot be ascribed to the movie's natural interpretation*—although there is probably a natural information-preserving relationship between the depiction and rocks, logs, and someone in an odd costume awkwardly negotiating these obstacles at said location. Surely that cannot be all there is to the movie's content. Surely anybody who knows anything about wilderness lore will tell you that it obviously depicts, well, a Sasquatch. They would be right. Yet how can motion pictures, or any other kind of representational system, refer to a non-existent entity or state of affairs? Isn't referring to imaginary things like swatting imaginary flies—that is, a failure to refer—akin to a failure to swat?

Pictures of, and discourses about, Sasquatches, like pictures of or words about any imaginary individual, are interpreted* by a certain concept of an imaginary thing, one that ascribes various attributes, including visible ones, to a mythic creature. Be it a sketch or a photograph, an image might depict a Sasquatch if some of its visible features are in an indicator relation to thoughts about this creature and the properties possessed by it. However, before an image can be of this cryptid, a further condition must be satisfied: The depiction must be made or used with the intention that it be interpreted by the Sasquatch concept and the various thoughts and imaginings that make up this idea. Hence "Sasquatch" is the interpretation*, though not the natural external significance, of the individual shown in Patterson's film. Although Bigfoot does not exist, and so cannot have its photograph taken, people's shared notions of this mythic beast are part of the causal order; and Patterson's knowledge of these notions is likely the main constraint on why the image, and the entity portrayed in it, look as they do. What the film refers to, and what guarantees its meaning, is a Sasquatch concept.

Nowadays, I suppose that Patterson knew that his footage describes only the concept of Sasquatch and not a genuine Bigfoot. And I suppose that he knowingly and deliberately used the footage to assert that a real Sasquatch in fact lumbered through the scenery, past his camera—the filmmaker hoping that audiences would mistake the film's interpretation* for its natural interpretation*. Thus, relative to Patterson's plans, the movie is a misrepresentation: The author would have us regard it as functioning naturally to indicate how things stood in reality, at a given location—that a particular kind of creature was present there; but no such entity was there.

However, it is only a contingent fact that the Patterson movie misrepresents reality. Without changing the visual track in the least, he could in some way have openly indicated that the footage is interpreted* by nothing more than an imaginary situation and invited spectators to make-believe that Sasquatches look just so, or to imagine that this one walked in front of his camera as shown. Or the filmmaker might have used the depiction to make assertions about the concept of the mythic forest dweller, rather than to assert that such a beast actually confronted him. In that case, his movie would have been interpreted* by an actual situation—a budget of publicly held ideas and beliefs. Any intention to describe that real thing, the concept of Sasquatch, has embedded within it a representation of an imaginary being, too.

Since we do not know exactly how the film was made, and since the world is a complex and often surprising place, I see no need to be dogmatic in our assignment of the Bigfoot movie's content to the category of the imaginary situation. Although it is not currently reasonable to believe that the creature exists, it is not impossible that one day Patterson will be vindicated, if it were to turn out upon careful investigation both that Sasquatch exists and that the footage in question actually depicts a real member of that species. If so, we will have to flip-flop and say that the film's natural interpretation* overdetermines its content. But no matter what the epistemic fortunes of its content, Patterson's incredible movie remains a work of non-fiction.

To talk about a special slice of a documentary's external significance, its content, in terms of situations captures some of the complexity of the cinematic constative's meaning. Although leaving reality well within the scope of motion picture representation, to talk of situations allows for meaning without associating it exclusively with reference to reality, and it licenses an anything goes approach to content without depriving us of a cogent description of what non-fictions represent. Consequently, even if they never have lived in Bluff Creek, Sasquatches now can be located on a map of non-fiction's native semantic turf.

Notes

1. The citations are from: Gregory Currie, *Image and Mind: Film, Philosophy, and Cognitive Science* (Cambridge: Cambridge University Press, 1995), 13; G. Roy Levin, "Introduction," in *Documentary Explorations: 15 Interviews with Filmmakers*, ed. G. Roy Levin (New York: Doubleday, 1971), 4; Lewis Jacobs, "Introduction," in *The Documentary Tradition*, ed. Lewis Jacobs, 2d ed. (New York: W. W. Norton, 1979), 2; Dziga Vertov, "The Essence of Kino-Eye," in *Kino-Eye: The Writings of Dziga Vertov*, ed. Annette Michelson, trans. Kevin O'Brien (Berkeley: University of California Press, 1984), 49–50; Noël Carroll, "From Real to Reel: Entangled in the Nonfiction Film," *Philosophic Exchange* 14 (1983): 17; Forsyth Hardy, "Introduction," in *Grierson on Documentary*, ed. Forsyth Hardy, 2d rev. ed. (London: Faber and Faber, 1979), 13; John Grierson, "First Principles of Documentary," in Hardy, *Grierson on Documentary*, 148; Richard Meran Barsam, "American Direct Cinema: The Representation of Reality," *Persistence of Vision* 3/4 (1986): 131; Carl Plantinga, *Rhetoric and Representation in Nonfiction Film* (New York: Cambridge University Press, 1997), 84; Michael Renov, "Toward a Poetics of Documentary," in *Theorizing Documentary*, ed. Michael Renov (New York: Routledge, 1993), 25; Jean-Louis Comolli, quoted in *Realism in the Cinema*, ed. Christopher Williams (London: Routledge and Kegan Paul, 1980), 226–227; William Guynn, *A Cinema of Nonfiction* (Rutherford, N.J.: Fairleigh Dickenson University Press, 1990), 41; Bill Nichols, *Representing Reality: Issues and Concepts in Documentary* (Bloomington: Indiana University Press, 1991), 110.

2. Plantinga, *Rhetoric and Representation in Nonfiction Film*, 16–17, 84–86.

3. Nichols, *Representing Reality*, 115.

4. In *Big Footprints: An Inquiry into the Reality of Sasquatch* (Boulder: Johnson Books, 1992), the cryptozoologist Grover Krantz performs a frame-by-frame analysis of the Patterson footage in an effort to prove its authenticity. To learn more about Sasquatch, consult Russel Ciochon, John Olsen, and Jamie James, *Other Origins: The Search for the Giant Ape in Human Prehistory* (New York: Bantam, 1990); David George Gordon, *Field Guide to the Sasquatch* (Seattle: Sasquatch Books, 1992); and John Green's classic, *Sasquatch: The Apes Among Us* (Seattle: Hancock House, 1978). With courteous regard to cryptozoologists, I note that to say we do not currently have adequate reason to believe in Bigfoot's existence is not the same as claiming that we will never have grounds to hold this belief. Maybe new and probative evidence will be uncovered one day, in which case the authenticity of Patterson's film should be reexamined. Or maybe such creatures

will appear on earth some time in the future. Of course, were Sasquatches eventually to win an uncontested niche in reality, Patterson's film would not suddenly become veridical. Its image track would not have the proper causal relation to an actual Sasquatch, given that it predates the appearance of the first such creature. And Patterson's intention is to make assertions, not future tense conditional predictions, about his referent.

5. Jon Barwise and John Perry, *Situations and Attitudes* (Cambridge, Mass.: M.I.T. Press, 1986).

6. Ibid., 29–31.

7. Ibid., 17.

8. In *Literary Knowledge: Humanistic Inquiry and the Philosophy of Science* (Ithaca: Cornell University Press, 1988) 261–263, Paisley Livingston recommends the use of literary fictions as models. Émile Zola's *Pot-Bouille*, for instance, could serve as a source of perspectives on and illustrations of the matrimonial economy; when read in relation to the appropriate body of social scientific research, it could function as a valuable heuristic that might lead to the refinement of social hypotheses and theoretical assumptions.

9. Jean-Louis Comolli, writing of direct cinema, says: "From the moment the camera intervenes a form of manipulation begins. And every operation, even when contained by the most technical of motives—starting with the camera rolling, cutting, changing the angle or lens, then choosing the rushes and editing them—like it or not, constitutes a manipulation of the film-document"; quoted in Williams, *Realism and Cinema*, 226.

10. By "take" I understand a single, continuous, unedited unit of motion picture footage. Although there are no cuts within it, it may well have been excised, as a whole, from a longer piece of footage. While the take is uncut, it can show evidence of pans, tilts, zooms, and other such camera movements. Besides recalling the remark that unrecognizable pictures cannot describe anything, (3) adds that there need be some requisite number of images projected or displayed at a specified speed before anyone will even be able to notice the moving picture let alone its content. Of course, you could take a single frame of motion picture footage, somehow display it, and examine it for its depiction of a scene. But this exercise would be fundamentally different from watching a movie. Readers who wonder whether we can be unconsciously aware of imperceptible imagery—for example, a twenty millisecond "subliminal" visual stimulus slipped into a television show, such that we have to fight the urge to rush out to buy kitty litter—should be warned of the paucity of empirical evidence for this phenomenon, as well as the lack of clear operational definitions for the associated concepts. An interesting volume on these and related topics is Geoffrey Underwood, ed., *Implicit Cognition* (Oxford: Oxford University Press, 1996).

11. Adopting a natural orientation entails no wishful or otherwise irrational denial, on the viewer's part, of the existence of the screen or the constructed, artificial status of the depiction—unless he or she is a less than minimally competent spectator, or just plain bonkers.

12. Viewers familiar with the publicity surrounding *Hoop Dreams*, or attentive to other clues arising later in the film, will identify the time as being the winter of 1987–1988.

13. Here I follow Bas van Fraassen's notion of unobservability, as laid out in *The Scientific Image* (Oxford: Oxford University Press, 1980). Hence microbes are unobservables, but a dinosaur is at least observable in principle: If one were to be alive, we'd be able to see it without microscopes, telescopes, cloud chambers, gauges, and what not. In *Fact and Method: Explanation, Confirmation, and Reality in the Natural and the Social Sciences* (Princeton: Princeton University Press, 1987), 359–363, Richard Miller points out that this definition, while a plausible way of specifying the kinds of things that anti-realist philosophers of science have the most trouble believing in, is still pretty coarse grained, and may seem arbitrary in some cases. The dimness of Pluto, for instance, is to be counted as observable, since astronauts without instruments and visual aids could, if they approached close enough, detect it with their eyesight. But Pluto's coldness isn't observable, since anyone getting near enough to detect it without instruments would be instantly killed. Hence anti-realists mandate confidence in modern astrophysics' claims about Pluto's dimness but will not accept the rationality of beliefs about its coldness.

14. The sequence currently under discussion is part of a longer sequence, detailing this test subject's performance from near the experiment's beginning on through to the debriefing stage, lasting approximately eighteen minutes. During this total time, there are eight edits (including three inserts and two straight cuts) and one dissolve.

15. I do not want to obscure an extremely important feature of both *Obedience* and the laboratory manipulation that it documents. By the time the segment in question begins, viewers have been unequivocally informed by the voice-over narration that the point of the experiment is to test obedience to authority, not the effects of punishment on learning; moreover, the learner is a confederate of the experimenter and is receiving no shocks. Hence the real situation, as the documentary describes it and as we grasp it, is that a team of psychologists is pretending to engage in certain activities for the purpose of discovering the test subjects' responses to a certain predicament. But the teacher's own understanding of the situation that he is in is fundamentally different, since he is not informed of the deception until after the test has finished.

16. The relation of constative to fiction-making intentions in *The War Game* is discussed in Chapter 4.

17. On the nature of imaginary documentaries, see Chapter 4.

4

Plans for Non-Fiction

In Chapter 1, I introduced the thesis that documentaries are products of purposive actions having a specific type of authorially designated effect as their goal. In this chapter and the two following, I expand and refine my case for regarding the filmmaker's intentions and plans as major, but by no means solitary, constraints on the movie's significance. The first orders of business are to spell out what I understand by "intention" and to elaborate on why certain measured assumptions about rationality and intentionality are crucial to a realistic account of how documentaries come to have their meanings.

I shall defend the idea that making a non-fictional motion picture is largely an exercise in practical rationality, that is, reasoning undertaken by somebody in order to resolve such questions as, "What do I do now?" or "How do I achieve X?" One way of building up this thesis is to explain the link between film production and cineastes' often complicated intentions with respect to force and content. Hence I propose to discuss the impact of planning and plans in the creation of cinematic works. By "plan," I wish to denote the representational content of an intention.

On this view, an intention to do X consists of a plan for X-ing, along with the appropriate sort of disposition to do X by following that route. Not all plans are incorporated within intentions. One might, for instance, possess an exhaustive plan—including screenplay, shooting script, budgets, and casting notes ("Get Harvey Keitel as L. W.")—for a thirteen-hour movie adaptation of Wittgenstein's *Philosophical Investigations* yet have no inclination to put this plan into action. Moreover, one might have spent many months formulating this scheme without ever being the slightest bit motivated to execute it. But the kind of plans that interest me serve, or could serve, an etiological function in an actual work's emergence, their causal powers deriving from an agent's special, "executive" attitude toward them. I use "planning" to refer to the activity of filling in and modifying the representational content of intentions; it is reasoning undertaken with a view to settling on and carrying through a course of action.

The thrust of my argument is this: no plans, no documentaries. What is more, the types of plans guiding the filmmaker are at least broadly determinant of the significant properties of his or her movie. On these grounds, it is defensible to maintain that a documentary's meaning is, indeed, must be, to a substantial degree under authorial control. A few readers will have trouble wholeheartedly embracing this claim. Some will find it counterintuitive, because it seems to suggest that there are no unforeseen elements in documentaries—an implication easily dismissed by reflecting on the conditions under which many films, like works of observational cinema, are made. Others will fault me for subscribing to an discreditable notion of authorship, one that privileges an autonomous, fully rational subject and that ignores the allegedly overwhelming influences of psychodynamic and social factors. Both charges can be defused.

From the moderate intentionalist view that I advocate, unforeseen features and effects, as well as properties not consciously intended by any single author, are part and parcel of the cinematic work. Furthermore, accepting the systematic dependence of meaning on intentions need not commit us to the notion of an author who exerts precise control over the movie's every significance, untouched by deep psychic motivations and sociological forces. My position is simply that an intentionalist psychology, in which meaningful cognitive states effectively guide action, is indispensable to the explanation of how motion pictures acquire their meanings.

Intention

In standard cases, the non-fictional movie's force and content are constrained by a finality that its maker has in mind. Roughly speaking, I think intentions do the constraining. It is in relation to these mental states that a work acquires much of its significance; characterizing their determinant role is our present objective. For maximum clarity, I begin with a definition of intention, including a description of its functions and how an intention may come to be held.

According to Al Mele, an intention is the specific underlying structure that mediates between, on the one hand, one having the motives to perform a given action (along with the abilities conducive to doing it) and, on the other hand, one actually performing that action.[1] Hence an intention can be characterized with reference to two important facets—one motivational, the other representational. Mele urges us to consider the motivational dimension in terms of the acquisition of an intending or executive attitude toward an action. Unlike the acquisition of even a preponderantly strong urge or wish to do something, an agent taking an executive attitude consists of his being settled upon X-ing.

At present my strongest desire is to watch reruns on TV, yet what I intend to do is finish this paragraph, even though I really do not feel much like writing at the moment. Between competing motivations (indulge my chief vice, work harder) the acquisition or, in this case, the formation—by actively exercising better judgment in the face of temptation—of an intention settles the practical matter of what it is that I will actually do. And here, settledness is understood to have the effect of triggering the sort of reasoning and behavior—thinking of ways to block out the urge to watch TV, focusing on the thought of how good I will feel for having written more pages than my daily average, staying at my computer and composing the next sentence—that the agent expects will lead to his doing or achieving X. All things being equal, we do, or try to do, what we intend to do. Granted, intentions can be defeated. I could die suddenly before typing another word. The computer could break down. Or I might reconsider and revoke my intention when my friend wanders past me, *TV Guide* in one hand, remote control in the other.

An intention's representational component is its content, and as such it is that toward which the agent takes the executive attitude. On this view, an intention's content is a representation of a goal state and a plan, however partial, for how to achieve that objective. Thus intending to do X entails having, and being guided by, some fixed ideas about steps conducive to doing or realizing X. The intention-embedded plan identifies a goal and supplies action directions.

To sum up, an intention's causal efficacy derives from it having two related properties: (1) an executive attitude component that initiates and sustains the implementation of (2) a representational component that guides behavioral output. As Mele insists, an agent's intentional performance of an action is not just contingent on his having a plan for so acting but also depends on his acting as he does because he is following this plan.[2] It just so happens that I have memorized a recipe for a triple chocolate terrine, one that I admire for its simplicity and its exquisite results. But given my current low calorie diet, the only attitude that will result in my making this coveted dessert—an executive attitude—is one I will not soon adopt. By itself, the plan has no motivational power. Thus an intention is that which determines the structure of an action (i.e., what the agent does), as well as that which ultimately triggers that deed.

I have already hinted at some of intention's main functions, now let's throw these and others into sharper relief. Intentions, as conceived above, are plausible candidates for the kind of psychological state that can initiate and motivationally sustain action. They help set people into action, and keep them in action until the goal is attained or the attempt fails, by bridging the gap between having motives to act and acting. Often, having a desire for such and such will straightaway produce action that would tend to satisfy that want. But in many instances, what we desire, even preponderantly desire, produces no movement toward a corresponding action or goal. Someone's constant craving for sweets need not automatically result in sweet-eating. By the same token, what we intend to do is not always identical to what we most want to do. An agoraphobic man's anxieties may be so intractable that he is currently most motivated to avoid going to his daughter's wedding; and he may strongly believe, on the basis of experience, that his fear will likely cause him to stay at home.[3] Yet if he has sought therapy and is taking steps to overcome his fear in order to be able to travel to the ceremony, it would be wrong to say that he **intends** to miss the wedding. On the contrary, he has settled on at least trying to go.

The motivational difference between desires and intentions leads Mele to contend that intentions have greater access to the mechanisms by which our actions and their consequences are generated. He regards intentions as the causal links between our wants and our actions, in the absence of which even the strongest desire will fail to trigger action. On this view, our desires incline us toward action by disposing us to form or acquire the appropriate intentions. With the help of a professional who shows him ways to stop his anxiety from defeating his intentions, the agoraphobe could surprise everyone, including himself, by going to the nuptials despite his persistent fear. In a gloomier scenario, his phobia might eventually overdetermine his conduct, disposing him at the last moment to settle on staying at home. What distinguishes the first from the second situation is the failure of a desire for **X** (staying securely at home), though disproportionately powerful relative to other wants, to settle the man on **X**-ing. Depending on our other wants and judgments, and on external conditions, we do not always intend according to our desires.

It is useful here to say a few words on the topic of how people usually come to have their intentions.[4] Mele argues in favor of recognizing both active and passive modes of acquisition. The active mode is identified with the agent's performance of some mental action of intention-formation, such as deciding. Generally speaking, this process consists of generating intentions from instances of practical inference—making them the output of reasoning performed with a view to answering the practical question about what to do now.[5] People do not, of course, always explicitly pose a query to this effect before acting; the supposition is merely that our behavior is largely motivated by settling on courses of action in the face of limiting and facilitating conditions, as we perceive them. These conditions have a psychological dimension, consisting of our various desires, values, beliefs, and reasons for acting. They also have an external dimension, consisting of physical and social environmental factors. The settling process unfolds by the making of inferences about the nature of these conditions and the behavioral options that they permit, require, and exclude.

Wanting to cross the highway, and believing that the oncoming eighteen wheeler is not moving fast enough to hit me if I run as quickly as I think can, I conclude that now is the moment to dash across the road, before the big rig gets any closer. Within Mele's schema for the etiology of action, the typical upshot of such an inference is an intention to perform the corresponding act. Employing the computer analogy of the default procedure, he would argue that, should I have no competing motivations or reservations, my practical judgment is likely to engender my intending to dash across the road, without my having to undertake a conscious intervening step, such as telling myself to run. Nevertheless, there are cases in which competing motivations make forming or executing an intention problematic. The agoraphobic father wants to be at his daughter's wedding and has compelling personal as well as social reasons for going. But the severe anxiety against which he struggles threatens to stop him from settling on attending, or else defeats his intention just as he puts his hand on the car door.

Many inferences are properly regarded as practical evaluative judgments. Someone who arrives at such a judgment holds a belief that it is better or best to do **X** than it is either not to do **X** or to do something else altogether. On occasion, this belief is based upon the agent's considered better judgment, insofar as it is supported by a consideration and ranking of many, if not all, of the individual's pertinent beliefs, desires, values, and so on. Alternatively, the belief may be prompted by a qualified judgment of the better course of action made from the limited perspective of a single value or concern that the agent regards as overriding his or her other interests. One might, for example, think that cheating on one's income tax return makes more sense, from a financial point of view, than not cheating—so much more sense that, if the individual were to take monetary considerations to outweigh others (such as the moral implications of the prospective deed), he or she would see cheating as the superior option.

In any case, an agent's practical evaluative judgments sometimes prompt him or her to put an end to the chain of considerations and regard it as simply best to do **X**. Mele refers to such attitudes as "unqualified best judgments," which rationally commit the agent to action. As long as you consciously hold the belief that you have better reason to do **X** than not to do **X**, it would be irrational from the standpoint of your own judgment not to go ahead and do **X**. Mele's further suggestion is that human beings are so constituted that, when things go smoothly, judgments that it is best to X trigger the default mechanism by which a corresponding intention to X emerges automatically. In turn, intending normally issues in doing, in a similarly automatic fashion.

The normal routes to intending are not, however, exclusively active. A passive mode of acquisition is said to produce intentions independently of an effort of to decide. Wanting another glass of wine before dinner, you straightaway pour yourself more wine. In the absence of a rival desire, nothing interrupts the progression from wanting more wine to acquiring and executing the corresponding intention to fill the glass. Similarly, the agoraphobe who has not sought treatment and has no confidence in his will power might never settle on a course of conduct at odds with his fear. Moreover, people engage in many unreflexive or habitual acts, like answering the telephone, that normally require no decision to initiate them yet are nonetheless poor candidates for the label of unintentional behaviors. After all, one can pick up the receiver on purpose, with the goal of finding out who is calling, without actively judging whether to pursue this goal. Provided that a rival want does not intervene (prompted, say, by a ringing doorbell), consciousness of the ringing phone will generate, as if by the operation of a default "instruction," the appropriate intention.

There is a final point to be made about an important relation between intention's motivational and representational aspects. Roughly speaking, intentions may initiate action either right away or at some moment in the future, depending on the plan component's content. A proximal intention is one that embeds a plan for immediate action and is therefore a propensity to execute that plan immediately. A distal intention contains a plan for later action and therefore disposes the agent to execute that plan at some appropriate time in the non-immediate future. Other intentions are temporally mixed, their plans featuring both immediate and future behaviors. An intention to travel from Montréal to Berlin has a proximal dimension because it specifies and initiates an action—getting on a flight today in Montréal—to be engaged in straightaway. It also has a distal dimension, insofar as it specifies something to be done—getting on a train after a stop-over in Amsterdam—a day later.

Now we return to intention's cognitive dimension. Which action or goal we settle on, and what route we take to it, depend on conduct controlling representational content. For instance: My intention to do some home maintenance produces the home-maintaining activities it does because a suitable plan guides and monitors the progress of my behavior. This plan need not be comprehensive from the outset. Deciding to devote the weekend to home improvements, I might initially leave open the matter of precisely which projects I ought to tackle. Yet this partial plan is, as Michael Bratman would say, a crucial filter on further practical reasoning and planning.[6] It rules out some activities (renting a bunch of old movies on video) while admitting others (making a list of what needs to be done, deciding what I can hope to do in two days, going to the hardware store, etc.). As time passes I may fill in additional steps toward my goal's realization, undertaking such reasoning as necessary to the plan's adjustment and completion. In this way, my settling on installing new storm windows prompts a review of my credit card balance, a glance at the Yellow Pages, and a trip to a store specializing in such items. Hence intentions typically exhibit a hierarchical structure, embedding at first general and preliminary, then increasingly more specific means, subplans, and intentions.

Note that the aforementioned example suggests some of intention's other normal functions. Settling on a course of action sometimes prompts an intender to undertake such reflection as is necessary to figure out how to achieve the specified goal; and once the intender has judged that she should do **X** to bring about that end, it is intention's settling dimension that terminates this line of reasoning. Mele, like Bratman, also attributes coordinative power to intention.[7] Intrapersonally, this function helps the agent to be consistent. Intending to **X** normally motivates one to align one's future activities and further developments in planning with what one is already committed to doing; for this reason, a decision to go to a movie tonight will tend to rule out inviting friends over for dinner and will promote reasoning about whether to take a cab or walk to the theater. Interpersonally, cooperative endeavors also benefit from intention's coordinative function. For example, sharing an intention to meet at certain restaurant at a given time gives both of us the motivation and information that we need in order to harmonize our actions in the specified way.

Moderate Intentionalism

In this section, I present the version of intentionalism best suited to explaining the grip that authorial intentions have on cinematic meaning. I emphasize that this version attributes authorial control to real, not implied, authors. Moreover, it is compatible with multiple authorship, as well as with the idea that the work may exhibit a variety of unforeseen or unintended properties. Moderate intentionalism also fills an explanatory gap left by psychoanalytic and sociological accounts of the production of cinematic meaning.

Like Paisley Livingston, I think there is a relatively small set of psychological states with a direct causal link to a movie's significance.[8] These effective communicative intentions are formative because they pertain to features and meanings that the author tries to make accessible to his or her audience. In other words, the filmmaker not only wants the work to have these features but takes steps to make it so and has good reason to believe that the properties and meanings so intended will be recognized by viewers, on the basis of available evidence and feasible reasoning.

It might well be the case that D. A. Pennebaker, director of *Don't Look Back* (1967), considers his subject, Bob Dylan, to be a Byronic character.[9] But barring a lucky guess, this singer-songwriter's resemblance to "the Byron legend" is not likely to occur to *Don't Look Back*'s audience. If Pennebaker had this analogy in mind while making his documentary, even if it in some way influenced how he undertook to represent his subject, he does not seem to have attempted to alert viewers to it. On the other hand, the representation in *Roger and Me* (Michael Moore, 1989) of its director's protracted quest to interview General Motors Chief Executive Officer Roger Smith is a good candidate for the sort of intention-constrained content that I wish to analyze. In shooting and constructing his film, it seems that Michael Moore was guided by a plan to get his audience to recognize a certain course of events, namely, a series of comically zealous, unsuccessful attempts to ambush and interview an apparently elusive industrialist. Evidently this plan reached into and controlled the movie's content from early in its inception, conceivably even before a single frame was shot.

So, when I refer to intentions constraining cinematic meaning, I have in mind effective communicative intentions. These determine a movie's significance by virtue of the author's commitment to expressing openly the content of the plans embedded within them. Hence the content of the plan is at least partly realized in the content of the motion picture.

Although no one could doubt their practical importance and efficacy in the production process, various sorts of intentions are not germane to the present discussion. A team's persistent, mutual intention to "make a film," although instrumental with respect to both intra- and interpersonal coordination, does not have the appropriately proximal bearing on what it is that the work shall indicate about this or that topic, or what sort of impact the film is supposed to have on its audience. Likewise, intentions to take the lens cap off the camera and drop the boom microphone a bit lower, both of which obviously serve the end of fixing a movie's content, nevertheless stand beyond the relevant kind of effective relation to meaning. The problem, again, is that their representational component does not specify or describe a situation or event that is supposed to be indicated by the cinematic work.

Although granting explanatory priority to agential plans, moderate intentionalism does not associate the work's real meanings with all and only those which are consciously intended by the author. The reasons why not should be fairly obvious. First of all, filmmakers sometimes fail to realize their intentions. Say, for instance, that Pennebaker did intend to put viewers in mind of Dylan's resemblance to Byron, that he did believe that he had taken steps to make this point, but that as a result of his directorial decisions, the analogy is too subtly implied for him rationally to expect a competent member of his target audience—someone aware of some of the documentary's explicit features intended to relate to this premise and able to infer authorial decisions on the basis of this available evidence—to have access to it. In this hypothetical example, the pop star's affinity to the poet is something that Pennebaker means to evoke by this or that sequence. However, owing to a lapse of authorial judgment or skill, he has not marshaled the representational system's tools and components in such a way as to provide viewers with sufficient evidence and reason to attribute this meaning to his work. Thus, despite his intention, the movie lacks this meaning.

Two other considerations tell against an exclusive alignment of meaning with intentionality; I shall briefly note both of these, returning to them in greater detail later. Often a work's external significance is partially the unintended by-product of its maker's efforts to realize another, intended goal. The author need not foresee, desire, or even be cognizant of this collateral information, conveyed by the movie as a result of natural or necessary dependencies. By selecting a certain lens or film stock in order to achieve a particular visual effect, the filmmaker, knowingly or not, creates an artifact with properties indicative of certain technical conditions having obtained in the course of its production. Thus a suitably knowledgeable viewer will be able to see by the given effect that such and such an optical device or material was used.

Notice that scholars tend to take for granted that movies also preserve similarly by-produced information with mental significance. A discussion of *Thy Kingdom Come* (Anthony Thomas, 1987), a documentary about the moral failings of America's religious right, might lead one to remark that elements of this motion picture's style betoken the filmmaker's immorality, too. Footage of and interviews with Kevin—a handicapped youth who serves as a spokesman for Jim and Tammy Bakker's Heritage USA charity in exchange for a largely solitary life in a showpiece shelter—might be said to evince director Thomas's "insensitive opportunism," since the cinematic representation of Kevin repeats the gesture of reducing him to a pawn serving somebody else's interests.[10] By realizing one of his plans, to impugn the Bakkers, the documentarian, it might be suggested, unwittingly but nonetheless graphically furnishes the alert critic with a sign of the documentarian's own opportunism.

Aside from being an accidental by-product of purposive action, significance can also be located in possibly unexpected or undesired meanings, the emergence of which is explicitly allowed for or supported by the author's intentions. Normally, filmmakers anticipate that visual and sound tracks will capture, and thereby indicate, actual states of affairs and events, the precise nature of which is not known or could not be known to the agent in advance. Thus, cinematic authors often work with plans to register that which transpires before the camera, whatever that turns out to be. Live coverage of competitive sporting events adheres to this model. Although producers have a schematic idea of what kinds and sequences of activities will occur, the actual specific occurrences are, from their point of view, highly contingent and sometimes entirely unanticipated. It is not hard to think of other vivid examples of contingency's intersection with documentary.

Although the makers of *Gimme Shelter* (Albert and David Maysles and Charlotte Zwerin, 1970), about the Rolling Stones concert at the Altamont Speedway, surely wanted and expected to depict the crowd's unruliness, the stabbing of a young man by one of the Hell's Angels hired as security guards by concert organizers is probably not a type of event even anticipated by the filmmakers. Yet their plans still seem designed to accommodate the representation of such a contingency, insofar as they deployed their camera operators with the intention of keeping a lens trained on the mob's antics, whatever those might turn out to be. That motion picture and sound apparatus can reliably allow us to represent real scenes in the absence of awareness of those scenes' properties is one attribute that separates cinematic from other representations.

It should also be stressed that moderate intentionality in no way implies the etiological autonomy of intention. Besides conduct-controlling executive attitudes, a great many other psychological as well as social and contextual factors are potentially involved in the movie's creation. In other words, intentions alone are not what motivate and govern a producer's activities. Yet they are pivotal. An intention to do **X**, or to do something leading to **X**, is a situated, historical item. Its formation or acquisition depends upon the condition of a particular agent's reasons for doing or wanting **X**, at a certain time and place.

Take, for example, the ordinary way in which we explain why someone has dropped out of school. We do not tend to regard dropping out as something that merely happens to a person, in the same way that being pointed northward is something that happens to a weathervane. Instead, we try to ascertain the beliefs, emotions, and desires upon which he acted, within the pertinent circumstances. Hence we cite his dissatisfaction with the curriculum, his opinions on how he is wasting his true talents on stupefying academic tasks, his wish to begin earning money and buying luxury items. We may even invoke psychological conditions that have escaped the person's own focal awareness; we might, for example, suspect that what has really motivated him is a characteristic fear of failure, which subtends his chronic inability to finish complex, long-term projects. Our reflections on this matter would likely also prompt speculation about actual as well as perceived opportunities and limitations currently facing the individual. Beliefs about the financial impossibility of continuing his education, or the immediate availability of an apparently lucrative job, can exert a powerful influence on an agent's choices of goals and actions.

Likewise, explaining why a movie has a certain feature, or why the work was made just as it was, would, presumably, sometimes involve citing its author's reasons for having deliberately given the work such and such a property or significance. Here "reasons" evokes a host of affective, perceptual, evaluative, doxastic, and conative states, along with personality traits and stable, long-term personal policies and projects (such as winning an Academy Award)—in brief, whatever might have motivated the filmmaker to make the movie just as he did.

Denizens of university humanities departments are also conversant with more specialized discourses concerning behavior, such as those which advert to familiar canons of sub-intentional and sociocultural items. It is not uncommon to encounter in cinema scholarship discourse about the crucial etiological powers exerted by internal and external forces of which filmmakers and viewers alike may be dimly if at all conscious.

In the present connection, it is hard not to think of Nichols's "epistephilic" account of the factors productive of the standard documentary, blending as it does the vocabulary of psychoanalysis with reference to supra-individual entities.[11] If I understand him, Nichols says that many non-fictions appeal to the audience's preponderant, perhaps even compulsive desire to gain knowledge of the world, especially of social-historical phenomena. The impetus for this pursuit is epistephilia: the desire for pleasure in knowing, where this pleasure is identified with the "sense of plenitude or self-sufficiency" that comes from knowing.[12] The documentary's appeal to this desire is apparently no accident. Nichols refers to the body of codes, conventions, and institutionalized practices associated with documentary realism as "a means of achieving specific effects one of which is the appearance of a nonproblematic relationship to representation itself."[13]

In other words, whether the filmmaker realizes it or not, his or her adherence to the codes of realism functions to promote the viewer's illusory impression of unmediated access to objective truths; and this impression is particularly apt to scratch the epistephilic itch.[14] Nichols also contends that the pleasure at issue is far from innocent. The spectator, permitted the satisfaction of imagining himself a knowing subject, is thereby disposed to accept as true what are in fact highly ideological images and messages tending to reflect or reinforce hegemonic social relations. The causes of the non-fiction's emergence and properties are therefore to be sought primarily in terms of anonymous, quasi-mechanical drives and supra-individual structures of gender, race, and class. These somehow operate in and through the activities of individual authors in such a way as to bring about the non-fiction's functional adaptation to the drive's gratification and the social relations' reproduction.

From the current intentionalist point of view, there is no question of whether a work's emergence can be intelligently explained on the basis of psychodynamic mechanisms and social totalities. Notice a commonality among such postulated determinants of cinematic meaning. The putative effects of all of the foregoing are mediated by intentions and intentional actions. Reasons, drives, social structures—the magnitude of kinds of things we discuss when trying to say why a work has its particular structure, content, and effects—are only effective if they influence or constrain somebody's intentional actions. Unlike the amount of ambient light or the focal length of a lens, these sorts of etiological items cannot directly determine a work's properties. Rather, their causal contributions must be filtered through the author's intentions. And it is intentions, in their mediating function, that necessarily bridge the gap between peoples' various imaginable motivations for doing X and their actually doing or achieving X.

Positing such a bridge is conceptually warranted for two major reasons, both having to do with intention's unique contribution to the generation of action by serving as its proximal cause. First, as previously noted, people do not always do what they are most strongly motivated to do; and there are many instances, both common and conceivable, in which they are subject to competing motivations. Intentions necessarily settle the issue of what the agent shall do, whereas relative motivational strength need not. Second, unlike being motivated to do X, intending to do X incorporates a plan for X-ing or realizing X. Intention differs from even the most irresistible libidinally or socially conditioned desire for some object, in that its representational content and guidance function specify, for a given agent at a certain location, how (best) to bring about that end.

Whether or not authors are so compelled, a propensity to make movies favoring the illusion of transparency is not etiologically equivalent to having and following a particular plan for making this movie here and now. The latter has more direct access to the mechanisms productive of action. Such a plan provides a path of action directed toward a particular goal state, one that allows for such reasoning and adjustments as required both by the tremendous variety of routes potentially leading to its realization and by the complications arising at various stages along the chosen route. Contending that an author had this or that motivation for making a work is an explanatory task different from indicating **how** having certain motivations could be productive of this work. Hence I focus not on the question of what motivating conditions and mental states might have disposed the filmmaker toward creating a certain kind of movie but on the special causal structure linking those conditions and states to the realization of the work.

I also underline that I subscribe to a thesis of real author intentionalism. Scholarship frequently refers to something along the lines of an implied author or authorial voice, where this entity is distinct from the person who actually made the work. For example, in their study of Wiseman's films, Thomas Benson and Carolyn Anderson prefer to attribute to "Wiseman as the implied author" or "Wiseman's camera'" responsibility for part of the meaning derived by the audience from a film.[15] Benson and Anderson are certainly not anti-realists about intention's causal role upstream in a movie's production, for they note that a Wiseman film (here, *High School*) provides "considerable inferential evidence about the filmmaker's rhetorical intentions." But they are unwilling to associate the film's meaning with authorially intended meaning. Their reticence has the standard sources: the implausibility of regarding all of a work's significant features as under its author's conscious, direct control; the inaccessibility of the filmmaker's actual psychological states; the possibility of multiple authorship in film production, and the difficulty of sorting out who really contributed what to the process of determining the work's features.

Nevertheless, Benson and Anderson also rule out a wholesale rejection of the notion of an authorial consciousness "behind the film," since audiences can often make sense of a movie only by asking what a filmmaker meant by this or that image or sound. They therefore assent to the idea that it is the wishes and attitudes of an implied author—a subjectivity that corresponds to no actual agent, is suggested by the work's properties, and reflects sensibilities, points of view, beliefs, and objectives—that spectators make reference to in deciding how they are to understand the film's meaning.

When the time comes, I shall highlight several weaknesses of implied authorship as an interpretive principle. At present, my rejection of it is merely programmatic, since the implied author has no application to the problem of stating how the motion picture in fact acquires those properties it possesses prior to and independent of reception and interpretive action. It should be stressed that I do not maintain that no genuine meaning can emerge as a result of an audience's reactions to a work. But I do insist that before spectators experience the work and construct any impressions of the nature and origins of its significance, it is endowed with an important and interesting array of stable meanings. The movie possesses these because, during its creation, certain commands are exercised over it in an effort to make a particular kind of artifact, elements of which audiences will recognize as already fulfilling various complex indicator functions. An implied author, and the various attitudes ascribed to it, are at best products or consequences of some other, real person's thoughts and actions. Completely lacking ontological and causal autonomy, an implied author cannot literally constrain the work in any way and thus cannot figure causally in an adequate explanation of how the movie comes to have the properties it exhibits.

Finally, a remark on multiple authorship is in order. Motion pictures are often created by groups of people. It is tempting to cite this fact as an objection to the idea that meaning can be associated with the author's intentions, since it is difficult to decide who is really responsible for what features. However, this worry is not an impediment to a moderate intentionalism, since it does not itself license the conclusion that plans do not constrain meaning. Multiple authorship, insofar as it presupposes that the etiology and exposition of meaning involves several individual agents engaging in practical reasoning and intentional action, is well within the ambit of the kind of explanatory framework that I support. Granted, collective endeavors pose the risk of our misattributing an intention to one person when it is properly ascribed to another or to the group as a whole. Moreover, the corporately produced work, no less than a solo project, might exhibit various perverse effects, resulting from peoples' efforts to share decisions, pass on instructions, and divide tasks; that is, it might contain accidentally emergent meanings unanticipated or undesired by any one of its makers. In any case, our job is neither to find a heuristic by which to decide whose personal vision or genius most informs the work nor to find a way to match each and every property with the sole intention of a particular person. On the contrary, a moderate intentionalism should not obscure the relevance of shared goals and intentions.

Movie making normally calls for the coordination of individual actions. If a completed film segment describes a certain situation, it may well be because the relevant doings of each member of a group were guided by the same or similar plan to create a sequence interpreted* by that situation. I say "same or similar," because, although these individuals may share the general intention to make a sequence describing **S**, the content of each person's plan will be subjectively appropriate to his or her role in the production and may add features unrepresented within the shared intention.

Forbidden by his subject to film in her home, Maximillian Schell went into the studio and marshaled a team of people in an effort to reconstruct from his memory part of Marlene Dietrich's Paris apartment. Those sequences of the documentary *Marlene* (1985) that feature this set have the content they do because various individuals, acting and interacting with a mutual intention in mind, executed a variety of sub-plans consonant with the realization of their overall goal. Although subordinated to the director's own plans, lighting, camera, and art direction personnel presumably will have all acted, within their particular domains of expertise, on effective communicative intentions to endow the movie with significant or expressive properties, some of which might not have been originally intended by Schell.

Although I have no evidence upon which to assert that this was the case, hypothetically speaking, it is not inconceivable that it was the cinematographer or lighting director who formulated the plan to evoke the luminosity of Dietrich's screen stardom by showing us bright light streaming through the French windows. That the depiction results from collective intentions, the contents of individual components displaying some degree of autonomy or improvisation relative to the overarching plan, no more requires the evacuation of intentionalist principles than do analogous examples of group action geared toward painting houses, preparing dinners, and editing scholarly anthologies.

Before moving on to the next, very technical phase of discussions of filmmaking pragmatics, I would like to offer a few remarks on one of my study's horizon questions—a problem I probably would have been better off analyzing before embarking on an investigation of agency's role in the production of meaning. Clearly enough, I think that movies have makers, that is, individuals who deliberately exercise control over force, content, and form—upstream of reception. I also think that many, if not all, cinematic works have a special kind of maker: an author.[16] But I am not sure what an author is, how it is different from a maker, and what the precise conditions are for saying of a work that it has one author, or several such makers.

Caught with unfinished homework, the best I can do for now is to extemporize a bit. Whenever I refer to a movie's author, I have the following in mind. I would propose a very stripped-down idea of authorship—having nothing in common with romantic notions of the auteur, that is, an all-controlling, individual genius who imprints his or her unique, personal vision on the film's every frame. Rather, "author" refers to the agent or agents who have the "A-plan." This structure of intentions might be fairly abstract, leaving much to be filled in as the project advances. Yet it is nevertheless a global, synthetic recipe regarding the finished movie's content, structure, properties, and effects, along with some of the practical routes to required to achieve these.

To give this conception of authorship intuitive appeal, it should maintain that the **A**-plan be largely formulated by the person or persons who mean(s) to execute it—thus we tend to exclude plans the content of which was randomly generated by computer programs or found at the bottom of wastebaskets on anonymous paper scraps. Also, the **A**-plan is distinguished from others by its constraint on the content of further, more regionally determinant and hierarchically subordinate plans. It is therefore likely, especially in the field of industrially produced, commercial cinema, that an authorial plan would be executed by virtue of its guiding and initiating other makers' intentions and actions. In such contexts, an author is someone who, in fact, effectively supervises and orients subalterns.

The author and the **A**-plan are, roughly stated, at the top of a hierarchy; the farther down and out we go along its lower branches of subaltern planners and subordinate plans, right out to the gaffers and grips and so forth, the less global their plans are and the less determinant their reasoning and intentions are with respect to content, form, and desired effects on audiences. We must, however, note two features of this arrangement. First, the concept of the **A**-plan may be relativized to one's production role. Bernard Herrmann, composer of *North by Northwest*'s (Alfred Hitchcock, 1959) musical score, is a maker of *North by Northwest*, not its author; but he is the author of its score. A similar claim could be made of actor James Mason and his performance, and of writer Ernest Lehman and his screenplay. Second, instead of being a rigidly top-down arrangement, the type of hierarchy we observe could be quite "tangled." Some movies are made in situations in which subalterns have significant opportunities for innovation and feedback, with authors being correspondingly accepting and disposed toward making adjustments. How the author is related to subordinates and collaborators might be a matter of great empirical variety.

One of my intuitions is that the concept of author, as defined above, is not synonymous with that of director, writer, producer, or any combination of such roles. I am also inclined to think that not all movies have authors. Perhaps some films result from nothing resembling an **A**-plan and fail to fall under the auspices of anybody functioning as an **A**-planner. Such works would have makers, without any individual or group having much of a global plan. Other works could have joint or collective authors, in which two or more people share in the formulation and execution of an **A**-plan; still another option would be multiple authorship, as in compilation films and anthologies, wherein each individual cooperatively contributes a largely independently authored work. However, these increasingly speculative remarks take me to outside the parameters of my current study and beyond my purposes. I do not here try to resolve the controversy over what an author is. Rather, I offer them as a first approximation of how I would analyze authorship, in anticipation of questions begged by discussions to follow.

Notes

1. Alfred Mele, *Springs of Action: Understanding Intentional Behavior* (New York: Oxford University Press, 1992). In preparing the present chapter, I have also found Michael Bratman's *Intentions, Plans, and Practical Reason* (Cambridge, Mass.: Harvard University Press, 1987) to be of value for its scope, depth, and clarity of exposition on the complex topic of intentionality. Two articles coauthored by Mele and Paisley Livingston, both treatments of the relevance of intentions to literary production, cast particularly strong light on the relevance of intentionality to matters of aesthetics and symbolic communication: Paisley Livingston and Alfred Mele, "Intention and Literature," *Stanford French Review* 16 (1992): 173–196; Alfred Mele and Paisley Livingston, "Intentions and Interpretations," *MLN* 107 (1992): 931–949.

2. Mele, *Springs of Action*, 136.

3. Livingston and Mele, "Intention and Literature," 178.

4. See Mele, *Springs of Action*, 228–241.

5. This question should be differentiated from its purely academic counterpart, "What would I do now, if I were to act?"

6. See Bratman, *Intentions, Plans, and Practical Reason*, 33.

7. Mele, *Springs of Action*, 137–38; Bratman, *Intentions, Plans, and Practical Reason*, 2–3, 108–109.

8. Paisley Livingston, "Characterization and Fictional Truth in the Cinema," in *Post-Theory: Reconstructing Film Studies*, ed. David Bordwell and Noël Carroll (Madison: University of Wisconsin Press, 1996), 167–168.

9. See G. Roy Levin's interview with D. A. Pennebaker, in *Documentary Explorations: 15 Interviews with Filmmakers*, ed. G. Roy Levin (New York: Doubleday, 1971), 266–267.

10. Bill Nichols, *Representing Reality: Issues and Concepts in Documentary* (Bloomington: Indiana University Press, 1991), 139.

11. Ibid., 31, 76–77, 178–180, 185–186, 194.

12. Ibid., 31.

13. Ibid., 179.

14. Self-reflexive movies that gesture toward their own constructedness and question the status of their own truth claims are said to disrupt epistephilia rather than appeal to it.

15. Thomas W. Benson and Carolyn Anderson, *Reality Fictions: The Films of Frederick Wiseman* (Carbondale: Southern Illinois University Press, 1989), 109–110. Other proponents of implied authorship include George Wilson, *Narration in Light: Studies in Cinematic Point of View* (Baltimore: Johns Hopkins University Press,1986), 134–139; and Gregory Currie, *Image and Mind: Film, Philosophy, and Cognitive Science* (Cambridge: Cambridge University Press, 1996), 243–246. An influential literary critical argument for the implied author is found in Wayne C.

Booth, *The Rhetoric of Fiction* (Chicago: University of Chicago Press, 1961), 71–76, 211–221.

16. Readers wanting intelligent introductions to the debates and hypotheses to which I can only now allude could not do better than to consult these two essays: Paisley Livingston, "Cinematic Authorship," in *Film Theory and Philosophy*, ed. Richard Allen and Murray Smith (Oxford: Oxford University Press, 1997), 132–148; Berys Gaut, "Film Authorship and Collaboration," in Allen and Smith, *Film Theory and Philosophy*, 148–172.

5

Planning for Content

I turn now to the job of showing how authorial intentions might determine non-fiction's content. This phase of the inquiry begins in the abstract. I suggest five principles as conceptual grounds for describing the ways in which particular kinds of authorial psychological states constrain the condition, hence the meaning, of the movie's representational states. These grounds make explicit what it is that a moderate intentionalist might prudently claim about the nature and extent of authorial control over one aspect of the documentary's significance. Then I propose two general categories of non-fictional content, reflecting the content-determining functions of two conceivable types of plans. Finally, the bulk of the present discussion is devoted to a more concrete examination of the role of planning and practical reasoning in an actual cinematic work's creation. Here I apply the central tenets of the moderate intentionalism that I recommend to an analysis of a canonical documentary, *Nanook of the North* (Robert Flaherty, 1922).

Explaining Content with Intentions

If we are to explain, as I think we must, the origins of a cinematic constative's meaning by saying that it exhibits dependency upon authorial rationality, then we are obliged to say how and why a film scholar may intelligently maintain that something as potentially obscure, muddled, and inaccessible as an idea "in somebody's head," so to speak, can exert a decisive influence over what the movie signifies to its audience. My response to this problem is to supply a budget of core methodological and explanatory principles in support of the hypothesis that the maker's intentions can be a source of meaning, even when authorial control is loose, only one factor among many, far from absolute, or itself subject to a variety of intractable external as well as internal constraints and forces.

These guidelines comport with the previous chapter's opening defense of moderate intentionalism, taking it one step farther in the form of five methodological dicta. That is why the first dictum recalls the definitive thesis of moderate intentionalism: To wit, not any and all of an author's intentions pertain to or manifest themselves in the movie's meaning. The privileged constraining states at issue are effective communicative intentions, the plan components of which pertain to those parts of the documentary's content that are to be expressed openly and explicitly to a target audience, or which the author reasonably expects competent members of that target audience to infer on the basis of their perceptions of the movie's features plus their relevant background beliefs and knowledge.

Second, plans with respect to content, being a species of communicative intentions, are plans to get viewers to notice or individuate various situations. "Situation" is the word we have been using to denote collections of individual objects having properties and standing in relations to one another at a given time and place or across spatial-temporal locations; they may be real, typical, or wholly imaginary. Thus effective communicative intentions help circumscribe the motion picture constative's external significance—that part of its meaning that we have been calling its interpretation*. To the extent they determine what scene shall be photographically depicted, and how that depiction shall appear to the viewer, plans also exert an influence over the work's natural interpretation*.

Third, given our previous discussions, we can say that documentary filmmaking intentions are plan-embedding executive attitudes that bridge the gap between the author having desires and ideas about his or her work's potential content and the realization of an artifact having that content. The plan component of the kind of effective communicative intention at issue here contains a mental representation of a situation to be described cinematically, along with a route to producing a cinematic description of that situation. So long as the filmmaker takes an executive attitude toward this plan—that is, engages in reasoning and action appropriately guided by its content—he or she will tend to (try to) take the relevant practical steps, including further efforts of reasoning, towards realizing a movie, a portion of the content of which shall exhibit non-accidental, intentional, counterfactual dependence on that of the plan. Plans and planning thereby initiate, guide, motivate, and terminate activities—choosing camera angles, decorating sets, scripting dialogue, editing imagery and sound, and so on—suitable to adapting cinematic tools and materials to the job of indicating how things stand with respect to a given state of affairs or event.

It follows that the effective communicative intention's plan component can accommodate two sorts of representations. It contains a description of a situation, the structure or condition of which it is the cinematic work's prospective function to indicate. The plan component also comprises a description of another situation or situations, namely, those constituting the steps to be taken toward realizing a filmic unit indicating this first situation. Both of these aspects of the intention's content may be more or less vague or schematic. Someone wishing to produce a documentary on whales in the St. Lawrence seaway might start off with only a rough, and distal, intention to depict the relevant species in their natural habitat, coping with pollution; embedded in this plan might be a similarly sketchy idea of how to make this depiction, for example, by sending an underwater cinematographer to a likely spot along the seaway and letting him shoot as much whale footage as the project can afford, then giving this material to the editor, and so on. Over time, and with respect to various stages and facets of the project, both aspects of the plan will be refined and revised and will branch off into sub-plans, in ways congruent with the initial intention to make a whale documentary.

A fourth principle holds that plans may constrain a work's mental significance, that is, that which the viewer can learn about the author's psychological condition from the condition of the representation. In such cases, the plan calls for indicating an actual or putative psychological relation—such as an attitude of belief, desire, or doubt—between a communicator and a proposition. The complex ways in which a particular kind of mental significance—namely, illocutionary force—is signaled will be dealt with in the next chapter. At present, our topic is the relationship between some of the movie's external significance and a narrow slice of the producer's mental states.

A fifth and final principle of moderate intentionality, then, pertains to the potential asymmetries between a non-fiction's content and its mental significance. Notice, for example, that a representation being interpreted* by a situation, **S**, is no automatic indication or guarantee that its maker believes that **S** is the case. The cineaste might be acting insincerely; recall the case of Patterson's Sasquatch film, which asserts the existence of a Bigfoot without its maker actually believing that the real pre-filmic object it shows is a Bigfoot. On the other hand, there may be content nested in a film of which the filmmaker is unaware. When people use movie cameras to produce photographic records of actual scenes, they often do so demonstratively and without precise beliefs regarding that which they are depicting; having recorded a crowded street corner, the filmmaker need not realize that he has depicted sixty-three people. Likewise, there may be an asymmetry between a work's actual content and the intentions that produce a representation having that content. In other words, that a representation is interpreted* by **S** does not mean that **S** exhaustively or accurately indicates the content of the author's plan, because the movie's content can include unforeseen and unintended features or properties of which the filmmaker is unconscious.

In a similar vein, a movie's content is at best conditionally indicative of its maker's motivations for producing the work or scene in question. The reasons, desires, temperaments, ideological leanings, or social, external forces that in fact prompted those involved to make the film as they did may be little if at all evident from the film itself. Deciding why a film has the content it does—why, say, Alain Resnais neglects, in *Night and Fog* (1955), to emphasize that the Jews were the Nazis' main targets, and what this omission means about Resnais' ethnic sensitivities and attitudes—often requires extensive empirical research into biographical matters, a film's production history, and institutional, economic, and other circumstances composing the proximal social conditions of the work's emergence.

Although researchers might care to investigate the intentional origins of a wide variety of cinematic properties, functions, and effects, my investigation currently centers on a very limited problematic: a rudimentary account of how intentions constrain the documentary's open and effective description of extra-cinematic situations. I do not tackle the problem of explaining the relation of authorial planning to persuasive, emotional, and other perlocutionary effects on the audience, such as transformative political and social engineering goals. Nor do I make a concerted effort to talk about the role of specifically aesthetic and artistic intentions, like those bearing on a maker's wish to create something beautiful, to imitate the stylistic traits of a certain tradition (e.g., film noir, German expressionism, the Griersonian documentary of the 1930s), or to find an aesthetic that reflects the illusory nature of objectivity and knowledge. I do not examine authorial attempts to express (or construct impressions of) their personalities or therapeutically work through their personal problems or obsessions by means of filmmaking.

One can make a documentary without seriously trying to mobilize the masses, achieve a particular aesthetic effect, or engage in self-actualization, but one cannot make a motion picture constative without ascribing content to it, in the very limited sense of content—openly describing situations—that I am here employing. I thus ignore certain kinds of intentions and goals not because I regard them as inconsequential or uninteresting but because, from the perspective of the present discussion, they are not essential to the production of non-fictions.

There is another job that I do not tackle, namely, the positing of a comprehensive typology of non-fiction styles and sub-genres. Such taxonomies are important to scholarship, for they throw into relief real differences that are undoubtedly significant to the study of non-fiction's formal properties, historical transformations, and relations to various rhetorical ends. However, within the confines of my present explanatory purposes, plans and intentions have priority relative to descriptions of categories and groupings of documentary styles and forms. Such insightful typologies as Bill Nichols's four documentary modes (expository, observational, interactive, and reflexive) are, to the limits of their historical and ecological validity, reflections of the kinds of plans that non-fiction filmmakers have thus far devised.[1] I offer no rival classification or workable alternative. Below I distinguish between two main categories of plans, corresponding to two broad strategies of authorially determining the content of non-fictional motion pictures. To a first approximation, then, here are two general schemas for explaining how agents' intentions, plans, and practical reasoning constrain cinematic meaning.

Type I Non-Fictions. Sometimes producers have only schematic plans and highly flexible commitments regarding what they will represent, and hence what cognitions, perceptions, emotions, and so forth they expect to trigger on the part of the spectator. Up to and including the time when their cameras roll, they might simply intend to show whatever it is that ultimately happens to be recorded on the resultant footage. In such cases, cineastes may well be following highly detailed plans concerning what images will be captured, plans encompassing stylistic considerations, logistics, budgetary constraints, and so on. Nonetheless, one facet of the content of this planning structure—the specification of what, exactly, will (likely) be shown—remains relatively abstract.

The incompleteness of plans with respect to cinematic content could be a function of one or a combination of any of three conditions: (1) The environment imposes constraints on the cinematic agent's activities that limit significantly his foreknowledge of what he can expect to depict and/or his influence over what he expects to depict and/or the means of depiction; (2) the agent prefers to try to minimize his influence over pre-filmic events; (3) the agent is to a greater rather than lesser degree uncommitted to using the motion picture representation to bring about particular perceptions and realizations on the part of viewers.

Consider an example of observational cinema. In movies like Wiseman's *Law and Order* (1968), the filmmaker is at the outset largely agnostic about what will wind up on the editing machine. Wiseman and his cinematographer, William Brayne, surely planned to represent certain kinds of law enforcement situations and must have engaged in extensive means-ends reasoning about feasible intermediate steps. They were, for instance, aware of the potential for witnessing police brutality and considered focusing on exposing the violence of the Kansas City officers to whom they had negotiated access.[2] However it also seems to have been part of their strategy to try to restrict their influence over their subjects' behavior before the camera and to put themselves in situations in which they would have incomplete knowledge of precisely what courses of events would unfold. So although Wiseman and Brayne counted on recording activities of, say, the vice squad, they operated under conditions of uncertainty that stopped them from settling in advance on a specific, narrowly conceived intention to secure audiovisual documentation of, say, an officer putting a stranglehold on a prostitute while telling her, "Go ahead, resist. I'll choke you till you can't breathe." In this sense embedded in their plan is a preference for working with a level of abstraction concerning that which would be portrayed in the day's footage.

Adherence to a Type I plan is no protection against kinky wayward causation. Although the filmmaker might take every step to avoid influencing those under observation, it is not impossible that awareness of the camera could either elicit or discourage subjects' responses. The agnosticism of a Type I schema can also accommodate *kinoki* who are quite sanguine about the chance that their presence may foster certain events. I am thinking of what Erik Barnouw labels "cinema verité."[3] Instead of simply trying to record events, the vérité filmmaker is a catalyst, in as much as he or she attempts to precipitate or contribute to the pre-filmic situation. Barnouw cites some of Jean Rouch's films as paradigmatic of participant observation. A case in point is *Tourou et Bitti* (1971), during which Rouch, in a voice-over, remarks that he hopes the camera's arrival at a ceremony will provoke a trance. Of course, an intention to try to trigger an event need not betoken a detailed plan regarding the actual features of that which will ultimately transpire and hence be depicted. The filmmaker might foresee and desire some of the ramifications of his intervention yet have only a vague idea of the kind of event that he would like to precipitate.

There is a post-filmic variation on Type I representations. Finding a length of previously recorded motion picture footage, a filmmaker or user could hit upon the idea of showing this material to an audience, intending that they take the attitude of belief toward whatever happens to be portrayed. The cinematic agent is still relatively undirective, insofar as he has but a general notion of what he wants to indicate by the image, along with a correspondingly loose idea of what he expects the viewer to see by the footage.

Imagine someone who inadvertently leaves his new home video camera on, the equipment registering a panoramic view of the living room. In the absence of the relevant sorts of intentional attitudes to initiate and guide it, the recording process itself falls short of being an act of non-fictional communication. But after he realizes what has happened, the accidental videographer resolves to send the tape to a relative with a note saying, "This is how our living room looks." Hence downstream from the generation of the video images, he formulates a plan pertaining to what effects he wishes to give rise to by displaying this footage. And this plan calls for nothing more specific than taking steps to give someone perceptual access to the grosser observable features of the room. The agent having played next to no role in the recording process; the movie's content is established by default. Although he probably would expect that anyone watching the tape could discriminate a vast array of perceptual items, he lacks a narrow commitment to showing that one of the paintings hangs crooked or that there are exactly ten compact discs stacked by the stereo. Instead of trying to guide the percipient's attention toward a specific region of the depiction or to dictate to her a particular meaning of the image, he is satisfied to take the opportunity to show her the look of the scene.

Type II Non-Fictions. Type II works are also shaped by stable structures of authorial choices and preferences. But unlike Type I movies, they result from intentions that are more rather than less restrictive of content. Type II non-fictions correspond to significantly more detailed plans concerning the depiction's discernible audiovisual properties and the facts that viewers are thereby meant to notice. The claim here is not that improvisation, spontaneity, or accident can play no part in the production of such a work; nor am I implying that the filmmaker ever achieves full lucidity and complete mastery over all aspects of the cinematic artifact's meaning. Yet a wholly defensible thesis would be that measures are sometimes taken to try to align the documentary's content with that of certain comprehensive plans, instead of allowing it to depend preponderantly on the emergence of unmanipulated, unforeseen, or undesired pre-filmic situations.

The Thin Blue Line (Errol Morris, 1988) would be an instance of documentary's content being finely adjusted to extensive future-directed schemes. Plans regarding blocking, lighting, shot composition, camera movement, the staging of reenactments, and so forth systematically oriented what is ultimately shown to, and noticed by, spectators. From the pre-production phases through to the shooting and cutting of this noirish film, its depictions were thus designed and achieved with the same meticulousness associated with Hollywood fictions. That a movie was made in a fashion typical of the fiction film is not itself sufficient reason to conclude that it is essentially a work of make-believe or is somehow a less straightforward piece of non-fiction. After all, the difference between fiction and non-fiction is one of force, not of style, form, or content. And in the case of *The Thin Blue Line*, it seems that various plans with respect to what would be represented, and how these representations would be constructed, were secondary to the principle goal of letting spectators know that it is appropriate to take the attitude of belief toward the greater part of that which is either explicitly shown or implied by the depiction.

The more general point is that a conceptual distinction between Type I and Type II non-fictions reflects no hierarchy of non-fictional status. That exemplars of the first category are often associated with standard, even institutionally prescribed practices or conventions of non-fiction filmmaking, issuing in certain stereotypical journalistic or "pure" documentaries, could be symptomatic of our normative suppositions about what makes for a good documentary but tells us nothing about the necessary and sufficient conditions for a movie being non-fiction.

Type II plans with respect to content can also be post-filmic, that is, bear directly on how the filmmaker or film-user will instantiate content by manipulating footage on which images and sounds have already been registered. For instance, having completed their shooting, documentarians more often than not discriminatingly assemble their material, adding narration, music, or other audiovisual features. To the degree that this processing is done with an eye to precipitating in the viewer certain cognitive perceptions and inferences, that which the movie depicts is at least partly the result of Type II post-filmic plans. The producers of *The Atomic Cafe* (Kevin Rafferty, Jane Loader, Pierce Rafferty, 1982) evidently appropriated extant audiovisual materials on the basis of comprehensive schemes for combining and altering them with a view to achieving certain meaningful ends. Excerpts from government propaganda films, military training movies, news footage, and music are combined so as to suggest an historical progression of public discourse about the bomb, from adulation to an increasing and perspicacious cynicism.

Distinguishing between Type I and Type II non-fictions reflects the intuition that there are genuine if not radical differences between, for instance, works of observational cinema and more theatrical documentaries—an intuition that can be developed through an examination of the cinematic agent's practical reasoning and action. Yet if talk of types of non-fictions is to be illuminating, it is best to locate such categories on a continuum. Instead of looking for mutually exclusive classifications, it makes more sense to situate films somewhere along a gradual progression from minimal to maximal prevalence of authorial intentions. In all likelihood the majority of works are a combination of Types I and II, one or the other kind of plan prevailing at certain production stages. For example, it is fair to say that in Wiseman's oeuvre Type I plans govern filmmaking up to and including the recording phase. But insofar as he carefully edits his images—thereby creating certain impressions and pursuing various rhetorical ends—Type II plans also perform a key role in the construction of his films.

Nanook of the North

To develop the foregoing points about types of authorial control over the cinematic constative, I turn now to another example, the details of which should serve to emphasize several of the pivotal roles that effective communicative intentions play with respect to content. This case also gives us a forum in which to examine the temporal dimensions of plans and planning, along with the influence such mental states exert over narrative and characterization. To avoid misunderstandings, I emphasize that my aim is not to make an empirical contribution to a body of film-historical evidence about how a certain film was made. Rather, in an effort further to conceptualize intention's role in the emergence of cinematic meaning I try to take what we do know or can legitimately infer from the existing historical record of a movie's production. Many of the facts about why Flaherty included the scenes he did are obscure or unknown to us. Hence any attempt to reconstruct the director's plans not accompanied by probative research can and should be given second-class epistemic status, from a historical and empirical point of view. But again, my aim is analytic and conceptual, geared to the formation of hypotheses about the contributions of plans and planning to cinematic meaning, not the solution of film-historical mysteries.

Flaherty's *Nanook of the North* has long been regarded as a prototypical non-fiction—one that not only inspired and influenced much subsequent work within the genre but that also rests squarely and fatefully within the disputed zone of non-fiction film's much contested relation to reality. An introductory title announces, "The picture concerns the life of one Nanook (The Bear), his family and little band of followers, 'Itivimuits' of Hopewell Sound, Northern Ungava, through whose kindliness, faithfulness and patience this film was made." In subsequent frames, Flaherty relates mundane as well as dramatic incidents from these nomadic people's lives, the narration extending in time from summer months until the depths of winter. Along with images of domestic habits and family activities, the filmmaker presents us with scenes of hunting, fishing, trekking, and the building of shelters—ordinary activities for the Inuit, but ones that Flaherty assures viewers are of the utmost urgency in an infertile land of scarcity and extremes.

Many of *Nanook of the North*'s sequences are relatively simple visual records of apparently unrehearsed or routine tasks, as when we are shown, in a series of three fairly long takes, the practice of fueling a fire with moss. Other filmic passages are considerably more elaborate. The story of a walrus hunt, conveyed in over forty shots of various lengths, angles, and perspectives, owes some of its interest to the hunters subduing their quarry in what was for them an idiosyncratic way. Later, in ostensibly depicting efforts to catch a seal swimming just below an ice floe, the film drifts toward burlesque comedy when it shows Nanook's tug 'o war with a spirited creature that, once pulled onto the ice, appears to be frozen solid.

Reading the literature on *Nanook of the North*, one notices an equally vigorous tug o' war between, at one end, those who consider it to be the quintessential movie of reality's revelation and, at the opposing end, those who find it emblematic of the inevitably artificial, manipulated qualities of both the documentary and the reality it purports merely to preserve.

Those pulling for the movie's privileged relation to reality include Frances Hubbard Flaherty, the filmmaker's wife and frequent collaborator. She labels her husband's work, beginning with *Nanook of the North*, a cinema of "non-preconception"—filmmaking as a process of discovery of and "surrender" to the extra-cinematic world, wherein the maker celebrates "freely and spontaneously, simply and purely" the "thing itself for its own sake."[4] From *Nanook* on, asserts Richard Barsam, Flaherty's method for discovering his referent "was to immerse himself in the subject, to shoot everything with the hope of capturing cinematographic images that would preserve the temporal and spatial realities of what his observant eyes perceived."[5] Paul Rotha likens Flaherty's approach to filming to that of an Eskimo carver who sets out to reveal that which is already in the unworked ivory.[6] An emphasis on the movie's self-effacing qualities is also found in Siegfried Kracauer's description of Flaherty's technique, which emphasizes the "found story" plucked from his subjects' lives rather than imposed upon them from without.[7] In a similar vein, Barnouw says that Flaherty applies the "machinary" of fiction film to "material not invented by a writer or director, not performed by actors. Thus drama, with its potential for emotional impact, was wedded to something more real—people being themselves."[8]

Attempts to draw *Nanook* closer to the side of artifice have from the start gestured toward the thoroughly contrived and misleading nature of many of its representations of Inuit culture. Iris Barry charges that, although the movie's images are undoubtedly of real Eskimo in their actual habitat, Flaherty's subjects are in fact "extremely sophisticated" individuals acting out an "enchanting romance" for the camera—one that "convinced us it was fact though it wasn't at all."[9] Vilhjalmur Stefansson equates the figure of Nanook, and the story in which he appears, with tales of such imaginary beings as Santa Claus.[10] Although Stefansson regards the Nanook fable as no more harmful to audiences than Santa Claus stories are to children, other critics have registered somewhat more alarm.

Commenting on the extent to which Flaherty altered the appearance of contemporary Inuit lifestyles, Roy Armes contends that "documentary as practised by Flaherty can never mean a scientific and objective recording, it is rather a sort of game. The Eskimos pretended they were living their normal lives, but in fact Flaherty's arrival totally disrupted their way of living."[11] Singling out the seal hunting sequence for commentary, James Roy MacBean faults *Nanook of the North* for mystifying the process of sealing as well as that of filming; the director, he contends, "gives the camera the classic privileged narrator's point of view that implies—but does not openly acknowledge—the godlike omniscience of the filmmaker while reinforcing the seemingly unimpeachable authority of the information provided by the image."[12] More recently, William Rothman revives the case against the documentary's purely revelatory status by remarking that the film distorts by portraying Inuit life as "unchanging, timeless, unthreatened" when it is really well on its way to "being destroyed by the social and economic structures of Western civilization."[13]

I do not cite the foregoing polarization (pun intended) of opinions so as to evaluate their relative merits or to state a preference for one side over the other. Indeed, I should like to underscore that there is a crystal of truth in both positions and that to inscribe one's self within either is to perpetuate a false dichotomy. But a description of *Nanook*'s content as either representing or misrepresenting reality is inadequate, since neither grasps Flaherty's ambitions with respect to his documentary's significance. Both views obscure the author's complicated and dynamic attitudes toward his film. An alternative approach is to regard *Nanook* as an opportunity to analyze the way in which a multiplicity of diverse intentions may constrain a work's meaning. Ultimately, this pragmatic explanation treats the film's content as a function of several strategically and reciprocally related plans.

The kind of analysis I have in mind starts by taking into account the decisive influence of long-term plans over the production of this documentary's meaning, from the earliest stages of filmmaking through to the termination of the filmmaker's communicative actions. Flaherty, it seems, was guided by a number of general plans, formulated at a time or times anterior to filming and persisting up until the end of the editing phase. From a practical perspective, such distal and temporally mixed intentions have an important utility for filmmakers: They extend the influence of prior deliberations and decisions over movie production by settling, sometimes well in advance, at least some questions of what to represent and the means by which to bring about those given ends. In other words, they provide ready-made partial solutions to the ongoing problems of determining what to put in the film and how to get that content onto the screen, thereby freeing authors from the necessity of reidentifying options for action, weighing their pros and cons, and reconsidering how to proceed at every stage of a complex project. Some of

Planning for Content 127

Flaherty's general plans regarding how to fill in the content of his discourses and depictions of Eskimo life represented, to varying degrees of abstraction, situations that he would, if given the chance, attempt in turn to represent to an audience. Others were in effect standing policies regarding how to go about deciding on the movie's content and what steps to take in order to assure the effective communication of this meaning.

One set of comparatively general plans, then, pertains to the types of individuals, situations, and events that the cineaste was from the start committed to portraying. The origins of these plans in the case at hand seem to have been as follows. Flaherty was, prior to his return to the Ungava region to film *Nanook of the North*, a veteran of four geological expeditions to the Canadian North. There is little to suggest that he took much care at the time to make anything approximating an anthropological study of either the cultural beliefs of the native peoples with whom he had contact or the impact of nonindigenous culture (including his own actions) on them. Yet it is clear from journal entries made during these trips, and writings published both before and after *Nanook*'s distribution, that he had taken a keen interest in observing and recording the grosser features of daily Inuit activities. Numerous admiring descriptions of the practical aspects of hunting, fishing, shelter building, transportation, and clothing suggest that Flaherty thereby associated a variety of such situations and actions with those he regarded as typifying Eskimo life.

Moreover, on two expeditions Flaherty made extensive use of a motion picture camera. Although some of the footage he shot was publicly exhibited between 1916 and 1920, none of it is known to have survived to this day. But other documents—such as newspaper reviews of screenings, the filmmaker's outline for the talks he sometimes gave at screenings, an unpublished article describing some of the film shot in 1914—provide at least a partial account of the lost footage. Among its scenes were depictions of travel by dog sledge, walrus and seal hunts, the construction of an igloo, and family life inside the igloo. Like *Nanook*, at least a portion of the earlier film focused on a single family.

In light of the homologies between *Nanook*'s explicit content and the kinds of objects in which Flaherty had expressed a previous interest, we may suppose that the director had settled on certain content-defining intentions well in advance of his return to Northern Ungava to film his new project. Although precise plans regarding which particular people, locations, and events to record had not yet been formulated, Flaherty, as soon as he had settled on the goal of producing a new movie, already possessed, before departing for Hopewell Sound, a schematic framework within which to undertake such planning.[14]

Among his general but nonetheless regnant ideas of a future movie's content, Flaherty also started out with three more specialized categories of objects and situations, corresponding to three more specialized representational plans. These concerned narrative, characterization, and confirmation.

Although we cannot judge the matter for ourselves, Flaherty reports having been bored by his early movies, which he says struck him as little more than ineptly executed, unconnected scenes resembling, at best, travelogues rather than dramas conveyed cinematically.[15] Reflecting on his thinking prior to the production of *Nanook of the North*, he remarks on his conviction that a successful film would be a biography of a typical Eskimo and his family: "Here is a man who has less resources than any other man in the world. He lives in a desolation that no other race could possibly survive. His life is a constant fight against starvation. Nothing grows; he must depend utterly on what he can kill; and all this against the most terrifying of tyrants—the bitter climate of the North, the bitterest climate in the world. Surely this story would be interesting."[16] Sounding as much like Cecil B. DeMille as like a sensitive documenter of traditional peoples, the director makes the point that, from its inception, *Nanook* was projected to describe a special kind of course of events—the kind indicated by a story or narrative. His nontheoretical version of what a story should be is fully accommodated by the concept of narrative that I shall employ.[17]

As I construe narrative, it consists of a representation of an agent or agents who, in trying to attain some goal, encounter an obstacle presenting a difficulty to that goal's realization. This representation must have at least one implicit or explicit teller, who expresses attitudes toward the story's content. The agents described need not be human but must be characterized as capable of generating purposive actions properly ascribed to them and not to someone or something outside of them. These individuals, and the course of events in which they are shown to be involved, can be either real or imaginary; and a narrative representation may be either (approximately) true or false, when understood to be about an actual course of events in extra-cinematic reality. Narratives may also be either constative or fictional, depending on the illocutionary force expressed toward them by their maker or teller. Normally, the goals and obstacles portrayed in a story are ones that an author thinks a given audience will find interesting, unusual, or otherwise compelling. Therefore, Flaherty's idea to show the struggles of an Inuit family to survive the hardships of their environment may be identified with an effective communicative plan to adapt the representation to the function of indicating the kind of course of events that we normally associate with a narrative.[18]

Like narrative, characters and characterization arise in both fictional and non-fictional contexts, across media. Novelist Jerzy Kosinski characterizes imaginary Chance the gardener as simple-minded and utterly genuine, it being true in *Being There*'s narrative make-believe that Chance has these traits; cineaste Hal Asby does likewise, encouraging us with moving pictures and sounds that his fictive protagonist, too, rises to the upper echelons of power because his lack of the guile and insecurities of others is taken by them as a sign that he naturally belongs among the powerful and self-possessed. Film documentarian Errol Morris characterizes real-life convicted murderer Randal Adams as more entangled in the charges against him the harder Adams struggles to prove his innocence—and from what I know of the case, Morris's characterization might well be true *simpliciter*.

In each instance, an author manipulates words, recorded images and sounds, or what have you with the intention of leading an audience toward determinate realizations about an individual's traits and dispositions. Under its minimal definition, characterization simply consists of an author intentionally attributing any property to an agent, real or imagined. Given that Flaherty's characterization of Nanook is consistent with his journal descriptions of previous Eskimo companions, it is plausible to maintain that the filmmaker had a pre-commitment to a schematic plan for describing Inuit figures in terms of such personal attributes as survival skills, courage, and fortitude in the face of hardship. As the time for filming drew nearer, his remaining task was to develop more detailed characterizations and to find ways to use cinematic means to get viewers to notice agents' ascribed characteristics.

Nanook of the North explicitly invites spectators to form a wide range of beliefs about Inuit life on the basis of the motion picture's presumed evidential status. Near the film's beginning, Flaherty mounts a series of shots showing how a cooking fire is kindled, interposing a title that asserts, "This is how Nanook uses moss for fuel." The director does this because he wants us to arrive at two realizations: First, that there is the aforementioned Inuit domestic technique; and second, that a certain truth-seeking procedure, consisting of Flaherty having traveled to Ungava and photographically recorded this scene, supports belief in that Inuit practice. Thus, in addition to narrative and characterization, a third wholly general plan constraining *Nanook*'s content, as well as its illocutionary force, was to engage in confirmative communicative action. Hereby the author sets about to represent a putatively actual (type of) state of affairs and to indicate a particular mental significance of that representation—namely, the expression of his belief in its object's existence along with his belief that there is a reason (here, the film itself) why the audience should adopt an analogous existential belief. This, too, was apparently one of Flaherty's standard intentions with respect to his public utterances.

He had on prior occasions exhibited film footage under such auspices as the University of Toronto, the Archeological Institute of America, and the American Geographical Society, accompanying these screenings with lectures on the North and its inhabitants.[19] We also know that some of Flaherty's supporters, including his wife, regarded his footage as scientifically valuable.[20] The filmmaker himself likely shared this opinion and wished to continue to make movies with the expressed interest of providing evidence of the folkways of the Eskimo, for he would later write that, in making *Nanook*, he "planned to depict an ethnoligical [sic] film of life covering the various phases of their hunting, travel, domestic life and religion in as much of a narrative form as is possible."[21]

Thus far I have remarked upon four categories of distal intentions that we may intelligently assume to have shaped *Nanook*'s content from its inception. What all of these have in common is that they possess a plan component representing, quite schematically, some kind of situation that the filmmaker was committed in advance to representing to his audience, if and when he were to make another movie. Yet Flaherty also resolved early on to adopt certain far-reaching methodological guidelines. These consist of plans not themselves representing a situation that is to be the movie's interpretation*. Rather, one of them contributes a strategy for generating further content-specifying plans and hence functions as an indirect but nonetheless significant determinant of content. The other is a set of intentions determining how to go about describing situations and unfolding the narrative.

As noted, Flaherty faulted his initial cinematic efforts for lack of finesse and for failure to convey the thread of a story by establishing relations between scenes. Although there is reason to hold that it had long been his wish to make a movie more closely approximating the structure and content of popular narrative fictions, it was not until *Nanook of the North* that he was satisfied that he had betokened such a work.[22] One of the conditions for this achievement is his having followed what I am calling a continuity policy.

At the very least, the content of such an intention specifies some steps deemed appropriate to ensuring that a succession of shots will describe a certain unitary situation, event, or course of events. A more robust notion of continuity—of the sort that Flaherty himself probably had in mind—would incorporate various evaluative and normative principles of what counts as a nontrivial or good instance of making and assembling shots toward this end. Flaherty's continuity policy, for instance, must have included the following kinds of directives: When feasible, photograph episodes from a number of vantage points; shoot scenes with a view to maintaining consistency of screen direction, so that individuals traveling left to right in shot **A** do not inexplicably move right to left in shot **B**; take care that, from shot to shot, objects do not mysteriously appear or disappear.

Because it extends one's judgments about how better or best to relay a movie's content throughout the production phases, a continuity policy is a quintessential temporally mixed intention. It is an input to deliberation, decision, and action at the time of filming, proximally constraining preferences for how shots should be composed and photographed in anticipation of the problems of editing these takes together into coherent scenes. Such a policy has a similar function at the time of editing, serving as a filter on choices between competing ways of arranging shot sequences. For example, Flaherty's desire to relate his story cinematically lead him to cross-cut footage of Nanook's igloo building with images of children at play, thereby showing the simultaneity of the two actions—an effect he could have achieved simply by showing the one event, then the other, linked by a caption stating that the children played while father worked.

Also, a continuity policy specifies actions to be taken now, at the filmic stage, in preparation for future deliberations and actions. By recording scenes from a number of perspectives, the filmmaker anticipates problems—and facilitates solutions, opportunities, and choices—during editing. Having shot Nanook kayaking among treacherous ice floes from a variety of angles, Flaherty was later able to relate this event from several progressive rather than one static visual perspective, without disrupting consistency of screen direction. On the other hand, in one shot in which Nanook is supposedly off by himself fishing, a second person's reflection moving in the water is for a moment clearly visible; presumably a lack of a suitable alternative to this shot—a failure of the continuity policy at the filmic stage—bootstrapped the filmmaker into a post-filmic continuity policy failure by limiting opportunities for avoiding this unintended lapse in narrative coherence.

In addition to the continuity policy, the cooperation policy furnishes, as I say, a strategy for generating further content-specifying plans, thus indirectly but nonetheless significantly determining meaning. It is part of *Nanook*'s production history that Flaherty and his subjects collaborated in the filmmaking process—a working method that Flaherty had employed on previous occasions.[23] Not only did local people help him with mechanical aspects of shooting and developing footage, they were also his on-camera performers; moreover, it was Flaherty's habit to screen the "rushes" for his Eskimo cohorts and elicit their suggestions for changes, improvements, and additional scenes.[24] Although it is unclear which scenes in *Nanook* were suggested by the filmmaker's Inuit confederates, and to what degree they participated in specifying any given sequence's content, we are surely warranted in assuming that it was normal for them both to share in the filmmaker's effective communicative intentions and to contribute decisively to the emergence of novel ones.

Although the following is incomplete as an analysis of the complexity of collective communicative intentions—not least of all because it leaves open the question of when a collaborator becomes an author or co-author—there are three fairly obvious ways in which the collaborative process could have manifested itself in the present case.

To simplify matters, assume that the object of cooperation is a representation interpreted* by a situation, **S**, and that we are talking about a single cooperator. One possibility, then, is that the cooperator shares Flaherty's intention to make a representation interpreted* by **S**; the content of his effective communicative intention, which need not be identical to the director's and will be appropriate to his own function in making the depiction, will nonetheless depend on what Flaherty plans to depict and what situation he intends his collaborator to plan to depict.

Under a second option, the cooperator is the effective author of a plan to make a representation of **S**, where: (1) The plan's content issues from and depends upon the cooperator's effort of planning and practical reasoning; (2) its content need not be any more detailed than a Type I plan; and (3) the collaborator need not himself take an executive attitude toward this scheme. Flaherty subsequently evaluates the plan in light of its consistency with some of his own immediate and long-term goals and then decides to adopt it, with or without modifications, thus embedding it in an effective communicative intention.

In a third scenario, the collaborator, somehow learning of Flaherty's plan to represent **S** (by watching unedited footage, by being verbally informed), modifies the plan's content by advising changes to the structure of **S** and/or by recommending a different way of depicting **S**; the filmmaker consequently evaluates the suggestions in light of his own preferences, better judgments, and intentions, elects to adopt them wholly or partially, with or without modifications, and embeds them in an effective communicative intention; here again, the collaborator himself need not take an executive attitude toward the resultant plan.

Notice that the second and third outcomes of the cooperation policy embody relatively stronger senses of collaboration, beyond technical assistance, consonant with what commentators invoke when they refer to the Inuit as "scriptwriters," to Nanook as a "chief fountainhead of film sequences," and to cooperation as having helped ensure that *Nanook of the North* "would present their [the Eskimo] point of view."[25] The cooperation policy's last two conceivable manifestations are also strategies by which Flaherty could try to loosen his authorial control over content, trying to elicit ideas that emerge more from his present context than from his own preconceptions. To be sure, this technique offers no assurance that the documentarian's interventions in Inuit life did not trigger unintended and undesired disruptions to their social fabric—disruptions that could be reflected in the documentary's content and mistakenly presented as authentically Eskimo when they are really a construct of interactions with the filmmaker's Western ideas. The cooperation policy itself neither means that Flaherty's romantic notions of Eskimoness did not prevail nor obviates the possibility of ethnocentrism and exploitation on his part.

The points that I have brought out support the thesis that aspects of *Nanook*'s meaning were determined by plans that were both comprehensive and schematic. These intentional constraints were comprehensive in the sense that had they been absent or different the film's content would have differed accordingly in a multitude of respects; furthermore, their etiological roles extended throughout the filmmaking process, across time, space, and successive production stages. Yet they were also incomplete, since they allowed for the filling in of additional, more detailed plans at later times, the emergence of unforeseen content, and the cineaste's adoption of Type I plans.

Likewise, it is apparent that Flaherty temporally updated his initial general intentions. Like anyone else, a filmmaker is a historical agent. With the passage of time, things can change for him, both psychologically and externally. A crucial feature of intentions is that they can accommodate such instability. Recall that Flaherty had distally intended to depict the Inuits' religious practices in *Nanook of the North*. At some moment, due to whatever exigencies or reasons, this resolution was obviously revoked. However, this modification did not entail the suspension of his overall intentional framework. On the contrary, rather than abandoning them entirely, Flaherty consistently updated his temporally proximal filmmaking plans from a perspective internal to his prior plans and policies, which continued, through to the project's termination, to provide the standards of relevance and admissibility for adjustments to content.

Given the option to film a polar bear hunt, the documentarian eagerly traveled many miles through severe weather in the hopes of recording a scene that, unfortunately, would not unfold. What must have made the effort seem worthwhile was the potential scene's affinity with his existing network of beliefs and desires pertaining to representation: Not only did the idea issue from a native source, but it also struck him as just the kind of dramatic and authentically Eskimo situation that he was, as a standing rule, committed to preserving on film.[26]

Here we turn our attention to those plans more proximally controlling the filmic and post-filmic production phases. As work on *Nanook* advanced to the recording stage, the filmmaker had to concretize his ideas about when, where, and what he would photograph. One way in which he resolved these matters was by adopting Type I plans to portray instances of those kinds of situations already specified within his more distal plans.

Presumably, Flaherty often allowed the content of his footage to be determined by opportunities and limitations deriving from his environment. One very basic respect in which Type I plans operated had to do with his surrender to the restrictions placed upon him by climate and season. Having resolved to track the seasonal and nomadic habits of an Inuit band, there could be no recordings of igloo construction in August. It also seems that Flaherty regularly sought to record whatever events were happening around him, while trying to minimize his influence over how those events would develop. Given the chance to shoot sledging, kayaking, or boat repairs, he would transport his camera to the appropriate location and photograph that scene, intending, in effect, that the resultant footage be naturally interpreted* by just that scene which it happens to register, however that pre-filmic event ultimately transpires.

In other instances, Flaherty would prompt or request a certain activity, or assent to record a scene proposed by someone else, going so far as to direct—or at least to caution that he might direct—participants to alter their actions in order to facilitate filming. Published accounts of the origins of the walrus hunt episode provide no clear indication of whose idea it was to perform the hunt as shown, when this decision was made, and whether the hunters' actions were ever interrupted either by Flaherty or the hunters themselves because of conflict with a cinematic interest such as getting a clearer shot or changing the camera's position. But it is known that this event was put on for the camera's benefit and that Flaherty had warned the hunters that it was the filming and not the hunt itself that was to be their priority.[27] Thus the representation of the hunt was surely constrained by a plan specifying such things as the conditions under which shooting should stop and the type of hunting activities that it would be desirable to show.

However, it was not part of the plan—not part of Flaherty's plan, anyway—to use a rifle to finish off the thrashing walrus.[28] Thus Flaherty's scheme was by no means a detailed model for that which would be depicted, Flaherty perforce having only a relatively abstract conception of how the hunt might progress, from the stalking to the harpoon's release to the ensuing battle to pull the wounded beast ashore. The plan, then, was also compatible with a demonstrative intention to represent a wide variety of unforeseen or only vaguely anticipated situations, as they arose before him.

The influence of more prescriptive intentions on the recording phase can also be surmised. As I remarked above, Type I and Type II plans are distinguished from one another gradually rather than by a sudden break; in *Nanook*'s case, a pair of imaginary entities suggests the contribution to authorship of plans that were more rather than less restrictive of the representation's content. First, watching the sealing sequence, one quickly suspects that upstream of the depiction was a fairly elaborate design for how the depicted event would occur. Nanook approaches the camera's fixed position from the distance, searching for a seal's breathing hole, which he finally "discovers" a few feet in front of the camera. Then, after he spears his prey, he is repeatedly dragged across the ice on his backside in a medley of pratfalls recalling the physical pranks of silent slapstick comedy. When it's pulled up onto the ice, the formerly recalcitrant seal looks to be frozen stiff. Viewers who do a little extra reading will not be surprised to learn of anecdotal evidence that a harpoon line, strung under the ice and connecting Nanook to a group of men out of camera range, might have helped achieve the impression of a lively confrontation between man and nature.[29]

Stefansson, himself a veteran arctic explorer, contends that no real Eskimo ever hunted seals in the way shown and that a seal would have to be "defective" to be killed by that method.[30] The content of this cinematic representation is far removed from its natural interpretation*. Instead, it is interpreted* by an imaginary situation, described initially and with some rigor within the content of an intention-embedded plan doubtless shared by Flaherty and several confederates.

The characterization of Nanook is also exemplary of a more thoroughgoing approach to planning for content. Flaherty's initial commitment to developing characters in his movie, and the outlines of his general plan for doing so, guided his various proximal steps toward identifying his protagonist. At first, this entailed selecting a man name Allakariallak to embody the title role, thereby ascribing to Nanook a set of physical properties.[31] A subsequent refinement to Allakariallak's screen persona was a pair of bearskin pants—wholly atypical of the contemporary Northern Ungavans' garb but apparently judged desirable by Flaherty as a way of vividly signifying to southern audiences his protagonist's ethnicity.[32] The filmmaker also thereby visually elaborated the association between this character and his namesake/personal totem: "Nanook" means "polar bear," traditionally a key symbol in Inuit culture, figuring in cosmogenic myths and shamanistic practices, as well as in concepts of male authority, potency, and hunting prowess.[33] Even if southern audiences were largely oblivious to these connotations, Flaherty's northern associates and audiences could scarcely have missed the symbolism.

Although the development of Flaherty's characterization plans may well have been complete by the post-filmic stage, it is nonetheless noteworthy that it was then that several finer points were added to the representation of Nanook. Intertitles, for example, identify him as "Chief of the Itivimuits" and "a great hunter famous through all Ungava"; later we are told that his catch for the year included "seven great polar bears, which in hand-to-hand encounters he killed with nothing more formidable than his harpoon." Allakariallak is not Nanook; and the traits ascribed to Nanook and constituting his character do not belong to an actual historical individual. Instead, the representation of Nanook is interpreted* by an imaginary entity, one that is the product of a plan driven by Flaherty's, and perhaps others', imaginings.

Other Type II post-filmic plans must have pertained to the construction of the narrative. During editing, whatever storytelling goals Flaherty had already set for himself—such as chronicling the survival struggles of an Inuit family over a year's time—were to be further realized in the form of image sequences selectively culled from the available footage. Such plans and their application would themselves be subject to various constraints. Proximal intentions for editing footage are likely to be at least partial realizations of distal plans for post-production, since filmmakers normally possess some notion, at the filmic stage, of the types of narrative events they desire in the finished film and the order in which they will occur.

At the filmic stage, other temporally mixed intentions, like those aligned with the continuity policy, will also have a decisive impact on post-filmic deliberations. And insofar as they influence the form and content of the raw footage available for editing, proximal filmic plans are still other inputs to the latter phases of planning. An additional source of constraints could be the physical condition of that footage, as well as the visual clarity of its images. We should also bear in mind that Type II post-filmic plans need not be immutable, all-encompassing structures. Although they are more rather than less restrictive of content, they are nonetheless compatible with the spontaneous emergence of intuitions and novel intentions. An initial intention to link three particular shots in such a way as to depict the progression of action, like guiding a sledge through chasms of ice, could give way, after a period of trial and error experimentation in which different combinations and durations are rejected as unsatisfactory, to the sudden acquisition of an insight and the subsequent intentional linking of the shots in a configuration not previously considered.

Earlier I commented on disagreement about whether *Nanook of the North* represents reality or projects a romantic fantasy of life among the Inuit. Both positions tend to efface Flaherty's goals for his movie, and neither fits very well with the evidence regarding his deliberations and choices. In fact, the documentarian was committed, over time and across production phases, to several representational schemes, the output of which is not so tidily described in the terms of either rival account.

Flaherty was definitely not just a recorder or revealer of reality, it being among his plans—some of these devised and shared, perhaps, with his collaborators—to describe various imaginary situations. Take, for example, the walrus hunt sequence. This narrative episode is introduced by the statement that some time has elapsed since the events of the previous scene, that food is again scarce, and that a herd of walrus has been sighted near where Nanook and his band are camped. Next a succession of images depicts the following: Nanook and his family scramble with apparent excitement to launch his kayak, as a flotilla of others crosses the water in the background; various brief angles show the kayaks traversing rough waters, all going in the same direction; cross-cutting shots of the hunters with inserts of the walrus herd and instructive intertitles, we watch as one animal is stalked, harpooned, and pulled back to the shore after a long struggle; finally, the hunters, who "cannot restrain the pangs of hunger," butcher their catch on the spot and eat some of its raw meat. A final image lingers on a walrus herd bobbing in the surf.

Flaherty had laid in a substantial stock of provisions and arranged to remunerate his Inuit colleagues and their families by giving them credit at the local trading post; this most likely meant that any serious shortages would not have arisen for the duration of filming.[34] Hence the urgent need to slaughter a walrus, though the sort of condition that might arise under other circumstances, seems in this particular instance to have been a bit of pretend put on for narrative purposes. Much the same can be said for the initial images of the commotion in the camp: As in the seal hunting scene, the camera is fortuitously positioned to record people bursting from their tent and rushing to the water, the flotilla passing by on cue in the background. Moreover, Flaherty asks us to believe not that it is Allakariallak and his companions who go hunting, but Nanook and three of his followers.

Now we have no grounds to assume other than that Flaherty was a moderately rational individual who knew there to be a difference between Allakariallak and Nanook; who knew that, thanks partly to his film project, the Eskimo he had chosen to help him were not on the verge of starvation; and who knew that there is a difference between people rushing to their kayaks because they are hungry and need to hunt walrus and people rushing to their kayaks on cue because someone has asked them to act as if they are in a hurry to hunt walrus. The filmmaker, in other words, not only designed a sequence of images, $i \ldots i_n$, to describe what was an imaginary course of events but knew that his plan to do so described an imaginary course of events.

Did Flaherty fully and genuinely want and expect this narrative episode, or others like it, to be regarded by audiences as literally true? The best answer to this question is, No—the implication being that such episodes were not unequivocally intended to function as representations of reality that would be epistemically invalidated by their failure to do so. Flaherty had settled well in advance on working hard to make *Nanook* as entertaining as any narrative fiction film. Concocting imaginary individuals and predicaments for the sake of generating suspense or levity was all part of the plan. Likewise, the director resorted to rather obvious contrivances to give *Nanook* approximately the appearance of a popular fiction, to help move the story along, and to keep up the viewer's interest. Rather than being a bid for "godlike omniscience" or "unimpeachable authority," a camera placed fortuitously at just the right spot to record a supposedly spontaneous event is as undisguised a sign of premeditation and artifice as any of the programmatic techniques of visual narration.

Of course, the author was far from careful to see to it that the difference between real and imaginary situations, true and false propositions, is clearly signaled to the viewer. Not wanting to spoil the impression that he has taken the camera into an authentic igloo, but having been forced by technical problems to build a special snow house without a roof, Flaherty accounts for the fact that the occupants' breath is visible by falsely claiming in an intertitle that room temperature must be kept below freezing to stop the interior from melting. Such reproductive illusions, too, were receptions he could live with, insofar as the audience's credulity helped them to enjoy the spectacle.

On the other hand, it was also the filmmaker's intention to embed representations of actual situations and events within the framework of this or that imaginary scenario. He sought not simply to describe imaginary occurrences but to draw the viewer's attention to those situations— sledging, fishing, igloo building, children at play with their toys—that really transpired before his lens, including those that transpired because his camera was present. A portrayal of Nanook hurrying in his kayak toward the walrus herd is, not coincidentally, footage naturally interpreted* by an Inuit man, Allakariallak, skillfully maneuvering his kayak through the water. The sequence meant to depict brave hunters desperately fighting to save their community from starvation is also meant to represent a real event, namely, a group of hunters harpooning a walrus in the traditional manner shown. Flaherty's plans with respect to content, from the shooting stage through to the editing, are to show viewers certain actual locations, individuals, and activities and to give them access to whatever facts about these depicta can be learned by visual observation of the depiction. The photographic picture perforce records an extracinematic reality, and it is this, too, that the filmmaker wishes to represent.

Flaherty invites his audience to take the attitude of belief toward the movie's content, even though he is less than fully committed to the believability of some of it. He did earnestly regard his work as ethnologically valuable, his conviction being that his intimacy with the Inuit, his collaborators' own input, the natural setting, and the photographic properties of the representations make *Nanook* a genuine record of the Inuits' lifestyle. Although uncommitted to the literal veracity of every scene and episode, Flaherty, it seems, considered his movie a legitimate source of knowledge, a sentiment reflected in his comments to a reviewer: "It seems to me that it is possible to record the life of primitive people in such a way as to preserve the scientific accuracy and yet make a picture which has vivid dramatic interest for the average man or woman."[35] This confirmative aspect of his plans, however, invites epistemological problems that Flaherty the amateur ethnographer was unconcerned, and unprepared, to resolve.

Taken literally, parts of his film certainly cannot be regarded as accurate descriptions of an indigenous people's culture, since his commitment to assuring "dramatic interest" for a lay audience apparently dampened any of his potential qualms about misrepresenting how seals are really caught or how igloos are actually warmed. Nor did Flaherty grant priority to disambiguating what exactly it was that he wished to assert as fact. It was not part of the plan, for instance, to distinguish between depictions of contemporary Inuit practices and depictions of people staging an activity, such as the walrus hunt, in order to recreate how they believe it used to be done. The line between real and imaginary situations is similarly vague, as is the difference between those parts of the movie's content that issue from the director's imagination and those parts that are meant to represent the Inuits' memories, imaginings, and self-images. Indeed, here we may raise doubts about the rationality, for Flaherty, of adhering to this confirmative intention, compromised as it is by some of his other representational plans. But absolute consistency between filmmaking plans, such that realizing one authorial intention is never hindered by or maladjusted to realizing another, is not a condition for achieving a modicum of genuine authorial control over meaning.

The case of *Nanook of the North* is significant not only for the degree to which this documentary fails epistemically. Rather, it is a truly paradigmatic documentary. It attests to non-fiction cinema's wholly contingent, not definitive, association with the representation of reality; and it bears out the thesis that truth claims need be neither central nor sincere and literal for a work to be non-fiction. *Nanook* is also exemplary of the pragmatics of cinematic meaning. It does not owe its content to a single, monolithic intention to portray reality or depict imaginary scenarios. Nor is its content reducible to that and only that which its author, in sole and complete control of meaning, wished to represent. Instead, *Nanook* derives its content from multiple plans, extensive practical reasoning, and the filmmaker's moderate success at executing some of his wishes.

Notes

1. Bill Nichols, *Representing Reality: Issues and Concepts in Documentary* (Bloomington: Indiana University Press, 1991), 32–76.

2. Wiseman has discussed his approach to making *Law and Order* in several interviews. On each of these occasions, he comments that his initial desire to "get the cops" gave way to a wish to show that police brutality is part of the violent, antisocial behavior that they face. See Alan Westin, "'You Start Off with a Bromide': Wiseman on Film and Civil Liberties," in *Frederick Wiseman*, ed. Thomas R. Atkins (New York: Simon and Schuster, 1976), 47–60; Janet Handelman, "An Interview with Frederick Wiseman," *Film Library Quarterly* 3 (1970): 5–9; Donald E. McWilliams, "Frederick Wiseman," *Film Quarterly* 24 (1970): 17–26. Shortly after finishing *Law and Order*, the filmmaker also authored a short article reflecting on some of his experiences in making this movie; see Frederick Wiseman, "Reminiscences of a Filmmaker: Frederick Wiseman on *Law and Order*," *Police Chief* 36 (1969): 32–35.

3. Erik Barnouw, *Documentary: A History of the Non-Fiction Film*, 2d rev. ed. (New York: Oxford University Press, 1993), 253–262.

4. Frances Hubbard Flaherty, *The Odyssey of a Filmmaker: Robert Flaherty's Story* (New York: Arno Press, 1972), 11–12, 43.

5. Richard Meram Barsam, *The Vision of Robert Flaherty* (Bloomington: Indiana University Press, 1988), 24.

6. Quoted in Arthur Calder-Marshall, *The Innocent Eye: The Life of Robert J. Flaherty* (New York: Harcourt, Brace and World, 1963), 69–70.

7. Siegfried Kracauer, *Theory of Film: The Redemption of Physical Reality* (New York: Oxford University Press, 1960), 245–259.

8. Barnouw, *Documentary*, 39.

9. Iris Barry, *Let's Go to the Movies* (London: Chatto and Windus, 1926), 57–58.

10. Vilhjalmur Stefansson, *The Standardization of Error* (London: Kegan Paul, Trench, and Trubner, 1928), 66–72.

11. Roy Armes, *Film and Reality: An Historical Survey* (London: Penguin, 1974), 32–33.

12. James Roy MacBean, "*Two Laws* from Australia, One White, One Black," in *New Challenges for Documentary*, ed. Alan Rosenthal (Berkeley: University of California Press, 1988), 216.

13. William Rothman, *Documentary Film Classics* (Cambridge: Cambridge University Press, 1997), 2.

14. As evidenced by his contract with Revillon Frères, which financed *Nanook of the North*, Flaherty must have resolved to make another film well before March of 1920. Part of this contract is cited in "Chronology," in *Robert Flaherty, Photographer/Filmmaker: The Inuit, 1910–1922: An Exhibition* (Vancouver, B.C.: Vancouver Art Gallery, 1979), 20. This exhibition catalogue, which consists of essays, a chronology, a filmography, and notes furnishes numerous references to and descriptions of otherwise unpublished archival sources, including material in the Robert J. Flaherty Papers, housed in the Butler Library, Rare Books and Manuscripts Collection, Columbia University.

15. Robert Flaherty, "Robert Flaherty Talking," in *The Cinema 1950*, ed. Roger Manvell (London: Pelican, 1950), 12.

Planning for Content

16. Ibid.

17. The definition of narrative that I privilege construes it as the product of a particular kind of agential action; further, this artifact represents agents responding to certain types of situation. See Paisley Livingston, *Literature and Rationality: Ideas of Agency in Theory and Fiction* (Cambridge: Cambridge University Press, 1991), 54–55.

18. Jay Ruby, "'The Aggie Will Come First': The Demystification of Robert Flaherty," in *Robert Flaherty, Photographer/Filmmaker*, 68, remarks that it is the presence of a dramatic story that sets *Nanook of the North* apart from the other non-fictions of its era. Barnouw, *Documentary*, 39, also appears to regard this film as having accomplished an innovation in non-fiction cinema because its author mastered the "grammar" of the fiction film.

19. "Chronology," 20; Ruby, "'The Aggie Will Come First,'" 55.

20. Ibid., 71.

21. Ruby, "'The Aggie Will Come First,'" 68, cites this passage from an undated, unpublished manuscript.

22. In a letter to Frances Flaherty, dated February 25, 1916—the month he began shooting the second of his now lost films—the filmmaker writes, "I am not going to try to take another self-contained film. I am taking this igloo building and my sledge runners, the seal hunting all over again and with other additions in the old—all of it in close-up—more vivid and in great detail for instance the seal hunt by itself close up as were our plans last summer"; see "Filmography," in *Robert Flaherty, Photographer/Filmmaker*, 61. Little is known about what models of cinematic narration Flaherty might have sought to imitate. However, Ruby, "'The Aggie Will Come First,'" 68, citing a journal entry about a viewing of *Birth of a Nation* as suggestive of at least occasional cinema attendance, notes that Flaherty did attend commercial films of his day.

23. See Robert Flaherty and Francis Hubbard Flaherty, *My Eskimo Friends* (Garden City, N.J.: Doubleday and Page, 1924), 126–127, 142–143; as well as "Filmography," 60–61.

24. Ibid., 126–127, 142–143.

25. The quotations are from "Filmography," 58; Barnouw, *Documentary*, 36; and Barsam, *The Vision of Robert Flaherty*, 16, respectively.

26. Flaherty and Hubbard Flaherty, *My Eskimo Friends*, 142–165, recounts this ill-fated polar bear expedition; the idea to film Nanook killing a bear in its den is attributed in this passage to Nanook himself.

27. Ibid., 134.

28. Robert Flaherty, "How I Filmed *Nanook of the North*," in *Film Makers on Film Making: Statements on Their Art by Thirty Directors*, ed. Harry M. Geduld (Bloomington: Indiana University Press, 1969), 58, recalls that the hunters shouted for him to use a rifle they had brought with them but that he pretended to not understand what they wanted. In the footage as it appears in the movie, viewers will see that one of the struggling hunters twice glances back over his shoulder, shooting what might (now) be understood as a frantic look at the camera.

29. "Filmography," 57.

30. Stefansson, *The Standardization of Error*, 68.

31. "Filmography," 62, supplies a partial, tentative list of some of the actual names of the performers in *Nanook of the North*.

32. See "Filmography," 57, for information about Inuit clothing of that region during the early twentieth century.

33. On the polar bear symbol, see Bernard Saladin D'Anglure, "Nanook, Super Male: The Polar Bear in the Imaginary Space and Social Time of the Inuit of the Canadian Arctic," in *Signifying Animals: Human Meaning in the Natural World*, ed. Roy Willis (London: Unwin Hyman, 1990), 178–185.

34. See Barnouw, *Documentary*, 36 and Armes, *Film and Reality*, 32–33.

35. Quoted in Ruby, "'The Aggie Will Come First,'" 73.

6

Planning for Force

To label a movie "non-fiction" is not necessarily to say that it contains no fiction or has no traffic with fiction. On the contrary, the documentarian may make or use fiction as a major part of a plan for achieving unambiguously constative purposes. In such cases, the author is guided by a plan consisting of multiple, hierarchized intentions regarding the illocutionary effects that the work is destined to have. This underlying complexity need not detract from the work's resolutely assertive force and hence non-fictional status.

I do not deny that real audiences can have real trouble deciding whether a given work is fiction or non-fiction. Everybody knows that it can be difficult to tell the difference, especially in these days of dramatic re-creations, simulations, "docudramas," and "fact-based fictions." Hence a sophisticated observer, fairly knowledgeable about (a) the range of stereotypical features currently attributed to cinematic fictions and non-fictions, (b) a particular work's properties, and (c) the context in which this particular work was produced and/or exhibited may still find that judging its illocutionary force requires making a tough call—one in which she may have less than complete confidence. But I strongly doubt any doctrine proposing that innovations and historical developments show the boundaries between documentary and fiction to be prone to subversion, to be fuzzy and in flux, or to be beyond hard and fast definitions.[1] Styles, techniques, and formal structures typically or normatively associated with documentary status may change over time, as may audiences' expectations that a given property normally indicates an author's assertive intention. But come what may, it is nonetheless the case that a cinematic work or part thereof is non-fiction if and only if an agent makes or uses it with expressed, effective constative intentions.

On the other hand, movie fictions will continue to result from effective fiction-making intentions, the nature of which I shall discuss below. And a genuine hybrid—a work mixing fiction with assertion—is one resulting from someone executing a plan in which are embedded both fiction-making and assertive communicative intentions. In the hybrid, the distinctions between fiction and non-fiction do not break down. All that dissolve are somebody's inhibitions against making a film in which both assertive and fiction-making illocutionary force are signaled. As I say, it is no part of my argument that spectators can always be sure of a movie's force. Nor do I suggest that a calculating or blundering filmmaker cannot either confuse an audience as to his work's genre or create the kind of work that begs the question of its genre affiliation. I merely claim that a movie's status as fiction, non-fiction, both, or neither depends proximally upon the intentions, plans, and practical reasoning that guide the author in making the work.

In what follows, I build up to an analysis of two contrasting kinds of hybrid motion pictures. By taking into account the role of communicative action and practical reasoning in their production, we can explain how filmmakers might establish instrumental relations between non-fiction and fiction—without our having to collapse the difference between those two communicative modes. Some movies use fiction toward non-fictional ends. They belong to a category of films identified by fiction's status as a subordinate element in a plan for achieving unambiguously constative purposes. Other complex illocutionary plans turn out to be mainly fictional, their standing as such unmitigated by their use of assertive force and their putative representation of certain real life events. But before we can delve into these matters, we need a working definition of fiction and a clearer idea of what it means to say that a movie is an illocutionary hybrid.

Fiction

Readers won't be surprised to learn that I prefer to approach fiction in a manner consistent with a commonsense attitude psychology and communicative pragmatics.[2] I will not here probe the various disagreements between the leading proponents of this kind of approach. Nor will I defend one version of it against any and all conceivable objections, except to say now that complaints stemming from anxieties over concepts of agency and intentionality may be met in the same ways as I have thus far dealt with them in my analyses of non-fiction.

Kendall Walton, for instance, is unlikely to be satisfied by my comments here because the last thing that he would want us to use to describe the nature of fiction is the concept of communicative action. For him, the idea of fiction attaches "most perspicuously to objects rather than actions."[3] What this means is that anything can function as fiction—including naturally occurring rock patterns spelling out "Once upon a time there were three bears . . . "—independent of whether or not it was made to serve that purpose. He is right, of course. People may treat whatever they want as fiction. Yet that fact does not preclude the existence of a certain class of artifacts, the proximal cause of which is an agent **A** attempting to indicate openly and accessibly to some target audience that this object, as **A** at a certain time and place is making or using it, is a fiction. Such an item's significance would have a very different etiology from that of either the rock formation or a particular linguistic item that, over time, comes to be viewed as fiction because a community somehow evolves a tradition or convention of considering it as such.

In the geological example, the object has no non-natural meaning aside from that which passersby ascribe to it. In cases of "social construction," the item already has a certain meaning, but a population of interpreters supplies it with another one on the basis of what they hope, desire, or believe that it means. Yet neither of these two sorts of cases make it any less conceivable that there is a kind of artifact, the force and content of which are produced by authorial forces. These constraints are imposed prior to and independently of reception and interpretation, by an agent seeking to adapt a physical object to representational and communicative purposes that are supposed to be discoverable by some other agent(s).

I do not dispute that these kinds of representations, like other artifacts, can acquire main functions unintended by the author or only peripheral to what that person meant the work to do. I do maintain that ascertaining the authorially intended functions, and the relations between them, is a privileged activity in most if not all communicative situations. To the extent that an object results from a communicative act, it is always a reasonable option for us to interpret its meanings and functions in light of what we can gather about its maker's intentions. So those sympathetic to Walton's outlook shall conclude that some of the things they regard as fictions fall as far beyond the horizons of my present study as do non-communicative non-fictions.

As I say, the scope of my discussion of fiction is narrow. I confine myself to outlining a selection of theoretical ideas in just enough detail to construct a framework for inquiring into strategic combinations of fiction and assertion. The most central of these principles hold that generally one imagines or make-believes the fiction's content and that a work is fictional if and only if its author communicatively intends that a given audience adopt the attitude of imagining toward its propositions.

Peter Lamarque and Stein Haugom Olsen make a useful distinction between imagining as a mental state and imagining as an activity.[4] Following Roger Scruton, they describe the psychological attitude of imagination as a reflective state consisting of "a form of attention, a way of holding something in the mind."[5] In taking that attitude, one entertains an idea or proposition non-assertively. Associating attitudinal imagining with the absence of a disposition towards assertion is, as we shall see later, somewhat questionable, but for now we will say that holding this sort of attitude towards an idea involves thinking that such and such is the case regardless of or without commitment to that idea's truth or falsity.

Roughly speaking, an agent can imagine that **P** independent of whether that proposition truthfully describes an actual situation. Just as I can take the attitude of belief or desire toward the content of the sentence "It's raining in Lisbon today," I can also imagine that this is so, whether or not it is in fact raining today in Lisbon. However, it seems difficult to adopt the imagining attitude to things that we believe or know to be true; and the more egocentrically vivid, salient, or focal the information is that supports one in suspecting that **P**, the harder it is to imagine that **P**. I cannot, for example, currently imagine that I am currently sitting at my desk, because I am aware of being currently seated at my desk and preoccupied by assertively held thoughts to that effect. Likewise, I find it impossible to imagine that the Trevi Fountain is in Rome—a lack of attitudinal imagination that I will return to in a moment.

When it comes to the activity of imagination, Lamarque and Olsen take the basically Humean position that it is a "combinatory activity of the mind" in which ideas are creatively assembled and reassembled.[6] I am even less eager to tackle a theory of imagination than a theory of fiction, so I will say little more than to reiterate the authors' claim that cognitively the imagination can be directed toward discovering and understanding the objective features of the world, as when scientists imaginatively speculate about the nature of things in the course of hypothesis formation; the imagination can also be the means of generating ideas of non-existent and fanciful things, ideas unconstrained by an interest in describing the world's objective features.

Like Currie, Lamarque and Olsen, Livingston, and others, I also think that a work's status as fiction is determined by its illocutionary force, not by its content. That a work represents strictly imaginary situations—ones that are the products of an agent's imaginings—no more makes that work fictional than positive truth content causes a movie to be a documentary. Obviously, fictioneers do often fill in the content of their films with imaginary individuals and events. But truth and reference are contingent properties of both fiction and non-fiction. Recall the case of Allakariallak, who is not a great Inuit chief named Nanook but plays one on the big screen. Although some of his characteristics do also belong to a real man named Allakariallak, the set of traits ascribed to Nanook and constituting his character do not belong to any actual historical individual. Instead, the representation of Nanook is interpreted by an imaginary entity, one that is the product of a plan driven by Flaherty's, and perhaps others', imaginings, in a creative and combinatorial activity that draws upon some of Allakariallak's own characteristics. Fictive though Nanook is, he is not the least bit fictional.

Even if it could one day be demonstrated that Flaherty had in mind the idea that Nanook is supposed to be a kind of fictional character like those he had seen in theatrical movies, Flaherty does not openly express the intention that we adopt the imagining attitude toward his hero's characteristics and deeds. All Flaherty does is invite us to believe that there exists a man named Nanook, and in the process of extending this invitation Flaherty preempts the viewer's capacity to distinguish between an imaginary entity and an actual person. Hence Nanook does not meet the criterion for fiction.

To say that fiction is by definition about imaginary or unreal things would be to impoverish drastically the concept by imposing arbitrary restrictions on both the set of objects to which it is regularly applied and the normal practices of fiction-making. After all, standard motion pictures are in one way or another inevitably about actual pre-filmic objects. An image of Darth Vader menacing Luke Skywalker with a light saber is a veridical depiction of, among other things, the behavior of an actor in a strange costume evidently waving a funny sort of stick. Many fictional works do contain representations that are demonstrably untrue if and when they are understood to be about extra-textual or extra-cinematic states of affairs. But whether by accident or authorial intuition, decidedly fantastic stories can turn out to be surprisingly accurate. Jules Verne's novel, *Twenty Thousand Leagues under the Sea*, manages to anticipate some of the technologies of submarine exploration. On the other hand, should Freud and Breurer's repression theory of the etiology of psychoneuroses be proved patently wrong, it will still belong within the category of constative communicative acts. By the same token, some non-fictions concern non-existent entities. As Walton remarks, William Hazlitt's early nineteenth century study, *The Characters of Shakespeare's Plays*, is largely about mere fictions yet is unambiguously non-fictional.[7]

It is a similarly bad idea to equate non-fiction with truth and reality. Some works are touted as "based on facts." But being based on facts, or simply true, is not obviously the same as, or determinant of, being non-fiction. Francis Ford Coppola's Vietnam War epic, *Apocalypse Now* (1979), is about an actual historical event; and Woody Allen's *Manhattan* (1979) not coincidentally provides viewers with a great many veridical depictions of New York City. Yet neither seems like a good candidate for the non-fiction shelf.

These remarks, which encapsulate several of my previous arguments, are here meant to highlight the confusion arising from the assumed blurring of categorical distinctions when documentaries contain falsehoods and imaginary entities, or when fictions contain facts. The solidity of the boundaries does not depend upon maintaining an arbitrary conflation of "fictional" with "false," "untrue," or "non-existent" and of "non-fictional" with "truth" and "reality." These arbitrary dichotomies do not define the genres in the first place; in the second place, their transgression does not nullify the difference between constative and imaginative illocutionary force.

Let me put a finer point on the condition that must obtain if a movie, or some part thereof, is to be regarded as fictional. A cinematic work is fictional if an agent makes it with the expressed, effective communicative intention that a target audience form or continue to hold the imagining attitude toward certain states of affairs, objects, situations, events, propositions, and so forth, where the relevant states of affairs and so on need not actually exist.[8] Looking at and listening to the movie, one discovers the content of the fiction, construed as the objects, situations, and events toward which one can appropriately adopt the attitude of imagining or make-belief. For example, in *Bullitt* (Peter Yates, 1968), it is fictional, as determined by what is shown and what the spectator can see and hear, that the protagonist drives a '68 Mustang coupe; and in light of the absence of the right kind of audiovisual information, it is not true in the story, so not authorized by the work as attitudinally imaginable, that police detective Bullitt opens a nightclub called "Chez Joey."

Individuating a fiction's content—the situations and events toward which we are to adopt the imagining attitude—is like individuating that of a non-fiction. What happens in the (fictional) story is determined by the movie's explicit, observable properties in conjunction with the filmmaker's effective communicative intentions, guided in part by expectations regarding his target audience's competencies and background beliefs. Consider Hitchcock's *The Birds* (1963). How does it get to be true in the fiction, and part of the propositional content toward which the imagining attitude is appropriate, that there are birds behaving badly, and in extraordinarily unnatural ways, in Northern California? Hitchcock and his team, with exacting plans, forethought, and technical ingenuity, took steps to show different species of birds amassing, flocking together, and randomly attacking human beings; moreover, these filmmakers, expecting their viewers to have the normal range of relevant experiences, counted on people to recognize that such a course of events would be bizarre and mysterious.

Fictioneers neither want nor expect that everything explicitly depicted or implied by the depiction shall be part of the story. Makers of naturalistic, mainstream, narrative movies would prefer that we ignore brief forays of boom microphones into the picture; they rely upon viewers to exclude such occurrences from their understanding of story events. Nor does it seem likely that filmmakers expect that all viewers will attitudinally imagine all aspects of the tale. It is true in the story of *The Birds* that seagulls are common on the Northern California coast, true in *Bullitt's* fiction that the '68 Mustang looks just so, and true in *La Dolce Vita* (Federico Fellini, 1960) that the Trevi Fountain is in Rome. To the degree that the producers of these movies suppose that potential spectators share their knowledge of certain facts pertaining to actual situations, the producers would expect these viewers to be no more disposed to adopt the attitude of make-believe to these facts than they themselves are.

Within an audience—especially when it is massive, or spatially-temporally or culturally removed from the context in which the work originated—there could in some cases be naive or under-informed persons who do not realize that embedded within certain story truths they are learning are also facts about how the world really is. Given their epistemic distance, such people would be ready and able to imagine a variety of propositions that other viewers, given their epistemic perspective, could not be expected to regard with anything but an attitude of belief.

Finally, a few words are in order about the specificity of visual fictions. Motion picture fictions are analogous to cinematic constatives in yet another respect: Much of their content, too, is determined by essentially visual means; and unlike interpreting linguistic artifacts, figuring out what is true in the story and what to make-believe depends on our capacities for visually sensing and perceptually recognizing both cinematic and extra-cinematic objects.

By showing us pictures on the screen, filmmakers indicate what happens in the fiction—that, for instance, spy X-27, played by Marlene Dietrich in *Dishonored* (Josef von Sternberg, 1931), is to be executed by military firing squad. Seeing the screen images, and recognizing their properties and the items that they depict, we thereby visually learn facts about characterization, narrative, and various other pre-filmic states of affairs; for example, we see by the depiction that X-27 stands elegantly attired before the soldiers. And thanks to the representation's photographic properties, we can see by Dietrich's facial expressions, and by the way she adjusts her stocking, that X-27, having betrayed Austria for her love of an enemy agent, stands composed, even ennobled, before her executioners.

Although I disagree with several key tenets of Currie's account of the movie spectator's perceptual experience, I do concur with him that our responses to films need only consist of "impersonal imaginings."[9] He disputes Walton's claim that movie fictions prescribe that spectators imagine they see the depicted events from the spatial positions defined by the intrinsic perspectives of successive shots. Walton's "Participation

Thesis" holds not that we falsely believe but that we make-believe ourselves to be standing in direct perceptual relations to the characters and events portrayed.

Hence while watching *Rashomon* (Akira Kurosawa, 1951), it is fictional that one sees the samurai being killed by his wife during the sequence illustrating her testimony, and the competent viewer responds to the scene by imagining he sees this murder as depicted.[10] Currie accepts fictional seeing as a possible mode of engagement but rejects the idea that it is either mandated by the work or the default norm of our interactions with films. It is his position, then, that visual perception is the major contributor to story comprehension because, in the absence of countervailing factors, what we see determines what we end up imagining to be the case in the story, without necessarily imagining ourselves to be seeing story events from the position implied by the camera. My arguments concerning the contributions of visual perception to basic feats of motion picture comprehension are given full rein in Chapter 7 and are intended to be compatible with theories of both cinematic fiction and assertion.

Fixed Boundaries, Mixed Intentions

My present objective is to try to explain in pragmatic, action theoretical terms how and why some movies are on the whole both fictional and non-fictional, or have both fictional and non-fictional components, or how non-fictional movies may not only contain but employ fiction for non-fictional purposes. This account is proposed as an alternative to claims to the effect that, for any movie(s), apparently mixed or ambiguous genre membership evinces non-fiction's indefinite or ambiguous nature.

I have already taken pains to establish the sterility of attempts to evoke, by observing the presence of falsities and purely imaginary items in documentaries, the indefiniteness of the fiction/non-fiction division. In a similar vein, it will not do to refer to the boundary-blurring effects of the documentarian's adoption of "imaginary techniques to tell the tale of actual occurrences."[11] There is nothing inherently fiction-making about narrative, characterization, staging, the use of actors, the scripting of dialogue, and the planning of content by the activity of imagining. These are at most contingently productive of fiction, depending on how they relate to the filmmaker's other attitudes and goals with regard to his movie.

Perhaps there is a more systematic way of showing that the generic demarcation is "fuzzy," one that also installs a principled basis for contending that there are real differences between documentary and fiction. In Wittgenstein's notion of family resemblance, Plantinga believes he has found just such a methodology. In *Philosophical Investigations*, Wittgenstein proposes that there are certain words that do not refer to a permanently fixed and exhaustively describable category of extra-linguistic objects. We use such words to pick out items with no essential property or list of properties entirely in common with each other. The philosopher's example is "game": Some of the items associated with this term are competitive, others cooperative, still others are both; some, like playing house or charades, involve pretending, whereas a game like racquet ball or pachinko does not; some are team efforts, others the pursuit of an individual, and so on.[12]

Surveying a sample of that which people refer to as games, one might have trouble finding those properties necessarily shared by all and sufficient to define any one of them as a game. Instead, the term applies to a family of entities, drawn together by a network of "overlapping and criss-crossing" similarities and characteristics.[13] Our concepts of such family resemblance terms and their referents are therefore open-ended, provisional, and ungoverned by an ultimate definition covering all possible uses of the word. In the absence of an intrinsic, defining property, one decides when to apply such open concepts by judging an item's similarity to other exemplary members of the category and by paying attention to how other speakers and practitioners classify that entity within a given context.

Plantinga steps into line with others who have tried to adapt the notion of family resemblance to the domains of aesthetics and culture.[14] If Wittgenstein is correct about the existence of family resemblance terms, he says, then documentary, like other film genres, may plausibly be regarded as an open concept. If so, we could say that a documentary film is not identified as such by a definitive non-fictional essence but rather by constellations of family resemblances, some more or less common, some more or less central. Hence the boundaries between fiction and non-fiction might be diffuse. Together with prototypical and central exemplars, there are increasingly peripheral members of the category that straddle adventitious boundaries or that cannot to any significant degree be situated within any current socially constructed version of that genre.[15]

Consider a pair of contrasting films, beginning with the prototypical documentary, *Vietnam: A Television History* (1983).[16] Within a given cultural and historical context, this film is attributed features thought central to the category of non-fiction. It is, for instance, indexed by its makers, exhibitors, and audience as adopting an assertive stance; it has a serious tone and subject matter; it uses currently standard documentary storytelling strategies, such as interviews, archival footage, and an authoritative voice-over narration, within a unified, unself-conscious structure. On the other hand, *Letter From Siberia* (Chris Marker, 1957) is not so clearly indexed as non-fiction. Although the work suggests itself to be a travelogue, its indulgence in witty word play takes precedence over any serious attempt to convey information about Siberia that would be at all useful to the traveler or geographer. The straightforward documentary characteristics, such as film footage of Siberia, are blended with irony, animated scenes, and "whimsical homages to the woolly mammoth"; thus it is "for our culture" at some remove from the core of the documentary category.[17]

Plantinga's "prototype theory" is supposed to allow for confident labeling of some works as documentary, without the need for an essentialist definition. This theory is also supposed to account for how non-fiction can be mixed with other genres by blending like two hues of paint the more or less prototypically documentary features with those of, say, fiction until the resultant work emerges several shades nearer non-fiction's periphery, or in the overlapping gray zone, or nearer to the vivid, central cases of fiction. For instance, *JFK* (Oliver Stone, 1991)—ambiguously indexed, serious of purpose, brimming with archival footage, containing flights of speculation and reenactments performed by famous actors—is said to fall within the gray zone of polymorphous films not prototypical of either fiction or documentary.[18] However, prototype theory is vulnerable to a criticism that makes it a less than satisfactory solution to the taxonomy problem.

The choice to treat non-fiction as a family resemblance term is a hasty one because it rests on an unexplored ontological assumption. Maybe "game," "art," "jazz," "fiction," or "non-fiction" **are** open concepts. But in advance of tagging one or another of these as such, another issue must first be settled. Wittgenstein and Wittgensteinians leave us with the daunting task of deciding when it is that a word or concept truly is fuzzy or inherently underdetermined because it cannot be associated with a single definitive regularity.[19] According to which heuristics, principles, and empirical criteria are we to decide whether a concept is truly "open"?

For any given term, we could point to a history of inconsistent usages, past failures to come up with coherent definitions, and current disagreements and debates over the precise nature of its referent. But past and present failures to specify an invariant sense or referent for a concept do not automatically mean that none exists or none will be found to exist in the future; nor does it necessarily indicate that none already exists, independent of what people think. Maybe one party to the dispute has the correct closed definition of the term or will propose such a definition. Perhaps unanimity will dawn in the future. Moreover, to make agreement a privileged condition for excluding a term from fuzziness would require an additional defense of a consensus theory of truth. I suggest that we take to heart Livingston's observation that it surely is prudent to resist presupposing that a term designates a real object with an unchanging essence, so long as the particulars it is used to pick out cannot be unified under a single overarching law or pattern—but endorsing that sort of prudence does not warrant embracing the further "preemptive assumption" that no such regularity exists.[20]

It is therefore not entirely obvious that "it is plausible to contend that 'nonfiction' and especially 'documentary' are open concepts too. If so a traditional attempt to define the documentary is bound to fail, since the concept has no essence."[21] Even if Plantinga were to modify his position, saying that the term "documentary"—in light of disputes, inconsistencies, and demonstrable failures to establish a definite pattern uniting the various particulars—is fuzzy as currently used, he would still most likely be wrong. I return to this charge in a moment. First, there is a question to answer.

Why does Plantinga hold that we should turn to an open concept of non-fiction? Clearly some of his reasons correspond to cinema and literary scholars' well-known, inconclusive, and largely confused efforts to describe a definite pattern uniting various actual and potential particulars under the rubric of non-fiction. Another motive must be the failure of objective definitions of documentary: There is apparently no intrinsically non-fictional formal or structural property of the text or work itself; rather, a movie is non-fiction only in relation to something else beyond itself. This inadequacy of objective definitions is manifested in the wide range of overlapping properties shared by particular documentaries and fictions, as well as by these genres in general. Plantinga's recourse to an open concept of non-fiction might follow in part from such motivations. However, the prototype theory's perceived warrant is ultimately Plantinga's reluctance to attribute the definitive role to authorial intentions.

Unless one is willing to espouse an ontology of autonomous, self-organizing textuality, in which linguistic and cinematic objects cause themselves to function as fiction or non-fiction, it must be either in relation to an author, a receiver, or community of receivers, or some combination of the three that a work acquires its documentary function. Plantinga elects the sociological option, thus making non-fictional status not the intended outcome of an individual or group's filmmaking actions but the by-product of the coordination of various individuals' and groups' attitudes towards the movie.

Recall Plantinga's thesis that films are non-fiction only insofar as they are indexed as making assertions. Indexing is a social phenomenon because it "lies within the domain of social convention": It begins with a filmmaker selecting characteristics that are, for a given population at a given point in time, to a greater or lesser degree usually associated with the making of truth claims; it is then taken up and completed by an audience, who may or may not accept the index applied to a film by its maker, distributor, and/or exhibitor.[22] Making a film's non-fictional status dependent upon a socially prescribed index makes sense only if one has reservations about authorship. Otherwise describing the specificity of (non-)fiction would become a matter of describing the nature of constative intentions and the ways in which they proximally govern the production of certain movies. In place of an analysis of assertion, Plantinga substitutes an analysis of indexing. Thus he removes authorial intentions from the running as the definitive constraint on documentary and fiction and thereby channels himself into an open concept approach to the description of the nature of these phenomena.

Plantinga's embrace of open concepts is, I think, premature. Generally speaking, the problem is that Plantinga has not given himself adequate reason to conclude that non-fiction probably lacks an essence and that a family resemblance approach is therefore preferable. More specifically, skepticism about intentionality is simply not evidence that documentary is an open concept. Even when circumstances deem it rational for us to question our access to a maker's mental states, doubting the possibility of knowing when an author has non-fictional intentions implies nothing about whether it is true that constative intentions are indeed what cause this particular movie, or movies in general, to be non-fictional.

If it is the existence of openly expressed, reflexive authorial intentions that he doubts, or their causal efficacy in determining genre membership, then Plantinga has yet to demonstrate either that (a) an individual author's intentions, or the shared intentions of a group of cooperating producers, do not/cannot themselves cause a work to be non-fiction or that (b) authorial intentions are purely private and cannot be openly signaled to an audience. And as far as I can tell, he espouses no anti-realism about the existence and powers of intentions. On the contrary, he frequently and explicitly refers to their motivational roles in both the filmmaker's and the viewer's actions, saying that viewers may use films for a variety of purposes and that "filmmakers cue the spectator to understand and evaluate what is shown as nonfiction."[23] Moreover, he seems to assume that there is something called an "assertive intention" that producers and viewers index non-fictional films as embodying. Is "assertive intention" also an open concept? For non-fiction to lack an essence, it would have to be. But Plantinga does not argue his case at this more fundamental level.

A family resemblance approach is, as it stands, uncompelling because we **do** have workable, precise, comprehensive, essentialist analyses of fiction and non-fiction. I reiterate that "essence" here refers to a stable pattern of regularities or constraints on a certain kind of artifact's emergence within human social contexts characterized by populations of agents subject to similar material conditions and possessing similar psychological traits, linguistic skills, communicative presumptions, and mutual contextual beliefs. I also remind readers that from speech act theory we inherit the possibility of hypothesizing the necessary and sufficient conditions for producing a variety of non-fictional communicative practices, constatives being but one subcategory of these.

Developing a prototype theory presupposes that the available analytic schemas for assertives, suggestives, predictives, and so on do not pick out the patterns of proximal causes giving rise to various actual cinematic works and hence do not afford a device for categorizing works. My fear, then, is that Plantinga has skipped over several steps in the path leading to a prototype theory—steps toward demonstrating that it is the ontology of non-fictional communication, and not just our ordinary as well as theoretical uses of words like "non-fiction," "documentary," and "fiction," that is fuzzy.

If not with reference to criss-crossing, overlapping features, and far from prototypical cases, how are we to deal with the biggest taxonomic messes, those being films that mix fiction with non-fiction or that appear to slip between genres? I begin my answer to this query by highlighting several of my own basic theses, beginning with the following. Authors engage in practical reasoning about how their works will be received. Sometimes this reasoning is highly complex. It not only allows for but also anticipates and aims to elicit more than one illocutionary uptake, that is, more than one judgment on the part of the target audience(s) about authorially intended force. Basic instances of this kind of communicative action have already been thoroughly analyzed in speech act theory. In the types of filmic cases I have uppermost in mind, production activities are guided by strategic plans in which more than one illocutionary goal is represented. These goals may be systematically and supportively related to one another and to other objectives pursued by the author.

A movie can contain passages that are non-fictional as well as passages that are fictional. Furthermore, a cinematic work, or a segment thereof, may on the whole be both fiction and non-fiction. There is no contradiction in this statement, as there would be in our saying that, simultaneously and in the same sense of the word "elm," something both is and is not an elm tree. Illocutionary force is not an objectival property but a relational one; it is a purpose to which the communicator puts some representational system. Such purposes can be varied. In principle, a filmmaker or user could, for example, functionally adapt an audiovisual representational system, $i \ldots i_n$, interpreted* by **S**, to the job of signaling his communicative intention to one intended audience that they imagine that **S** and to another audience that they should believe that **S**. Therefore the classification of a work as non-fiction is not exclusive of its classification as fiction, and vice versa.

The possibility of using a work with more than one illocutionary intention in mind renders the distinction between the concepts and conditions of fictionality and non-fictionality no less precise. What can be obscured by the expression of multiple communicative goals is the nature of a filmmaker's purposes in creating or showing a particular work and the connections between those purposes. Indeed, a work's illocutionary force or forces can become controversial—blurred, so to speak—from the spectator's point of view under a variety of conditions. The following would be among the more obvious situations tending to confuse reception:

1. A work, **W**, exhibits stereotypical features presumed within a social context or community, **C**, at time **t** to belong to more than one film genre.
2. **W** is explicitly labeled as non-fiction (or as some sub-genre of non-fiction, e.g., reportage, ethnography, biography, etc.) by its producer or distributor, but it also exhibits or is ascribed, by an interpreter, properties stereotypically associated by **C** at **t** with another genre, such as fiction, where these other properties are thought by members of **C** to be antithetical to non-fiction and/or to undermine the possibility of decisively ascribing **W** to any genre.
3. **W**'s author fails or neglects to express an effective communicative intention with respect to force.
4. Members of **C** lack some property or knowledge, Φ, necessary to recognize **W**'s force(s).

With the exception of number 3, the foregoing do not necessarily instance cases in which **W** has no stable, determinate force or forces—although what these forces are and why they are combined as they are may be baffling or impenetrable to spectators. And although the superficial characteristics stereotypically associated with fictional or non-fictional status actually know no borders, none of the above sorts of cases perforce betokens a blurring of the defining differences between the kinds of illocutionary acts that humans perform with language, sound, and moving pictures.

Note that in numbers 1 and 2, the confusion may stem largely from the viewer's faulty assumption that the presence of certain properties means, say, that the work must be wholly or partially fictional or that it cannot be (principally) non-fictional, when these are really only superficially or highly contingently indicative of fictional status. In number 3, it may be the intractability of the communicative presumption—the mutual belief within **C** that whenever an agent manipulates a representational system he is doing so with overt illocutionary intent—that contributes to the audience's confusion by leading them to persist in the suspicion that there must be some kind of recognizable force, even when there is none. Finally, with respect to numbers 1, 2, and 4, that **C** is perplexed or unable to reach a (correct) judgment about **W**'s force(s) does not itself establish that the work's force is undecidable or indefinite, nor does it demonstrate that a stable referent for the term "non-fiction" is illusory. Obviously the condition of the work, the context in which it is encountered, and variables pertaining to the state of the spectator can present obstacles to a successful uptake, insofar as success is possible. But local failures either to express or detect them do not justify global skepticism about the existence of determinant, genre-specifying, effective communicative intentions, including plans composed of mixed but rationally related intentions.

At this juncture, I remind readers of one of my framework assumptions. To the extent that $i \ldots i_n$ is a cinematic work, it is crafted or used by somebody who thereby endows it with various features for whatever reasons. The myriad reasons that might come into play—from the very personal and even private, to the economic, the aesthetic, and the practical, to propaganda motivated by a fascistic attempt at social engineering or by a genuine care for the welfare of others—will not all be accessible to us nor equally relevant to determining how the movie acquired its properties and what effects the author sought to have on a target audience by making it in the way he or she did. On the contrary, only a relatively limited budget of motivational and cognitive states have a direct etiological bearing on production.

In the case of many familiar sorts of representational movies, the work owes at least some of its features to effective communicative intentions. A work has many of its properties and meanings because somebody acted on the belief that making an artifact with certain features would be a way of openly indicating certain states of affairs to an audience and thereby achieving various further effects on those people, such as giving them (mis)information, getting them to recognize external and mental significance, causing them to be amused or angry, and so forth. This teleological constraint, and the spectator's tacit acceptance of it, is one of the conditions that makes it possible to tell the difference between works per se and mere jumbles of unrelated audiovisual material thrown together into the same scrap bin. Granted, someone could make a "found footage" movie from these *disjecta membra*—but that would require work, in the purposive, practical reasoning sense of the word.

I reiterate these points as a basis for several additional hypotheses about movies that mix fiction and non-fiction. If we spectators normally assume that movies are works, then for heuristic purposes we may coherently start from the supposition that when fiction-making and assertion coincide, it is toward some designated end. Obviously this heuristic rules against assuming from the outset of our investigations that hybridization is generally a-rational or a matter of sheer accident, the unintended and unforeseen by-product of something else the author was trying to do. Moreover, this heuristic is a positive alternative to the assumption that mixtures of fiction and non-fiction are signs of a postmodern collapse of absolute generic differences and of the blurring of boundaries between fact and fiction, representation and reality. Such an alternative strategy is desirable because it does not require a commitment to false oppositions and skeptical ontological theses.

Complex Illocutionary Plans

It is not always clear to audiences whether a cinematic work is fictional or non-fictional. One can imagine cases of a movie's author not being entirely clearheaded about what his or her objective is—there is no reason to believe that everyone who makes a film **always** does so with a clear communicative purpose in mind or is invariably efficient at signaling their illocutionary aims. Yet granting the truth of these observations in no way counts against the plausibility of the kind of explanatory hypothesis that I am constructing, since these observations are quite compatible with the truth of the proposition that often people do have coherent, feasible communicative goals in view, some of which they subsequently take successful steps towards realizing.

In many instances in which a movie displays traits normally associated with more than one genre (like documentary and fiction), and/or in which an audience is unable or unwilling to assign that work to a single category, the artifact in question is a genuine illocutionary hybrid. The pertinent sort of movie embodies the performance of more than one illocutionary act. It results from someone following a plan in which is embedded both fiction-making and constative communicative intentions, where these intentions may be instrumentally linked. Illocutionary hybrids are not unclassifiable. Rather, they are to be grouped according to the kinds of plans that produce them. Nor does hybridity necessarily mean that a work does not essentially belong within a single category.

Below I single out four initial types of complex illocutionary plans: temporally mixed plans; hierarchically constructed plans in which fiction serves constative goals; hierarchically constructed plans in which assertion subserves fiction-making; and plans to confound an audiences inferences regarding illocutionary force. I focus in particular on the two categories of hierarchical plans, in which the popular and controversial "docudramas" and "fact-based fictions" are best situated. This typology is not supposed to be exhaustive or indelible. As a departure point for scholarship, it provides a number of abstract, simplified models of illocutionary complexity—models that might serve to orient empirical investigation and ongoing conceptual clarification and that would in turn be subject to revision in light of this continued research. To streamline the exposition, I shall occasionally resort to the following notation. Let **S** stand for (a portion of) the content of a given cinematic representation, that is, some state of affairs, situation, or event described by $i \ldots i_n$. F indicates the expression of any constative illocutionary force; **FF** is the expression of fictional illocutionary force, that is, the intention that the spectator take an imagining attitude toward the content.

Some plans with respect to force are temporally mixed. They specify a sequence of different illocutionary uptakes during a work's reception. *Daughter Rite* (Michelle Citron, 1978) is an experimental film, partially fabricated from home movies of a woman with two small girls, accompanied by the voice-over narration of a woman reminiscing about her mother and meditating upon their relationship; portions of this visual track are optically manipulated, for example, slowed down and repeated in a looping effect. Much of Citron's film, however, consists of stereotypically documentary footage and content, it being apparent that the camera is merely recording its subjects' unrehearsed and spontaneous activities. Talking to one another and, so it seems, at times to an off-screen interviewer or director, two young women speak candidly of their relationship to their mother, in whose house they are visiting. Their discussions and bitter complaints about this absent person are recorded in various rooms, an unsteady camera sometimes lagging behind its subjects' movements. As the movie advances, we watch them with the growing impression both that the daughters' comments are as revealing of themselves as of their mother and that they are engaging in hapless repetitions of some of the maternal behaviors toward which they express contempt.

Later in the movie, it might also occur to viewers that the extra-cinematic events may not have been entirely unrehearsed, for there are times at which the subjects' actions appear to have been coordinated with the camera or "blocked" in order to accommodate the dictates of framing, camera movements, and preparations for continuity editing. When the credits finally roll, the audience learns that the two on-screen women were only pretending to be sisters; two actors had performed those roles partly by improvisation, partly according to a script.

Daughter Rite's complex illocutionary plan calls for at least two stages of uptake. Initially, we are to take the attitude of belief toward its content. But in a second moment, in light of newly available information, we are to realize that an imagining attitude would be more appropriate—an attitude that we are to adopt retroactively to the same content that we had initially regarded as asserted. More formally, *Daughter Rite* is the kind of film in which the author indicates at t^1 that she is **F**-ing that **S**, at t^2 that she is **FF**-ing that **S**.

Not all temporally mixed schemes call on viewers to make a retroactive adjustment to their inferences about a movie's or scene's intended force. Take, for instance, Dusan Makavejev's *WR: Mysteries of the Organism* (1971), which interweaves fictional and non-fictional sequences. The early part of this film is composed largely of interviews, some of them shot at the Wilhelm Reich Museum near Rangeley, Maine, with followers of maverick sexologist Wilhelm Reich. Amidst the "orgone accumulator," the "orgone gun," and other artifacts of the psychiatrist's strange career, interview subjects tell of his inquiries into the mysterious human energy that, if deprived of its natural outlet in carnal love, leads to individual psychological and physical pathologies like criminality and cancer and that supports such group pathologies as fascistic and totalitarian regimes.

Later scenes in the movie recount the story of Milena, a Belgrade beautician and staunch Reichian who attempts to seduce peoples' artist Vladimir Illich, a champion Soviet figure skater visiting Belgrade with the Moscow Ice Follies. Illich eventually kills Milena with his skate blade. But with the only slightly surprised policeman and morgue attendant looking on, her head comes back to life, and Milena, talking directly to the camera, condemns state-sponsored orgone retention for the violence and lovelessness of "Red Fascism."

Makavejev's temporally mixed plan thus specifies a covariation of force with content. At the earlier point in the movie, t^1, he signals that he is **F**-ing that **S**; at a later t^2, in a scene as grotesque as it is whimsical, he signals that he is **FF**-ing that **S'**. In fact, a property of the movie as a whole is that it oscillates between these two forces.

Encountering mixtures of assertion and fiction, we might wonder how these communicative acts fit together. Is there a bigger plan or ulterior objective that their juxtaposition helps to realize? Here I wish to add a new dimension to our understanding of the pragmatics of cinematic communication. In combining assertion with fiction, filmmakers typically pursue various rhetorical and aesthetic ends. For instance, Annette Kuhn suggests that Citron, inspired by contemporary theory, is trying with *Daughter Rite* to snap viewers out of their complacent acceptance of documentary's authenticity.[24] Walton, remarking on a less highfalutin motive behind such literary forms as the factual fictions and non-fiction novels of the New Journalism, notes that the "vivacity of the reader's imagination" may be enhanced by knowledge that a work's contents are to some degree true.[25] Walton would probably say much the same of motion picture analogues to these forms. But in combining fiction and nonfiction, filmmakers could also be pursuing a special kind of illocutionary objective—a communicative act, the workings of which have yet to be examined by cinema researchers. I identify this act with reference to plans to make one illocutionary force subserve another.

A plan to mix fiction and assertion may specify their hierarchical arrangement, relative to one another. Two kinds of hierarchized plans seem to animate a great many popular as well as experimental movies. Let the lower case letter indicate the subserving act. In one schema, generating works that are effectively fictional, the author is **f**-ing that **S** as part of a plan to indicate to an audience that he is **FF**-ing that **S** or **S′**. In another, effectively productive of constatives, the author **ff**'s that **S** in order to **F** that **S** or **S′**.

Consider again Makavejev's *WR: Mysteries of the Organism*, in which fiction is a means to an end. It is make-believe that Milena delivers a postmortem discourse on the origins of Red Fascism. But presenting us with this fiction is one of the strategies that Makavejev uses to draw our attention to his apparently literal, quasi-Reichian assertion that socialism fails for having stopped short of a sexual revolution. *Daughter Rite* is amenable to a similar analysis, its temporally mixed illocutionary forces also being combined with a plan to subordinate fiction-making to constative intentions.

Ultimately, Citron would have us not believe but imagine that two daughters say and do such and such during a visit to their mother's house. Yet the significance of this fiction is not simply that viewers cannot be wholly secure in their presuppositions about the documentary representation's authenticity. Citron could have reminded us of that banal truism without going to the bother of thoughtfully constructing a series of fascinating models typifying the repetitive behaviors and imitative psychology of some aspects of mother-daughter relationships. The director's revelation, then, is not that the preceding scenes consist of merely fictive situations that are only meant to be imagined by us; and the viewer's expected payoff or satisfaction, possibly disgruntled by the deception, is not the pleasure of an ex post facto imaginative engagement with the imaginary characters and their actions. Rather, our discovery is that embedded in the fiction are various assertions, that is, detailed and vivid illustrations of actual kinds of interpersonal psychological phenomena toward which we are to take the attitude of belief.

Complex plans to make one illocutionary force subserve another are not a radically novel, uncharted category of communicative pragmatics. As I construe them, they belong within the ambit of what speech act theorists call indirect illocutionary acts.[26] Suppose that you and I have an argument that terminates with me saying to you, "There's the door." By asserting that the door is over there, I request that you leave. In speech act terms, the requestive is the indirect act, because it is performed subordinately, in the logical sense, to the assertive. My utterance is such that its success in securing your comprehension depends upon you identifying the request by way of first identifying the assertion. But logical priority does not imply teleological priority. The function of my utterance is clearly not only or even principally to assert the door's location. I assert that the door is over there because I want to signal my intention to request you to leave, not the converse.

The meanings of some indirect acts, like "Do you know what time it is?" are highly conventional; others, like "There's the door," are more context specific. There are also nonliteral indirect illocutionary acts, such as "I'm sure the professor wants you to cheat on the exam." I shall not pause here to examine all of the intricacies of this kind of discourse. But in advance of discussing the intricacies of docudramas and fact-based fictions, it is worthwhile to underscore the following. Works of the sort that I wish to analyze surely employ indirection: one illocutionary act is performed in virtue of performing another, different one; the two acts are not parallel but instrumentally related, such that recognizing one depends upon recognizing the other. However, they are a good deal more complex than the paradigmatic linguistic cases. As a result, for a given hybrid movie, which illocutionary act is recognized first may vary between individual spectators and across reception contexts, depending on such variables as prior knowledge of the work and expectations about what kind of viewing experience (entertainment? current affairs information?) the movie shall provide.

Moreover, with respect to very complex films, recognizing one of the illocutionary forces may not guarantee successful uptake of the other. Alan Rosenthal, for example, regards *Daughter Rite* as strictly fictional.[27] Viewers in a quandary may also waver between conclusions about whether a film is really fiction or non-fiction, without (immediately) considering that it could be a means-ends conjunction of both. I also underscore that my emphasis is on the teleological rather than logical subordination of one act to the other. It is to this dimension of indirect acts that I now turn.

Identifying the nature of a linguistic or cinematic communicative act on the basis of its primary purpose should be, generally speaking, no more (or less) problematic than doing so with any other human action. Within the spheres of moral, legal, and ordinary practical reasoning about our own and others' conduct, we classify and evaluate intentional deeds by referring to the states of affairs to which they are a means. We forbear the anxiety and pain that medical professionals inflict on us when they intentionally probe and cut because we believe that these actions are extrinsically motivated parts of larger, means-ends, rational, hierarchized plans to make us well. If one were to suspect that the doctor is acting with only a vague or irrational plan in mind, or that he is cutting for its own sake, for the pleasure it gives him, one should be alarmed. The kinds of actions we perform, and their meanings both for us and for others, depend upon the plans that govern them. Illocutionary acts are no exception to this heuristic.

The intuition that hybrid movies can be motivated by instrumental relations between hierarchized illocutionary intentions implies that, in some cases, classification of a film as fiction or non-fiction can be made according to its primary purpose. This is not an uncontroversial thesis, for it is explicitly rejected by Walton.[28] He does accept that a work could have an array of functions, some of which could predominate over others. But he argues that the paradigmatically non-fictional functions—"cognitive aims," construed broadly so as to include both imparting information about reality and promoting understanding of actual typical or particular human social and psychological phenomena—are not "the proprietary property of non-fiction" as they may also be the "primary purpose[s]" of paradigmatically fictional works. So in the case of hybrids, it is no use trying to settle the work into the non-fictional category by saying that fiction is subservient to non-fiction, since the main goal of the fiction itself can be cognitive. Hence Walton maintains that a work is non-fiction if and only if it completely lacks the specifically fictional function of serving as a prop in a game of make-believe; any work having this function is "definitely fiction in our sense, no matter what other purposes it might have and how insignificant this one may be."[29]

Cognitive aims are certainly not non-fiction's "proprietary property"—but Walton here implies that assenting to that fact compels us to define non-fiction negatively, as conditional upon absence of fiction. That conclusion is controvertible. The alternative is to define the genre positively as the expression of constative force toward a unit of content.[30] Indeed, one of the reasons we would be eager to adopt this definition is precisely that it does accommodate the knowledge that both fiction and assertion may have significant cognitive and fact-preserving dimensions, yet still somehow be basically different from each other. More importantly at present, if non-fiction is defined by presence of assertive force rather than absence of fiction, then a work might contain fictional properties without compromising its status as non-fiction. It need be the case only that the author's principle aim be to make non-fiction.

Notice that the expression of constative force need not be undermined by a fiction's cognitive functions. On the contrary, the fiction's cognitive value could even support achievement of that illocutionary objective, insofar as the presence of facts about and insights into reality help the audience to recognize that the author is mainly interested in making assertions. The possibility of subordinating fiction-making to assertion is attractive because it coheres with the commonsense, as well as linguistic, assumption that some actions are systematically linked in complicated means-ends structures. The surgeon cannot fulfill his intention to cure the patient's cancer directly, in the same way that he can more or less directly fulfill his intention to move his desk calendar a little to the left. Instead, executing his medical intention requires forming and executing a series of other intentions; performing tests, analyzing their results, scheduling surgery, and making an incision and removing the tumor are intermediary stages of reasoning and action in support of the overall plan. Likewise, I can, if I choose, perform one communicative act, asking you to leave, by performing another, telling you where the door is.

I think it's a good idea to assign genre membership on the basis of primary purposes, with one caveat. When talking about a work's dominant or primary purpose, we ought to avoid confusion by understanding this term to refer to its main **illocutionary** purpose; and let it also be understood that the non-fiction's illocutionary purpose is distinct from the work's possible cognitive functions. Veridicality and cognition may very well be crucial roles of any work, be it a homogeneous instance of fiction or assertion or a hybrid of the two; but of no work are these the primary, in the sense of definitive, functions. In the current sense, the primary function of non-fiction is to indicate an intention that the attitude of belief be adopted; and the primary function of fiction is to signal that the imagining attitude be taken.

We would never want to suggest that a work's primary purpose is its only purpose, for people usually have complicated motivations for communicating. Thus a modification is in order. A communicative act, having a given illocutionary/primary purpose, is **intrinsically** motivated when it is performed for its own sake or as an end. Intrinsically motivated asserting would consist of assertion for the sake of realizing assertive perlocutionary effects, namely, getting the receiver to: (1) recognize that a given belief is being expressed; (2) recognize that the communicator intends that the receiver form or continue to hold that belief; (3) acquire that belief, subsequent to and because of 1 and 2. Intrinsically motivated fictioneering would consist of fiction-making for the sake of getting an audience to imagine that such and such is the case, where imagining is presumably a kind of activity having an inherent attraction distinct from, but not necessarily unrelated to, believing such and such to be the case.

Extrinsically motivated communicative actions are pursued for their conduciveness to some further ends.[31] The making of assertions, fiction, and their various hybrids may all be animated by the agent's interest in achieving sundry aesthetic, political, economic, as well as cognitive aims. When multiple, these extrinsic motivators might themselves be arrayed in a hierarchy of differentially weighted, more or less central or dispensable goals. Finally, illocutionary acts may be extrinsically motivated relative to one another. In other words, fiction-making is sometimes extrinsically motivated relative to assertion; and assertion is sometimes extrinsically motivated by fiction-making goals.

Peter Watkin's *The War Game* (1966) is one of those films in which fiction-making is extrinsically motivated by constative plans. Interestingly, Nichols seems to be of two minds about this film. At one point, he calls it a "conditional tense documentary"—a comment he soon amends by noting that, although it employs many "conventions of documentary," it shares "a fundamental trait of fiction" because it presents a view of an imaginary world rather than of the actual historical world.[32] Later he includes it, along with *Daughter Rite*, among "fictions disguised as documentaries."[33] True, this British film consists of fictional depictions of the conditions leading up to and following a fictive nuclear attack. It also asks us to imagine that the imagery we are watching bears a natural counterfactual relation to the terrible events in question. But in prescribing these grim imaginings, Watkins has an undisguised, ulterior, predominant motive.

It is not simply Watkins's intent that we make-believe that Britain's citizens and civil defense systems could not withstand such a disaster. The instrumental point of the graphic pre-constructions is to express predictions about the likely outcomes of a nuclear attack, thereby signaling that it is appropriate for viewers to take the attitude of belief toward certain propositions concerning possible future states of affairs. Over a series of scripted scenes in which nonprofessional players act out dramatic situations and problems, Watkins invites spectators to imagine that the film footage they are watching is of the terrifying events leading up to and following a nuclear attack on a civilian target in Kent, much of the footage of this attack having been shot to achieve the look of documentary or news coverage of current events.

The narration of this make-believe story, however, need not be considered antithetical to the pragmatics of non-fiction, for it is only part of yet another relatively complex tactic for asserting that something is, or could eventually be, the case. Thus Watkins would have us imagine that we are watching events precipitating and following a Russian nuclear strike against Britain, while also wishing us to see by the unfolding drama that certain things are likely actually to happen, should Britain ever come under such a barrage. Here the mode of assertion is decidedly predictive and conditional, insofar as Watkins indicates what he believes (or believed) would transpire at some unspecified future time, if the cold war were to reach a nuclear flash point.

It need not be assumed that the movie's complicated brand of "constructedness" is antithetical to its capacity for conveying to viewers the idea that they are to adopt various beliefs as to what might transpire in case of nuclear war. A competent viewer of *The War Game* will thus recognize that he or she is watching, say, a fictional portrayal of a homeowner's refusal to shelter evacuees; but at the same time, the viewer will see that this scene is meant to assert a number of propositions about the probable unreliability of civil defense mechanisms in the advent of an actual disaster. In other words, one realizes that it is make-believe that **S**, that is, that a homeowner of such a description refuses to house evacuees; and one thereby recognizes that it is asserted that **S′**, that is, that implementation of a certain kind of disaster response plan will be problematic in roughly the sorts of ways implied or explicitly shown by the staged scene.

Note that before the movie ends, it is made explicit that the contents of its speculative representations have been selected in order to correspond with a number of empirical hypotheses regarding the immediate as well as long-term effects of a nuclear war. So even if it is only make-believe that the individuals on screen are the victims of a massive firestorm, we are to recognize both that the reason for this elaborate pre-construction is the expression of an assertion to the effect that this kind of suffering could occur, and that we should believe that it could occur because the filmmaker has undertaken various truth-seeking procedures, such as consulting the appropriate experts and investigating the historical records concerning the destruction of Dresden and Hiroshima.

The film's confirmative dimension does not, of course, automatically entail its epistemic validity as a source of facts and evidence supporting a belief that any actual or postulated atomic blast will have the specified observable properties. At most, *The War Game*'s vivid models of various hypotheses are only as epistemically justified as this body of extra-filmic evidence and reasoning—research to which the filmmaker adverts in an effort to garner the viewer's assent to various audiovisually communicated propositions.

Some of the movies that some critics refer to as docudramas certainly do fit the present category of illocutionary complexity—think, for example, of Paul Cowan's combination of documentary and narrative fiction in *Democracy on Trial: The Morgentaler Affair* (1980). The director informs us, in an initial title, that the movie contains actual interview footage as well as "dramatized recreations . . . based on interviews and official transcripts and records. The facts of the case have not been altered." In the course of this staged material, some of the actual key participants in a series of police and court actions against a Canadian abortionist reenact prior events in which they were involved. For instance, Dr. Henry Morgentaler plays himself in the film's story of his legal and political struggles against Canada's abortion laws. However, I am not especially interested in associating the concept of docudrama with a pragmatic analysis of motion pictures that are the products of an intention to make assertions by way of fiction.

The term "docudrama," like others that are often used interchangeably—"drama documentary," "fact-based fiction," "faction," "documentary fiction"—already has some unfortunate associations that make it difficult to use with precision. To begin with, there is certainly no consensus as to whether a docudrama is fiction or non-fiction. Some people use the word to refer to basically fictional works, whereas other commentators understand it to be a basically documentary mode. Yet both parties collude with one another, insofar as they tend to subscribe to the same misconceptions regarding the distinction between fiction and non-fiction.

Jerry Kuehl stipulates that the drama documentary, although non-fictional to the extent that it deals with real events, slides mostly into fiction because it shows what the camera had not or could not have recorded at the time of those events and/or dramatizes them, where dramatization involves using "the conventions of naturalistic drama" and encouraging viewers to identify with the "dramatic *personae*" by exploiting "the skills of writers and directors, actors and actresses, to get beneath the surface of characters remote in time and space."[34] Nichols characterizes docudramas as "essentially fictional" stories, "based on fact but performed by actors and scripted from both documents and conjecture."[35]

Another perspective situates docudrama mainly within the orbit of non-fiction. Thomas Hoffer and Richard Nelson construe the genre as providing "accurate recreations of events in the lives of actual persons"—reenactment and restaging being the source of the docudrama's fictional aspect.[36] Although he does not develop it in action-theoretical terms, Richard Kilborn has an interesting intuition when he reserves "drama documentary" to refer to programs, the "primary intention" of which is "to provide a documentary chronicling of events, with dramatic reconstructions employed to make the account more persuasive or to illustrate things which could not be depicted using traditional documentary means."[37] But he, too, supposes that documentary is a matter of representing or trying to represent reality, whereas fiction is a matter of dramatization, recreation, scripting, acting, and conjecture.

Earlier I implied that *The War Game* has another significant and, from a taxonomic perspective, potentially confusing feature. Watkins prescribes that we imagine that Kent suffers a nuclear strike; and one aspect of the film's content is interpreted* by the imaginary situation, **S**, of Kent being in that condition. There is, however, more to *The War Game*'s make-believe, as we are also asked to take the imagining attitude toward two further situations, namely: (1) that the motion picture we are watching is a documentary about **S**, the bombing of Kent and (2) that this documentary contains film footage that is naturally-counterfactually interpreted* by **S**. The content of (1) and (2) is interpreted* by a corresponding pair of fictive situations, **S'** and **S"**, respectively: an imaginary documentary, consisting of a narrative, a voice-over narration, various propositions about the causes of the Third World War, and so on; and imaginary footage of the nuclear catastrophe. Hence embedded in *The War Game* is a fictional non-fiction—an imaginary documentary toward which viewers are intended to adopt an imagining attitude. In this way, Watkin's film resembles the farcical *This is Spinal Tap* (Rob Reiner, 1984), in which we are to imagine the director's constative intentions regarding a fictive heavy metal band. Unlike *This is Spinal Tap*, Watkin's imaginary documentary is extrinsically motivated, insofar as his primary aim is to make actual assertions about events that could occur in reality. For this reason, *The War Game* contains a fictional documentary but overall is itself an actual one.

Watkins makes no effort either to deceive viewers into believing that the aforementioned imaginary situations are real or to give them reason to believe that he is sincerely asserting that Kent is burning. Rather, he relies on his audience to share his background knowledge that England has never come under nuclear attack and thereby to infer the fictional and imaginary status of the relevant parts of his film. Contrast his illocutionary plans with those of Citron. At the beginning of *Daughter Rite* spectators are led to gather both that they are watching audiovisual recordings of two women exchanging intimate details of their relations with their mother and that in showing us this material the producer is asserting that such and such was at an earlier time said and done by the sisters. Later Citron throws the alert viewer some clues that perhaps the film presents a theatrical scenario in which the women pretend to be engaging in the aforementioned activities. Later still it is explicitly avowed that the sounds and images represent staged scenes of imaginary situations, toward which an imagining attitude is more appropriate.

Although I am uncommitted to this further hypothesis, I have often wondered whether it was not also Citron's aim to get us to imagine, retroactively, that the relevant parts of her film constitute a piece of vérité cinema. I am more committed to the thesis that one of her goals in making the movie as she did is to puzzle her audience as to her work's force, in such a way as to prevent viewers, at given points in the reception process, from being altogether confident in their judgments of whether the work is fiction or non-fiction, a depiction of imaginary or actual situations. The pragmatics of *Daughter Rite* thus include a fourth type of complex illocutionary plan, to deprive the watcher (temporarily, in this instance) of certainty about whether the filmmaker is asserting that such and such is actually the case or indicating that we ought to take an imagining attitude toward an imaginary situation.

Not all complex illocutionary plans deploy fiction for constative ends. Although I cannot here explore in depth the practices of fiction-making, I would like to conclude this discussion of illocutionary complexity with a few remarks on one possible role of assertion in some fictions. Sometimes the hierarchy of force is reversed: the filmmaker f-ing that **S** in order to **FF** that **S'**. Here, assertion is secondary to the maker's further desire to direct an audience to take an imagining attitude toward various situations implied by or explicitly portrayed in the movie. This strategy of fiction-making is distinguished from fictioneering in general by one of the producer's effective communicative intentions; namely, significant authorial choices are made with a view to eliciting or maintaining a target audience's credulity towards parts of the movie's content.

It is difficult to think of a fiction, be it highly naturalistic or utterly fantastic, that is not meant to represent some believable and even factual situations. The Trevi Fountain really is a Roman landmark decorated with elaborately sculpted figures, and Fellini no doubt expected the relevant section of his film to be consistent with these facts and supportive of such corresponding beliefs as he and his viewers have about this location. But we haven't much reason to suppose that Fellini was committed to alerting viewers to his intention to make any particular assertions about the Fountain; nor does attributing constative intentions to him help us to make sense of or appreciate the narrative events that unfold there.

When assertion is exploited for the purpose of fiction, that which is asserted may be signaled explicitly, implicitly, or in both ways. *Laughter and Tears: The Joan and Melissa Rivers Story* (Oz Scott, 1994) begins with a voice-over announcer stating that, "Joan and Melissa Rivers star as themselves in their own story of heartbreak and healing," while we read the on-screen title, "Based on their own story."[38] Given the rough consistency of the narrative with the circumstances of Joan Rivers's life, it is also likely that the producers want and expect viewers to think that they mean to claim that certain events represented in the film, such as Joan's dismissal by her talent agent, happened in the protagonist's actual life. *Battle of Algiers* (Gillo Pontecorvo, 1965) presumes its audience will recognize its efforts to chronicle the course of the Algerian uprising, since it represents well-known (especially in France) recent developments (as of the movie's debut) in the history of France's political relations with one of its colonies.[39] *The Day After* (Nicholas Meyer, 1983), somewhat like *The War Game*, graphically forecasts the possible consequences of a nuclear war and attributes part of its content to the expertise of various scientists and physicians; notice of its constative dimension would also have been aided by the film's consonance with what was, at the time of its release, a prominent public debate about the probable effects of nuclear war.[40]

The aforementioned works are, however, ultimately designed to channel spectators into a fictional mode of reception. In asserting that such and such is (was, could, or will be) the case, the author also fills in the content of the make-believe. As I say, the makers of *Laughter and Tears* seem literally and sincerely to claim that shortly after her husband's death, Rivers's talent agency refused to represent her, citing among other reasons their belief that a recently widowed comedian whose last television series was a flop would be unemployable. This assertion, which some fans may regard as a touching biographical tidbit, has a special function within the movie's narrative context. It contributes a premise to a description of a fictive situation, one that is the product of someone's imaginings and that is not entirely constrained by facts about what really happened nor wholly intended as a literal and sincere representation of those past events.

Think of this situation as a description of an individual's or group's concepts or ideas of, among other things, how the scene looks and sounds when Rivers's talent agent lets her go. The cinematic representation—a product of screenwriting, staging, performance, cinematography, editing, and so on—is adapted to the job of describing to the audience the content of these ideas. Hence many of the facts we perceive and infer—about Rivers's physical appearance, her states of mind, her gestures, the way the agent and his office looks, what he says and how his client responds to him—are facts about what is imaginary. It is, for example, a fact about what is imaginary that the comedian's agent says to her, "No one wants to see the widow of a suicide making jokes" and then tells her that his bosses "feel our relationship with you is no longer mutually productive." Yet given what is known of Rivers's career, it makes sense to interpret this character's dialogue, which may or may not record the exact words someone said to her, as an implicit assertion of the end of relations with her talent agency.

If this episode from *Laughter and Tears*, and scenes like it in this and other movies, is the vehicle for assertion, why is the film not merely a documentary, or a documentary subserved by fiction? Although the authors avail themselves of an opportunity to make or imply an assertion by means of an imaginary scenario, the kind of movie in question here uses assertion as a subordinate element in a plan to make fiction. Asserting that **P** is not done for its own sake; nor is fiction-making motivated by non-fictional ends. Rather, the role of the asserted content is mainly to supply premises to the make-believe. Even if non-accidentally true, such a movie's assertions—that Rivers was dumped by her agency; that Claus Von Bulow, in *Reversal of Fortune* (Barbet Schroeder, 1990), was accused of attempting to murder his wife and defended by Harvard law professor Alan Dershowitz—are made to facilitate the construction of imaginary situations. In turn, the spectator is generally invited to adopt an imagining attitude toward those situations, although she is also expected to recognize that they embody or suggest various literal assertions.

There are no law-like, unconditional signs that a movie is fiction. As a rule of thumb, we are justified in judging that the work's primary purpose is to serve as fiction if that hypothesis makes the author's actions, in producing the work as he did, seem the most reasonable and appropriate. Some combination of a number of more specific heuristics can help us to draw such conclusions. Normally, one clue is the film's reliance upon thoroughly scripted and theatrically staged performances by professional actors pretending to engage in various actions and to be people (including themselves at another time or in an imaginary situation) other than their present selves. Another hint is that the content of these imaginary scenes is not obviously intended to model specific aspects of an actual situation or type of situation.

For example, apparently embedded within the previously mentioned scene from *Laughter and Tears* is an assertion, but it is in no way established to what degree the features of the cinematically described imaginary situation are intended to correspond to those of an actual anterior situation, such as a real meeting between Rivers and an actual talent agent. For all we know, she was dismissed over the telephone. Contrast this work to the likes of *The War Game* and *Democracy on Trial*, which employ such instruments as voice-over narration and interviews to guide the spectator toward information about which parts of the depiction are meant to describe real states of affairs. *Laughter and Tears* is also analogous to *The Glenn Miller Story* (Anthony Mann, 1954), which surely reflects some incidents in the bandleader's life without the producers making a concerted effort to distinguish between those parts of the story that are indicative of their beliefs about Miller's biography and those parts that are the results of their imaginings. In the absence of such explicit distinctions, we require special reasons to classify theatrical movies exhibiting the stereotypical traits of popular fictions as anything more than fictions themselves, despite their constative elements.

Notes

1. Bill Nichols adopts this view in *Blurred Boundaries: Questions of Meaning in Contemporary Culture* (Bloomington: Indiana University Press, 1994). Similarly, Carl Plantinga, *Rhetoric and Representation in Nonfiction Film* (New York: Cambridge University Press, 1997), maintains that the borders between fiction and non-fiction tend to dissolve as one moves from the genres' central, prototypical exemplars out toward the periphery of the two categories.
2. Gregory Currie, *The Nature of Fiction* (Cambridge: Cambridge University Press, 1990); Peter Lamarque and Stein Haugom Olsen, *Truth, Fiction, and Litera-

ture (Oxford: Clarendon, 1994); Paisley Livingston, *Literature and Rationality: Ideas of Agency in Theory and Fiction* (Cambridge: Cambridge University Press, 1991), 69–80.

3. Kendall Walton, *Mimesis As Make-Believe: On the Foundations of the Representational Arts* (New York: Cambridge University Press, 1990), 87.

4. Lamarque and Olsen, *Truth, Fiction, and Literature*, 243–244.

5. Ibid., 243. Roger Scruton gives his description of the imagining attitude in *Art and the Imagination: A Study in the Philosophy of Mind*, 2d ed. (London: Methuen, 1982), 94–99. Noël Carroll offers a similar version of attitudinal imagining under the rubric of "suppositional imagination"; see "Fiction, Nonfiction, and the Film of Presumptive Assertion: Conceptual Analyses," in *Film Theory and Philosophy*, ed. Richard Allen and Murray Smith (Oxford: Oxford University Press, 1997), 173–202.

6. Lamarque and Olsen, *Truth, Fiction, and Literature*, 243.

7. Walton, *Mimesis As Make-Believe*, 74.

8. Although I will skip over the technical details of fiction-making, I direct readers interested in such an analysis to Gregory Currie's Gricean definition of fiction in *The Nature of Fiction*, 31–33. My definition is intended to be compatible with his own description of the communicative pragmatics of fiction-making which, in its first approximation, is as follows (where **P** is a proposition, **S** is a sentence, and **U** is a speaker or writer):

S is fiction if and only if **U** utters **S** intending that the audience will:

(1) recognize that **S** means **P**;
(2) recognize that **S** is intended by **U** to mean **P**;
(3) recognize that **U** intends for them (the audience) to make-believe that **P**;
(4) make-believe that **P**;

And further intending that:

(5) (2) will be a reason for (3);
(6) (3) will be a reason for (4).

9. See Gregory Currie, *Image and Mind: Film, Philosophy, and Cognitive Science* (Cambridge: Cambridge University Press, 1996), 179–180; and "Impersonal Imaginings: A Reply to Jerrold Levinson," *The Philosophical Quarterly* 43 (1993): 79–82.

10. Walton, *Mimesis As Make-Believe*, 345. See also Jerrold Levinson, "Seeing, Imaginarily, at the Movies," *The Philosophical Quarterly* 43 (1993): 70–78.

11. Nichols, *Blurred Boundaries*, ix.

12. Ludwig Wittgenstein, *Philosophical Investigations*, trans. G. E. M. Anscombe, 3d ed. (New York: Macmillan, 1958), 32.

13. Ibid., 32.

14. For Plantinga's influences, see Morris Weitz, "The Role of Theory in Aesthetics," *Journal of Aesthetics and Art Criticism* 15 (1956): 27–35; and George Lakoff, *Women, Fire, and Dangerous Things: What Categories Reveal About the Mind* (Chicago: University of Chicago Press, 1987). Bill Nichols, in *Representing Reality: Issues and Concepts in Documentary* (Bloomington: Indiana University Press, 1991),

12, implies that he, too, may be inclined toward some sort of Wittgensteinian family resemblance definition of non-fiction.

15. Plantinga, *Rhetoric and Representation in Nonfiction Film*, 14–24.
16. Ibid., 15.
17. Ibid.
18. Ibid., 23–24.
19. Paisley Livingston, *Literary Knowledge: Humanistic Inquiry and the Philosophy of Science* (Ithaca: Cornell University Press, 1988), 154–163, performs a probing critique of family resemblance and its perceived utility as an organizing concept within literary and other humanistic and cultural studies domains.
20. Ibid., 161.
21. Plantinga, *Rhetoric and Representation in Nonfiction Film*, 15.
22. Ibid., 21.
23. Ibid., 20, 19.
24. Annette Kuhn, "Theories of the Feminist Documentary," in *New Challenges for Documentary*, ed. Alan Rosenthal (Berkeley: University of California Press, 1988), 100.
25. Walton, *Mimesis As Make-Believe*, 93–94.
26. Kent Bach and Robert Harnish, *Linguistic Communication and Speech Acts* (Cambridge, Mass.: M.I.T. Press, 1979), 70–76. See also John Searle, "Indirect Speech Acts," in *Pragmatics: A Reader*, ed. Steven Davis (New York: Oxford University Press, 1991), 265–277; and Herbert H. Clark, "Responding to Indirect Speech Acts," in Davis, *Pragmatics: A Reader*, 199–230.
27. Alan Rosenthal, "Introduction," in *New Challenges for Documentary*, ed. Alan Rosenthal (Berkeley: University of California Press, 1988), 513.
28. Walton, *Mimesis As Make-Believe*, 94.
29. Ibid., 93.
30. During his discussion of the inadequacies of a speech act definition of fiction, Walton says little about his understanding of how communicative pragmatics has defined assertion, although he does note that speech act theorists "attempt to understand language fundamentally in terms of actions that speakers perform rather than properties of words or sentences" and that for them "the notion of assertion applies primarily to human actions." But he says no more about how assertions might be identified; nor does he mention whether he might be inclined to share any of communicative pragmatics' theses about the nature of constatives, interrogatives, requestives, and so forth. See Walton, *Mimesis As Make-Believe*, 86.
31. See Alfred Mele, "Motivation: Essentially Motivation-Constituting Attitudes," *The Philosophical Review* 104 (1995): 391, for a cogent tour of the distinction within the psychological and philosophical literature between internal and external motivation.
32. Nichols, *Representing Reality*, 112.
33. Ibid., 161.
34. Jerry Kuehl, "Truth Claims," *Sight and Sound* 50 (1981): 274.
35. Nichols, *Representing Reality*, 160.
36. That there are probably several sub-varieties of docudrama, defined by variables ranging across content and form, is not an unusual idea. For instance,

Thomas Hoffer and Richard Nelson, "Evolution of Docudrama on American Television Networks: Content Analysis, 1966–1978," *The Southern Speech and Communication Journal* 4 (1980): 149–163, propose nine kinds of docudrama content, ranging from the verbatim staging of court transcripts to highly speculative and theatrical restagings of actual, distant historical events.

37. Richard Kilborn, "Drama Over Lockerbie: A New Look At Television Drama-Documentaries," *Historical Journal of Film, Radio and Television* 14 (1994): 61. For additional discussions of the docudrama, fact-based fictions, and so on, see Thomas Hoffer, Richard Nelson, and Robert Musburger, "Docudrama," in *TV Genres: A Handbook and Reference Guide*, ed. Bryan Rose, (Westport, Conn.: Greenwood Press, 1985), 80–111; Derek Paget, *True Stories?: Documentary Drama on Radio, Screen, and Stage* (New York: St. Martin's Press, 1990); Eric Breitbart, "From the Panorama to the Docudrama: Notes on the Visualization of History, *Radical History Review* 25 (1981): 115–125; Alan Rosenthal, *Writing Docudrama: Dramatizing Reality for Film and TV* (New York: Focal Press, 1994).

38. Despite its adamance and its connotations of truth and knowledge of intimate details, the proposition that this made for television movie is derived from the stars' "own story" is, from a rhetorical point of view, a remarkable piece of circumlocution. An audience eager to see representations of events they have already heard about and to learn new bits of inside information about the Rivers family is likely to conclude that this program promises to give them all that and more—a conclusion that the opening proposition encourages them to reach. Indeed, what follows rehearses many of the publicly reported facts about the suicide of Joan Rivers's husband as well as her previous and subsequent career and personal troubles. Yet "Based on their own story" does not literally mean "true." One seeking protection from litigation or criticism for having distorted facts could reply that the claim is equivalent to saying "basically a product of imagination" or "basically an imaginary course of events that the Rivers wanted to turn into a movie." That's show biz.

39. For its North American release, the filmmakers added a title noting that the movie consists entirely of reconstructions of actual events. Viewers are thereby alerted to its basis in historical fact and to the absence of actual footage of these historical events, even though the film is shot according to a documentary style.

40. It was around this time that *The Atomic Cafe* (Kevin Rafferty, Jayne Loader, and Pierce Rafferty, 1982), a compilation film of pro-nuclear propaganda mostly from the 1950s, and *If You Love This Planet* (Terri Nash, 1982), built around pro-disarmament lectures by Helen Caldicott, president of the American chapter of Physicians for Social Responsibility, appeared on screens. The renewal of cold war tensions in the early 1980s also spawned Jonathan Schell's revealing *The Fate of the Earth* (New York: Knopf, 1982), a best-selling book that examines the ecological, health, and social effects of nuclear war.

7

Perceptual Access to Cinematic Meaning

Up until now, I have been concentrating on those constraints that make a constative of a movie. At this stage of my exposition, I shift attention onto matters of uptake, that is, those conditions and processes supporting the viewer's comprehension of the work. It is now my purpose to lay down part of the groundwork for the next two chapters' consideration of some interpretive and epistemic aspects of documentary spectatorship. Since any exposition of how spectators derive meaning and knowledge from movies in general, and cinematic constatives in particular, must eventually confront the difficult topic of visual perception, I begin the study's new phase here, with a discussion of the complexities of the relation between seeing something and understanding something about what one is seeing. In so doing, I substantiate some of the perceptual assumptions behind my previous discussions of depiction and representation.

A motion picture's capacity to mean anything to anyone depends, in part, on what it looks like, since many of its visible properties are significant to the viewer to the extent they stand in an indicator relation to something beyond themselves. The spectator perceives these visible features, visually recognizes what they indicate, and thereby sees that the work has a given significance. This process is roughly what I intend by my use of the term "perceptual access." The process normally consists of the discovery of a great many facts about cinematic as well as extra-cinematic entities and situations—facts concerning visible as well as non-visible states of affairs. I therefore treat visual perception as a particular mode of comprehension, that is, the acquisition of knowledge and beliefs by visual, versus aural or olfactory, means.

Watching *The Thin Blue Line* (Errol Morris, 1988), we can, for example, see that it contains reenactments; and we can see by those reenactments that witnesses claim to have seen Randall Adams shoot a policeman.

Rather than being fraught with illusion and error, our visual experience of the imagery gives rise to various realizations concerning not only the images themselves but also the director's plans, the movie's form and content, and how a policeman supposedly met his end. Unfortunately, the nature of visual perception and its role in motion picture spectatorship are complicated, contested issues. The questions immediately arise: What is the nature of our visual experience of motion picture imagery? How immune is that experience to illusion? How exactly does seeing contribute both to movie comprehension and to learning about the world by watching movies? These are the fundamental problems to which I now turn.

Visual Perception

In discussing visual perception, it helps, I feel, to begin with a distinction between sensory and cognitive perception.[1] The difference I have in mind is captured by two sentences:

1. Wesley sees a Portuguese Water Dog.
2. Wesley sees that the dog is a Portuguese Water Dog.

Report number 1 describes a sensory perceptual experience, that which is ordinarily called the look (sound, smell, or feel) of a thing. For number 1 to be true, it need be the case only that said dog actually has some appearance to Wesley. This situation, sensing something by visual (as opposed to aural, olfactory, or tactile) means, in the first place consists of a relationship between a person and a scene before him. Normally we conceive of this relation in terms of a particular kind of causation, entailing the stimulation of photoreceptors and neural pathways by patterns of light reflected from some actually existing, external object.[2] The parameters of this type of perceptual feat might be further specified as consisting of a sensory representation.

Seeing, under this description, is more than a relational state. It is also an internal state of the subject himself, the etiology and content of which usually depend on his being in the appropriate sort of contact with an object in his environment. It is by having this sensory representation that the percipient sees that which is before him; in contrast with sightlessness, the external scene looks some way to him. Attaining such a state is an interpretation-independent, cognitively neutral mode of perception to the extent that its content neither depends on nor is determined by the percipient's having any beliefs, thoughts, or other attitudes about that which is seen. Wesley himself could be a pretty exotic creature, one who has never seen a dog before, knows nothing of them, has no schema, concepts, or words for "Portuguese Water Dog," "dog," or even "fur ball," and lacks the reasoning skills to figure out that he has finally encountered any such things. Yet he could still see that object, the Portuguese Water Dog, as clearly as the President of the American Kennel Club would see it. "Total ignorance is not a condition for total blindness."[3]

The second report, if true, describes more than Wesley's sensation of the dog. It also tells us about the agent's states of mind, that is, the thoughts and beliefs that are the usual concomitant of visual experiences. In cognitively seeing the Portuguese Water Dog, Wesley also realizes or **sees that** there is a Portuguese Water Dog nearby. Such cognitive perceptions have an epistemic outcome: Wesley learns a fact about his environment, that it includes this kind of animal, partly as a result of being in visual contact with a certain object in his vicinity. Such perceptions also have an epistemic condition: Wesley's ability to acquire new beliefs, or confirm old ones, as a result of his visual experience depends upon his previous beliefs, knowledge, and associative abilities. Already knowing a little about dog breeds, and recognizing several telling features of the present specimen, he lights upon the idea that there is a Portuguese Water Dog in front of him. Cognitive perception is thus strongly influenced by such higher-order cognitive factors as having and applying a myriad of concepts and background beliefs. It is this post-sensory exploitation of our visual experiences that we invoke when we say that we notice or recognize an item or state of affairs. Equally important for our purposes, cognitive perception introduces the possibility of visually acquiring information about one object, not present to the senses, by directly perceiving another.

The nature of vision is currently the topic of intensive research within empirical as well as philosophical circles, and the foregoing model responds to various corresponding debates. I will not unpack all of its implications, just two that strike me as pivotal and far-reaching. One key premise is that there is a distinction to be made between seeing objects and seeing facts. The former, sensory perceptual mode comprises early and intermediate visual processes that are largely "modular," which is to say that the visual system's execution of these processes does not necessarily depend upon or contribute to any of the percipient's higher-level mental states, such as her stored beliefs about the world. At this rudimentary level, visual access consists, as I have said, of some sort of physical connection of receptors to objects, plus sensory representations or "percepts" of those items.

In advance of decisive scientific findings, it is hard to say just what processes make up object perception. One venerable research tradition holds that all visual perception involves operations that may be described in thought-like, inferential terms. Constructivist theories posit that visual systems must actively extract and organize the information borne by the signal; this process is often said to involve the system in problem-solving operations, like a detective who forms conclusions on the basis of memory, experience, inference, and available evidence.[4] Whether the totality of processes constituting visual acuity, from detection all the way up to recognition, are any more literally intelligent than those of a cheap hand calculator remains contentious. Rival direct theories of perception hold that the patterns of stimuli reaching the observer are themselves so information-rich as to determine unambiguously the character of the corresponding perceptual experience with little or no computation by the visual system.[5] Perhaps normal sensory perception, seeing objects, might be a non-rational, physiological process culminating in a representational structure that preserves in analog form that information about objects which is carried by reflected light. It is at this stage of visual processing that the percept makes available to the percipient, in serviceable form, data about the environment's visually perceptible features.

Cognitive seeing, seeing facts, occurs when the individual exploits this percept's content, thereby recognizing objects and events, noticing states of affairs, seeing that such and such is the case. So understood, cognitive seeing is the agent's normal response to having a sensory experience, one that is contingent upon the coupling of cognitive and sensory structures and the content of the agent's cognitive repertoire.

Responding in their input-driven, mechanical way, a being's detector components pick up and represent the information that, say, a predator approaches. But the system containing these mechanisms has not detected anything—has not itself had a genuine perceptual response—until it has extracted from this input the relevant information and has realized the fact that the object is a predator.[6] Perception is thus ultimately a mode of cognitive uptake for some agent. It is how we identify objects, and what they indicate, when we see them. At this level, perception is clearly not modular. In generating a response to what one of its components has detected, the character of the cognitive uptake depends at least as much on the system's repertoire of concepts and associative powers as on the input's character. Lacking a Portuguese Water Dog concept, I will not have the canine fancier's uptake. Perceptual relativity—people seeing things differently—is precisely the result of the influence of language, conceptual schemes, world views, and such on higher-order perceptual access.

However, the influence of language and linguistically acquired beliefs on the cognitive dimension of perception does not mean that cognition itself is an essentially linguistic phenomenon.[7] Knowledge of language no doubt facilitates thought and reasoning, but it would be wrong to assume that mental representation depends on storage of and operations upon linguistic tokens all the way down to the lowest levels of consciousness and mentation. As I have already tried to show, film theorists do not currently have satisfactory grounds to assume that all artificial representational systems are necessarily essentially linguistic. It would thus be a mistake for us to form an a priori and unqualified conclusion that mental representations must be irreducibly linguistic.

Philosophers, psychologists, and cognitive scientists are only just beginning to debate an arena of difficult questions about: how concepts and content in a language of thought, and the processing of them, would be physically instantiated; how symbol manipulation in one's innate mental language would be correlated with a conventional natural language; whether "mentalese" would be sufficiently like a natural language to be called a language at all; whether the nature and functioning of this language would be ultimately explained at a lower, nonlinguistic level of mental operations and structures. To the extent that these questions are relevant to film theoretical claims concerning the nature of perception and interpretation, scholars might wish to familiarize themselves with some of the main theories thus far posed to address them.[8] But except for this brief digression, my own discussion takes no particular stance on the language of thought debates.

Dretske makes another crucial distinction, this one between primary and secondary cognitive perception. Many of the beliefs we get by visual means are mediated in some way. In such cases, "our visual knowledge of A depends on, and derives from, our visual knowledge of B."[9] Consider this example: By seeing that the fuel gauge registers E, one sees that the car's gas tank is empty. That the tank is in a certain state, emptiness, is a secondary cognitive perception, a fact learned by virtue of the way that some other object looks to the percipient. The gauge is the primary sensory-perceptual object. It is that which is non-cognitively seen. Moreover, the cognitions arising from visual awareness of this object are, in the first place, cognitions about it—that it is a gas gauge, that it is in a particular state. Now provided that the agent has key pieces of background knowledge regarding the kind of relationship that can be expected to hold between gauges and gas tanks, he or she can also exploit this primary cognitive perception to learn about an item that is not present. You see by the gauge that the tank is empty because you are aware that somebody designed this mechanism to take advantage of a convention (E means "empty") and the physical connections (the wiring between the gauge and the tank) that constrain the meter to look a particular way when the tank is in a given condition. Hence looking at the gauge straightaway permits you visually to acquire the relevant information without you having to infer or guess what the gauge's visible state has to do with how things stand with respect to the tank.

Perceptual Access to Cinematic Meaning

Research into perception is pertinent to cinema scholars insofar as we regularly hold forth on such matters as the viewing experience's specificity and effects on spectators, what it is that viewers see, and how it is that they derive the beliefs they do from watching movies. I contend that the foregoing model of perception has a positive contribution to make to our debates over these matters. My own opinion is that it is the best currently available framework within which to describe the various perceptual achievements feeding into the spectator's visual experience and comprehension of the movie; although its real value derives more from its introducing into cinema studies a conceptual alternative that has yet to be adequately explored by us.

Henceforth my comments will be apropos of a refinement to how we explain visual perception's role in film spectatorship. The concept of visual perception is often vague or confused, or subject to a restrictive association with direct, unmediated, purely sensory awareness of images. Perception's function as an input to movie comprehension is thereby plunged into the dark. Alternatively, we could take up the task of analyzing how agents perceptually discovers facts, pertaining both to cinematic and extra-cinematic states of affairs, by cognitively utilizing sensory experiences of motion picture imagery. So my next concern is to identify some of the kinds of cognitive perceptions constitutive of spectatorship.

Seeing That D Is a Motion Picture. Motion picture comprehension is to a large extent, though not often exclusively, a visual achievement. One of the reasons this statement is true is that spectatorship is conditional upon visually sensing some object. In that respect, understanding movies has the same foundation as a gamut of entertainments, from visual reading to watching live plays to gazing at paintings. So the specificity of the movie viewer's activity must be elsewhere. In my account, it resides in the area of his or her primary cognitive perceptions. Shown a film, the viewer's primary perceptual object is the representational medium; and the facts perceptually learned are primarily facts about it. The competent spectator is just someone who can recognize, by visual means, one such fact concerning this immediate object, namely, that it is a cinematic depiction.

By "competent," I refer to the kind of agent who goes into the viewing situation with some accurate if nontechnical beliefs about the nature of movie technology and imagery and who can mobilize these beliefs when necessary. For example, beset by squeamish discomfort at the mere thought of crawling bugs, Scott manages to endure a documentary on humanity's battle with insects if every so often he says aloud to himself, "It's only a movie, it's only a movie." The competent spectator would also be able to grasp the source of the naive subject's confusion. In the absence of compelling empirical research, we can if we like muse about the existence of otherwise rational folk who for whatever reasons, when seeing motion picture imagery (perhaps for the first time), have a belief to the effect that they are seeing the photographed object directly.

In one of his memoirs of his time among the Inuit, Flaherty reports that upon seeing a movie for the first time, his audience "completely forgot the picture—to them the walrus [depicted in the film] was real and living."[10] Depending on circumstances, it might be challenging but not impossible to help such agents satisfy the norm of competent spectatorship. More readily imagined are individuals who are confused or under-informed about the nature of the relationship between image and object but who, owing to their intuition that an unusual perceptual situation obtains, do not automatically jump to the conclusion that they are seeing the photographed object in the exact same way—primarily and directly—as they see objects live and in person. Indeed, Flaherty, attributing lack of understanding rather than full-blown illusion to them, elsewhere characterizes the Inuit audience as just such agents.[11] As long as the root of their bewilderment is a lack of background knowledge rather than ensorcellment by the cinematic apparatus, such spectators too could be trained to proficiency.

Seeing That D Represents An/The O. Recognizing that **D** is a movie is probably best considered part of a parcel of interlocking cognitive perceptions. For conceptual purposes, another member of this package of perceptions can be described as seeing that the representation itself has a certain visible appearance and properties. Here again we are describing the viewer's primary cognitive perceptions. In reference to naturalistic movies, an important class of these perceptions consists of seeing that certain types of objects are depicted. Identifying, for example, the various stereotypical visible features of steam locomotives, the percipient thereby sees that the picture represents a token of that kind of train. Similarly, the viewer may see that a depiction represents a particular object, like the Statue of Liberty. I add that not all primary cognitive perceptions of images involve noticing representational content. **Seeing that D is P**—that it is bright, grainy, wide, clear, fuzzy, technicolor, black and white, and so on—involves recognizing the visually observable properties of the pictorial medium itself.

Seeing By D That O Is P. The realization that something is a motion picture ramifies into still further, secondary, cognitive perceptions. While watching *Alien Autopsy: Fact or Fiction?* (Tom McGough, 1995) one sees that something, which on-screen narrator Jonathan Frakes (an actor in popular science fiction television programs and movies) has suggested could be an alien, has a gaping leg wound. The alleged spacenik is the extra-cinematic, secondary perceptual object; any facts we visually learn about it—that it is a real E.T. or an elaborate prosthetic device—are cognitively secondary to those we visually learn about the depiction. In other words, knowledge of various bygone states of affairs concerning a non-present object derives from knowledge of current and directly perceivable states of affairs, namely, the movie image's visible properties.

Just as one sees by a fuel gauge that a tank is empty, one sees by the motion picture that the little alien has a leg wound. You see by the gauge that the tank is empty because you are aware that somebody designed this mechanism to take advantage of a convention (**E** means "empty") and physical connections (the wiring between the gauge and the tank) that constrain the meter to look a particular way when the tank is in a given condition. Hence looking at the gauge straightaway permits you visually to acquire the relevant information without having to infer or guess what the gauge's visible state has to do with how things stand with respect to the tank. The film spectator's perceptual situation is fundamentally the same. That person is in sensory contact with a given object, namely, the representation. He or she visually recognizes some of that item's visible properties. To the degree that the sensory object's visible properties preserve information about the visible features of something not sensed, the viewer is able cognitively to see that the latter obtain by sensing and cognitively seeing the former. He or she can see that some other, non-present (and bygone) state of affairs looked a certain way because he or she knows that, owing to the causal conditions productive of photographic depictions, the picture would not look as it does if an actual distal scene had not looked a particular way.

To be sure, there are differences between the movie image and the gauge. The picture gives rise to a perceptual experience similar to that one would have were one to see, directly, the kind of scene specified by the picture. The gauge, on the other hand, is a non-pictorial representation. Also, the former visually conveys many more facts about its object's visible state than the latter. Not only does the image indicate that a humanoid form lies on a slab, but nested in this representation are a plethora of facts concerning what the scene of that humanoid lying on that slab looks like. The gauge's appearance shows only that there is little or no gas, without providing any other information about the appearance of the tank and gas. The gauge is not even intended to indicate the tank's visible condition so much as its content's volume or weight. Yet in terms of **how** (by visual means) an observer picks up facts about external situations (the container's emptiness, the shape of the unearthly cadaver's leg) the analogy holds.

Note that these secondary cognitions are not a necessary and inevitable consequence of non-epistemically seeing the image. Like Wesley's primary cognitive feat of seeing that the dog is a Portuguese Water Dog, these cognitions are highly contingent. Seeing by the depiction that such and such was the case in pre-filmic reality depends upon the agent's awareness of various systematic relations and constraints, plus her possession of relevant background knowledge. Some key constraints are nomic. Causal relations bearing on cinematographic recording and exhibition processes support information-conveying or indicator relations between two very different situations: viewing at a given time and place a depiction of **O**, and **O**'s actual condition in a different location at an anterior time. Cognizance of these systematic relations permits the agent to exploit the former so as to learn about the latter.

Although grounded in natural laws, the connections between images and objects themselves hinge on certain conditions being met. Generally speaking, connections hold if photographic technology is used in a particular way within a conducive environment. And even then the image's indicator function will not necessarily help us to discover facts about an alleged alien autopsy that occurred in 1947, since you cannot see by the depiction that such an event transpired unless you already have a concept for extra-terrestrial and know when the recently "found" archival footage was supposed to have been shot.

The movie spectator's perceptual access, I propose, is to situations well beyond the representation's own visible condition. Viewing Terry Zwigoff's *Crumb* (1995), most people cannot but notice that underground artist Robert Crumb is tall, thin, and wears thick spectacles. Provided you haven't forgotten your big thick eyeglasses, you will have no problem seeing that this is the case because you know that the image's appearance naturally means that Crumb looks a certain way. You might also realize that part of the footage, and some of the observable doings it depicts, have a non-pictorial, non-visible external significance. Arguably, by looking at depictions of his roughhousing with female friends, his piggyback rides on women, and his sketches and cartoons, one can see that Crumb has a misogynist streak. If so, you see by the imagery that he has this psychological trait because you are able to bring a certain visual input under a particular concept. Your cognitive perception of Crumb's character may be facilitated by sundry non-perceptual factors, like background beliefs and information gleaned from the explicit linguistic assertions of interview subjects, including Crumb himself. By the same token, facts discovered by visual means are an aid to our attempts to test and verify what interviewees say about the artist's attitudes toward women.

There are definitely no guarantees that each of every spectator's cognitive perceptions will always be perfectly accurate. Mistakes due to inattention or lack of information are as endemic to movie watching as to any perceptual enterprise. Nor is it uncommon to fall prey to the author's calculated manipulations of the depiction. Maybe some not necessarily intellectually unsophisticated people will, upon viewing *Alien Autopsy*, judge that they have seen suppressed footage of an actual top secret postmortem. We cannot even assume that viewers of the popular television show *America's Funniest Home Videos* realize that a "wild track" of studio audience reaction shots is used, such that people shown laughing, apparently in response to one video, may really have been laughing at an altogether different one. However, the lesson here is not that cinema studies' reigning assumption should be one of skepticism about the possibility of achieving perceptual knowledge. Rather, the point is that the sensory seeing/cognitive seeing distinction, as an explanatory construct, allows for perceptual errors as well as successes; seeing anything, including a cinematic image, is no assurance of either an entirely positive or negative epistemic outcome, since the encounter's result depends on the percipient s capacity to exploit the sensory input.

Aestheticians have long held that access to the content of pictorial representations is not easily construed as a purely sensory accomplishment. There is a history of complicated debates, none of which I can summarize here, over the degree to which the spectator's grasp of pictorial as well as non-pictorial significance is to be attributed to that individual's mobilization of a variety of non-sensory factors, broadly referred to as conventions.[12] To avoid misunderstandings of my position, I am anxious to emphasize the following points.

First, cognitive perception, as I understand it, accommodates the hypothesis that successful picture perception may involve knowledge of conventions, but it does so without committing us to the idea that perception involves conventions, codes, rules, or ratiocination all the way out to the periphery of sensory processing. This reluctance to associate all vision with computational or quasi-rational processes should not be confused with an endorsement of the notion that we can experience a pure perception whereby we apprehend things just as they are, without our own subjectivities making a significant contribution to how we experience those objects. To maintain that sensory seeing is nonrational, hence nonconventional, is not to propose that it transcends the limitations and structures imposed on it by the organization and material composition of the human agent's sensory organs, so as to constitute a form of unmediated contact with the world or the art object itself.

Second, to accept that knowledge of conventions can influence the viewer's cognitive perceptions is not to accept that visual works are literally read or decoded in a manner analogous to linguistic comprehension. The kinds of conventions mobilized in either the reception or production of pictorial representations may be different from that which is identified with the technical sense of conventionality that I have used throughout my study, and which I associate with a defining feature of properly linguistic artifacts and activities. To this point I add a third, namely, that I have no trouble accepting the general idea that knowledge of sundry traditions, iconographic or symbolic associations, technical schemas and rules about how to achieve certain visual effects, as well as familiarity with historically or culturally relative pictorial styles, might greatly enhance comprehension of a work's meaning and value. But my approach does not support the conclusion that the success of one's cognitive perceptions of any given work inevitably depends upon knowledge of such conventions, loosely conceived.

For argument's sake, imagine an appropriately naive subject, someone from a culture very different from your own, a culture having (from your perspective) unusual modes of visual representation and lacking such traditions as painting, cubism, and photographic depiction. In terms of his social environment, learning history, and psychological development, this individual is substantially unlike anyone else you know. He is not stupid but, rather, a moderately rational human being with a history of normal visual experiences of a wide range of perceptual objects.[13] Presented with Picasso's *Portrait of Daniel Henry Kahnweiler* or Cindy Sherman's *Untitled Film Still #54*, the subject described here could have some trouble seeing the same facts that you might be able to recognize at a glance. But his lack of knowledge of the specific conventions influencing the form, appearance, and content of these works does not necessarily mean that he will have no perceptual access to correct interpretations.

It is safe to assume that this spectator will not see that Picasso's painting is cubist nor that Sherman's is photographic, since concepts like "painting," "cubism," and "photography" are unavailable to him. By the same token, it is unlikely that the agent will tell at a glance that the painting is a picture of a face. However, based on the available sensory information (which is not fundamentally different from your sensory information), and whatever concepts he does possess, it might not take him long to see that there is an image of a face before him; likewise, he might visually discover, perhaps even immediately, that there is or could be a kind of (to him, unorthodox) representation or picture before him. Without needing to learn about cubism from other sources or look at other such works, the untrained viewer could be able to recognize or soon infer some of the portrait's significant properties, depending on the strength of numerous factors, including: what concepts are available to him (i.e., ideas at least partially coinciding with our notions of "representation" and "picture");

his expertise in their use as heuristics for identifying unfamiliar exemplars; his powers of recall, reasoning, and association; his capacity visually to recognize ordinary objects like faces even when external conditions (trees, fog, darkness) obscure his vision somewhat. In short, perceptual acuity, agent rationality, and cultural background—not simply knowledge of conventions—are crucial inputs to interpretive success.

Much the same can be said of our imaginary subject's engagement with *Untitled Film Still #54*. Given his limitations, he will not be able to see that the image depicts the photographer herself, masquerading as Marilyn Monroe. Nor should we expect him to see by the lighting, composition, angle, and pose struck by Sherman that the picture is staged to suggest the predatory nature of the spectator's gaze at the female popular cultural icon. Yet these limitations do not automatically rule out the possibility that the subject will be able to see that there is a kind of picture before him and will recognize some of the objects shown.

Finally, the more a conscious act of deliberation or decision enters into the comprehension process, the less specifically visual one's knowledge becomes, and cognitive perception thereby shades into an increasingly non-perceptual mode of comprehension. To the extent that you have to **decide**, with reference to various pictorial or other conventions, that the unicorn appearing in a given painting here symbolizes chastity, you do not cognitively see that the picture has this meaning.

At this stage, it would be helpful to locate my chosen model of perception in relation to four other claims about the nature of the movie spectator's visual experiences. Illusion, participation, transparency, and representation theses all, I believe, have problems avoided by my position. In so arguing, I have an opportunity to expand on some of my own claims, as well as defend cognitive perception against the charge that it is not a kind of seeing at all.

Projective Illusion

Some scholars suggest that film's mimetic function is so fascinating that under ordinary viewing conditions, spectators, their wits addled by the cinematic apparatus, tend to acquire a strong impression that they are looking straight at objects, oblivious to the fact that what is being directly viewed is a representation rather than reality itself.[14] Although I do not wish to elide subtle differences between proponents, illusion theorists typically seem to contend that spectators are in visual contact with one thing that they somehow misperceive as another. Richard Allen has proposed a thoughtful and detailed reconstruction of this position.

Allen asserts that film viewing can give rise to a projective illusion (PI).[15] What he means is that viewers occasionally experience a particular kind of sensory illusion that gives rise to the thought that they are seeing before them the cinematically portrayed object or event: For at least a moment, it sometimes looks to the percipient as if the pre-photographic scene is right before his or her eyes.[16] Allen compares this experience to that of certain optical illusions, like the Müller-Lyer figure in which parallel lines of equal length appear to the observer to be unequal. What is interesting about such illusions is that they are perceptually compelling even in the absence of epistemic failure. The percipient could know very well that the lines are actually the same length, but they will nonetheless look unequal to him or her. PI, says Allen, is a weaker variety of this kind of "sensory deception."[17] He stresses that it is a weaker type of illusion because it is not an inevitable part of the viewing experience—consciously held countervailing thoughts pertaining to the fact that the depiction is just that can prevent PI's onset or break its hold.[18]

Allen maintains that film viewing is a rational activity; there never is any doubt in our minds that the only thing right in front of us is a picture.[19] Yet given the proper circumstances, it is possible that the qualities of the movie image will promote a sensory impression that triggers not the belief but the non-assertively held thought, without commitment to its truth, that one is directly viewing some item or event. Various features of the depiction—resemblance to extra-filmic objects, photographic lifelikeness, projection, movement, linear perspective, sound, color, and so on—facilitate this train of sensation and thought.[20] The spectator's mental states also factor into this effect's emergence. One contributor is belief (true belief, according to Allen) in the image's transparency.[21] Another is a predisposition toward benign disavowal, consisting of the suppression of awareness that one is only watching a movie in order better to fulfill the wish embodied by the cinematic fantasy.[22]

Allen should be applauded for abandoning one of film theory's most enduring but least enlightened dogmas, that is, the notion that spectators ever literally believe themselves to be in direct perceptual contact with anything other than a cinematic depiction. But his evidence is inadequate to warrant concluding that the content of one's sensory experience of a movie image—how it looks to one—is sometimes such that it triggers thoughts of the pre-filmic object's immediacy.

First, the analogy between how motion pictures and certain geometrical optical illusions appear to observers is unsound. As with Müller-Lyer figures, Necker cubes, and Gestalt switch pictures, any equivocation, ambiguity, or error at the level of the film viewer's internal, sensory representation would have to be traced to the ambiguity of the visual display and/or the visual system's failure to extract or compute correctly the available information.[23] The case for sensory misrepresentation of imagery is plausible only on the basis of evidence of the paucity or ambivalence of cues to such features as: two dimensionality, and the unmanipulableness of the depicted objects; edges; the manifest discontinuity between screen space and viewer space; the magnification or diminution of the items pictured, and so forth. Yet Allen offers no compelling grounds for assuming that the array of reflected light is anything but rich in information pertaining to those properties of the distal stimulus (the movie image) unequivocally specifying it as a depiction. Nor does he suggest how visual detection and lower-level processing could be so flawed as to generate an inaccurate sensory perception of the moving picture. On the contrary, he seems to assume that processing of the available information is generally accurate and reliable, since the thought of the object's presence is neither inevitable nor indefeasible: The image often looks like an image to the spectator.

In lieu of demonstrating that lower-level processing is prone to generating erroneous sensory representations, Allen might still advocate his position by emphasizing that certain of the observer's other, higher-order psychological states can overdetermine how things appear to him or her. After all, thinking "rabbit" thoughts can help you to apprehend one aspect of a Gestalt switch picture, a feat someone lacking that concept might have trouble performing. Because Allen does not refer to any specific explanation of visual perception's relation to cognition and affect, it is hard to say how he would account for the visual experience's putative distortion by expectations, wishful thinking, and emotions. Any such account of perceptual change and relativity requires a clearer description of what it is that is supposedly being altered.

Obviously, our perceptual beliefs and judgments are subject to mental influences. Somebody pining for a lost love might momentarily misrecognize that person's face in a crowd, as the combination of a lovelorn frame of mind and the brevity of perceptual contact trigger this misapprehension. Less obvious is that the content of the lover's **sensory** perception depends upon his longing. Remove this desire and what is nonepistemically seen might remain unchanged, while the belief about what is seen is brought into line with the fact that it is only a stranger approaching. Less obvious still is how one's sensory perception of a movie image as the object itself could be induced by other mental states. Advocating this position would commit Allen to a number of conceptually as well as empirically problematic claims unsupported in his argument as it stands. He would, for instance, wind up implying that the processing of a steady, unambiguous flow of stimuli is potentially less constrained by the visual display's actual features than by certain psychological states—states so strong as to alter the competent viewer's sensory experience despite his or her true and justified beliefs about the perceptual situation's actual nature.[24]

A second problem with the PI thesis concerns "loss of medium awareness," which Allen calls a "prerequisite to the experience of projective illusion."[25] Just as one cannot enjoy the picture's duck aspect while looking for its rabbit features, one cannot have a PI if one focuses on the disillusioning properties of the depiction, like its edges, and consciously dwells on the knowledge that the image is merely that, an image. The phenomenological specificity of sensory perception of movie pictures, then, is that it tends to inhibit your focal attention to the fact that the image's frame circumscribes a photographic recording rather than the limits of your own visual field.[26]

But Allen's appeal to loss of medium awareness as a condition of PI's emergence is ill-founded, for the claim that a viewer can experience such a lapse is itself question-begging. Although we cannot be sure what, for Allen, counts as awareness, it need not be restricted to propositionally formulated thoughts of which one is focally conscious. Some models of human cognition, like those incorporating a duplex theory of memory, equate active awareness with a subset of beliefs in short-term memory.[27] As opposed to the comparatively dormant beliefs in long-term storage, the content of this working memory plays a continuous functional role in the agent's current reasoning and action, as these internal structures steer the agent's interpretations of and responses to her environment. Hence, being attentive to or engrossed in the depicted events need not be taken as a sign of obliviousness to the fact that one is looking at a cinematic work.

Seeing a movie leads to comprehension of, and emotional responses to, the depicted individuals, events, and actions because one is aware, in the aforementioned sense, that one is watching a movie. It is difficult to conceive of a viewing situation in which the visual display, no matter how sensational or engrossing, incapacitates our active network of beliefs and background assumptions to the effect that what we are watching is a selection and organization of images resulting from somebody's rational, deliberate actions for the purpose of narrating a story. Consider, for example, *Twister* (Jan De Bont, 1996).

Storm-bound, Jo and Bill, two tornado hunters, lash themselves to a pipe in a wooden shed and are nearly sucked up feet first into the vortex's eye. This episode is represented in a series of images, including: (a) an exterior view of the shack as a swirling black tempest of dust and debris gradually rips its planks away; (b) Jo and Bill, in close-up, watching their shelter torn from around them; (c) the shack, seen from a medium-long distance, which now appears all but destroyed, as the protagonists huddle beneath the pipe and the dust eventually obscures our view of them; (d) a shot establishing Jo and Bill's position in the funnel's center, replaced by a Spielberg moment, namely a medium shot looking down on their facial expressions of wide-eyed wonderment, followed by a point of view shot (roughly consistent with either character's perspective) showing two pairs of legs floating skyward. We thrill to this segment of the film story if and only if we see by the depiction that such and such happens in the fiction. And we understand the fiction's content if and only if we realize that an image track has been systematically manipulated as a way of indicating the characters' predicament, and changes in that predicament, at a certain time and place.

Despite the discontinuities between visual perspectives, we interpret this ensemble of pictures as a chronologically ordered series of informative views on a single, developing course of events, namely, the tempest's gradual engulfment of Jo and Bill, its impact on them, and their reactions to this crisis. Noticing significant overlaps of content between shots, and recognizing that images are juxtaposed so as to show the progression of cause-effect chains, we see that this course of events occurs over a brief, continuous time, instead of over some longer period in which minutes or hours elapse between cuts. Were they truly to induce loss of medium awareness, these images would be experienced as a bewildering succession of visual sensations, rather than as a coherent cinematic passage. The excitement they arouse would be due to the observer's confusion about the origins of his perceptions, the inexplicable perspectival discontinuities to which his visual field is apparently subject, the reasons for and relations between these discontinuities, and their inconsistency with his impression of being stationary and comfortably seated at some remove from the evident danger. Thus it is the imagery's meaning in the context of the narrative that ultimately would be lost to the medium unaware viewer.

Allen makes the point that familiarity with narrative conventions of either classical or art cinema usually smooths the way for onset of loss of medium awareness and PI.[28] One's introductory encounter with shot-reverse shot editing, jump cuts, long takes, and so on might initially draw one's attention to the structure of the film itself. Yet with subsequent exposures to such practices, one learns how they serve to advance the story, whereupon they no longer interfere with absorption in watching characters and their actions as if they were immediately present.

My intuitions on this matter are different. In learning to drive, you must make a focal and concerted effort to make the steady stream of small steering and speed adjustments necessary to control the car. But once you are accustomed to making those adjustments, you can perform them more or less automatically, even while holding an engrossing conversation. At this stage, you have not graduated to loss of steering awareness; knowledge of when and how to make corrections is still functionally engaged in a part of short-term memory that corresponds to a task that you are actively thinking about and doing. Familiarity with cinematic properties and practices, encountered within one work or across a given category of works, is similar to this example.

Suppose that **N** is a narrative strategy, like Chantal Ackerman's repeated procedure, in *Jeanne Dielman, 23 Quai Du Commerce, 1080 Bruxelles* (1975), of signaling an impending cut by letting the camera linger on remaining objects after the character has left the scene. Learning that **N** means that **P**, that a transition is in the offing, does not constitute or favor loss of medium awareness—it **is** medium awareness. In other words, the viewer thereby acquires a capacity to mobilize knowledge of **N** within active memory, after which he is able to see by **N** that **P** without having to form, deliberately and consciously, a judgment about what it is that this procedure means in the present context.

Be it narration of the spectacular exploits of tornado jockeys or of Jeanne Dielman's enervating household routine, story comprehension depends on appropriate beliefs and expectations about the visual display's cinematic nature operating within our cognitive system; this belief set includes the premise that camera angles and movements, editing, spatial and temporal ellipses, and so forth are subordinated to storytelling goals.

Imagined Seeing

In keeping with his participation thesis, which holds that people use representations as props in games of make-believe, Kendall Walton claims that audiences typically think of themselves as directly seeing that which pictures and movies depict.[29] The premises of Walton's argument, as I understand it, are as follows. When a spectator watches a movie, he is in direct perceptual contact with a representation. Unlike the PI thesis, this contact is not said to involve a sensory misrepresentation of the image as its object. Hence it does not look to the perceiver as if the pre-filmic scene is directly before him. Moreover, as a consequence of seeing the picture, the viewer winds up with a package of veridical beliefs: that he is looking at a picture, that it is a picture of such and such an object or kind, that the pre-filmic object is in a given condition and has various properties (is thin, wears glasses, is sitting in a restaurant), that the representation itself has certain features (e.g., it is a color video image appearing on a small television monitor). However, Walton says that there is another, specifically pictorial dimension to the viewer's visual experience: imagined seeing. It is here that the fun starts.

I say that it is with imagined seeing that the fun starts because it is to this aspect of image spectatorship that Walton ascribes an essentially non-epistemic value. Although we can and frequently do examine depictions in order to gather important information, imagined seeing is a perceptual phenomenon that can be experienced for its own sake, without a view to learning about either the image or the extra-cinematic situation. Hence it is without effort of conscious decision or will, "more or less automatically" as a consequence of perceiving a picture, that the spectator imagines his actual visual experience of, say, seeing a video image of R. Crumb to be the experience of seeing R. Crumb directly.[30]

If, for example, the artist is shown in close-up profile, from a low angle, then the spectator will imagine seeing him from the perspective dictated by that camera angle.[31] This phenomenon is specific to picture perception. The visual experience you would have were you actually sitting across the table from Crumb would not trigger it because you would indeed be seeing him directly. Nor would reading a written description of the artist induce imagined seeing because you would not be looking at the right kind of prop, that is, something that looks like Crumb. So imagined seeing seems to be predicated on the truism that the experience of looking at a picture is analogous to that of gazing upon the pictured object. But I have already shown—and will continue to show—that these two perceptual experiences are dissimilar enough to rule out various kinds of substitutions, in the minds of viewers, of the one for the other.

For investigations of the nature of visual non-fictions, Walton's present thesis raises a particular concern. It suggests that photographic non-fictions are nonetheless indissociable from fiction because they are normally props in viewers' games of make-believe. Looking at a family or news photograph, or at a documentary movie, the onlooker imagines seeing the depictum itself; hence, as Walton says, "it is fictional that [one] sees Aunt Mabel directly, without photographic assistance."[32] Unless there were reasons to draw back from the imagined seeing thesis, we would need to treat it as a challenge to our position that the categories "fiction" and "constative" are defined by authorially expressed illocutionary intentions and that these two categories do not coincide except when that author has the right kind of complex illocutionary plan. Luckily there are grounds for withholding our assent from imagined seeing.

One of imagined seeing's shortcomings is semantic, as it is not immediately obvious what kind of specifically perceptual experience, if any, such a locution describes. Visual perception is, in the first instance, a relational state subject to an existential constraint. For **S** to see **O**, there must be an actual percipient within whom arises an actual percept the content of which is counterfactually dependent on the existence of an actual object external to the percept itself. Strictly speaking, imagined seeing is oxymoronic.

Although his term's phenomenological specificity is fuzzy, Walton clearly does not maintain that the spectator's perception of the image is a purely psychological matter. He insists that imagined seeing is not a higher-order conceptual abstraction, distinct from any actual, vivid sensory experience but a genuine perceptual mode of engagement with pictures. In other words, it is not his contention that imagined seeing consists merely of entertaining a mental proposition to the effect that I see such and such. To imagine seeing **O** is not to imagine that "I see **O**." Nor is Walton claiming that one experiences **imaginary** seeing in response to movies—as when I close my eyes and have an imaginary visual experience of frolicsome dolphins in the surf. So imagined seeing must refer to the percipient's psychological relation to something he really does sense by visual means. It is apparently another cognitive upshot of sensory perception. The viewer has a more or less unmediated sensory-perceptual experience of the picture; subsequently he acquires all manner of beliefs and attitudes concerning that sensation, including a non-assertively held thought of seeing the depicted scene directly. Somehow, due to the interplay of the pictorial properties of the stimulus and the workings of the brain, this thought is elicited as spontaneously as the recognition of the picture's polychromaticity and Crumb's thinness. The viewer imagines that his occurrent visual sensation is of Crumb. This sentence does not here refer to or imply an instance of either propositional make-believe or imaginary seeing, that is, a thought of how a scene looks that is devoid of actual sensory content and free of the existential condition on bona fide seeing. It simply refers to that which Walton attributes to the spectator: a passively acquired psychological attitude toward the internally represented sense data—one among other such attitudes the spectator has regarding this percept.

Whatever "imagined seeing" denotes, it has neither empirical nor conceptual priority over a gamut of other perceptual feats. Were it not for our actual sensation of the picture, and the accompanying recognition of its form and content, there would be nothing to imagine. Borrowing a remark from Christopher Peacocke, imagined seeing, as a statement of the nature of our perceptual experiences of depictions, suffers from an insufficiency problem: "It seems that imagining a face, say, on some part of a canvas is never guaranteed to be sufficient for *seeing* a face in the painting, and it is such experiences of seeing that depiction exploits."[33]

The question thus arises, What does imagined seeing explain? Walton would undoubtedly reply that it evokes a particularly aesthetic, versus epistemic, aspect of our involvement with the work. Although not a mode of sensory acuity nor a source of further information about either picture or depictum, imagining one's self to be looking right at the scene could make the viewing experience more engrossing, moving, or pleasurable. A thorough challenge to this thesis would therefore include a meta-aesthetic investigation of whether the audience's experience of a work would be less affecting, and their appreciation of it more shallow, without imagined seeing. The topic of such a probe would ultimately be the norms of appreciation, that is, what kinds and degrees of engagement with visual art works we can reasonably expect of human agents. Investigation of the question of whether a competent, mature aesthetic appreciation of a movie depends on the experience of imagined seeing falls just beyond the horizon of my present discussion. But the rest of my comments would not support embracing imagined seeing as a mark of spectator success, insofar as they cast doubt on its cognitive feasibility.

The thought that one is looking straight at the depicted scene is an unlikely consequence of viewing pictures because it is incompatible with one's actual sensory- and cognitive-perceptual responses. A friend of Walton's thesis is bound to retort that perceptual evidence usually is at odds with the things people imagine. When young Erik, playing with a gigantic cardboard box, thinks of himself as walking on the deck of his pirate ship, his occurrent make-beliefs are falsified by his occurrent sensations, his ongoing cognitive perceptions, and his background knowledge. But Erik's state of mind admits of no real confusion or cognitive dissonance because he is uncommitted to the truth of the content of his imaginings. He is, after all, only pretending.

However, the participation thesis calls on the movie spectator to execute a very specialized type of imagining. The spectator's achievement entails more than using his visual perceptions as aids to help him conceive of external objects—help him think, for example, of the world as being in a certain condition, or entertain the idea of some non-actual external state of affairs, or make-believe himself situated within a non-actual environment or course of events. As Walton would have it, the objects of his imaginings are his own visual perceptions.

Thus conceived, imagined seeing implies a psychological operation that strikes me as counterintuitive. The trouble is twofold. The first problem is that as a cognitive upshot of seeing a depiction, it is disfavored by the stimulus and inconsistent with the viewer's other cognitive perceptions. Hence the physical, input-driven, causal triggers of imagined seeing are obscure, as are the spectator's reasons for responding in this manner. Walton proposes the following. Viewing a cinematic depiction of, for instance, Crumb, the percipient somehow manages to misrepresent to himself his occurrent subjective perceptual states. Although (indeed, partly because) the agent supposedly has a stream of information-preserving sensory impressions, he imagines that his occurrent visual sensation is of Crumb. So it is in the absence of any sort of sensory deception that he spontaneously thinks of himself as having visual experiences qualitatively opposed to the character of his actual sensory-experiences and what he knows them to be about.

Unlike the Müller-Lyer design, there is nothing about either the input or the nature of lower-level sensory processing of pictures that causes the percept to represent the image of Crumb as anything but what it is, an image of Crumb. The movie picture of Crumb continuously looks to the percipient like a movie picture of Crumb. Moreover, during the course of this perceptual event, in league with noticing sundry connected facts pertaining to the image and its referent—such as the angle of the shot and the actions of its subject—the percipient also recognizes that the picture is the primary perceptual object, whereas Crumb is the secondary object. Note as well that the imagined seeing response changes nothing about how the scene actually appears to the percipient: Crumb does not suddenly look to him like the primary perceptual object. Nor does it entail modification or distortion of the spectator's beliefs; he does not become confused about what the primary perceptual object really is or whether the secondary object appears to him more like a direct object.

We therefore have the right to ask of the imagined seeing proponent how and why the pictorial properties of a visual display would more or less automatically prompt the viewer to think of his sensation of the picture as a sensation of the pre-photographic object, even though (a) there is unequivocal information about the depiction-depictum relation available in both the picture and the agent's percept; (b) it continuously looks to him like he is seeing a picture; (c) he all the while knows that he is seeing a picture. Since the experience of imagined seeing is dependent upon and coextensive with feats of veridical sensory and cognitive perception, the task facing the proponent is to explain why these feats necessarily support rather than undermine either the physical causation of or the psychological motivation for this phenomenon. On this basis alone we are currently in a better position to doubt than adopt Walton's thesis.

Although **they** can misrepresent the external world, one's own perceptions are not obviously the kinds of states that can be misrepresented to one's self while one is in their grip. This remark introduces a second criticism to which imagined seeing is vulnerable. Contrary to the implications of Walton's thesis, visual perception, referring both to sensory and cognitive seeing, is characteristically vivid and compelling. Here are some examples of what I mean.

Sometimes we cannot correctly identify our visual object, yet we are nonetheless aware that it looks a certain way to us. Someone who has little or no information about computer technology will be unable to bring a credit card-size internal modem under the precisely appropriate conceptual category. If pre- or non-linguistic, that individual might even lack the sorts of size, shape, and color concepts that other percipients would deploy in the process of recognizing at least some of this item's superficial features. Although perhaps unable to describe its function or appearance to anyone, including herself, the individual will still know that the modem looks a certain way to her. Likewise, on seeing the Müller-Lyer picture, a naive subject experiences cognitive as well as sensory deception. Yet there is one thing about which this subject is not mistaken: He knows that the lines appear unequal to him.

One's knowing how things appear to one is, as I say, a feat qualitatively different from knowing how things really are in the world. But no matter how epistemically imperfect they may be, our beliefs about the world tend to be in alignment with how the world looks to us. If I see an object, **O**, and **O** looks to me like a stick, then **O** will look like a stick to me, and I will continue to hold thoughts to the effect that it looks like a stick to me, until one or both of two conditions change: A change in the visual stimulus, or in my physical relation to it, could alter its appearance to me; or a change in me, such as the sudden onset of astigmatism or my bringing the display under a different concept, could change, respectively, my sensory impression of **O**'s appearance or my thoughts about what it looks like. Given a shift in these conditions, **O** might suddenly look like a snake to me or I might now think that it looks this way—with or without a subsequent belief that I see a snake.

Now suppose that **O** is in truth a long, serpentine stick; and further suppose both that **O** looks just so to me and that my ongoing beliefs reflect that fact. Is there any clear sense in which I could also be accurately described as thinking of myself as seeing a snake? Surely not—not if that description's truth does not require a change in either of the two aforementioned conditions but does require that I think of my sensory impression of the stick as a sensory impression of a snake. To be sure, I could form or acquire thoughts of how this stick looks like a snake, but that involves no imaginative misrepresentation to myself of how things look to me. I would merely be entertaining higher-order, conceptually abstract ideas pertaining to the respects in which something I currently know to look to me like one thing, a stick, visibly resembles another kind of thing.

The experience of seeing objects is thus vivid and compelling because it entails our sensory and cognitive preoccupation with how things appear to us. To see an item is to be occurrently and focally aware of how that thing looks to us and to know more or less immediately that it looks that way to us. When something looks red, our most vivid sensory impression will be of its redness; and our most spontaneous, persistent impressions and thoughts will be of its redness and will be consistent with the thought that it looks red. Moreover, the object will continue to look red, and we will continue to be preoccupied with thoughts of its redness, unless and until the two previously cited conditions change. In other words, **O**'s looking **L** to us is typically accompanied by thoughts aligned with that sensory experience.

As Alexander Bain noted long ago, perception is largely a matter of "innate credulity."[34] When something looks some way to you, you usually acquire the corresponding beliefs that it looks that way and that the object has the properties that it appears to have. In the case of picture perception, Walton asks us to abandon this assumption. He would say that the spectator's default response is to imagine that his sensory experience is of Crumb, even though (a) Crumb appears to him to be the secondary object and (b) he knows (a) to be the case. We are thereby asked to accept that the pictorial properties of the visual display prompt an idea that is contraindicated not only by reality but by the other, vivid sensory and cognitive states that Walton himself ascribes to the competent viewer.

If "imagined seeing" describes an occurrent, non-abstract, resolutely perceptual response—one that is part of the "particular nature of the visual experiences that pictures provide"—it is hard to see where it fits in relation to the rest of the spectator's perceptual repertoire.[35] It is much easier to accept that when an external scene (an image of a man in a restaurant) looks a certain way to us (like an image of a man in a restaurant), our subsequent realizations are merely about how it actually looks (we recognize that it is an image of . . .), since the coupling of sensory perceptions and perceptual beliefs tend to exclude from our focal awareness other, non-actual and non-veridical sensations of and ideas about that scene's appearance.

Transparency

As mentioned earlier, claims that movie viewers experience projective illusions can be justified with the notion of transparency, construed not as the viewer's irrational belief in the depicted object's presence but as the moving as well as still photograph's actual relation to its object. In defending his account of non-illusionistic transparency, Walton observes that "even photographic motion pictures in 'living color' are manifestly mere projections on a flat surface and are easily distinguished from 'reality.'"[36] He posits that without being at all uncertain of whether they are looking directly at images or objects themselves, viewers really do see the photographed scene by or through the media of still and moving pictures: "We *see*, quite literally, our dead relatives when we look at photographs of them."[37] Walton feels this conclusion is sound because, although manifestly indirect, one's contact with the photographed item is of the same kind as one's mediated contact with something seen through a telescope or corrective lenses or in a mirror. In all such cases, the medium purportedly maintains rather than interrupts the subject's perceptual contact with the object. Apart from distortions and enhancements due to the instrument or the way it is used, each of these visual situations shares a condition with situations in which something is seen with the naked eye.

This condition is natural counterfactual dependence. If the object were to have different visible properties, the (photographic, telescopic, optical) image would be correspondingly different, owing to the way the relevant apparatus functions under the given natural laws. Unlike the relation of the painting to its object, this sort of counterfactuality is independent of the depictor's state of mind. Once the proper lens and camera angle are chosen, Paula Abdul appears taller in her music video than she does on the set not only because the director wants her to look that way but because of how her actual visible dimensions are mechanically rendered by the recording device under the prevailing conditions. Holding fixed all the other variables, a change in Abdul's physique would produce a corresponding difference in the image. In contrast, how she is portrayed in a painting depends on the artist's beliefs about the singer's appearance and his goals regarding how he shall picture her. Without also altering the painter's intentions, a change in his subject's proportions would not automatically yield a change in the image's visible features.

Walton says that natural counterfactual dependence, although a necessary condition for perceptual discrimination, is not sufficient. The printouts of a light sensitive device capable of mechanically generating accurate verbal descriptions of visible scenes would surely not constitute transparent visual contact with the world. Perceptions, Walton notes, are also structurally analogous to the structure of reality.[38] He argues this point on the grounds that perceptual errors are likely to correspond to actual similarities between things themselves: Although the words "house" and "barn" are unlikely to be confused with one another, houses are sometimes mistaken for barns because there are real, structural homologies between these two sorts of items, homologies that are preserved by the perceptual process. Since photographs also preserve these similarity relations, they, too, count as a perceptual mode of discrimination.

Responding to Walton, Currie adopts a defensive posture. Instead of providing his own version of perceptual discrimination's necessary and sufficient conditions, he settles for offering reasons why Walton has done nothing to undermine preference for the relatively less controversial view that we perceive representations of things when we see photographs rather than the things themselves. I will refer to this position as Currie's representation thesis. It is supported by his complaint that Walton is mistaken about the conditions for perception and therefore has not established a fundamental commonality between seeing things and seeing photographically produced images of things.[39]

Currie begins his rejoinder by noting that one could be said to see something even in circumstances not usually associated with the etiology of vision. He refers to Malebranche's thesis that in the absence of natural causal connections God could mediate between our visual experiences and the scenes before our eyes, thereby benevolently maintaining counterfactual dependence. Although such a process would exhibit intentional rather than natural dependence, to "see all things in God" would nonetheless still be seeing.[40] The point of this thought experiment is that an authentically visual state could conceivably be brought about in a variety of non-standard, exotic, yet functionally equivalent ways, contrary to the teachings of causal theories of perception.[41] Stating the kind of etiological relation to something—**how** one purportedly sees something—does not settle the question of whether one is really seeing it. Thus by invoking natural counterfactual dependence Walton has isolated neither a definitive feature of seeing nor a basis on which to conclude that looking at photos is a mode of seeing the referent.

Jointly, natural counterfactual dependence and the preservation of similarity relations fair no better as grounds for transparency. Currie asks readers to consider two clocks, **A** and **B**, where the first is hidden from sight.[42] By way of radio signals, **A**'s hands mechanically govern the orientation of **B**'s hands; since its appearance would be correspondingly different were the orientation of **A**'s hands to be different from what they are at any given instant, **B** exhibits natural dependence on **A**. What's more, **B**'s visible structure is analogous to that of **A**. With clock **A**'s hands in the 08:06 position, their configuration is closely similar to what it would be were they at 08:07; **B**'s appearance preserves this similarity, along with the potential for discriminatory error concerning **A**'s hands. Although this example meets transparency's criteria, Currie finds implausible the claim that one can see "or perceive in any way" clock **A** by looking at **B**.[43] Instead, one's sole visual contact is with an object having the status of a natural representation of something that remains unseen. **B** is in this respect like a thermometer, with the added feature of an extensive overlap between the visible properties of the indicator and the indicated. Still and moving photographs have the same indicator capacity; they are natural representations that give us visual information about things without maintaining our perceptual contact with them.

Like Currie, I doubt that I could offer the definitive statement of what constitutes visual perception. And like Currie, I am partial to the position that the movie spectator's only visual contact is with pictures. Since a photographic image's properties proximally depend not just on the depictor's relevant wants, plans, and doings but also on the laws of optics and light figuring in its etiology, there is a genuine distinction to be made between a cinematic, natural representation and an intentional representation such as a painting or sketch. Yet the former's special etiological difference does not add up to what Walton means by transparency.

My previous remarks about sensory perception bear on this topic. This kind of seeing, the reader will recall, involves a relation between a percipient, **S**, and an object, **O**. Both must actually exist and they must somehow be in appropriate contact with one another. To say that a person has a sensory perception **of** something is to say that such a relationship obtains. Under this description, "seeing" is like "stepping on," as you can neither see nor step on that with which you are not in contact. The transparency thesis's weakness, then, is in its construction of what it means to be in sensory contact. It invites us to ask why looking at Brad Pitt's picture should any more mean sensory-seeing Brad Pitt than treading on his likeness should mean stepping on Brad Pitt.

Walton's thesis rests on the truism that when one sees a photographically made image, there is a complex natural causal linkage between one's internal sensory representation, a depiction, and a distal stimulus. But according to a plausible alternative model of perceptual processes, this chain does not constitute sensory contact with the pictured item. The reason the depiction, **D**, should be privileged as the sensory object proper is that the viewer's percept gives "primary representation" to it rather than to the extra-cinematic object.[44]

More precisely, **S**'s sensory state represents some of **O**'s properties only by means of representing **D**'s properties. As it pertains to **O**, the content embodied by the percept—e.g., the information that Harrison Ford is wearing a bow tie—depends on the percept's capacity to represent **D** and its properties. Information thus conveyed by the sensory representation is made available for cognitive exploitation by the competent viewer who, given the right sort of background knowledge, will recognize that Mr. Ford wears a bow tie. But presently, what is most significant about this visual situation is that the percept carrying information about **D** exhibits no dependence on **O**: It is not by representing **O** that **S**'s percept indicates the state of **D** and its visible features. Although Ford's standing in front of the camera is just as much a cause of the viewer's experience as the light reflected by the photograph, **S**'s relation to **D** is unique for the information that it carries.

One hypothesis, then, is that to sense something is to have a primary representation of it within a given sensory modality; hence the spectator's sensory contact is with no more and no less than the depiction. Here we have one nonarbitrary way of resolving the controversy over what objects movie viewers really see. The hypothesis acknowledges that there may well be important causal similarities between seeing a photo of a thing and seeing this thing in the normal way, but it also identifies significant difference in the information provided by these two visual sensations.[45]

The Representation Thesis

Much of what I have argued thus far lends credence to Currie's representation thesis. But my agreement with him is limited. In general, I have reservations about the perspicuity of the model of perception that he recommends to film studies; and in particular, although I grant that the only objects spectators sensory-see are depictions, this admission does not automatically support the idea that one does not "perceive in any way" the prephotographic referent, unless one confuses seeing objects and seeing facts.

To articulate the extent of my disagreement with Currie, I need to sketch his position in a bit more detail. He adheres to a constructivist view, according to which visual perception is to be identified with certain sub-personal processes at the middle range of the mind's systemic hierarchy.[46] Therein resides a "not very intelligent" subsystem—a "homunculus," below the level of the person, charged with tasks about which the agent need know nothing and over which he or she might have no control. Although this visual unit is described in modular terms, that is, as a set of input-driven, largely automatic mechanisms, Currie also says that it can execute ratiocinations: Seeing a horse, for instance, requires this subsystem to match visual stimuli with available stored models of known objects, since perception entails that the homunculus exercise its horse recognition capacity.

Although, as I say, Currie does not attempt to spell out his own version of the necessary and sufficient conditions for seeing something, one assumption that he does make is that vision consists of perceptual contact with that which is seen.[47] Thus bona fide perception occurs only when a person sees an **O**; and **O** is seen only when there arises in someone an internal sensory representation of it, computed by the visual homunculus, the content of which is somehow dependent on the visible features of **O** itself. The **percipient's**—the person's—attainment of any realizations about that which is seen is itself not part of the perceptual process, although Currie allows that visual experience typically causes the agent— the system of systems—to attain distinctively "perceptual beliefs," the structure and content of which display rich counterfactual dependence on **O**'s visible properties.[48]

I think a budget of problems issues from Currie's commitment to constructivism and his restriction of visual perception to seeing objects. These difficulties are the focus of ongoing philosophical and empirical investigation, and I make no claim to be offering anything on the order of solutions; at most, I should like to suggest a few reasons why the philosophically minded cinema scholar might want to consider one coherent alternative to Currie's approach.

Much of the difficulty at issue here arises from how Currie, following other researchers, attempts to specify the nature of the processes responsible for object perception. Although he wishes to associate one's visual experience of an object with a specialized subsystem's identification of that item, Currie also supposes that there are more or less "brute causal powers" involved in the detection and delivery of input for recognition.[49] This allowance for noncognitive factors ultimately begs the question of whether there is not a full-fledged visual experience, like when Wesley sees the Portuguese Water Dog, preceding any properly cognitive states and events.

Think, for instance, of Currie's assertion that "my visual capacity to recognize a horse is the capacity to associate some visual feature of what I see with the concept *horse*, thereby enabling me to bring what I see under that concept."[50] This formulation seems to imply a conceptual distinction between seeing and recognizing an object, such that the former, although devoid of the epistemic content characteristic of the latter, is no less visual a state. Then again, Currie could simply be misstating his case. Maybe he would rather maintain that detection and early casual mechanisms are pre-perceptual and nothing is really seen prior to recognition. Part of the trouble, then, is that he is unclear as to when in the sequence of visual processing perception occurs, and how thought-like or inferential perception's antecedents, especially at its lower levels, need be. Like Jerry Fodor, Currie might be inclined toward describing the whole perceptual process, starting from its extreme sensory periphery, in terms of an intelligent operation entailing the coding of data in the form of hypotheses that must be tested before the stimulus is identified.[51] If so, there would be no distinctively noncognitive stage of seeing the horse prior to bringing the input under the appropriate concept.

But if seeing the horse depends on recognizing it, who or what does the recognizing? This is really a question about when it is that the incoming signal becomes meaningful to some part of the system. Although I do not know which components he has in mind, Currie supposes that there are "ground floor" visual mechanisms that respond as they do because of straightforward causal interactions governed by natural laws.[52] He might therefore agree that the signal having the meaning it does—its being about a chestnut mare—is not what triggers, say, photosensitive rods and cones and subsequently the ganglion cells. Instead, it is the physical properties of the signal that activate these components—just as it is physical and not semantic relations, how she sings and not what is sung, that explain why a soprano's vocalizations can shatter glass. Yet Currie's story is that somewhere along the line, prior to one seeing the horse, there is a homunculus who must sort through the information carried to it by the external receptor. Although no rocket scientist, the manikin has a flair for understanding the visual input's content, that is, what it indicates about how things stand in the world, and for noticing when it is like some other thing such as the stored model of a horse's visible features.

It is hard to say how committed Currie is to the literal truth of the view of visual processing as a thinking subsystem able to recognize, infer, and match. Perhaps he is merely adopting an intentional stance as a metaphorical description of obscure sub-intentional, neurosensory conditions. Such a ratiomorphism is what Daniel Dennett calls a "black box theory," equivalent to saying that the signal goes in one end, then the brain processes that data, and then you see a horse.[53] In any case, I have no idea whether anything like homunculi, to whom it is appropriate to ascribe intentional attitudes, exist in the head with the function of finding for us the meaning of things.

From a philosophical perspective, it is surely not uncontroversial to try to explain agent rationality with reference to hypothetical sub-agential cognitive centers that mimic feats of rationality—such as acquiring knowledge by perceptual means, which is exactly what the visual micromorph does—that have yet to be explained in the first place. Within a folk metapsychology, it is relatively more tenable to maintain, as I do, that **we** are currently the best candidates for the kinds of creatures who identify, categorize, and find meaning in things, including the information delivered to us by our sensory components.

There is another problem I am eager to avoid. Being a quick and dirty operator, the visual homunculus, says Currie, might not discriminate between pictures of horses and horses themselves. Citing two reasons, he calls this errancy "illusionism we can live with."[54] On the one hand, it supposedly attests to that which makes cinematic and photographic depiction realistic: Because it is by way of likeness or resemblance, instead of convention and codedness, that images represent their depicta, the recognition of depicted objects and the recognition of objects themselves are basically similar operations. On the other hand, any illusion at the level of the visual module is corrigible further up the hierarchy: Taking into account experience, memory, other sources of evidence, and context, the person judges that he is looking at an image representing a horse rather than that he is looking at a horse.

In reply, if the cost of your theory of cinematic realism is illusionism at any level of perception, you might be paying too much. The cheaper but nonetheless high quality alternative is set apart by a theory of perception that is realist all the way down. What we have been calling the sensory representation or percept is an internal representational state standing in some sort of causally efficient relationship to an actual object. Although there is surely some loss of information between the stimulus and the detector mechanisms, this state might preserve enough information about the visible properties of a (still or moving) horse picture to specify it as just that, a **picture** of a **horse**. The percept is not fooled by anything—does not confuse horses and donkeys, depictions with depicta—because it is a fundamentally non-epistemic stage of the total visual process. It simply represents whatever is out there to be represented.

Note that a strong theory of perceptual realism would hold that although such factors as the sensory representation's physical properties condition how things look to us, it is not because we (or our visual homunculi) perceive this internal representation that we see the object. Instead we see the horse (picture) by internally representing the horse (picture).[55] Thus the percept is that stage in the perceptual process at which the agent consults the world, rather than a representation of the world that has been constructed by a visual system or subsystem in a quasi-rational process of inference and recognition.

Cognitive seeing occurs when the individual exploits this percept's content, thereby recognizing objects and events, noticing states of affairs, seeing that such and such is the case. So understood, cognitive seeing is the agent's normal response to having a sensory experience, one that is contingent on the coupling of cognitive and sensory structures and on the content of the agent's cognitive repertoire.

What sort of mental event is it to see a fact, for example, that there is a movie picture of a horse on the screen? Currie contends that judging a given item to be a depiction of a horse is something that the agent does.[56] However, he leaves open the question of what route lies between seeing the object and judging it to be an image. Ordinary visual situations like looking at photographs, watching television, and viewing movies projected onto the big screen do not, as far as I can tell, compel us to undertake conscious, deliberate mental acts of deciding whether we are gazing at a depiction or the depictum itself. On the contrary, we simply see that there is a still or moving picture of a horse before us, no intervening act of judgment being necessary. In agents endowed with the appropriate background and not faced with any competing, contrary information, occurrent sensory perceptions lead, as if by default, to the realization that **D** is a picture of a horse. Cognitive perception is typically a passive mode of acquiring beliefs and knowledge, the automatic and often veridical epistemic upshot of visual contact with some object. As C. S. Peirce remarks, perceptual judgments, if not infallible, are at least involuntary.[57]

In the final analysis, the trouble with Currie's version of the spectator's visual experience is that it takes into account only one dimension of perceptual achievement. In spite of his intentional stance and his talk of computational homunculi, he privileges seeing objects, that is, unmediated visual contact between the percipient and an external object, over seeing facts. This restriction forms the basis of his representation thesis. Granted, sensory seeing is a fundamental stage of visual perception. Yet from a functional perspective, that is not all there is to perception. Rather, perception is a mode of recognition—a process by which a highly integrated cognitive system, namely the agent, selectively (it could not possibly take it **all** in!) extracts and classifies information made available to it by an incoming signal as embodied by the sensory representation. The percept is itself a-rational, since it neither requires, embodies, nor necessarily triggers judgments about the object. The output or terminus of visual processing is the acquisition of beliefs and knowledge, the percipient's coming to certain realizations.

Those still unconvinced of my model of seeing and its application to cinema studies might be particularly critical of the idea of secondary cognitive seeing, that is, seeing by the depiction that such and such is or was the case in pre-filmic reality. An opponent could complain that you do not see that **P** by seeing the cinematic image. You simply infer that **P** from seeing the picture. Genuinely to see that something is the case is exclusively a matter of seeing the object that constitutes the state of affairs that is the content of your perception. Thus nothing "secondary" to the image itself—people, places, objects, actions, events, and so on—can be seen.

Opposition to secondary perception would likely be predicated on objections to the idea of cognitive perception in general and to the adherence to a claim to the effect that seeing proper is to be equated with the sensory representation of objects. Like primary cognitive perception, secondary cognitive perception provides an answer to the question "How does the agent know that something or other is the case?" that is distinctively visual. The only difference between the two modalities is that the latter exploits a sensory relation to a certain object in gaining perceptual access to something not itself sensed.

It is the way other things—the image and its properties—look to the viewer that allow him to see that Audrey Hepburn once stood outside a display window at Tiffany and Company in New York. What makes this exploitation possible is the viewer's possession of an extensive set of background beliefs regarding underlying conditions. Some of this knowledge pertains to natural, law-like regularities: The cinematographic depiction would not look the way it does if the actress had not stood, just as she did, in front of Tiffany's window. Other background information will pertain to the identity of the actor, the location, and the visually discernible objects—information without which it would be impossible to recognize Hepburn and notice that she is wearing a black Givenchy evening dress and dark glasses, holding a croissant and a paper cup, and standing outside Tiffany's. Believing the underlying conditions to be as described, the spectator is able to see by the depiction that some things were once the case in extra-cinematic reality and, subsequently, that such and such is the case in the fictional story of the character Holly Golightly.

Another big objection would be that the visual specificity of secondary seeing is canceled by the role of inference. I think this charge is groundless. Secondary, like primary, cognitive perception involves the generation of cognitions and beliefs about objects and situations by visual means. The processes by which these judgments are acquired may well be, at some level of description, reasoning-like or computational. But cognitive perception in general, and secondary seeing in particular, need not involve any conscious intellectual procedures of forming judgments on the basis of visual evidence. Seeing that the cat is on the sofa, seeing by the gauge that the gas tank is empty, and so on do not entail acts, however swift, of deliberation or justification. On the contrary, they short-circuit inferential exercises and discursive processes that might otherwise stand between seeing and knowing.[58]

Hence the sensory state's informative properties might straightaway cause a suitably constituted viewer to recognize a depiction of Hepburn and to see by the image that she had stood before Tiffany's. Maybe a good rule of thumb is that where the boundary between cognitive perception and epistemic achievements in general is vague, "seeing that" and "seeing by" locutions fail to denote distinctly visual accomplishments to the degree that conscious inferential processes intervene between seeing O and coming to any realizations about O or a situation systematically related to it.

Notes

1. Fred Dretske, "Meaningful Perception," in *Visual Cognition*, 2d ed., ed. Daniel N. Osherson and Stephen M. Kosslyn (Cambridge, Mass.: M.I.T. Press, 1995), 331–352; "The Percept in Visual Cognition," in *Minnesota Studies in the Philosophy of Science IX: Perception and Cognition: Issues in the Foundations of Psychology*, ed. C. Wade Savage (Minneapolis: University of Minnesota Press, 1978), 107–127; *Seeing and Knowing* (London: Routledge and Kegan Paul, 1969). Some of the conceptual roots of Dretske's distinction between seeing objects and seeing facts can be traced to G. J. Warnock, "Seeing," *Aristotelian Society Proceedings* 55 (1955): 201–218. See also Frank N. Sibley, "Analyzing Seeing (I)," in *Perception*, ed. Frank N. Sibley (London: Methuen, 1971), 81–132.

2. Say that the currently accepted, or any future new and improved, description of the causal sequence associated with seeing an object turns out to be false; or that it does not begin to explain how creatures on other planets see; or say that we discover a person demonstrably able to see things on the other side of a concrete wall, without the light reflected by those things reaching his eyes by any means. Because it is not a causal theory of perception—it does not propose to define what seeing is in terms of a given causal sequence A-B-C—Dretske's concept

of sensory perception would be no less descriptive of one kind of visual feat, even if the causal processes giving rise to it are unknown or obscure to us. The point he wishes to make, and the one I want to reiterate, is that a perfectly ordinary usage of the verb "to see" is constrained by two conditions. Although one could desire a unicorn without there being any unicorns, one cannot see a nonexistent unicorn any more than one can ride on a nonexistent unicorn. So seeing is in the first place a relational state between a viewer and an actually existing object. And second, the visual object must look some way to the percipient, without that person necessarily having any associated beliefs.

3. Dretske, *Seeing and Knowing*, 17.

4. For the constructivist account of perception, consult Richard L. Gregory, *Eye and Brain: The Psychology of Seeing*, 3d ed. (New York: McGraw-Hill, 1978); Jerry Fodor and Zenon Pylyshyn, "How Direct Is Direct Perception?: Some Reflections on Gibson's 'Ecological Approach,'" *Cognition* 9 (1981): 139–196; David Marr, *Vision: A Computational Investigation Into the Human Representation and Processing of Visual Information* (San Francisco: W. H. Freeman, 1982); Irvin Rock, *The Logic of Perception* (Cambridge, Mass.: M.I.T. Press, 1983).

5. See J. J. Gibson, *The Ecological Approach to Visual Perception* (Boston: Houghton Mifflin, 1979).

6. Dretske, "The Role of the Percept in Visual Cognition," 114.

7. Against David Bordwell's reluctance, in *Narration in the Fiction Film* (Madison: University of Wisconsin Press, 1985), 30–31, to assume an identity between cognitive and linguistic structures, John Champagne doubts that one can easily "imagine cognition outside of language." He goes on to imply the implausibility of Bordwell's claims by posing a number of rhetorical questions: "Bordwell's analysis thus requires us to posit the drawing of inferences, the testing of hypotheses, and the reckoning in probabilities as nonverbal activities. Even if we could think this as a possibility, how might it work in actuality? How does a brain rid itself of language in the act of cognition. How might one even demonstrate Bordwell's proposition that cognition is nonverbal?" Champagne is, of course, right to ask for the details and substantive hypotheses indeed lacking from his nemesis's discussion; and no one denies that the question of how mental states represent and have meaning is a tough one, the best available answers to which are for now very tentative and underdetermined by empirical evidence. But one gets the impression that Champagne has not in fact tried to find out what the best currently available rival hypotheses are, which problems they share, which premises they have in common, and how they differ.

He has not, for instance, considered a question that frames investigation on both sides, namely, the question of whether mental representations and operations may not be instantiated as operations on linguistic propositions all the way down, from the "higher" levels of consciousness (what I'm thinking to myself right now as I write) to the lower levels (how linguistic structures and relations between them are ultimately executed, represented, and stored within my brain's neural networks). Champagne's remarks are found in "'Stop Reading Films!' Film Studies, Close Analysis, and Gay Pornography," *Cinema Journal* 36 (1997): 95.

8. A good introduction to some of the ideas covered in this paragraph can be found in Colin McGinn, *The Character of Mind: An Introduction to the Philosophy of*

Mind, 2d ed. (Oxford: Oxford University Press, 1997), 82–106. See Jerry Fodor, *The Language of Thought* (New York: Crowell, 1975) and P. N. Johnson-Laird, *Mental Models: Towards a Cognitive Science of Language, Inference, and Consciousness* (Cambridge, Mass.: Harvard University Press, 1983) for more technical and detailed arguments for and against privileging a language of thought model of the mind.

9. Dretske, "Seeing, Believing, and Knowing," 133.

10. Robert Flaherty, "How I Filmed *Nanook of the North*," in *Film Makers on Film Making: Statements on Their Art By Thirty Directors*, ed. Harry M. Geduld (Bloomington: Indiana University Press, 1969), 60.

11. Robert Flaherty and Frances Hubbard Flaherty, *My Eskimo Friends* (Garden City, N.J.: Doubleday and Page, 1924), 135–136.

12. For a sample of the positions in the debates over the conventionality of pictorial representations, see E. H. Gombrich, *Art and Illusion* (London: Phaidon, 1960); Nelson Goodman, *Languages of Art* (Indianapolis: Bobbs-Merrill, 1968); Richard Wollheim, *Art and Its Objects* (New York: Harper, 1971); Kent Bach, "Part of What a Picture Is," *British Journal of Aesthetics* 10 (1970): 119–137; J. J. Gibson, "The Information Available in Pictures," *Leondardo* 4 (1971): 27–35; Max Black, "How Do Pictures Represent?" in *Art, Perception, and Reality*, eds. E. H. Gombrich, Julian Hochberg, and Max Black (Baltimore: Johns Hopkins University Press, 1971), 95–129; Göran Hermerén, *Aspects of Aesthetics* (Lund: LiberFörlag, 1983); David Novitz, *Pictures and Their Use in Communication* (The Hague: N. Nijhoff, 1977); Gregory Currie, "The Long Goodbye: The Imaginary Language of Film," *British Journal of Aesthetics* 33 (1993): 207–219.

13. In fact, you can, if desired, entertain a version of this thought experiment in which the subject is molecule for molecule organically identical to yourself, although not psychologically identical to you.

14. Frequently this point is made by saying that, as the quasi-mechanical effect of gazing at the cinematic image, the percipient implements a "naturalized" mode of perception, attending strictly to what such images represent, having forgotten or suppressed the fact of looking at a highly "coded" or conventionalized representation made according to techniques that conceal the social as well as technological conditions of production. See Bill Nichols, *Ideology and the Image* (Bloomington: Indiana University Press, 1981) and John Ellis, *Visible Fictions* (London: Routledge and Kegan Paul, 1982). Both are adherents to the notion that, owing to the operation of various psychic mechanisms, spectators overlook the fact that they are looking at constructed representations. False ideas about the nature of both the perceptual experience and the object portrayed are triggered insofar as the perceiver fails to bear in mind that what he or she is looking at is only a picture.

These theorists, like many others, argue that there is a corresponding ideological dimension to this naturalization effect. Along with the impression of the cinematic image's transparency, viewers accept as self-evident and necessarily true an array of highly normative and politically motivated messages. Indeed, the means of delivering these messages—widespread practices of cinematography, editing, narration; the use of linear perspective; and so on—are themselves labeled as being in the service of ideology in as much as they allegedly foment the impression that the representation is authorless and results from no particular class, gender, or race specific interests. Readers seeking a careful and thoroughgoing critique of these allegations should refer to Noël Carroll's *Mystifying Movies: Fads and Fallacies in Contemporary Film Theory* (New York: Columbia University Press, 1988). Although maintaining that the content and rhetoric of some movies may well promote the communication of contentious falsehoods that would, if adopted as beliefs, tend to obscure important social, economic, and political facts, Carroll denies both that the cinematic apparatus is essentially ideological and that films are a uniquely effective means of disseminating ideology.

15. Richard Allen, *Projecting Illusion: Film Spectatorship and the Impression of Reality* (New York: Cambridge University Press, 1995).

16. Ibid., 100.

17. Ibid., 99–100.

18. Ibid., 101–102.

19. Ibid., 139.

20. Ibid., 88.

21. Ibid., 86, 112. Allen's authorities on this matter are Kendall Walton, "Transparent Pictures: On the Nature of Photographic Realism," *Critical Inquiry* 11 (1984): 246–277 and Roger Scruton, *The Aesthetic Understanding* (New York: Methuen, 1983).

22. Allen, *Projecting Illusion*, 122, 136.

23. For a comprehensive discussion of the causes and conditions favoring the emergence of various types of optical and geometrical illusions, consult J. O. Robinson's *The Psychology of Visual Illusion* (London: Hutchinson University Library, 1972).

24. Presumably Allen would not opt for the alternative defensive move, suggested by his reference to the spectator of George Romero's *Night of the Living Dead* (1968) as imagining that he or she perceives a world inhabited by zombies (107); that is, he could fall back to the position that, prompted by the vivid, lifelike qualities of the cinematic representation, spectators actively imagine themselves in direct visual contact with the pictured items and events, without those depicta actually looking to the spectator as if they are present. Since there is no question here of "sensory deception," this revision takes the illusion out of PI and effectively reduces Allen's argument to a variation on Kendall Walton's claim that audiences, without experiencing any sort of illusion, sometimes imagine seeing that which movies depict. See Walton's *Mimesis As Make-Believe: On the Foundations of the Representational Arts* (Cambridge, Mass: Harvard University Press, 1990), 345. His "fictional seeing" receives support from Jerrold Levinson, "Seeing, Imaginarily, At the Movies," *The Philosophical Quarterly* 43 (1993): 70–78. I offer my criticisms of this thesis in the pages below.

25. Allen, *Projecting Illusion*, 89.

26. Ibid., 107.

27. A useful discussion of duplex theories of memory, and their pertinence to philosophical inquiry into agency, rationality, and psychology, can be found in Christopher Cherniak's *Minimal Rationality* (Cambridge, Mass: M.I.T. Press, 1986), 52–55.

28. Allen, *Projecting Illusion*, 115–118.

29. Walton, *Mimesis As Make-Believes*; and "On Pictures and Photographs: Objections Answered," in *Film Theory and Philosophy*, ed. Richard Allen and Murray

Smith (Oxford: Oxford University Press, 1997), 60–75. An early version of his thesis can be found in his "Pictures and Make-Believe," *Philosophical Review* 82 (1973): 283–319. See also the supportive arguments in Levinson, "Seeing, Imaginarily, At the Movies." George Wilson, *Narration in Light: Studies in Cinematic Point of View* (Baltimore: Johns Hopkins University Press, 1986), 55–56, urges a conclusion similar to Walton's when he states, "The spectator *knows* that he is in the theater, but *it is make-believe for him* that he is watching from within the space of the story." Note that Walton endeavors to account for viewers' responses to all pictorial representations, photographic and other. I will be referring only to the experience of photographically generated pictures—although I hope that my observations, too, could eventually be applied to any other pictorial medium.

30. Walton, "On Pictures and Photographs: Objections Answered," 61.

31. Gregory Currie, "Visual Fictions," *The Philosophical Quarterly* 41 (1991): 127–143, has complained that imagined seeing would regularly require spectators to hold bizarre and dissonant thoughts. Here are some examples, based on his objections. Watching *2001: A Space Odyssey* would induce us to imagine being in the vacuum of space for much of the film. The close-up of Crumb entails thinking of one's self as hovering with one's nose virtually in Crumb's ear; a sudden shift in camera perspective to a long shot of the subject as seen from the opposite side of the restaurant would require just as sudden a jump in our imagined position; some movies (including music videos) demand dozens of such shifts in our orientation during less than a minute. In some narrative fictions, it is explicitly part of the story that nobody is present to witness an event, in which case the audience would be called upon to entertain the contradictory thoughts that they are seeing the unseen murderer. Walton's response to these kinds of objectionable examples are satisfying enough to dissuade me from pursuing complaints similar to those of Currie.

In imagining seeing **O**, one just imagines having the visual experience of directly seeing **O** from the stipulated perspective, without imagining being at the apparent spatial-temporal position of the camera at the moment of recording. And when there are transitions between shots or points of view, one need not imagine any of the transitions' implications. The spectator just imagines the one visual experience and then the next, without entertaining the thought of being transported between locations. In the event of an unseen killer, Walton proposes that it need not entail the viewer's imagining the contradictory conjunction **P** (I see the villain) and **-P** (the villain is unseen). Here he appeals to a distinction between what is true of the spectator's pictorial experience and what is true in the fiction. Hence the movie induces people to imagine seeing the killer as a way of indicating to them that the killer is unobserved by the characters in the fiction. See "On Pictures and Photographs: Objections Answered," 64–65. Although I cannot elaborate on this point at present, I do accept Currie's argument, also in "Visual Fictions," that it is not normally part of the movie's propositional fiction—that is, true in the story—that the audience directly sees the narrated events, as if they were standing slightly behind the camera.

32. Walton, "Transparent Pictures: On the Nature of Photographic Realism," 254.

33. Christopher Peacocke, "Depiction," *Philosophical Review* 96 (1987): 391–392.

34. Alexander Bain, *The Emotions and the Will*, 3d ed. (London: Longmans and Green, 1875), 511. Bain adds that we are not the dupes of our senses, insofar as it is also within our abilities to doubt and reflect upon their veracity and to compensate for their inaccuracies.

35. Walton, "On Pictures and Photographs: Objections Answered," 61.

36. Walton, "Transparent Pictures: On the Nature of Photographic Realism," 249. See also his defense of transparency in "On Pictures and Photographs: Objections Answered," 67—72.

37. Walton, "Transparent Pictures," 252.

38. Ibid., 270–272.

39. Gregory Currie, "Photography, Painting, and Perception," *Journal of Aesthetics and Art Criticism* 49 (1991): 23–29. See also his *Image and Mind: Film, Philosophy, and Cognitive Science* (Cambridge: Cambridge University Press, 1995), 52–78.

40. Currie, "Photography, Painting, and Perception," 25. David Lewis provides a number of intriguing, and occasionally macabre, variations on Malebranchean seeing; see his "Veridical Hallucinations and Prosthetic Vision," *Philosophical Papers*, 2 vols. (New York: Oxford University Press, 1983—1986), 2:273–286.

41. An influential philosophical exposition of the causal definition is H. P. Grice's "The Causal Theory of Perception," *Proceedings of the Aristotelian Society*, supplementary vol. 35 (1961): 121–152.

42. Currie, "Photography, Painting, and Perception," 27.

43. Ibid., 26.

44. Here I follow Fred Dretske's analysis of the nature of perceptual objects in *Knowledge and the Flow of Information* (Oxford: Basil Blackwell, 1981), 153–161.

45. When looking at a mirror reflection, or at an object through a window or binoculars, you see—i.e., are in sensory contact with—the reflected object or the thing on the other side of the window or lens. Although the properties of the optical device in each of these cases causally contribute to your seeing **O**, your sensory state's capacity to carry information about that object does not depend upon the state's representing information about the properties of the intermediary itself. Unless you want to look at the mirror, glass pane, or lens, you need not represent those objects to see something else. Hence these media, unlike photographs, are transparent.

46. Currie, *Image and Mind*, 80–88, 182–185. For background on the hierarchical, modular nature of mind, one might consult Daniel Dennett, *Brainstorms: Philosophical Essays on Mind and Psychology* (Montgomery, Vt.: Bradford, 1978); Fodor, *The Language of Thought* and "Précis of *The Modularity of Mind*," *Behavioral and Brain Sciences* 8 (1985): 1–42; John Haugeland, "The Nature and Plausibility of Cognitivism," *Behavioral and Brain Sciences* 2 (1978): 215–260; William G. Lycan, "Form, Function, and Feel," *Journal of Philosophy* 78 (1981): 24–50; Zenon Pylyshyn, "Computation and Cognition: Issues in the Foundations of Cognitive Science," *Behavioral and Brain Sciences* 3 (1980): 111–132. Currie owes his constructivist model of visual perception to Marr.

47. Currie, *Image and Mind*, 71.

48. Ibid., 182–183.

49. Ibid., 84.

50. Ibid., 81.

51. See Fodor's *The Language of Thought* for a defense of this degree of computationalism.

52. Currie, *Image and Mind*, 84.

53. Daniel Dennett, *The Intentional Stance* (Cambridge, Mass.: M.I.T. Press, 1989), 74.

54. Currie, *Image and Mind*, 86.

55. On the theory of direct realism, see Dretske, "Meaningful Perception," 338–340; Alvin Goldman, "Perceptual Objects," *Synthese* 35 (1977) 257–284; and Roger Chisholm, *Perceiving: A Philosophical Study* (Ithaca: Cornell University Press, 1957). For accounts of the rival indirect or representative realist camp, which holds that our perceptions are mediated by awareness of mental representations, consult Frank Jackson, *Perception* (Cambridge: Cambridge University Press, 1977) and Moreland Perkins, *Sensing the World* (Indianapolis: Hackett, 1983).

56. Currie, *Image and Mind*, 84–85.

57. Charles Sanders Peirce, *Collected Papers of Charles Sanders Peirce*, 8 vols., ed. Charles Hartshorne, Paul Weiss, and A. W. Burks (Cambridge, Mass.: Harvard University Press, 1931–1958), 5:115.

58. Dretske, *Seeing and Knowing*, 120–122, 158–160; see also *Knowledge and the Flow of Information*, 91.

8

Aspects of Interpretation

I have been unfolding a thesis about the nature of motion picture non-fictions: Many such productions can be accurately categorized as cinematic constatives. More specifically, most non-fictions are representational systems, made to discharge a certain type of communicative function. This sort of thing is an artifact, that is, an object made by someone in order to serve one or more determinate purposes. The actions involved in creating the movie produce a material structure having certain intrinsic physical properties adapted to perform certain functions. Most importantly, in making this structure, the producers, acting on diverse communicative and expressive intentions, take steps to exploit that structure's representational capacities. Unlike other artifacts, a cinematic work is devised and used to fulfill indicator functions. It is constructed with a special goal in mind, so that people attending to one or another of its states can learn the condition of something external to the movie itself. What it indicates ultimately depends not upon the structure of its intrinsic physical properties, nor upon its formal properties, but upon relations imposed during the production phase(s) between its representational elements—images, sounds, and sequences thereof—and extra-cinematic objects and states of affairs. Some of these indicator relations consist of natural or nomic dependencies, whereas others are subject to intentional constraints like the author's plans with respect to force and content. Meaning inheres in these systematic relations, which exist independently of the work's reception.

My central claim implies a corresponding thesis about interpretation. Though elementary and perhaps self-evident, its inner workings must now be made explicit. The core of this thesis is that an important and ordinary class of interpretive activities aim toward discovering the aforementioned objective meanings of the kind of work just described. Interpretative action, in the current sense, is a standard component of human symbolic interaction. Among other enabling conditions, it is supported by mutual contextual beliefs structuring the situations in which linguistic, cinematic, and other symbolic artifacts are created and received. Authors expect their audiences to engage in this kind of action and make their works accordingly; audiences anticipate that authors will direct their efforts toward making meaning accessible to interpretive action and in turn infer and deliberate according to this expectation. A modest amount of such coordination is the hallmark of communication.

There can be no doubt that producers sometimes fail to make their communicative intentions clear or accessible to their audience; in certain instances, this failure is part of the producer's deliberate suspension of communicative assumptions, a deviation that itself is meant to be intelligible to an audience of cognoscenti. Nor can there be any doubt that spectators are not always or only concerned with apprehending the work's objective meanings; sometimes they become absorbed in their own or other viewers' reactions to it, with little regard either to that which someone intended to communicate or to what this or that feature of the work necessarily indicates. However, such limit cases undermine neither the prevalence nor tenability within any given social group of commitment to specifically communicative interests. Nor do they rule out the occurrence of communication per se.

The foregoing remarks bring us to this default assumption about the nature of cinematic constatives. An audience's encounter with that sort of work is normally constrained by a presumption to the effect that it was made with recognizable communicative intentions and designed to have mental as well as external significance. It is therefore plausibly argued that one kind of interpretive response is to learn, or try to learn, what objects, situations, and events it is the work's function to describe and what attitudes are being expressed towards this content. Generally speaking, this reaction mobilizes a wide range of the agent's perceptual and cognitive abilities and involves inferring authorial intentions and plans that shaped the representational system prior to its reception, as well as the natural constraints on its emergence. In effect, the interpretive response serves to answer three sorts of questions—although for present purposes we need not assume either that viewers always focally and deliberately set out to answer these or that all non-fictions are erotetic narratives.[1]

One question concerns the representation's force. Another question pertains to that which is true in the non-fiction. Once we identify something as a cinematic constative, we usually care to find out what it is that is being asserted, who is asserting it, and whether or not they sincerely hold the beliefs that they are expressing. Also, asserting that **P** usually implies that there is reason to believe that **P** is the case. Hence it is often appropriate for us to attend not only to the issue of whether it is true that so and so (sincerely) asserts such and such but also to whether the assertion that **P** is more or less accurate, when understood to be about some actual, extra-cinematic situation. A third question thus bears upon ascertaining the truth of the non-fiction—the topic of my final chapter.

So, an interpretation is a belief or beliefs about what a representational artifact means. Interpretation is the generation of beliefs and hypotheses about what is true in the non-fiction and about what is true of the condition of some portion of the extra-cinematic world, in light of the facts we learn about the condition of the non-fiction. Belief acquisition and formation are guided by perceptual acumen, reasoning about intentions, and other, sometimes more context-specific, principles of reasoning and inquiry. As I construe it, an interpretive response to a work is a personal response; it is an act of judgment that an individual performs in and through learning about the meaningful properties of a certain kind of object and is not the result of merely learning someone else's response.

The content of an interpretive response, or of a statement reporting it, is to be understood quite liberally. It includes both descriptive and explanatory statements; statements about explicit or implicit features, obvious or nonobvious (relative to a given observer) properties. "*Titicut Follies* depicts inmates of the Bridgewater Hospital for the criminally insane" can be an interpretive statement. "*JFK* is non-fiction because its makers subordinate fiction-making intentions to a constative plan" is one, too, as is the proposition, "The finale of Fellini's *I Clowns* symbolically resurrects the tradition of clowning by the power of the director's artistic fantasy." What all of these statements share, as interpretations, is their articulation of judgments regarding aspects of some representational system's mental or external significance.

Arguably, there are many kinds of interpretive practices, many kinds of interpretations, and many intelligent opinions about what constitutes a good or valid interpretation. Physicists interpret the behavior of subatomic particles under experimental conditions; geologists interpret rock formations; radiologists, X rays; psychoanalysts, dreams; anthropologists, rituals; judges, laws and statutes; literary critics, novels. Although the practices of these groups may admit of commonalities and shared foundations, they also admit of some obvious differences. Indeed, it seems that a cogent, uncontroversial statement of the necessary and sufficient conditions for saying of a statement that it is an interpretation has yet to be publicized.[2]

Perhaps there are several kinds of interpretation and which one you pursue depends on your expressive, communicative, cognitive, aesthetic, or other motivations and their relative importance. Maybe this plurality exists even **within** given fields, such as those of the humanistic study and criticism of literature, cinema, theater, painting, and so on. For example, some interpretation could largely consist of a type of creative engagement, aiming toward a certain kind of understanding of the work, the condition for which is not only or mainly a matter of getting the facts right about the author's intentions or the history of the work's production but of trying to express one's own responses to the work or else "render the work coherent in a way that promotes appreciation."[3] In other words, we could equate some modes of interpretation with imaginative rather than confirmative activity, whereby the having of a satisfying experience of a work can be served by, say, an extremely anachronistic reading or the ascription of meanings unintended by the author and unsupported by the text.[4]

Pluralism should not stop us from presuming that one ordinary, defensible, and useful idea of interpretation refers to people's engagements with artificial representational systems, of the sort that have two special kinds of mental and external significance: force and interpretation*. The **activity** of interpretation is the detection of those two features, insofar as it is possible by means of reasoning and perception. But here we must stress that this sort of interpretation cannot be radically dissociated from other kinds. Documentaries are in one way like rock formations and X rays—they have natural meanings, access to which depends upon knowledge of nomic and necessary constraints. What's more, interpreting non-fictions, in the current sense of "interpreting," often depends upon, or conduces to, other types of interpretive practices. Given a broad notion of interpretation as analysis and explanation, a social psychologist viewing Milgram's *Obedience* (1965) is likely to mobilize a number of specialized interpretive practices—topic-specific background knowledge and methodological principles—in order to describe and explain the actual pre-filmic situations represented by this work and to evaluate the truth of Milgram's assertions about these situations.

Finally, the content of one's interpretive responses can sometimes be epistemically justified. Actually, this thesis extends to the verification, by the work's interpreter(s), of three kinds of beliefs: beliefs about what is true in the non-fiction; beliefs that are expressed in the non-fiction film, by the author, an interview subject, or any other character; and beliefs about extra-cinematic reality that viewers acquire in the course of spectatorship. This thesis puts me squarely within the epistemic realist camp. Although the overall satisfactoriness of any theory of non-fiction hinges, I think, on abandoning dogmatic skepticism, I do not undertake a proper philosophical defense of epistemic realism; nor do I survey either the arguments for realism or those on behalf of realists' anti-realist opponents. For overviews of the difficult problems facing contemporary, post-positivist realists as well as their critics, I refer readers to recent exemplary works of epistemology.[5]

However, throughout the discussions in this chapter and the next, I do try to outline how epistemic justification, for spectators, might proceed. In doing so, I take a fallibilist approach. Justification, on this conception, is not absolute, mind-independent, or ahistorical. Instead, it is gradational, that is, one may be more or less justified in believing something to be the case; it is also personal, insofar as the justifiability of one agent believing in a proposition's truth may reasonably differ from that of another agent and depends upon the information and evidence available to each agent at a given moment. And how justified one is in believing that **P** may change with the addition of new evidence.

I also subscribe to a concept of justification having both internalist and coherentist aspects. Internalism is the idea that the subjective contents of one's sensory states can provide direct evidence for one's belief; perceptual experience thus provides a partial foundation for empirical justification unanchored in any further beliefs. From coherentism comes the notion that beliefs sometimes receive pervasive, noncircular mutual support from one another.

This kind of justification strategy has recently been proposed by Susan Haack, who likens justification to the filling in of a crossword puzzle, where there is pervasive mutual support without viscous circularity. Some entries, the analogues of beliefs, overlap at multiple points, and their intersection makes it reasonable to regard them as support each for the other. Clues are the analogues of perceptual-experiential evidence, which lend a degree of support to each entry independent of that entry's relation to any other already completed intersecting entries. Like a crossword entry, the epistemic justifiability of a belief thus depends on how well it fits with available evidence that is not itself wholly and regressively anchored in concepts and beliefs, as well as on how well it fits the comprehensiveness and coherence of one's background beliefs and on how reasonable those other beliefs are independently of the belief in question.

First Principles of Documentary Interpretation

Notice that "interpretation," as I use the word, is not defined with respect to some set of specialized inferential procedures and cognitive processes specific or unique to the comprehension of motion pictures in general, and documentaries in particular. Instead, interpretation is identified with a certain objective: grasping the force and (natural) interpretations* of (cinematic) representational systems. The kind of interpretive achievement that interests me is largely the outcome of our deployment of basic inferential and perceptual skills not essentially different from those we normally rely upon in non-cinematic contexts when explaining people's actions and extracting knowledge of the world from visual experiences. Moreover, if I were doing a study of movie fictions, I would say that the pertinent sort of interpretive success depends upon these same skills.

In a simplified account of interpretation like my own, the objective is to explain how it is that people's beliefs about a work's significance might coincide with some of that artifact's objective meanings. We know from everyday experience that this convergence is a calculated, frequent occurrence; the onus is on those skeptical of this framework assumption to prove that it is more likely right for us to think that people are not generally interested in communication or are mostly unable to converge on the communicator's meaning.

It is no fluke that your request for the pepper mill results in your dining partner's pepper mill passing behavior. Nor was the change in your behavior an accident the last time you confidently avoided the freeway because you saw and heard a television report about a traffic jam on that route. In standard cases of communication, the way audiences think about a given message or representation is systematically and appropriately adapted to how that item was made. Upstream of their encounter with a communicative artifact are certain constraints on how it is produced—dependencies that establish meaningful relations between the condition of some of its properties and how things stand with respect to select extra-representational situations. Downstream of the artifact's emergence are audiences' intelligent responses to it—many of which are guided or constrained by knowledge and assumptions about how the artifact came to have just the properties that it (apparently) has. The constraints on interpretation thus reflect suppositions about the proximal determinants directly involved in the work's production.

Describing the interpretive process is, from the current perspective, primarily a matter of describing the appropriate constraints bearing on the spectator's judgments. To this end, I posit three sorts of conceptual tools—the rationality heuristic, real author intentionalism, and a bundle of perceptual truisms—that play privileged roles in guiding the agent towards a successful uptake of the communicative act. For researcher and spectator alike, these are serious candidates for the label of "first principles." Abandoning these conceptual tools, unlike abandoning beliefs concerning, say, the role of conventions in guiding the viewer's reception of a work as a documentary, would literally leave spectators without an alternative way of discovering the cinematic constative's force and content; such abandonment also would leave scholars without a way of explaining how interpreters arrive at an understanding of such communicative acts in those cases in which they pursue their interest in attuning themselves to the work's upstream meanings. As explanatory principles, these truisms have priority relative to talk of such entities as conventions, codes, institutions, and formal properties.

The rationality heuristic is a way of understanding people's behavior.[6] It consists of the assumption that sense can be made of what individuals say and do, and valid explanations of many of their observable acts can be obtained, by attributing to them the gamut of familiar "folk psychological" mental states and attitudes: beliefs, desires, emotions, expectations, plans, intentions, and so forth. This approach to understanding behavior proposes that many of a person's actions depend upon the content of his or her reasons (which need not be reasonable reasons) and plans, and upon nonrandom connections between those mental items and the individual's actions. The rationality heuristic does not imply that all thought and action is inevitably wise, deductively sound, prudent, means-ends coherent, or successful at securing its goal. Nor does it commit us to the idea that we are always in a position to know why an agent acted as observed or what his or her intentions were. Nor does it maintain that all behaviors are the results of beliefs, desires, and so forth. It is a default assumption that should be suspended only when one has grounds to believe that some piece of conduct is not dependent upon the agent's mental states and attitudes. Thus the rationality heuristic is a *"privileged but fallible"* approach to understanding behavior.[7]

As an interpretive principle, the scope of the rationality heuristic is extremely broad. Its application extends to the spectator's comprehension of the actions of the persons represented in the movie's content—actual and imaginary characters, interviewees, interviewers, on- and off-screen narrators, agents caught unawares by the camera, and so on. The rationality heuristic also extends to our understanding of authorial action, insofar as it guides our judgments about what intentions and plans constrained the work's production and what the work's features indicate about the author's state of mind. The rationality heuristic is therefore consistent with—and, we should say, the foundation for—real author intentionalism.[8]

Real author intentionalism holds that movies (like all other artificial representational systems) are products of authorial actions—that is, behaviors guided by intentions and reasons—and that the interpreter's task, to the extent that this person wishes to discover whatever meaning the work has independent of acts of interpretation and reception, is to a significant degree to ascertain (as far as he or she can) the real author's effective communicative intentions and plans.

Taken together, the rationality heuristic and real author intentionalism reflect the thesis that only agents make communicative artifacts and that we must therefore turn to these individuals in order to resolve a great many questions about meaning. This thesis rules out attributing the significance and emergence of such objects to anonymous, a-rational, supra-individual structures and forces. Whatever else they might connote for us, collective consciousness, the spirit of the times, codes, conventions, discourses, ideology, and institutions do not describe the kinds of entities that can be proximal causes of either an individual's actions or a representation's production. Such items have no intrinsic properties that do not depend on anyone having any particular intentions or attitudes toward them. These objects do not meet the basic material requirements for being the sort of entities capable of attaining cognitive and volitional states, acting on the basis of beliefs and desires, and so on. They lack irreducible, autonomous causal powers because the changes they undergo and the forces they exert upon other parts of reality all require the contribution of some rather complex human intentional, affective, cognitive, and inter-individual operations.

It follows that accounts of, say, an institution's properties, transformations, and effects require descriptions and explanations of the relevant thoughts and actions of agents. Note that although the current description of agency is meant to clear up questions regarding who does what and how within the arenas of representation and communication, it does not imply a reduction of all human phenomena to descriptions of individual psychology. Denying that collectives, institutions, conventions, and other human artifacts are genuine, meaning-producing agents does not cause us to lose sight of the existence and specificity of these objects in reality.

Individuals act, interact, act together, and act with reference to one another—and in so doing they produce certain phenomena, some of which are not intended, understood, or even noticed by the agents involved. Just because its effects must be explained in terms of the thoughts and actions of individual rather than collective beings, we need not conclude that the social domain of reality does not have its own regularities, patterns, and properties (institutions, discourses, conventions, traffic jams, etc.) that emerge as the consequences of people adjusting and coordinating their thoughts and actions in response to one another. We simply want to deny that these properties can have consciousness and can exercise agency and self-control. In so doing, we retain the insight that groups or collectives of agents can share beliefs, desires, intentions, values, actions, and so on and can act with reference to (their perceptions of) other agents' intentional attitudes.

The foregoing brings us to the gist of real author intentionalism: Those intentional constraints having a proximal, effective bearing on the generation of the work's meaning belong to an actual historical agent-author; it is about these intentions that we reason, and it is these that we may discover when interpreting the movie. Working from the production side of cinematic communication, I have already argued that skepticism about the transparency of authorial intentions provides no good reason to think that filmmakers do not formulate and successfully execute content-controlling plans.

Might it be more compellingly argued that, during the interpretive phase, it is the wishes and attitudes of something along the lines of an implied author—a subjectivity that corresponds to no actual agent, is suggested by the work's properties, and reflects sensibilities, points of view, beliefs, and objectives—that spectators make reference to in deciding how they are to understand the film's meaning and whose sensibilities the movie evokes? Many critics seem to think so, including Nichols, who once employed the word "voice" to denote "the text's social point of view, of how it is speaking to us and how it is organizing the materials it is presenting to us. In this sense, voice is not restricted to any one code or feature, such as dialogue or spoken commentary. Voice is perhaps akin to that intangible, moirélike pattern formed by the unique interaction of all of a film's codes, and it applies to all modes of documentary."[9]

Plantinga, acknowledging the proximity of his to Nichols's use of the term, says that a film's voice is the perspective from which information is presented and the "implicit stance or attitude toward what it presents." "Like a person reporting an event to an audience, the discourse of a nonfiction film may manifest voice as ostensibly objective as in television news, as angry and hostile as in the *Why We Fight* series, blatantly or subtly ironic as in Michael Moore's *TV Nation*, sympathetic and praising as in *Say Amen, Somebody*."[10] And Thomas Benson and Carolyn Anderson embrace the following implied author thesis in their discussion of the rhetoric of "Wiseman's camera":

> The meaning of the film is not in "what the filmmaker meant," although, as we shall try to show, the meanings experienced by the audience are constructed by the filmmaker, who is also constructing what Wayne Booth calls the "implied author." Partly, audiences make sense of films by asking what filmmakers meant, and that part of the audience's understanding, drawn from what it sees and hears in the film, must also be taken into account in a rhetorical reading.[11]

When they say that filmmakers construct the meanings experienced by the audience, Benson and Anderson grant what every good researcher knows, that movies result from agential actions. But they simultaneously undermine this sentiment when they stipulate against associating a film's meaning with "'what the filmmaker meant.'" The only way to resolve this internal conflict is to suppose that Benson and Anderson would assent to the following argument: Part of a movie's meaning is produced by a filmmaker's intentional actions, but these intentions are inaccessible to the viewer and not always made manifest in the work's explicit properties; however, interpretation necessarily proceeds by attempts to infer authorial intentions; hence there is warrant for positing a hypothetical intermediary between spectators and meaning, since it describes precisely "whose" designs the viewer is really inferring. Benson and Anderson do not openly say as much, but let us also assume that actual authors need not know that they are, as an effect of their authorial activities, creating an implied author; and audiences are probably not aware that the intentions they posit may not belong to an actual historical maker and are only indirectly, and very likely waywardly, the consequences of that agent's actions.

If Benson and Anderson are reasoning in roughly the manner that I have outlined, they have the interpreter grasping at air. Implied authors are non-agents; non-agents are incapable of producing either plans or artifacts; and unwitting attributions of real intentions to non-agents who the viewer mistakes for real authors are false attributions. If you are unperturbed by thinking of interpreting cinematic non-fictions as a feat significantly different from comprehending conversations and academic essays, and if it does not disturb you to be asked to assume that movie viewers like yourself ordinarily hold a number of illusory beliefs about whose intentions they are seeking, you may want to consider some further implications of an implied author thesis. For example, on the current model, apparently we must conclude that even cases of one's discerning the real author's actual effective communicative intentions betoken interpreter irrationality, because learning of these plans is the (accidental?) by-product of the spectator's irrational attempts to grasp the real author's intentions. Indeed one of the chief tricks of the implied author thesis is to get us to suspect that there is something epistemically illicit about interpretive preoccupation with authorial intentions, without stretching its own credibility by asking us to be anti-realists about intentions or proclaiming that authors can never have or realize determinant intentions with respect to force and content.

Now suppose that the fan of implied authorship allows that there will be cases in which the interpreter is under no illusion of ascertaining anything but the implied author's intentions. The documentary theorist might, for instance, take up Currie's suggestion regarding literary and movie fictions, namely, that the implied author is "a heuristic device that no one need believe in, and reference to him is easily eliminated; that the implied author intends P to be fictional means just that the text can reasonably be thought of as produced by someone intending the reader to recognize that P is fictional."[12] Saying that **P** is non-fictional is thus equivalent to saying that the film may reasonably be thought of as made by someone intending the audience to recognize that **P** is non-fictional. The reasonableness of this thought is precisely the question that remains to be answered.

After all, identifying some of the work's meanings by way of an implied author heuristic still leaves us with the problem of devising principles by which to individuate those implied or hypothetical intentions. Why is it any easier or more verifiable to reconstruct an implied author's intentional attitudes? An implied author thesis leaves us with the same problem we started with: identifying which intentional constraints bear upon meaning—only now we are prevented from talking about the kind of entity who can really exercise such constraints. Moreover, rather than relieving us of the burden of the rationality heuristic, the implied author thesis simply displaces its focus onto a hypothetical entity. And if one is a causal realist about the role of intentions in aesthetics and communication, implied authorship as an interpretive dictum is inconsistent with the principles by which the work's emergence is to be explained.

When theorists use the concept of voice, they often do so in order to describe an overall impression of an authorial consciousness or persona projected by the movie's structure and content. It is accepted critical practice not to identify this construct with the actual author. Hence Plantinga comments that the filmic **discourse** is **like** a person in as much as it may manifest various attitudes towards what it presents. Although Michael Moore, in his on-screen and voice-over narration of *Roger and Me* (1989), characterizes himself as a bumbling rube, the former editor of *Mother Jones* magazine is really not the sort of person who would have trouble figuring out how best to try to get an interview with the head of General Motors.

Surely it is wrong to assume that every belief, psychological perspective, or personality trait evoked by a film is really a property of, or sincerely asserted by, the real author. But we may acknowledge this fact while insisting that a work's voice, if one chooses to use this term, is an intentional artifact—not merely a "moirélike pattern formed by the unique interaction of all of a film's codes," but the product of authorial plans. On those occasions in which the attitudes expressed in a movie diverge from those truly held by its maker, we might nonetheless have grounds to hold that they truly belong, in some appropriate sense, to the real author. More precisely, expressing those attitudes may belong to the maker's repertoire of effective communicative intentions—in the same sense that my intention to express an overt but insincere belief that you look fabulous in your new lime green leisure suit belongs to me.

Inside the perspective of real author intentionalism, one way of dealing with concepts of voice is to reduce them to the underlying concept of authorial attitudes. The governing intuition here is that we can avoid displacements and reifications by supposing that what we call "voice" consists not of one of the movie's formal properties, nor of a hypothetical entity seemingly projected by the movie, but of a relational property; that is, the representation's condition indicates something about the psychological condition of the actual author. A cinematic constative, like any communicative act, has mental significance. In the first place, such a work gives us information about its makers illocutionary intentions. Likewise it usually discloses what its makers know or believe, or want an audience to think they know or believe. But filmmakers, like other communicators, are hardly limited in the range of dispositions, tempers, and frames of mind they can attach to their material. Normally, by emphasizing the relative importance of certain facts or assertions over others, producers afford us insight into how they assign relative importance. Frequently they express conative stances, like desires and wishes; documentarians also typically give the content of their movies emotional intonation or valence; and they often indicate various political, ethical, and moral evaluations and stances.

To construe voice as mental significance, we need not suppose that the authorial subjectivity implied by the movie is always and certainly an attitude, disposition, or trait, **f**, sincerely held by the work's actual historical maker(s). Our thesis must leave room for at least four distinct explanations of the origins of the film's voice. Schematically put, these are the possible scenarios: (1) the author actually has **f**, and openly and sincerely communicates that fact; (2) the author openly expresses **f**, but does so insincerely, as he or she does not really have the specified attitude or does not actually believe him or herself to be the kind of person describable as having **f**; (3) **f** is an authorial property, but in as much as the author does not mean to express or indicate that fact, the movie conveys it waywardly, as collateral information; (4) as a perverse effect of the representational process, or relative to a particular audience or reception context, a movie gives the impression that the author has **f**, in turn leading the viewer to misattribute **f** to the author.

In actual critical practice, ascertaining a work's mental significance is a matter of identifying which of the four scenarios we want to describe and then offering reasons and empirical evidence sufficient to warrant a claim that a given psychological item or state constrained the state of a certain movie. Here, as always, such constraints are highly conditional. No part of mental significance—not even collateral information about it—is nomically indicated by the cinematic work's objective properties. I therefore disagree with the idea either that "an indexical bond exists between the image and the ethics that produced it," or that "the photographic (and aural) record provides an imprint of its user's ethical, political, and ideological stance as well as an imprint of the visible surface of

Aspects of Interpretation 225

things."¹³ No meaningful natural counterfactual dependence exists between the appearance and style of the photographic record and the filmmaker's attitudes toward his movie's subject. We achieve access to authorial stances by reasoning about agent rationality, not by looking at the kind of "gaze" the film trains on the world. Form and style are but clues that leave us to fill in the details of how the author having **f** might have constrained the work to look or sound as it does.

Assumptions pertaining to rationality are key to the interpretive process, but they are not **the** key to it. As already argued, visual perception is also a decisive and reliable input to motion picture comprehension. Typically a stream of primary and secondary perceptions facilitates the spectator's interpretive access to various cinematic and extra-cinematic states of affairs. One sees that a given item is a motion picture, that the image itself has certain visible properties, and sees that it represents a certain (kind of) object. One can also see by the state of the depiction how things stand with respect to a specified pre-filmic object. Relying on their visual experience no less than on the rationality heuristic, viewers assume that their perceptual experiences are fallible sources of facts about the movie's properties as well as about situations systematically related to those properties. In other words, competent spectators interpret according to certain truistic principles concerning the nature of their visual experiences.

Although the average spectator's portfolio of folk theories of visual cognition and cinematic depiction is pre-analytic and mainly non-technical, everyday observations of people's responses to motion pictures, accompanied by our previous conceptual spadework, suggest that some elementary perceptual heuristics would include background beliefs along the following lines.

1. The photographic image is not the pre-filmic object and does not make that distal item directly present to the viewer; looking at the image is somehow a substantially different perceptual situation from looking at the object itself. This commonsense non-identity thesis would, for instance, include the assumption that by walking around the image (or the surface on which it appears) one does not thereby walk around the pre-filmic object.
2. Perceptual experiences of many standard, naturalistic photographs of **O** are like but not identical to perceptual experiences (that one might expect to have) of **O** itself. They afford similar sensations and similar opportunities for learning about a piece of the world by visual means. One knows by looking at it that the image presents, in altered and degraded form, a selection of information about how the pre-filmic scene actually looks/looked.

For example, naturalistic images of medium-sized objects usually indicate the approximate shapes, colors, and patterns that would be revealed to a person with normal eyesight directly encountering the object under normal conditions from a position roughly analogous to that of the camera. Information about the image's size, flatness, surface, edges, and other medium-specific properties are also made available by one's sensory-cognitive experiences of it. When the depicted object looks somehow different from how one would expect it to look, this condition is to be explained by the production or reproduction process, for example, by the use of distorting lenses, unusual lighting, monochromatic or technicolor film stock, magnification by projection onto a big screen, special effects, and so on.

3. Assumptions about the image and its object are also sometimes guided by certain elementary principles of optics that form part of a modern audience's general knowledge. One of these, which has in fact been around since Anton Leeuwenhoek's first experiments with rudimentary microscopes in the 1670s, is as follows: An instrument of visual detection is reliable if it seems to make clear and distinct that which was previously blurry or invisible to the unaided eye.[14] Such a principle is relevant in relation to imagery produced by means of slow motion mechanisms, macrophotography, and so forth.

4. The image, by virtue of the way it is mechanically produced, can reveal things about the external scene as well as the process of its own production without the maker having intended to reveal these things.

5. Images, singularly and in connection with one another, and images' appearances are products of human action and technology and are subject to a tremendous variety of manipulations and uses by people who are not necessarily good, trustworthy, bias-free, or all-knowing, or who are not primarily motivated by a concern with morality or truth.

These perceptual principles are entirely within the realm of general knowledge and common sense; one need not be a rocket scientist or a film theorist to know and apply them, since learning them is more a matter of ordinary observation and experience than of inquiry into theories of optics, perception, and representation. Notice, too, that viewers' assumptions about the nature of their visual experiences need not stand alone. Principles 4 and 5, for instance, garner the support of the rationality heuristic, along with background beliefs about who makes movies for what conceivable reasons. As I shall explain later, framework assumptions about perception can combine with other, more specialized epistemic and evidential principles if and when it becomes necessary to seek a higher degree of justification regarding judgments of, for instance, a depiction's truth-value or the confirmation it supplies for a given assertion.

The above perceptual principles are, as I say, heuristics. Following them is not always conducive to interpretive success and truth. More specifically, each is in some respect potentially defeasible in particular contexts. The advent of some sort of whizbang holographic technology might, for instance, require the revision of principle 1 in order to incorporate the potential for three-dimensional motion pictures suspended in midair; this would not, of course, require the suspension of the nonidentity thesis itself. Trickery and deception, of the type that becomes harder to detect with the refinement of computer imaging technologies, render the perspicacity of principles 2 through 4 conditional upon the viewer's knowledge of how the depiction was in fact made. Principle 5 could turn out to be inapplicable to the degree that the imagery is the result of an accident or a deviant causal chain that minimizes the role of human agency in the image track's emergence.

Like the rationality heuristic, our perceptual guidelines are prima facie principles that should be granted so long as there is no definite reason not to accept them. But when there is evidence available to the viewer that a principle is inapplicable, or in cases of epistemic stress in which an interpretation is called into question or there is a premium on justification, conclusions need to be checked by considering the most likely contrary causal accounts of why the work has the properties it does and by trying to eliminate them in a process of causal comparison. Otherwise, the rationality heuristic and perceptual principles function as truisms that no reasonable person would deny or hesitate to mobilize. In response to the sorts of experiences that almost all human beings routinely have, reason and evidence generally commit us to accept these principles. Someone who claims not to accept them takes on the burden of proof, which entails citing special reasons and evidence why their own or anyone else's interpretive judgments are not or should not be reliant upon these principles.

Illocutionary Uptake

For interpreters to fulfill their end of the communicative transaction, the following issue is to be resolved in relation to a cinematic representational system: What is the illocutionary force of $i \ldots i_n$? In *The War Game* (1966), is Watkins asserting that Kent was attacked as shown or is he eliciting the audience's make-belief towards a proposition to this effect? Does Buñuel, by way of *Land Without Bread* (1932), want us to believe that he is sincerely asserting that the Hurdanos are a depraved tribe of subhumans, or are his propositions about these unfortunate souls emitted with obvious insincerity? These are matters of uptake, as it relates to ascertaining the force expressed toward a unit of content. Audiences will try to detect the illocutionary intentions of interviewers, interview subjects, on-screen characters and narrators, voice-over narrators, as well as the intentions subtending any verbal titles. To streamline discussion, I shall focus on efforts to get a handle on the work's overall illocutionary force, as constrained by the author's plans.

I hope already to have made a sufficiently good case for supposing that many cinematic productions are unambiguously constative and hence facilitate their audience's more rather than less spontaneous recognition of their force. Recall the example of Bateson and Mead's *Trance and Dance in Bali* (1952), undeniably devised to assert that a certain kind of ritual performance has the depicted features. An attribution of assertive intent makes the most sense, insofar as it is consistent with the film's observable properties, along with our knowledge of the circumstances under which the film was made and of its authors' research agenda. In many situations—watching news broadcasts and investigative reports, political debates, daytime talk shows, antismoking advertisements, and so on—the viewer's background knowledge, the context in which they encounter the work, the work's explicit features, and the plans governing its production are likewise such that evidence and reasoning support no simple, undogmatic conclusion other than the ascription of constative force. Yet there are also cases in which judging the work's force requires more complex inferential activity, an effort of interpretive action and justification in the face of rival intuitions.

Oliver Stone's *JFK* (1991) helps to illustrate some potential complexities and problems of interpreting force. Readers familiar with this film about who shot Kennedy will remember it for Stone's remarkable blending of genres and his sometimes nearly seamless combinations of archival with staged footage; one might have equally strong recollections of the public controversy surrounding the veracity and political significance of this highly entertaining and theatrical dramatization, starring famous actors playing actual historical figures, of a pastiche of conspiracy theories.[15] With good reason, commentators have been apt to question whether this movie is fiction or non-fiction. *JFK*'s form and content seem like ample support for concluding that this film is simply one of those postmodern cases of category evanescence, such that classification as fiction or non-fiction is, if not impossible, then "fuzzy at best."[16]

There is, however, a competing interpretation even better supported by the available evidence. *JFK* is an instance of complex illocutionary plans. It deploys fiction for constative purposes. Thus, on balance, it is non-fiction.

Aspects of Interpretation 229

Within a fictional narrative, it openly and obviously represents some (supposedly) real situations and events; the truth of these representations, if and when they are true, is putatively non-accidental. And here, fiction-making is extrinsically motivated, being subordinated to constative illocutionary purposes. Producing and exhibiting make-believe is a means to an assertive end. In this account, *JFK* on balance has a certain mental significance: Stone primarily wants to make various assertions and suggestions. This significance is publicly accessible: *JFK* is made with a communicative intention, and a reasonable expectation, that an audience can find an inferential path to the movie's main authorially prescribed force.

Although a viewer might come to an inference about Stone's goals via other routes, and at different moments in the movie, one way of securing the uptake goes like this. As the film progresses by means of staged scenes, it is clear that much of the narrative involves the presentation of actors pretending to be, say, and do such and such. For example, we are to make-believe that Kevin Costner is New Orleans District Attorney Jim Garrison and that events in his prosecution, early in 1969, of businessman Clay Shaw look just so. We thereby recognize that the sounds and imagery pertain to how we are to imagine Garrison, his clothes, behavior, the court room, and other people at that place to sound and look L at t. The representation shows and tells what we are to imagine about what his physical gestures are and how they look, what words he and others speak and how those utterances sound, what it looks and sounds like as he tries to convince a jury that Shaw had been part of a conspiracy to kill the president and that Lee Harvey Oswald could not have been the lone assassin, how Garrison appears and feels when his efforts fail—where the values of L are determined by the pertinent pre-filmic features of Costner and the other performers, their actions before the cameras, the mise-en-scène, shot selection and composition, film editing, the movie's observable audiovisual properties, and so on.

Yet under the circumstances, it also seems that there is an identifiable, calculated relation between Stone's fiction-making and the making of various assertions and suggestions. The grounds for this inference are partly a function of the movie's properties and partly a function of certain mutual contextual beliefs (MCBs) shared by the filmmaker and his target audience. It is a matter of fact that *JFK* makes reference to a number of actual incidents and individuals within recent American history. By the same token, its makers, employing research and sources that are signaled explicitly in the movie's credits, have gone to great lengths to represent certain historical events and various people's beliefs and claims about these and other alleged events. On the other hand, the actual existence of many of the people and events in question is easily grasped by members of Stone's mass audience. Assuming him to be moderately rational, it makes the best sense to assume that he expects that his viewership will expect that he shares with them various beliefs about Kennedy's death and some of its well-known consequences, like the Warren Commission Report. Publicity and criticism surrounding *JFK* also help to create a context in which its connections to actual events and persons, to a body of conspiracy literature, and to ongoing public debates and suspicions would be identifiable as desired and planned.

The relevance of the represented fictional situations to (popular discourses about) actual historical incidents thus prompts the assumption that Stone is not merely fictioneering. Why, under these circumstances, would he show us the situations and events that he does if not in anticipation that viewers shall recognize their systematic relations to assertions about actual and hypothesized situations? The filmmaker does not want viewers to make-believe that Garrison tried Shaw, that a single bullet could not have killed President Kennedy and wounded Governor Connally, and that a conspiracy to kill Kennedy has been covered up. Rather, he is asserting some of these propositions, suggesting others. Stone's plan must be to **ff** that **S** and thereby **F** that **S'**.

An advantage of the foregoing interpretation is its affinity with Stone's own statements about *JFK*. During the furor over this movie, the beginning of which predated by several months its release, the filmmaker frequently availed himself of opportunities to reply to his critics and expound his objectives. At various times, Stone has made it abundantly clear that his goals go well beyond fictioneering, as when he expresses hopes that his film "will at least move people away from the Warren Commission and consider the possibility that there was a coup d'état."[17] Elsewhere, he refers to his intention "to explore the various credible assassination theories," to "pose the view that Kennedy's desire to wind down the cold war and the Vietnam War is a possible motive for the murder," to "promulgate [Garrison's] theory" of a cover-up, and to assemble "several layers of research from the '60's, '70's, and '80's . . . in a seamless jigsaw puzzle that will allow the audience, for the first time, to understand what happened and why."[18]

Another of Stone's comments—that he sets out in his movie to disagree with the Warren Commission's findings—points to another dimension of the film's non-fictional status.[19] Many scenes, such as the courtroom illustration of the single bullet thesis, belong to the category of disputative constatives. Here the rationale of the fiction is not to so much to assert that such and such is the case. Rather it is a vehicle for signaling an intention that the viewer believe there is reason not to believe that a given proposition is true.[20]

On several occasions, Stone has commented that *JFK* presents a "myth." On another occasion, he says that his film is a "counter-myth" to the official Warren Commission myth of the lone assassin.[21] I admit to being puzzled by what exactly he understands by these two terms.[22] However, neither trying to represent "the true inner spiritual meaning" of Kennedy's murder nor proposing an "artistic interpretation" of events relating to the assassination is necessarily antithetical to the making of assertions.[23] And even if the Warren Report were substantially false or wishful, it still would not be fictional.

It should be noted that the audience's successful comprehension of the work's complex illocutionary strategy does not require that they reach an accurate conclusion, or any conclusion at all, about the sincerity of the film's assertions. To assert that such and such is or could have been the case usually manifests the communicator's knowledge or belief that **P**; as I have said before, one standard conversational presumption consists of the mutual belief that speakers in fact possess the attitudes that they express. But this is a defeasible assumption, the suspension of which need not get in the way of either signaling or grasping illocutionary force. One does not need to believe that **P** in order to assert that **P**. Although we may be curious about whether Stone—or the other conspiracy mongers upstream in the cascade of conjectures and allegations informing Stone's film—really has the attitudes expressed, individuating many of the author's actual beliefs could require biographical information not necessarily available from the movie itself.

Part of what Stone considers myth-making might consist of "hypothetical speculation," which could include the depiction of events that may be more imaginary than actual. But speculating, as contrasted with asserting literal historical truth claims, draws a work no closer to fiction.[24] Speculation—like conjecture, hypothesis, guessing, and suggestion—is a constative communicative act whereby the communicator indicates that there is reason, but not yet sufficient reason, to believe that such and such could be the case.[25]

The current interpretation of *JFK*'s illocutionary force is also compatible with the idea that the filmmakers are not literally asserting or suggesting everything that is shown or implied by the representation. Having noticed that the film is constructed partly from imaginative stagings and theatrical performances, surely audiences will not suppose that every detail of the imagery, sound track, acting, and mise-en-scène supports an assertion of a putative fact about an actual historical situation. Few will be tempted to believe that Stone would have them believe that Garrison **actually** described the so-called magic bullet's trajectory in just the manner represented in the movie, or that the character constructed by Costner, co-screenwriter Sklar, and Stone is meant to have only or principally a fact-preserving relation to the appearance, personality, thoughts, and actions of the real Jim Garrison.

In the current example, as in other works resulting from complex illocutionary plans, embedded within cinematic representations of fictional and imaginary situations are representations, which can be relatively schematic, of actual or purportedly actual situations towards which we are intended to adopt the attitude of belief. Establishing which parts of the movie are literally asserted, and which are deliberate departures from literal assertion, is an interactive phenomenon of use. In other words, much of *JFK* is made with the mutually-recognized intention on the communicator's part that the audience actively adjust their responses, searching for and reasoning about textual and contextual clues in order to settle on an appropriate interpretation. Spectators need a reliable basis for distinguishing between that which they are intended to imagine, for the pleasure of imagining, and that which is literally asserted or suggested. Inferences exploiting MCBs serve as just such a filter.

Here is what I mean. In several episodes, some incorporating Abraham Zapruder's footage of the assassination as well as Stone's reconstructions of that scene, Kennedy is represented as being struck in the head by gun fire, thus incurring a devastating head wound. Most spectators will already believe that, roughly speaking, this is what happened one day in Dallas. They will not be disposed to make-believe that Kennedy died as shown. They likely will be disposed to believe that Stone believes, and expects them to believe, that the murder looked thus and so. On these grounds, viewers can infer that the filmmaker could be asserting—indicating that they should form or continue to hold a belief—only that the moment of the assassination transpired in pretty much the way shown.

Now consider the following. In the climactic courtroom scene, the Garrison character uses two other characters, his colleagues, to illustrate the weaknesses of the single bullet thesis. Viewers may or may not go into the screening room already believing that there is such a thing as a single bullet thesis, that it is the cornerstone of the Warren Commission's conclusions, and that it has been renamed the magic bullet thesis by those who doubt that one projectile could have done all the damage to Kennedy's and Connally's bodies. But even the uninitiated will have grounds to think it inappropriate to make-believe that there is a single bullet thesis, and so on. Here, again, an MCB comes into play.

Generally speaking, *JFK*'s target audience is aware that there is a controversy surrounding who killed the president and how, that there are public claims of conspiracies and cover-ups, and that there are popular doubts regarding the official account's veracity. We can be reasonably sure that Stone, during *JFK*'s production stages, counted on such background beliefs and suspicions being common among his target audience.[26] Under the circumstances—in light of the representation's explicit content, the relevant MCBs, and the presumption that Stone must have some sort of communicative goal in mind—it makes best sense to assume that certain assertions and suggestions are being made about the single bullet thesis and its role in the cover-up of a conspiracy.

As I say, not all of *JFK*'s content is expressed with constative force. Hence there must be some conceivable inferential route connecting the viewer's uptake to that which is fictional. Again, think of the courtroom scene. This staged, play-acted scene, just as it is presented on screen, is surely not designed only or even mainly to correspond with that which viewers already know or believe about the details of the actual trial and events connected to it. Furthermore, viewers are unlikely to believe that Stone or anyone else literally believes or claims that the cinematic representation corresponds exactly with the sights, sounds, and constitutive events of the real 1969 trial. On the contrary, the pertinent MCB is that much of the representation is the product of performance, cinematic craft, and imagination. In the absence of a countervailing belief that a given feature, such as a unit of spoken dialogue, coincides with a fact, belief, or claim about the real trial and its content, we deem it appropriate to adopt an imagining attitude toward that feature.

Finally, *JFK*'s status as non-fiction in no way precludes its being the product of other sorts of plans. For example, the filmmakers evidently put a lot of effort into making it hard for spectators to tell the difference between some fictive imagery and actual footage of real and alleged historical events. Likewise, in a sentiment echoed by Plantinga, many commentators in the popular press pointed out that it seems to have been Stone's strategy to obscure the distinctions between what is being represented as conjecture, what is asserted as known fact, and what is purely imaginary.[27] Perhaps triggering such confusion is another facet of what Stone regards as an "artistic interpretation" of historical events. In any case, the kind of interpretive achievement that we wish to attribute to viewers is not predicated on complete success and absolute certainty regarding what is asserted, what is make-believe, what is imaginary, what is factual. Rather, their illocutionary uptake, to be moderately successful, need secure only the inference that the filmmakers are on balance using fiction for non-fictional purposes.

Truth in Non-Fiction

Audiences are often interested in discerning what content an author is asserting to them. They want to know what situations are being described, what states of affairs are being represented, what propositions are being made—their interest is in gaining access to the content toward which the producers would have them adopt the attitude of belief. Interpretive response then focuses on something like this question: What can be truthfully said about the non-fiction's believable content? Justifiable answers to this question are moderately intentionalist in character. In other words, substantiating claims about what is true in the non-fiction—or, for that matter, the fiction—entails reasoning jointly about the author's effective communicative intentions and the work's explicit features, in light of one's sensory and cognitive perceptions of the work.

I suspect that the above query, or something to its effect, is the default setting for our rational engagements with constatives in whatever medium. From the outset, interpreters assume that it is desirable and possible to grasp some of the producer's plans regarding a constative's external and mental significance. If my hunch is correct, the reader of this book is, right now, assuming that the writer has various communicative purposes in mind; subsequently, the reader is interested in and, when uncertain, inclined to make an effort to reason about, what propositions the writer wants to make and the attitudes he wishes to express towards them. Evaluating the book (and its writer's professional achievements!) depends upon the interpreter's ability to operate on these assumptions and form these judgments.

The term "truth in non-fiction" underscores that there can be a disjunction between the truth-value of our statements about the non-fiction's content and the truth-value of the non-fiction's content. Thus an accurate description of the non-fiction's content—the situations that it represents—is not necessarily an accurate description of how things stand in some part of extra-cinematic reality. It is true in *Nanook of the North*'s non-fiction that an igloo's interior temperature is below freezing; and it is true in the non-fiction of a classic advertising campaign that the Pillsbury Doughboy wears a chef's hat. But it is not true *simpliciter* in reality that it's frigid inside an igloo, nor that there exists a risible, dough-based intelligent life form who wears a chef's hat. The current point fits nicely with some facts about non-fictions. Their meaningful content is not restricted to representations of reality or putatively real states of affairs. They themselves are often "interpretations," in the sense of being constructive or creative treatments of certain topics or material, guided by the author's self-expressive intentions, fantasies, desires, biases, or misconceptions. Finally, that which is true in the non-fiction need not be identical to that which it is true that the filmmaker (sincerely) believes.

That which is true in the non-fiction is that which the filmmaker effectively means to be truthfully said of the work's content. This intentional constraint on meaning need be only very loose. The demonstrative intentions composing Type I plans—as when one trains a camera on a busy street, turns it on, then leaves it alone to let it record whatever events transpire within its range—commit the filmmaker to subordinating truth in

Aspects of Interpretation

non-fiction to what we have called the imagery's natural interpretation*, unless or until someone acting in an authorial capacity comes along to manipulate that imagery in such a way as to give it a symbolic interpretation*. On the other hand, there are many instances in which the work's content depends much less on natural meaning and much more on what someone means by showing us an image or sequence. In any case, the viewer's task, in justifying his or her ideas about what is true in a non-fiction, is to cite the constraints making it a function of $i \ldots i_n$ to indicate that such and such is the case. We have grounds to attribute a given external significance to the work when we can specify which constraints determine that it be the function of $i \ldots i_n$ to describe that situation.

Here, then, is how I conceive of interpretive success: The spectator acquires or forms a belief to the effect that $i \ldots i_n$ is interpreted* by **S**—or naturally interpreted* by **S**, just in case meaning is subordinated to natural meaning—when $i \ldots i_n$ is in fact (naturally) interpreted* by **S**. If and when observers attain interpretive success, it is more or less jointly conditional upon their warranted inferences regarding effective authorial plans, along with their veridical sensory and cognitive perceptions of the motion picture and situations systematically related to it. A few comments on these conditions, and their conjunction, are thus in order.

Some of a non-fiction's content is represented explicitly, relative to the spectator's perceptual abilities and background beliefs. Apprehending such content is a matter of cognitive perception rather than of an act of judgment that intervenes between sensory experience and settling on what it is that is believable. Provided one already knows what German military uniforms look like, one sees that in *Night and Fog* (Alain Resnais, 1955) German officers are shown ferrying on their backs concentration camp dead to mass graves; indeed, one can see by the depiction that such an event actually transpired in extra-cinematic reality.

Notice as well that some explicit content is intended, in the sense of being the result of an authorial execution of Type II plans. In a sequence from *High School* (Frederick Wiseman, 1968) an adult male hall monitor is pictured peering through a window in a door; the very next shots depict teenage girls exercising in a gymnasium; and these images tend to emphasize the adolescents' bottoms and legs. Given a prior knowledge of standard practices for indicating spatiotemporal and sequential relations by means of shot juxtapositions, strategies of the sort to which this sequence adheres, one may thereby see that the hall monitor is peeking at these young women. A viewer thus recognizes without inferential effort the sequence's interpretation*—a significance generated by editing and describing a situation that might not really have existed.

Other facets of explicit content are, frankly, unintended. When we see that a group of police officers are shown striking a man as he drops to his knees, we are visually recognizing one of the natural interpretations* of Holliday's video footage; the videographer and subsequent users have elected to subordinate meaning to demonstrative, Type I plans with respect to content.

However, not all veridical cognitive perceptions are to be identified with successful interpretive uptake. Near the end of *Salesman* (Albert and David Maysles and Charlotte Zwerin, 1969), traveling Bible peddler Paul "The Badger" Brennan worries aloud about his ongoing sales slump. His partner, Ray "The Bull" Martos, sitting across from him in their motel room and distractedly counting his many sales receipts, reacts by saying, "You get a week or two of good production under your belt and you'll be OK." A first-time viewer might not notice an unusual but fairly explicit attribute of this scene: In a movie made with direct sound, the sound coming out of the "The Bull's" mouth is visibly out of synchronization with the movement of his lips; and the aural quality of that utterance is different from that of the rest of the sound recording, since the speaker's utterance was apparently recorded at a different location and post-synchronously dubbed over the present scene.

Now if one sees and hears that the audiovisual tracks have been tampered with, one does not thereby discover that it is true in the non-fiction that "The Bull's" dialogue is out of sync with his mouth, and so on. Like a boom microphone dropping into a scene in a naturalistic fiction, it is appropriate to exclude this feature from our decisions about the work's communicated content. Presumably, it is not part of the filmmakers' plan to represent a tricky bit of sound editing but, rather, to use this trick in an effort to describe something quite different, namely, one salesman's antipathy to another's failures.

The foregoing alludes to another factor in interpretive uptake because a principled exclusion of the stated feature requires reference to authorial intentions. For instance, we might want to contend that it makes the most sense to assume that the producers do not want us to think it true in the non-fiction that "The Bull's" dialogue is out of sync with his lip movements, since it is apparent from the rest of the movie that they have otherwise attempted to make the production apparatus as unobtrusive as possible; on the other hand, a scene describing antipathy to failure would be thematically consistent with the content of other scenes and would cohere with some of the Maysles's own remarks about this sequence's significance and the ways in which they used editing to foreground certain themes, even if it involved constructing scenes out of disparate components recording different pre-filmic events.[28] Here, as in cases in which meaning is implicit or ambiguous, reasons for preferring one interpretation over another mobilize judgments of the author's communicative plans. Support for such judgments may come from many quarters, in-

Aspects of Interpretation

cluding explicit textual features; background knowledge and extra-textual evidence pertaining to the history and context of the work's production; information about mutual contextual beliefs shared by the author and his or her target audience; and insights into authorial intentions drawn from letters, biographical information, interviews, writings, production notes, or analyses of his or her other movies.

In reasoning about authorial attitudes, an interpreter's successful inferences will be those that hit upon the filmmaker's effective communicative intentions. The non-fictioneer may have countless beliefs concerning what this or that segment of his film means, not to mention a budget of genuine but failed aspirations with respect to content. If these sorts of attitudes are not actual constraints on the representation's content or are inaccessible to the target audience, then ascertaining them is no reliable guide to that which is determinately true in the non-fiction.

The following is a concrete example of the point I want to make. In *Titicut Follies* (Frederick Wiseman, 1967), there is a scene during which we are shown a couple of images of a man off by himself in one of the Bridgewater hospital's exercise yards; we watch as his head and shoulders tilt and jerk a little, and as his hand fidgets inside his pants pocket. To some viewers, including a Superior Court judge presiding over a legal action to suppress Wiseman's documentary, it looks as if the subject is masturbating.[29] Nothing about these images themselves, nor about what we can perceive of the inmate's physical appearance at a certain time and place, is necessarily inconsistent with this impression. Indeed, other parts of the movie seem to raise the possibility that we are supposed to think of the image as depicting masturbation: Prior to this scene, we have been shown full frontal nudity, disturbing conduct on the part of both inmates and their keepers, and an exchange between another patient and his doctor during which masturbation is an explicit topic. Another "sordid" spectacle would hardly be unexpected. However, the information provided by the image track is compatible with an alternative conclusion, namely, that the man's head and hand movements belong to a repertoire of nonerotic nervous habits. Wiseman himself asserted in court that he did not believe the man to be masturbating and that he edited this sequence thinking only of his actual nervous habits, with which the cineaste claimed familiarity; several guards corroborated his testimony as to the nature of the hand movements.[30]

Do the documentarian's own beliefs about the depiction's content settle the question of how we are to interpret this controversial scene? Do his professed attitudes establish that it is true in the non-fiction that the man fidgets innocently? The answer, I think, ought to be no. Wiseman may well have thought his subject's gestures nonerotic, but aside from executing a Type I plan to show us the look of that individual's behavior at a given location from certain camera perspectives, he has taken no steps to convey those beliefs to his viewers. Subsequently, the ambiguous nature of the pre-filmic situation itself is reflected in the movie's content. There is, perforce, a fact of the matter regarding the imagery's natural interpretation*; and quite possibly it is that natural interpretation* that Wiseman desires to be true in his documentary. But in as much as that meaning is equivocal, for viewers, the director cannot regard it as an explicit, unambiguous part of the film's content, despite his own beliefs. And we cannot justifiably cite his beliefs as actual constraints on the scene's meaning and on how we are intended to interpret it, although we can cite them as one piece of evidence suggesting that the footage has this or that natural interpretation*.

For authorial attitudes to be a guide to our interpretations to what is true in the non-fiction, they must function, as we have often said, as effective communicative intentions. What this means is that they must exert some decisive influence, by way of controlling the author's relevant filmmaking actions, over the condition of the cinematic representation; and they must be openly indicated, in the sense that it is reasonable for the filmmaker to expect a given target audience to be able to grasp his desires with respect to content.

Regarding the current scene, Wiseman's beliefs about content fail to satisfy these criteria. As I say, his demonstrative intentions see to it that the pre-filmic situation's ambiguity is preserved in the depiction itself. Having eschewed voice-over narration—and neglected to include other shots and on-screen or voice-over commentaries that might offer clarification—Wiseman makes no further effort to steer the viewer toward a convergence with his own beliefs. On the other hand, textual evidence and background assumptions about the kinds of individuals one might encounter in an institution such as Bridgewater make the masturbation hypothesis a relevant and appropriate alternative, to which some of the film's other features lend a degree of support. Moreover, given the context in which the shots occur, a lay audience, possessing no particular knowledge of this patient and no specialized diagnostic skills, could not be expected, on the basis of the limited visual information about the pre-filmic situation, to come to any automatic and certain conclusions regarding the innocence of the inmate's behavior.[31]

It seems, then, that in the current example that which is true in the documentary, like that which is true *simpliciter*, is ambiguous.[32] On the one hand, that which the imagery indicates about the pre-filmic situation is equivocal, at least for an audience lacking specialized knowledge of this particular patient and his psychiatric condition. On the other hand, the filmmaker has failed or did not intend to produce a representation in which it would be possible to make a principled choice between interpretations on the basis of his attitudes toward the pre-filmic scene—even though it may well be that, in his mind, there is a fact of the matter concerning what the inmate is doing.

When we turn to intentions for support for our judgments about content, we must therefore restrict ourselves to inferences regarding the sorts of action-orienting attitudes that a filmmaker would have good reason to think publicly accessible, and that we would have good reason to attribute to the filmmaker. Such interpretations of implicit content might proceed along the following lines. In *Night and Fog*, Resnais and poet Jean Cayrol, writer of the film's voice-over narration, try to give viewers an indelible impression of the Nazi concentration camp prisoner's subjective experience of internment. Their subtle but harrowing filmic essay seems to suggest that detainees, though conscious of the daily reality of their torment and degradation, were actually profoundly uncertain as to the nature of their situation and failed to grasp the structure of the institution in which they were plunged and the magnitude of its violence. At one point the narrator labels the "camp's reality" as *"insaisissable par ceux qui la subissent"* (inapprehensible to those who suffer it).

During his analysis of *Night and Fog*, William Rothman proposes that the above statement refers to a different psychological phenomenon, the prisoner's "struggle to survive" by "denying that the present was the real world."[33] Rothman links this affair to two related conditions. Prisoners, he suggests, take the "image" of reality on the other side of the fence for the real reality; their self-contained, bounded camp reality they regard as less real or unreal, "for the real world encompasses everything that exists ... it has—can have—no fence around it." His interpretation extends from an overarching premise that in *Night and Fog* the concentration camp fence is identified symbolically with a movie screen. According to Rothman, the fence makes the extra-camp world present to the detainee as a quasi-inaccessible slice of reality cropped or framed by the barbed wire boundaries—much like "a movie screen upon which the world is projected" makes a portion of the temporally anterior world present, in both the physical and temporal sense of "present," but unreachable to the viewer. Thus the fence provides prisoners with a re-presentation of reality—for them, a past reality of freedom—that somehow helps them adaptively and wishfully to suppress thoughts or beliefs about their current condition as prisoners.

Rothman's comments—inspired by Bazin and the leading contemporary Bazinian, Stanley Cavell—beg a number of philosophical questions about the nature of cinematic depiction and its purported identity with its pre-filmic object. But it speaks more directly to our interpretive issue to ask whether we might intelligently doubt that the filmmakers had a commitment to alerting audiences to a fence/movie analogy embedded in something to the effect of a Bazinian identity thesis. True, in archival footage, we are shown a view of a village as seen through the wire, a vista described first as "the real world of peaceful landscapes, the world of the [prisoner's] past" then as merely "an image, for the deportee." But this is the only occasion when the prisoner's relation to the outside world is characterized as similar to that of a viewer to an image. It is a nonliteral claim underscoring the virtual hopelessness of breaching the camp's perimeter and regaining one's prior normal life. To be understood, it does not require belief on our part that the authors believe or mean either (a) that the barrier making the outside world inaccessible to the camp inmate is in some way itself like a surface upon which a photograph is projected or printed, or (b) that filmic images are ontologically identical to their pre-filmic objects, or (c) that the inmate's actual psychological and perceptual relation to the scene on the other side of the fence is similar to that of the spectator to the pre-filmic item. Nor does Rothman offer any further grounds—in the form of explicit textual features, or analyses of the authors' likely representational plans, or evidence of their own beliefs—that would lend credence to the idea that the authors' want and expect their audience to recognize either (a), (b), or (c) and thus took steps in that direction.

Not long after the narrator's figurative assertion, Resnais confronts us with material in which a relevant disanalogy between camp fences and movie theater screens is apparent: In a series of stills, we see two men, gunned down or electrocuted, hanging dead on the barbed wire. The kinds of inaccessibility imposed by guarded fences and screens are, evidently, dramatically different, as are the sorts of beliefs that prisoners and spectators would sincerely and understandingly assent to concerning the nature of their respective "barriers" and their perceptual relations to that which they can see through the fence and that which they can see by the photograph.

Resnais and Cayrol surely represent life within the concentration camp's borders as having an extraordinary, otherworldly quality. Any location containing, as we are shown, an orchestra, a zoo, hothouses, thousands of naked and terrified people, and watchtowers from which some of those people would occasionally be killed by listless soldiers is an alienating place, the reality of which is difficult to conceive. Indeed, from the average prisoner's own perspective, the logic of such an environment would be unlike that of ordinary life as they had known it and hence very difficult to penetrate. But it is far from obvious that the authors attribute to the prisoner a belief to the effect that, because he or she is detained within a fence, the reality therein is less real than that of the outside world because, after all, you can't put a fence around the real world.[34]

There is, however, a much more plausible thesis pertaining to how the filmmakers wish to describe one facet of the prisoner's psychology.

Aspects of Interpretation 241

Rather than denial of the camp's reality, Resnais and Cayrol emphasize the sort of cognitive breakdown that attends the deportee's experience. Onwards from the time of their deportation, they are literally trapped in a course of events, none of which, to put it in ordinary terms, add up, from their subjective perspective. It is their progression from one bewildering situation to the next that the filmmakers graphically chart.

Massing at the train station, the nature of their destination unknown, deportees are shown moving back and forth in confusion before they are loaded into suffocating box cars in which they cannot differentiate between day and night. Upon their arrival, the narrator tells us that they were "driven at gunpoint, while dogs barked and searchlights wheeled," through gates promising *"ARBEIT MACHT FREI."* "First sight of the camp" is depicted with a close-up of a man's face, eyes and mouth wide open. Amassed again, but now naked, rows of people fill a yard; the voice-over notes, "It is another planet." Soon the inmates are tattooed, and clothed in uniforms bearing numbers, letters, or coded icons; now they are "caught up in the game of a still incomprehensible hierarchy" of racial prisoners, political detainees, common criminals, prisoner-functionaries, guards, S.S. officers, and bureaucrats. The authors go on to stress the uncertainties faced by those living in a locale in which a walk through the yard or a trip to the latrine could end in death from a random gun shot or at the hands of a drunken Kapo. Finally, over images of inmates staring at their liberators from behind barbed wire, the narrator describes these people as looking on "without understanding. Are they free? Will life recognize them?"

Apart from these textual features, there are concrete biographical and historical reasons why it makes sense for us to interpret *Night and Fog* as referring to the prisoner's condition as one marked by an inability to surmount a limited or deficient understanding of the nature of his or her situation. Cayrol, himself a camp survivor, would have been intimately familiar with the uncertainty and cognitive limitations that historians of the Holocaust have documented as integral parts of the experience of internment. In the present context, a comment by Wolfgang Sofsky is especially telling:

> Surrounded everywhere by death, they were incapable of seeing the camp as a whole and gauging the extent of the dying there. Their horizons were limited to the immediate proximate world around them. Tomorrow the fellow prisoner who had been toiling next to them today might disappear— transferred to another block, the hospital, or another camp, or beaten to death somewhere. The foreigners who understood no German often had no idea where they were and for whom they were working. They learned nothing about the activity of the resistance group and the fierce rivalry between

the prisoner-functionaries. The average prisoner eked out a miserable existence, locked in an unfathomable cage of terror.[35]

Spectatorship is not telepathy; nor are movies magic windows opening directly onto the contents of their creators' minds. Yet there are times when a documentary's explicit features, along with relevant pieces of historical and biographical background knowledge, strongly recommend the attribution of certain action-orienting communicative plans to the author. Assuming the filmmaker moderately rational, and his movie the outcome of purposive action, we may judge that a work such as this likely realizes plans such as these. In light of the available evidence, it is the judgment that makes the best sense of why the work is constructed as it is. In such cases, our reasoning about authorial intentions can give us sufficient grounds for preferring one interpretation over its rival.

Notes

1. Erotetic narratives and narration proceed by generating questions about the actions and events represented in a movie and then answering them, or most of them, in ensuing scenes. For discussions of the workings of this type of narrative in fiction films, see Noël Carroll, *Mystifying Movies: Fads and Fallacies in Contemporary Film Theory* (New York: Columbia University Press, 1988), 171–181. Carl Plantinga offers a substantive commentary on the role of this narrative mode in non-fiction film, during which he describes "formal voice" non-fictions as partaking in erotetic narration: "They perform two significant operations: (1) they pose a clear question or a relevant and coherent set of questions (or they elicit such questions on the part of the spectator), and (2) they answer every salient question they pose"; see *Rhetoric and Representation in Nonfiction Film* (Cambridge: Cambridge University Press, 1997), 107.

2. For a cogent introduction to this problem, and one possible solution to it, see Annette Barnes, *On Interpretation* (Oxford: Blackwell, 1988).

3. Robert Stecker, "Relativism About Interpretation," *Journal of Aesthetics and Art Criticism* 53 (1995): 14; see also his "Incompatible Interpretations," *Journal of Aesthetics and Art Criticism* 50 (1992): 292–298.

4. Susan Feagin, "Incompatible Interpretations of Art," *Philosophy and Literature* 6 (1982): 133–146.

5. Robert Audi, *The Structure of Justification* (Cambridge: Cambridge University Press, 1993); Susan Haack, *Evidence and Inquiry: Towards Reconstruction in Epistemology* (Oxford: Blackwell, 1995); Richard Miller, *Fact and Method: Explanation, Confirmation, and Reality in the Natural and the Social Sciences* (Princeton: Princeton University Press, 1987); Paul K. Moser, *Knowledge and Evidence* (Cambridge: Cambridge University Press, 1989).

6. The term "rationality heuristic," and the way in which I am using it, derives from Paisley Livingston, *Literature and Rationality: Ideas of Agency in Theory and Fiction* (Cambridge: Cambridge University Press, 1991), 45.

Aspects of Interpretation 243

7. Livingston, *Literature and Rationality*, 45.

8. I owe the term "real author intentionalism" to Gregory Currie, *Image and Mind: Film, Philosophy, and Cognitive Science* (Cambridge: Cambridge University Press, 1995), 243, who associates it with the idea that the task of the interpreter of narrative fiction is to discover the author's intended meaning for the text. It should be clear that I attach a somewhat different sense to the term, while retaining reference to the idea of privileging the actual author's intentions. Note as well that Currie goes on to reject this interpretive principle, as he construes it, in favor of implied author intentionalism (see *Image and Mind*, 245–249).

9. Bill Nichols, "The Voice of Documentary," in *New Challenges for Documentary*, ed. Alan Rosenthal (Berkeley: University of California Press, 1988), 50.

10. Plantinga, *Rhetoric and Representation in Nonfiction Film*, 99–100.

11. Thomas W. Benson and Carolyn Anderson, *Reality Fictions: The Films of Frederick Wiseman* (Carbondale: Southern Illinois University Press, 1989), 109–110.

12. Currie, *Image and Mind*, 245.

13. Nichols, *Realism and Representation*, 77, 79.

14. Miller, *Fact and Method*, 468, discusses the origins of this truism and its role in an argument against skepticism about the existence of unobservables.

15. Those looking for a handy overview of the fracas will want to take advantage of this one-stop *JFK* shopping: Oliver Stone and Zachary Sklar, *JFK: The Book of the Film* (New York: Applause Books, 1992). This compendium includes a version of the movie's screenplay annotated with research notes; the script is followed by reviews, opinion and editorial pieces culled from popular journals, and responses from and interviews with Stone; along with this material, a selection of declassified government documents and a bibliography of assassination and conspiracy writings are presented.

16. Plantinga, *Rhetoric and Representation in Nonfiction Film*, 24.

17. Oliver Stone, quoted in Lance Morrow and Martha Smilgis, "Plunging Into the Labyrinth," in Stone and Sklar, *JFK: The Book of the Film*, 298.

18. The quotations are, respectively, from: Oliver Stone, "Stone's *JFK*: A Higher Truth?" in Stone and Sklar, *JFK: The Book of the Film*, 199; "Who Is Re-Writing History?" in Stone and Sklar, *JFK: The Book of the Film*, 276; Oliver Stone, quoted in David Ansen, "What Does Oliver Stone Owe History?" in Stone and Sklar, *JFK: The Book of the Film*, 295; Oliver Stone, "Oliver Stone Talks Back," in Stone and Sklar, *JFK: The Book of the Film*, 352. Zackary Sklar, co-screenwriter of *JFK*, observes that the movie "presents the hypothesis that Kennedy was assassinated because those institutional forces with a vested interest in the cold war perceived him as a threat"; see Zackary Sklar, "Exchange: Jousting After Camelot," in Stone and Sklar, *JFK: The Book of the Film*, 473.

19. Stone, "Stone's *JFK*: A Higher Truth?" 202.

20. Kent Bach and Robert Harnish, *Linguistic Communication and Speech Acts* (Cambridge, Mass.: M.I.T. Press, 1979), 43, define disputatives—demurring, disputing, objecting, protesting, questioning—as the communicator's expression of (1) a belief that there is reason not to believe that **P**, despite what is claimed by a hearer or is otherwise under discussion, and (2) the intention that the hearer believe that there is reason not to assent to **P**.

21. Stone, quoted in Morrow and Smilgis, "Plunging Into the Labyrinth," 298.

22. In what comes closest to a substantive remark on his use of "myth," Stone writes that "the importance of a historical episode is not just its factual content but its emotional and ethical significance as well. Why did it happen? What does it mean? Was it a triumph or a tragedy? For whom? This process of evaluation, when undertaken by a whole society, eventually leads to the creation of a cultural myth. Unlike children's fairy tales, myths have always expressed the true inner meaning of human events. Myths are dynamic. They reinterpret history in order to create lasting, universal truths. For example, artists for centuries have tackled exactly the same historical and religious stories and produced a Christ with a thousand faces." He goes on, in the next paragraph, to say, "From Griffith to Kubrick, moviemakers have operated on the principle that the dramatic force of a story transcends the 'facts.' With *JFK*, we are attempting to film the true inner meaning of the Dallas labyrinth—the mythical and spiritual dimension of Kennedy's murder—to help us understand why the shots in Dealey Plaza still continue to reverberate in our nightmares"; see Stone, "Oliver Stone Talks Back," 356.

To analyze these comments in depth is to risk attributing to them more sense then they really possess. They simply beg too many questions for one to extract from them a coherent thesis about what kind of activity *JFK*'s cinematic myth-making is supposed to be. Not the least of these questions is how the director would differentiate between, on one hand, something special called a historical episode's "inner meaning" and, on the other hand, factual descriptions and explanations of (a) the event's proximal and distal causes and (b) a given population's beliefs and feelings about that event. And I cannot decide whether he is implying that he as an artist is making up a "true meaning" of Kennedy's murder and offering it to the public as a palliative for their putative trauma, or if he is discovering the transcendental significance of this event and merely reporting it back to spectators. Readers of documentary film theory may detect a probably unintended Griersonian tone to Stone's statement. To them, it might sound as if a myth is a creative interpretation or treatment of actuality, where creativity in no way precludes insight and truth. More cynically, one might suspect that Stone is responding to heavy criticism by saying something to the effect that he might be mistaken about—or indifferent to—a lot of the facts, but that he's convinced that he knows better why Kennedy was killed.

23. The phrases in quotation marks derive from: Stone, quoted in Morrow and Smilgis, "Plunging into the Labyrinth," 298; and Stone, quoted in Roger Ebert, "Interview with Oliver Stone," in Stone and Sklar, *JFK: The Book of the Film*, 251.

24. Plantinga, *Rhetoric and Representation in Nonfiction Film*, 23–24, implies that hypothetical speculation somehow contributes to the movie's ambiguous relation both to fiction and to non-fiction.

25. For an analysis of suggestive communicative acts, consult Bach and Harnish, *Linguistic Communication and Speech Acts*, 43–44.

26. See, for instance, Stone, "Stone's *JFK*: A Higher Truth," 199; herein, Stone professes his belief that the "conclusion that Lee Harvey Oswald acted alone is not believed by most people." This article appeared while the movie was still in production, over six months before its general release. A *Washington Post* poll in

May of 1991 showed that only 19 percent of Americans think that Oswald acted alone; this information is cited by George Lardner Jr., "On the Set: Dallas in Wonderland," in Stone and Sklar, *JFK: The Book of the Film*, 198.

27. Plantinga, *Rhetoric and Representation in Nonfiction Film*, 23.

28. See G. Roy Levin, ed., *Documentary Explorations: 15 Interviews with Filmmakers* (New York: Doubleday, 1971), 279.

29. Benson and Anderson, *Reality Fictions*, 45, 82. Benson and Anderson's detailed account of the Commonwealth of Massachusetts's attempts to censor *Titicut Follies* is both an excellent research resource and a fascinating read.

30. Ibid., 45. The authors quote from the court transcripts.

31. Referring to Wiseman's letters and production notes, Benson and Anderson, pages 12–13, mention that the filmmaker had foreseen broadcast of his documentary on National Educational Television as well as exhibition in educational and public institutions for training and teaching purposes.

32. My conception of ambiguity is borrowed from Paisley Livingston, "Characterization and Fictional Truth in the Cinema," in *Post-Theory: Reconstructing Film Studies*, ed. David Bordwell and Noël Carroll (Madison: University of Wisconsin Press, 1996), 166.

33. William Rothman, *Documentary Film Classics* (Cambridge: Cambridge University Press, 1997), 48. All of the following citations from Rothman's discussion can be found on this page.

34. The theme of denial is nonetheless pervasive in *Night and Fog*. Indeed, the film makes a special point of illustrating the self-deception of the commandant and other keepers. The commandant, pictured standing at an observational post above the camp but looking away from it, toward the camera, is characterized as "feigning ignorance of the camp." Later, we are shown him, his wife, and his dog, ensconced in a nearby villa, visiting with guests, managing to maintain a social life, as if living "in any other garrison town." These images are part of a long sequence describing the "semblance of a real city" within the camp: Among other amenities, there is a hospital (where pseudo-medical atrocities are perpetrated), a residential district (barracks jammed with prisoners), and a brothel (where privileged prisoner-functionaries prey on women, better fed than most, but still captives). Perhaps the facade of urban planning facilitates self-deception on the part of guards, S.S. men, and Kapos and thereby helps alleviate the psychological dissonance between believing one's self to be an ordinary, decent person and participating in a daily genocidal routine.

35. Wolfgang Sofsky, *The Order of Terror: The Concentration Camps*, trans. William Templer (Princeton: Princeton University Press, 1997), 151.

9

The Truth of Non-Fiction

To assert that **P** usually manifests belief or knowledge that **P**, which makes it generally appropriate to take an interest in the assertion's truth. Indeed, during communicative exchanges, there is often a burden—sometimes a quite heavy burden—on the interpreter to make a determination, at least tentatively, about whether the asserted content is probably true, or about what true beliefs might be derived from that content. If a friend tells you that there is a storm system coming, bringing a severe blizzard today, and you have not put snow tires on your car; or if your physician tells you that your test results are inconclusive, and that she now has doubts as to whether you are cured, what you will do next, and how you shall feel about it, depend on what you believe about how well a statement indicates how things really are. Interpreting cinematic constatives is like interpreting constatives in general. Usually the spectator has, to some extent, a cognitive or practical interest in whether or not they are accurate; and usually communicators have some interest in leading an audience to believe that the constative is true.

Often one makes top-of-the-head judgments about whether a representation is true or false, without much in the way of confirmation procedures and explicit reasoning; sometimes one merely assumes that there is some degree of truth preservation, as when watching the nightly news. Maybe reporters only ever report the lies that the ruling elite want them to report; but if the White House correspondent says that the president announced today that Oceania is our ally, one can be reasonably sure that the president really made that announcement. In other cases, what we know or believe about its relation to how things actually are or were in reality help us to decide if a work, such as *JFK*, is best classed as non-fiction. For these reasons, the question of the truth of non-fiction is integral to the topic of interpretation.

This final chapter examines the reasons we sometimes have for regarding cinematic constatives as true and as inputs to the spectator's acquisition of knowledge. What follows is mostly a constructive enterprise. My project is not to refute the sweeping skeptical, anti-realist suggestions and claims made by Bill Nichols, Michael Renov, Trinh T. Minh-ha, Brian Winston, and others. I suspect that I broadly agree with their sentiments, since I, too, presume that both making and viewing non-fictions provide abundant opportunities for misrepresenting reality and for subsequently helping to foster corresponding irrational, imprudent, unjust responses to problems, especially human and social troubles. The causes and consequences of these cognitive failures—including factors and effects involving desire, ideology, and distorted ethical-political thinking—deserve serious inquiry. But my further assumption, which takes me beyond the present study's bounds, is that such inquiry requires at least tacit commitment to the idea that there are facts, that we can know them, and that learning them helps us attain a measure of insight, control, happiness, and human goodness within our environments.

I doubt that our goals—as researchers, teachers, cultural critics—within academic cinema studies are coherently stated and best served when shackled to the professed rejection or questioning of the possibility of insight and knowledge. Hence my own small contribution to our understanding of the epistemological aspects of cinematic representation and interpretation is to plant the first step toward an explanation of how non-fictions might be more or less true and how it might be that interpreters sometimes come to have good and sufficient reason to regard some of their cinematically derived beliefs about reality as approximately accurate.

I propose that cinematic constatives sometimes facilitate epistemic access to features of the world. By "epistemic access," I intend information gathering, especially when this process results in somebody acquiring approximately true beliefs for which they have a degree of justification.[1] Watching motion picture non-fictions usually puts us in the position passively or actively to learn facts about both cinematic works and extra-cinematic realities. Loosely stated, one way in which we enjoy the second kind of success is by encountering representations the contents of which we have grounds to believe are true, where truth involves preserving facts about the world. But often it can be difficult for spectators to ascertain which facts this content makes available. In such instances, the epistemic access a representation affords depends more rather than less heavily on our efforts to justify our beliefs about what is actually indicated about reality.

Truth As Correspondence

Currently there is no uncontroversial definition of truth available to us. For the sake of my argument, I adhere to this minimal correspondence definition, as recently defended by Paul Moser: "The claim that a proposition, P, is true means that things are as they are stated to be by P."[2] Traditional correspondence theories require that propositions or their constituent elements faithfully picture reality or be somehow isomorphic with how things really are in the world. But philosophers find the notion of a representation mirroring or matching the structure of the world difficult to explain and defend.[3] How can we believe that a proposition is true if we cannot grasp a clear sense in which it is isomorphic with some extra-propositional thing? It is for this reason that Moser proposes a version of minimal correspondence, where truth is a relation between a proposition—the content of a belief, statement, or any sort of representation—and how some part of reality is. We believe that a proposition is true when we believe that it indicates how things are. Representation—successful representation, when the system fulfills its function of indicating that its object is in such and such a condition, when that object is in that condition—is precisely this sort of minimal correspondence.

In the current definition, the idea of truth being a description of "how things are in reality" is surely not radically independent of reference to the conceiver. For a true proposition to be of any epistemic interest as an input to somebody's knowledge it has to be the kind of thing that can be formulated or possessed by a conceiver. What's more, reality, to be knowable, cannot be wholly mind-independent, because then it would be inaccessible to us. And some of the realities that we come to know are one another's beliefs, intentions, desires, and other psychological states—that is, mind-dependent facts. But the minimal correspondence definition also requires that truth be a relation between a proposition and the world, and not entirely the product of a relation between a conceiver and a proposition, such as the act of conceiving, uttering, or assenting to the proposition. A belief is not true or false because someone, or everyone, ardently believes or desires it to be (not) true. It is true because it states how things actually are. Let us also stress, with Moser, that the minimal correspondence definition is **not** a criterion for discovering whether a representation is true.[4] It is just a definition of truth. We must look elsewhere in epistemology for definitions and strategies of justification, so that we have grounds for holding that any given proposition permits us access to how things are in reality.

There is another intelligible sense in which a proposition's truth depends upon the conceiver or inquirer. A proposition truly or falsely describes an actual situation only if it is supposed to indicate how things stand with respect to that situation. Generally speaking, which situation(s) an artificial representational system describes depends on what a maker or user gives it the job of describing. Prior to and independent of the arrival of the right kind of observer, any particular region of pebbles on the beach is just a bunch of pebbles on the beach. It is not "about" anything. But when you and I come along, we notice one situation, an a-rational random pattern, that puts us in mind of another situation, Marcello Mastroianni's face; subsequently, we amuse ourselves by employing the fortuitously shaped bunch of pebbles as an approximately accurate depiction of the great actor; this region's truth-bearing correspondence with something beyond itself results from a functional adaptation that we perform on it.

Or recall Chapter 2's commentary on misrepresentation.[5] An image produced with the aid of a massively distorting fish-eye lens, so that its pre-filmic subject looks as if she has one giant eye and a nose wrapping behind her head, is not a misrepresentation, hence not false—not unless we have reason to suspect that its maker rationally expected or intended for a target audience to interpret it as a literal and sincere description of how its subject looks pre-filmically, in reality.[6] Contrast this case with a more subtle optical manipulation, as when a photographer adjusts lens and lighting in order to get viewers to believe falsely that a pop idol is taller and thinner than he really is.

Assessing truth and falsehood is a matter of ascertaining which situations it is the representation's function to represent. Generally, we determine this with reference to its maker's or user's intentions. Watkin's *The War Game* (1966) cannot be accused of misrepresenting Kent as suffering a (past, present, or future) nuclear siege, because he openly and effectively communicates to his audience that his film is, in the relevant respects, interpreted* by an imaginary attack on this location. If there is to be an evaluation of his documentary's truth value, we must, instead, focus on its indicator relation to some (putatively) actual state of affairs. *The War Game*'s fictive destruction of Kent itself serves, as we have seen, a further representational function as a model. It is supposed to describe how things really stand with respect to certain actual and future states of affairs and thus is a vehicle for making literal assertions and predictions about Britain's civil defense policies and procedures, their likely effectiveness in the event of nuclear war, and the types of consequences that such a catastrophe can be expected to have for a civilian population. *The War Game*'s truth or falseness is therefore relative to that of its models of certain realities.

Although I shall return to this topic below, I should now make a special point of saying that a non-fiction's truth, in the current sense, is not necessarily compromised or supported by the presence of a narrative. As I understand narrative, it has nothing essentially to do with "assertion," "truth," "fiction," "fictive," or "false." It is merely a particular kind of representation—of some agent(s) meeting and responding to an obstacle to the realization of a desire or objective. Such a representation may be lodged within fiction or non-fiction; and it might describe either imaginary or real occurrences. Hence the narrative course of events described by Les Blank's *Burden of Dreams* (1982)—roughly, Werner Herzog's protracted struggles in the Amazonian jungle to make his movie, *Fitzcarraldo* (1982)—is true to the extent that it corresponds to an actual course of events and the various cause-effect relations between them, that is, some of those constituting Herzog's protracted struggles in the jungle to film *Fitzcarraldo*.

A proposition's status as true is like its status as non-fiction, in as much as there are many factors having no essential bearing on a work's veracity. Truth is independent of form and style of expression, presence or absence of narrative, and the motives that drive the inquirer. Consider the following proposition: "Child labor, corporate tax avoidance, and the closing of North American factories are consequences of increased international trade and the transformation of the world into a single market." Now consider all of the ways of communicating this alleged information to a target audience: I could stand in a bucket wearing a clown suit, shouting in a silly, high-pitched voice; I could publish an article, accompanied by statistical analyses, in an economics journal; I could hire a famous actor, dress him in fabulous clothes, and film him against a beautiful Mediterranean backdrop as he looks straight into the camera and says, "Hello, I'm a famous actor, you're watching a movie that is an ideological construct of bourgeois Western culture, and I've been paid to tell you that the filmmaker believes that child labor, corporate tax avoidance . . . "; I could spray-paint the appropriate sentence in big, fat, multicolored letters on the side of a bank; I could hire the Mormon Tabernacle Choir to sing something to this effect, to the tune of "Amazing Grace"; or I could pay Oliver Stone to produce a *JFK*-esque movie in which a famous actor, playing a real economist, recreates the "true life story" of someone's struggles to convince politicians and investors that child labor . . . .

Moreover, my motives for concluding that **P** and publicizing it just as I do can be extremely diverse: an interest in the truth, confidence in the results of careful research performed according to my field's methodological and theoretical principles, anticipation of what my audience wants to hear, desire for professional advancement, conservative leanings, Marxist leanings, a wish for my mother's love, raging epistophilia, self-aggrandizement, self-loathing, and so on. Presumably, some contextual and motivational factors and some rules for the conduct of inquiry are more conducive to learning facts, others less so; wishful thinking, delusions of grandeur, and a methodology based on tarot card readings may be more a hindrance than help to knowledge production. Similarly, not all rhetorical strategies and modes of communication will efficiently and convincingly transmit the belief that **P** to every audience. A documentarian's plans for how she will gather, record, and communicate information and beliefs obviously influences whether or not this material will be epistemically reliable and accessible to her audience's assent.

But it is important not to conflate the condition for a proposition's truth—minimal correspondence with reality—with the myriad possible conditions serving the discovery and communication of truth. In other words, even a tarot card-reading, epistophiliac, falsetto clown in a bucket can speak the truth, sometimes. Truth isn't guaranteed by style or rhetoric, but neither is error and falsehood. By definition, representation and correspondence are not properties of the representational system's intrinsic structures and organization but of its real relations to something else.

Even those generally sympathetic to the idea of knowledge tend to regard a definition of truth as a prelude to a more serious problem, that of judging whether any given proposition is true. If, for example, truth is correspondence, how is one supposed to establish that the correspondence exists? People do not enjoy totally concept-free access to reality, unfiltered and unconstrained by the contents of their minds and the dictates of their cultures—meaning that it is not as if one need only glance over one's shoulder for a direct and unmediated look at how reality actually is, in comparison to how the proposition describes it to be. Ascertaining the truth or falsehood of a movie constative, or a belief derived from viewing one, is therefore like establishing that of any other type of representation or belief. It requires an indication of truthfulness. It demands epistemic justification.

Non-Fiction Cinema and Justification

We need not assume that all cinematic constatives spring from a nontrivial, substantive interest in discovering or conveying truth. All in all, *Alien Autopsy: Fact or Fiction?* (Tom McGough, 1995) is mainly supposed to confuse people and encourage their incredible beliefs. But some non-fictions do partake of a significant interest in truth; it is one such artifact that I shall examine closely in the context of the present discussion. I should like to be emphatic about this discussion's framework. Its target is the justification of epistemic, not legal, moral, or political, beliefs.[7] It is restricted to the truth value of judgments pertaining to the movie's content—that is, an external state of affairs that it is the representation's function to describe. Finally, the discussion's focus is the context of serious inquiry.

Often people spontaneously make up their minds that a non-fiction is true or false, or jump to a conclusion concerning what it means about reality, without trying to justify their conclusions by carefully weighing the cinematically presented evidence in relation to other information culled from a further effort of investigation and from knowledge-seeking procedures. In this comparatively passive mode of reception, they might simply rely on assumptions about the trustworthiness of the representation's source. Perhaps they will also lean on a "judgmental heuristic." For example, a jobless person watching a report on unemployment might be inclined to accept the more dire estimates of the unemployment rate; given that his own situation is most salient to him and that his daily activities, such as visits to employment agencies, likely bring him into contact with other job-seekers, his sense of what a correct estimate is could be cognitively skewed by the vivid sample of evidence subjectively available to him.

Another heuristic applies resemblance or "goodness of fit" criteria to problems of categorization and causal explanation; for example, the *Titicut Follies* (Frederick Wiseman, 1967) viewer might be inclined to account for an inmate's violent emotional outbursts in terms of affective and personal tumult, overlooking possible sub-personal, biochemical roots.[8] Quick and dirty inferences may sometimes be rational and successful. But there are also scholarly and other special circumstances when we need to become more actively engaged in what ought to be a principled judgment of a representation's truth value and of the support it lends to certain of our beliefs. George Holliday's videotape of Rodney King's beating by Los Angeles police officers has certainly occasioned a few such engagements.

Although the situation it describes is anything but simple, Holliday's video, shot from the balcony of an apartment building, is a rudimentary cinematic constative. It is the product of a Type I plan, its maker having photographed the scene below in one continuous take, unbeknownst to the participants in the drama down on the street; then he took it to the media with the intention, reproduced by subsequent users, that viewers take the attitude of belief toward whatever it is that is depicted. A more formally and stylistically complex non-fiction, the result of extensive Type II planning, could confront the spectator with different obstacles to gaining knowledge of the world (more on this below). But in taking a conscientious epistemic stance toward the Holliday tape, one must solve the same problem one encounters upon taking that stance toward any constative, that is, determining what one may now reasonably believe about how things stand with respect to a given, putatively real extra-cinematic situation. And in response to any cinematic constative, the basic answer to the question "What possible justification is there for believing that **P**?" is fundamentally the same: The more perceptual evidence and other beliefs that support one's belief that **P**, the more justified one is in believing that **P**.

It has been said that we cannot rely on the Holliday video to give us epistemic access to reality because its significance is, in large part, con-

The Truth of Non-Fiction

tingent on the viewer's interpretive frame—the a priori concepts, assumptions, prejudices, fears, and desires that one applies to the footage, thereby pressing it into service as confirmation of those presuppositions.[9] Thanks to its indexical properties, the image may be an authentic "imprint" of an actual historical event, but the meaning of this recorded event, as Nichols puts it, "remains the result of interpretations applied and accepted."[10] Thus an all white jury in Simi Valley, California, might believe that the imagery shows a dangerous black male threatening a team of law enforcers doing their duty at great personal risk; whereas to African-American television viewers in South Central Los Angeles, its meaning will likely be profoundly different.

Let us grant that the meanings audiences ascribe to the tape are potentially relative to their attitudes, experiences, and biases. The fact of the matter is that some interpretations—but no interpretations*—are framework relative. There are probably a great many contexts, as when inquirers share a serious interest in truth-seeking, in which we would agree that such "readings" are strictly speaking **mis**interpretations. In any event, ascription is not the only kind of relation that gives rise to meaning. To the extent that it is a product of various constraints exercised on the emergence of a representational system's condition, upstream of any reception processes, the video exhibits a gamut of meanings—external and mental significances—among its objective features. Rather than inevitably enforcing their own, interpreters can discover these objective meanings and thereby achieve a moderate form of epistemic access to a prior course of events.

One activity of interpretation, I have said, consists partly of the detection of a movie's (natural) interpretation(s)*. Holliday's video owes its emergence to its author's execution of a Type I content plan. In making and exhibiting this document Holliday's aim was, and continues to be, to portray whatever situation was emerging at some distance before the camera, at a particular location, and in so doing to yield to nomic and necessary connections to ensure the video records a selection of information pertaining to that situation. Its interpretation* is thus subordinated to its natural interpretation*—that course of events (**COE**) to which the depiction is necessarily related and that it partially describes, owing to the condition of its natural indicator elements. Which situations and events are described is not, however, entirely clear—although some claims with respect to the video's content are much less trouble to justify than others.

Due to its natural pictorial significance, the Holliday video preserves a host of facts about the visible properties of a pre-filmic scene. By watching the video, one can acquire or form true beliefs about, roughly speaking, the look of that **COE**. This claim does not deny that there is loss of information between image and scene; obviously it is a limited and degraded slice of information available to viewers, since many of the pre-filmic scene's visible traits are obscured by the condition of the footage or simply not depicted; they are indiscernible even if we slow or freeze the frame. Yet a wide variety of such properties are perceptually and cognitively accessible to us, including: the appearance of objects, agents, and their doings; spatial, directional, and distance relations between individuals, and changes thereof; the sequence, duration, speed, and intensity of events; superficial cause-effect relations between events. Thus the tape indicates that: King, on the ground in such and such a position, is hit by **n** baton blows from Officer Wind, n^1 being faster and harder than n^2, n^2 closer to King's head than n^3; later Officer Briseno steps on the back of King's neck, which forces King to flatten out against the pavement; momentarily, King tries to rise again; and so on.

So what grounds do we have for regarding these beliefs as true, that is, as themselves preserving facts about the **COE**? The quick answer is that we can see that these facts are the case. But that is shorthand for a longer justification, one having a partial foundation in experiential evidence that is not itself exclusively dependent upon any further beliefs. Watching the video, the observer does not literally see King and the police. Instead, he or she has sensory contact with a depiction that contains sensory information about the extra-cinematic **COE**; it is by having a sensory representation of the former that he or she is aware of the visible properties of the latter (and not vice versa). In this way, a person receives visual information about the **COE**, has a visual experience of some of its visible features, without being in properly sensory contact with that scene itself. And in this way, one aspect of the observer's subjective perceptual experience preserves facts about reality—about both the imagery and the earlier **COE**—that are not themselves derived from the content of or connections between the observer's (nor anybody else's) subjective conceptual states or other psychological attitudes.

As some contemporary epistemologists stress, such a perceptual experience is an evidential basis that does not come from us but from the world.[11] Presuming that there can be a one-way causal relation between sensory experience and cognitive uptake, facts about the world, unmediated by any further beliefs, become available to agents as constraints on the contents of their empirical beliefs. Insofar as humans endure within their environments, routinely avoiding or overcoming obstacles to their survival, it seems probable that such constraints exist. This thesis should not be confused with the fantastical idea that there exists a mind-independent, absolute assurance for the perfect correspondence of our beliefs with reality; nor does it underwrite the assumption that desire, confusion, and limitations of our cognitive capacities never stop us from exploiting the information made available to us by experience. It merely holds that the chain of epistemic justification can sometimes terminate with successful reference to how things stand in the world. What justifies our belief that n^2 lands closer to King's head than n^3? Our visual experience of n^2 landing closer to King's head than n^3.

Allowing for the relevance of a nonbelief, experiential anchor for knowledge does not require justification exclusively by sensory perception, without support from other beliefs. On the contrary, such a belief, **P**, as "at t^n Briseno steps on the back of King's neck" is only warranted to the degree that it is supported by a branching "tree of reasons" constituting a set of beliefs mutually relevant to the issue of whether **P** is true. Here I have in mind Haack's counterproposal to the assumption that chains of justifying beliefs are inevitably circular.[12] Such chains may generally be more like pyramids or "inverted trees of reasons": the belief that **P** is supported by beliefs **Q**, **R**, and **S**; the belief that **Q** is supported by the beliefs **T** and **U**; the belief that **R** is supported by **U** and **V**; that **S** is supported by **W**, **X**, **Y**; and so on. Haack notes that this schema allows for the emergence of loops without the coherentist having to concede that legitimate mutual support has been replaced by vicious circularity: Although it could be the case that **P** is one's reason for believing that **Y**, **Y** need not have a role in justifying **T** or **R**.

Hence an observer is to a greater rather than lesser degree justified in holding that **P** provided that this belief is further supported by beliefs that the video is photographically related to the actual incident in question, that it is not the product of Holliday staging and shooting a recreation of the events, that the depiction's appearance preserves information about the event's appearance, that one's experience of the video is the product of sensory contact with a video rather than an hallucination caused by a bump on the head or a scientist's thought-control experiment, and so on. Aside from their relation to further beliefs still, some of these beliefs can carry a degree of independent justification, in light of specific pieces of additional evidence as well as general experiences and truistic principles that no reasonable person would normally be in the position to doubt.

Recall, for instance, perceptual principles 1 through 5. Each of these would play, to varying degrees, a role in securing the observer's beliefs, upon watching (at normal or slow speed, or in freeze-frame mode) the Holliday tape—including the fifth principle, which reminds us that agents' uses of imagery can be skewed by desires and non-epistemic motivations, such as a defense lawyer's commitment to protecting his client. Additional, physical principles are also germane: for example, the force of one object is transferred to the other when they collide. Nor should we forget the relevance to justification of certain anthropological truisms, like the assumption that human behavior, rather than being random or controlled mainly from without, has a ratio; it often results from meaningful and regular relations among such mental states as beliefs, desires, emotions, fears, and intentions.

Some theorists are inclined to endorse the following proposition about people's experiences of the Holliday video: What one sees on this tape depends on one's attitudes prior to viewing because "people generally do not come to believe things *after* seeing them; they see things only when they *already* believe them—based on their prior *Lebenswelt* and media exposure."[13] I hope already to have shown that, taken literally, this relativist claim is patently false. There is no belief condition on sensory perception; and there are conceptual as well as empirical grounds for maintaining that a uni-directional relationship obtains between sensation and belief acquisition. Adjusting for the obvious types of differences in visual acuity, perspectival relations to the imagery, and favorability of viewing conditions, people see pretty much the same thing on their television monitors. Moreover, they must share many cognitive perceptions, even if, for whatever fanciful reasons, there can be important differences in cognitive uptake.

To be charitable to the relativist, we can render his claim as a truism about epistemic perception: One's capacity to perceive facts may be both positively and negatively affected by one's background knowledge, conceptual schemes, desires, affiliations, and so forth. Observers are not epistemically infallible; sometimes we think that we see that such and such is the case when it is really not that way. But sometimes our cognitive perceptions are veridical—we actually do see facts. In turn, these veridical cognitive perceptions can be crucial inputs to more general, inferential feats of epistemic access.

In the case of the Holliday video, cognitive perceptions and the judgments in which they figure are, indeed, likely to diverge. The root of the problem is easy to grasp. As I argued in Chapter 2, pace its causal connection to the depicted agents' actions, this depiction is not a natural counterfactual indicator of those people's psychological states. How much easier jurors'—and film scholars'—duties would be if video were the kind of representational system that, say, necessarily or nomically glowed red in case of racial malice, blue in case of lawful professional conduct violating no civil or human rights. But intentionality is one kind of non-pictorial external significance that is only conditionally indicated by the imagery's appearance. This contingency helps channel scholars toward the conclusion that, as far as the mental states of King and the officers are concerned, the tape's meaning is indeterminate. As Plantinga says, although "the video clearly showed the man's beating, it remained mute about his or the police men's intentions and motivations."[14]

The Truth of Non-Fiction

Nichols takes this premise one step further, offering it as grounds for the relativity of meaning to interpretive framework: "The meaning of the tape (as opposed to its indexical correspondence to a prior event, the actual beating), however, is the signified of the interpretive frame's signifiers, not an external referent."[15]

I think we ought to reverse this judgment. Although the videographer did not undertake further truth-seeking procedures (e.g., recording interviews with witnesses moments after the incident), and did not execute a post-filmic Type II plan to manipulate the images in order to comment on or clarify what scene (he believes) they show, the tape is no more mute about motivations and intentions than are the visible features of the officers' deeds. Rather, these sorts of unobservable, psychological features of the **COE** can be conditionally and implicitly indicated. The onus is then on the observer to gather up this implicit and often ambiguous information, relying upon the representation's properties along with other pertinent information and background beliefs that help individuate the agent's effective psychological states. The significance and epistemic value of the representation is, in the present respect, analogous to that of any outwardly observable aspect of an individual's behavior. The latter is a conditional indicator of a subjective meaning, that is, the beliefs, desires, and intentions with respect to which he or she performs the act in question. The constraints that the contents and motivational strengths of these subjective states exercise over the observed deed are what make that deed an action and what identify it as the kind of action it is. So provided that there is a determinate fact of the matter regarding what action a depicted agent is/was executing, there is a determinate fact of the matter regarding what action the imagery records.

For problem-solving purposes, suppose for a moment that the proximal cause of Briseno's stepping on King's neck is the following mental item: an intention to hurt this man prompted not exclusively nor even primarily for the sake of subduing an uncooperative suspect but, rather, for its own sake, in order to hurt him, where Briseno acquires this desire because he sees that the suspect is black. Now suppose, as we must, that a chunk of Holliday's tape depicts Briseno stepping on King's neck. What event does $i \ldots i_n$ record? The obvious answer is that it is naturally interpreted* by whatever action it is that Briseno performs at that time, that is, intrinsically motivated racial violence against King. This answer will be right if the video's production and/or use was guided by a Type I plan to exploit its natural indicator elements to represent some of the visually observable features of a pre-filmic scene, and if the policeman was engaged in the stated action. It is not required that the imagery be any more naturally indicative of the agent's mental state than are his overt physical gestures themselves. The video just means what this person's actions conditionally, intentionally-counterfactually mean about his state of mind, what he intends to accomplish by acting as he does. Thus we rely on the video's natural pictorial significance to bootstrap the representation's content to a dependency on some of the psychological attitudes of those depicted. Without believing or desiring it, the police and King exert wayward intentional constraints on the video's meaning. So the tape's meaning is the "signified" of an external referent, after all.

There are facts of the matter regarding what actions the agents shown on the Holiday tape are engaged in, hence there are facts of the matter regarding the tape's meaning with respect to what these agents are doing. Yet because the image track supplies only a thin slice of information pertaining to a **COE** that began before the camera started rolling, and because the recorded portion of this pre-filmic social-psychological **COE** is itself extremely complex and maybe a touch chaotic, those facts are bound to be obscure to spectators. The next obvious question is: Even if the tape simply means whatever a given individual means by acting as he does, how can we as observers of the tape apprehend this information and be sure of the truth of our judgments about the identity of the represented action?

Justifying claims about the identity of an actual extra-cinematic action is analogous to justifying claims about agential actions in general. In light of the available evidence, background beliefs, truistic and specialized principles, and reasoning, observers are sometimes to a degree justified in believing that the observed individual is or was performing such and such an action. One very general truistic principle is, of course, the rationality heuristic. In day-to-day interactions with others, we assume, unless we have special reasons not to, that people's behaviors are somehow guided by various psychological attitudes—mental states that need not be the sole determinants of conduct and that may themselves be constrained or influenced by certain extraneous factors (like threats or hallucinogens) but that nonetheless mediate between what acts we see them perform and what sense those acts make to the agent. Our encounters with the Holliday footage are no exception to this heuristic, for we can veridically see that the individuals portrayed are in fact agents rather than cyborgs or elaborate puppets; neither the tape itself nor any outside source stands as evidence to the contrary. Thus many of our claims about the pre-filmic situation—that it shows a beating; that "Briseno steps . . . "; "King rolls . . . "; "Powell followed the accepted procedure of . . . "— embed well-founded beliefs that the events in question can be adequately described and explained only in terms of conscious agency.

However, when trying to give a reasoned, defensible explanation of what it is that we see the police and their suspect doing, we need to go well beyond the rationality heuristic and our perceptual experiences of the tape in an effort to comprehend the relevant unobservable, non-pictorial properties of the represented **COE**. Here formulating, testing, and assenting to hypotheses about intentionality and motivation call for research and confirmation procedures. There's no need to be parsimonious about the types of resources and investigations that might be brought to bear on the problem. Mutually relevant material could include further sources of physical evidence, eye-witness and participant testimony; biographical and career information about those involved; evidence concerning police attitudes toward and encounters with minority citizens; accounts of similar altercations; documentation and analysis of relevant police procedures; existing social-psychological research into the various personality, cognitive, affective, and situational factors involved in the instigation and escalation of violent conflicts between law enforcers and their suspects; and so on. The more relevant the research and evidence one has taken into account are, the more favorable the reasons and evidence are to one's belief relative to its rivals; and the more independently secure the reasons and evidence supporting that belief are, the greater the degree of justification one has for believing that an agent did such and such with the specified intentions and motivations.

The kind of epistemic access motion pictures afford us is not a fully self-validating, god's-eye view transcending all weaknesses of human cognition by looking directly out onto the hidden-most structures of reality. Non-fictional movies help us to achieve epistemic access to the world when their properties are in indicator relations with actual extra-cinematic states of affairs. Sometimes these relations are more rather than less a-rational and law-like. In many other cases, the representation's capacity to indicate how things stand in reality is dependent upon such highly conditional factors as somebody's intentions.

The video indicates that Powell used a police baton, not a baseball bat, to beat his victim, because there is a nomic connection between the imagery's visible condition and the weapon that Powell actually wielded. The video indicates that this officer executed the action of striking King—that he intentionally hit and hurt this man for whatever subjective reasons, and that he did not swing his baton in the mistaken belief that he was playing baseball—only because certain agential attitudes played an effective role in generating the observed behavior and the imagery's content. Likewise, *The Thin Blue Line* (Errol Morris, 1988) indicates certain facts—that a man was convicted of a murder because various people had little interest in either learning of or acting on the truth—only because the film's director has knowledge of these facts and has engaged in complex planning and action consistent with passing them on to his audience.

Morris thereby presents us with some of his justification for believing that Adams is innocent. We, in turn, may adopt the film's content as part of our justification for assenting to this belief.

Symbolic Meaning, Narrative, and Epistemic Access

The Holliday video is a cinematic constative, without being paradigmatic of what most of us think of as a documentary. Documentaries are supposedly not mere recordings of unstaged pre-filmic scenes. Rather, they emerge from expressive, creative shapings of recorded material and perhaps also of that which transpires before the camera. When theorists wax skeptical of non-fiction film's rapport with knowledge, they often do so with that supposition in mind. It becomes a premise of their critique of documentary, a critique holding that the symbolic structures such movies embody, and the ways in which these are generated, are anathema to the cognitive purposes non-fictions are ordinarily thought apt to serve.

Anyone who deals in earnest with documentary cinema will be attentive to the question: Are the complex, mind-trammeled processes of representation, belief-formation, and communication that produce such works ever truth-conducive? My position is that figurative and narrative elements one finds in many documentaries are sometimes compatible with knowledge, that is, with the formation of beliefs that an inquirer has some warrant to regard as true.

I have already shown that photographic depictions are best regarded as adaptable to truth-preservation. Now I want to give reasons to hold that highly symbolic manipulations of the cinematic representational system's indicator elements may be epistemically valuable, too. As a concomitant of my realism, I propose that all manner of intentional processes undertaken by non-fictioneers can contribute to the representation of justified, true belief. Figurative and symbolic representation, narrative, and imagination are thus not to be identified with quasi-autonomous "tropological processes" that inevitably booby-trap truth-seeking. Instead, they are strategic components in someone's plan to indicate how things stand in some part of the world. Whether they help realize this plan and result in an audience's successful cognitive uptake depends on a variety of factors. These include their designated epistemic function within the representational system, the spectator's acuity, and the reliability of the author's truth-seeking and recording procedures.

Some critics admire, and would apply to cinema studies, Hayden White's suggestion that the language, narrative formulae, and concepts used by historians to identify and describe anthropological and social-historical domains of reality constitute "interpretations" of those domains.[16] In his view, properties and relationships ostensibly inherent in the object fields themselves are actually imposed upon the messy magma of history by investigators in the very act of representation. For instance, one historian might interpret the French Revolution as a satirically grotesque narrative; whereas another will "encode" the same events as tragedy.[17] Neither historian, however, reveals the true nature of the events usually associated with the French Revolution.

Discourse thus bears not a transparent but a tropic relation to truth: The figures of speech and thought historians employ, and the narratives and plots in which they organize their data, cause representations to veer away from representing things as they really are; the human sciences' mimetic-analytic prose discourses are prevented from describing reality by the overdetermining, inward pull of figuration and consciousness. Suspicions about historical writing have, as I say, girt some theorists for their assault on non-fiction cinema. Renov, citing White, identifies the documentary movie as one of those discourses that inevitably "'*constitutes* the objects which it pretends only to describe realistically and to analyze objectively.' Every documentary representation depends upon its own detour from the real, through the defiles of the audiovisual signifier (via choices of language, lens, proximity, and sound environment)."[18]

Renov, White, and their compeers strike me as granting unqualified priority to embellishing an idea of non-fictional discourse as naturally destined toward epistemic failure. The intentionality of representation, because ultimately tropic, turns the representation away from correspondence with reality and back into the recesses of metaphor and imagination whence discourse allegedly emerges. Now I realize that the parties involved are unlikely to endorse the main tenets of the view of intentionality that I advocate. Their writings typically presume the underlying sources of meaning to be powerful autonomous forces beyond the ken and control of rational agency. It frequently sounds as if, say, "epistephilia" or the "codes of realism" are themselves supposed to be at the helm of documentary filmmaking. Nevertheless many of the sorts of things that theorists single out as "problematizing" representation and knowledge overlap with that which I treat as reducible to mental, intentional phenomena: codes, conventions, norms, traditions, styles, gazes, institutions, figuration, symbolism, rhetoric, point of view, choice, selection, imagination, creativity, invention, expressivity, abstraction, subjectivity, consciousness, desire, bias, emphasis, voice, signification, interpretation, construction, attitude, plot, narrative, characterization, manipulation, discourse, and so on.

My current task is to state why I do not think that these phenomena are inherently and preeminently vehicles of misrepresentation. I glance at more complex cinematic representational systems, those characteristically nearer the Type II end of the spectrum of non-fictional plans and planning. Apropos of such documentaries, "the defiles of the audiovisual signifier" can be remarkable not because they impose a detour away from "the real," but for adding to our knowledge of reality.

To bolster this claim, let's begin with the use of storytelling in *The Thin Blue Line*. Interestingly, the story in Morris's documentary bears more than a faint resemblance to some familiar narrative attributes of the suspense and film noir genres. The filmmaker himself alludes to this fact. Commenting on the contribution of Glass's musical score to the construction of a foreboding sense of inevitable doom and desperation, Morris refers to these traits as "part of the film noir aspect of the story."[19] Although there are plenty of disanalogies between *The Thin Blue Line* and the master's paradigmatic suspense films, it is also tempting to remark on the documentary's Hitchcockian dimensions. Regardless of whether Morris made an effort to emulate Hitchcock, *The Thin Blue Line* shares elements of a well-known narrative formula.

Randall Dale Adams is no Roger O. Thornhill—he lacks even the modest finesse of a Manny Balestrero—but he is the wrong man, whose accidental intersection with a young, roguish stranger marks the eruption of everyday life's underlying insecurity and the stepwise progression of the rule of law's failure to shield him from persecution and misplaced guilt.[20] Moreover, if Morris's telling of this tale generally strikes a dramatic chord, it is not without contrasting moments of drollery. Part of Adam's earnest monologue about his activities the night of the murder is, for instance, dubbed over a sampling of cheerfully foolish scenes from the softcore sex movies he and Harris watched at a drive-in theater.

It seems that *The Thin Blue Line*'s narrative illustrates the point of Renov's comment that elements of a documentary's style, structure, and exposition can "draw upon preexistent constructs, or schemas, to establish meanings and effects for audiences."[21] For this is surely a case in which the filmmaker counts on aspects of his narrative to resonate with subjects and motifs familiar to consumers of popular suspense, mystery, and crime fictions. Indeed part of a discriminating aesthetic appreciation of Morris's achievement would, I think, involve recognizing how the themes of his tale and the tone of its telling recall movies like *The Wrong Man* (Alfred Hitchcock, 1956) and *Detour* (Edgar G. Ulmer, 1945).

What's more, its story events are packaged and presented within a certain form. This form, rather than strictly corresponding to or following the order in which events supposedly occurred, is in various ways extraneous to it. Thus it is true in the story (and apparently in reality) that David Harris's brother drowns when they are both small boys, then Officer Wood is gunned down in 1976, then Adams is tried for Wood's murder, then he is convicted and sentenced to death row. But in its telling, the narrative is organized otherwise. The depiction of Wood's murder occurs long before Harris's childhood is described; and we are told of Adams's sentence before Harris relates episodes during which prosecutors, preparing their case against Adams, coach Harris as to how he should testify at the trial. Likewise, the stopping of Harris's car by police and the fatal shooting moments later are pictured in at least eleven flashbacks, each correlated with a witness's recollection of the scene.

Notice as well that, pro forma, historical stories and acts of storytelling, like their fictional counterparts, have beginnings and endings determined at least as much by exigencies of narrative communication as by how the world itself is pieced together. Morris, for instance, starts narrating his tale by showing us Adams, in prison, recounting how he arrived in Dallas in October 1976 and quickly found a job. Perhaps the director preferred this opening as a means of creating suspense in his audience over what and how things will go astray for Adams. Yet he could just have easily elected to begin with a description of the murder or of Harris's boyhood traumas. Narrative structure is not a pure distillate of prefilmic events but largely an imposition upon representational content according to the maker's sundry rhetorical, artistic, entertainment, and generic preferences.

Documentary narratives are potentially underdetermined by reality, overdetermined by the processes of story-making, and telling in two more respects. First, narrative, as I understand it, is partly defined by a psychological component. A story's teller or tellers must express one or more attitudes toward the narrative course of events. Thus a necessary component of the narrative is mental as opposed to external significance. Obviously one kind of attitude directed at a story is illocutionary force. But as I have said previously, documentarians express a wide range of dispositions toward their material. They may emphasize the relative importance of certain assertions or story elements over others; frequently they indicate the desirability or preferability of certain states of affairs; documentarians also typically give their movies an emotional intonation or mood; and they often express various evaluative judgments about the situations their movies describe. There can be a deeply subjective, highly contingent aspect to the attitudes embodied in a work. *The War Game* registers alarm about the presence of nuclear weapons on British soil—an attitude not shared by government critics of the movie at the time of its release. Nor is it naturally comical that Adams and Harris watched soft-core sex movies a short while before Officer Wood's demise. In both cases, other filmmakers with different sensibilities would have expressed different attitudes toward the same facts and events. But not all narratively expressed attitudes are purely arbitrary or prescriptive. Normally, assertive illocutionary force is an expedient and effective means of signaling that beliefs and knowledge are being communicated. Likewise, *Night and Fog*'s tragic tone and moral condemnation of mass murder seem to me to be morally appropriate and correct.

Second, when interpreting documentaries, it is important to bear in mind the distinction between that which is true in the narrative and that which is true *simpliciter*. At one point in Morris's film, the police cruiser carrying Wood and his partner is depicted as pulling away from a fast-food restaurant, the restaurant's brightly lit sign reflected against the car's hood. Notwithstanding its aesthetic value and its role in advancing the story, the shot in question does not seem to have any further cognitive import as a literal and sincere illustration or report of what anyone saw or how the scene supposedly looked. In relating stories, cineastes may fail, neglect, or not want to describe all and only those individuals, states of affairs, situations, and events that really exist(ed) and occur(red). Hence the truth of a statement about what happens in a documentary does not automatically entail its truth as a statement about the world.

Narrative documentaries frequently contain elements of style, structure, attitude, and content that need not describe how things stand in some part of reality and that serve ends and have effects distinct from and/or incompatible with conducting information about representata. But a story's inclusion of such non-referential and tropological elements, as Renov and White might call them, doesn't settle the matter of its epistemic value nor give us enough reason to be skeptical as a rule. Couched in positive terms, the underlying requirements for a veridical documentary narrative are as follows.

There exists some real course of events in which an agent or agents, in trying to attain a goal or satisfy a desire, encounter an obstacle to its realization. As usual, we'll name this collection of items—and its constituent individuals, states, situations, events, and properties, and the relations (causal and other) between them—**COE**. Of equal necessity, there exists a narrative representational system that is supposed to indicate how things stand with respect to this **COE**. Truth as minimal correspondence allows that a narrative can be true to the degree that things are as they are stated to be by this representation. To capture the sense of the phrase "true story," we can say that a narrative is true just in case it states that the specified agent or agents encounter a given obstacle, where this agent or these agents in reality have or had this difficulty. Overall, the story is therefore true to the extent the aforementioned **COE**'s constituent elements are as described.

The minimal correspondence thesis does not ask that movie representation be an adequate substitution for the world or anyone's experiences of it. It does not presume that the documentary ever can or should be full re-presentation of reality. It makes no demand on the narrative to be wholly or absolutely true. It contains no predicates regarding how the representation is to be made and what processes are to be the proximal determinants of its form and content. It does not stipulate the absence of figurative elements or of features deriving from the maker's imagination. It is neutral with respect to the representational system's material composition, organization, and structural properties. Nor does the minimal correspondence thesis maintain that the representation is true because it has a certain illocutionary force or because someone expresses (or does not express) a certain attitude toward its content. Rather than making truth contingent upon the absence of certain types of properties or upon an impossible circumventing of relations between the symbolic object and its maker's consciousness, minimal correspondence only needs the narrative to be interpreted* by an actual course of events, to a greater or lesser degree. What a narrative is interpreted* by is a pragmatic matter of intention and functional adaptation.

The work gets its interpretation* when someone gives it the job of indicating the condition of a particular **COE**. Normally this indicator function is established upstream of reception, during the production processes, when makers carefully deploy at least some of the indicator elements in an effort to accommodate their representation's features to the features, or perceived features, of the world, thereby describing the **COE** or what they believe about the **COE**. But as we have already said, a representation's fact-preserving capacity can be an accidental by-product.

Let's say that *The Thin Blue Line* is a super-tropic movie; scene by scene, shot by shot, the whole story and its structure came to Morris in a dream; the director believed throughout production that the content of his new film is purely a spontaneous outpouring of his imagination's wellsprings. He hires actors, scripts interviews, and plans ultimately to release his film as a make-believe documentary about fictive characters named Randall Adams, David Harris, Emily Miller, and all. Only later, after the final edit is made, does the director learn of the real-life trials and tribulations of actual historical entities named Randall Adams, David Harris, Emily Miller, and all, each of whom is identical in appearance to the hired actors. Owing to the natural and intentional constraints on its production, this movie is not, in the first instance, about Adams's predicament. Yet the director decides to take advantage of the uncanny coincidences by using his movie to describe to an audience—without deceiving them about the lack of footage naturally interpreted* by interviews with the real people, and so on—Adams's predicament. In this case, the film is made to take a detour toward reality, despite its origins in confabulation. If Morris now uses segments of his work to describe Adams as convicted of murder by biased belief and perjury, and Adams was convicted of murder by biased belief and perjury, then those relevant parts are true to the extent that their features correspond with features of the actual world. So in principle, narratives can be truth-conducive.

One might accept that narratives can be true and still think that there are other, fairly common elements of documentary representation that are perforce cognitively unreliable. At issue are the cinematic counterparts of linguistic tropes, such as irony, simile, and metaphor. An utterance of this sort has a meaning that, taken literally, is highly incongruous or patently false. Take, for instance, this figurative comparison: Alluding to *Star Wars*, a leading rival of the Microsoft Corporation describes his competitor as the Empire.[22] Bill Gates and his colleagues are dissimilar in countless ways from fictive aliens who lived a long time ago in a galaxy far, far away. Perhaps now we have encountered a form of representation that does lead us on a merry chase through the defiles of the signifier, without conducing to a single fact.

I suggest an alternative conception, rooted in the idea that figuration is a kind of communicative action. To paraphrase Robert Fogelin, communicators communicate figuratively, but representations do not intrinsically have figurative meanings.[23] Like other deliberate departures from literalness, figuration is an interactive phenomenon of use. On this view, figurative meaning in general is indirect and nonliteral. It is indirect in the sense that there is a mismatch between literal meaning and context, such that what is meant by the utterance does not seem exhausted by its face value. It is nonliteral because it is made with the mutually-recognized intention on the communicator's part that the receiver not accept the utterance's meaning at face value but actively correct or adjust it in order to square with the context.

Figurative comparisons, as in similes and metaphors, are therefore invitations to participate in a further adjustment, that is, to search among the salient features of one thing for those applicable to another thing. Working out the aforementioned metaphor thus entails making a qualitative similarity assessment. Using what we already know or believe about two objects, we make sense of an odd juxtaposition by extracting and compiling a set of features that, in the present context, seem to match. Putting aside the apparent incongruities between the imaginary Empire and the real Microsoft, the suggestion is that the latter is monopolistic, malevolent toward competitors, and possesses extraordinary control over activities in a (terrestrial) marketplace.[24]

It's not unusual for Type II non-fictions to administer images, sounds, and language toward figurative effects, without thereby depriving the cinematic representation of substantial truth. *The Thin Blue Line* is particularly rich in this respect. To cite but one example, readers might remember a sequence beginning with interview footage of Adams's protests that Officer Wood's partner changed her eyewitness testimony after she met with police department representatives. When Adams concludes his remarks, the image cuts to a brief shot of a milkshake container tossed into midair. The reprise of this striking slow-motion image, first seen during a reconstruction of the murder, is initially baffling, for it bears no obvious relation to the footage immediately before or after it. Adams has not mentioned anything about dairy drinks sailing through the void. So viewers must search for the import of this visual insert. Finding it is partly a matter of recalling facts we already know about the movie, for example, more explicitly literal images and verbal comments were previously used to describe the partner as seated in the cruiser, jettisoning her milkshake only as she reacts to shots fired at Wood. Hence we adjust our responses to the insert so as to produce a good fit between it and the relevant facts. In doing so, one warranted judgment is that the image, punctuating Adams's remarks as it does, makes oblique and highly symbolic reference to the likelihood that the officer, having failed to back up her partner according to correct procedures, was vulnerable to departmental pressures to testify against Adams. This response to the insert further squares with the context, insofar as it is consistent with the theme of non-epistemic motivations distorting truth-seeking procedures.

Figurative assertions like the foregoing are no less true for requiring of interpreters a participatory response. Provided that the figure can be adjusted effectively to describe a given situation, and if that situation obtains more or less as described, then the figure conveys some information about it. On the other hand, being a phenomenon of use, figuration may also be inaccurate, vague, ill-conceived, or otherwise cognitively disabling. A figurative comparison from *Obedience* (Stanley Milgram, 1965) helps make this point. Near movie's end, Milgram summarizes one of his key findings, namely, that the level of obedience to a destructive command varies with changes to the physical proximity of the subject (or "teacher") to the learner and the experimenter. For example, when the learner is hidden from his sight, the subject is likely to be more compliant with requests to deliver ever deadlier shocks; but when the experimenter leaves the room and gives orders by telephone, compliance falls off. On screen, a drawing of three balls appears. Two of these are surrounded by concentric circles, and the third is enmeshed by the lines emanating from the other two balls. In voice-over, Milgram says, "It would appear that something akin to fields of force diminishing in effectiveness with increasing psychological distance from their source have a controlling effect on the subject's performance."

In his documentary, as in his early writings on his obedience research, Milgram elects to conceptualize his findings in very empirical terms.[25] Hence the physicalist metaphor locates the determinants of the test subject's actions in certain observable, external features of that individual's situation—the structure of the laboratory setting and the spatial relationships between the teacher and the other two agents, the visibility of the participants to one another, the availability to the teacher of immediate feedback from the learner, and so forth. In print, Milgram refers to these as "the situational variables responsible for" the subject's obedience.[26] The graphic, then, apparently drives home that the experiment demonstrates that the subject's responses depend on extra-personal elements of structure and proximity. The learner and experimenter don't literally give off unseen waves or particles that regulate the teacher's comportment. Yet there is at least a covariation of compliance with situational properties, and this relation is suggested by the figurative use of imagery and language.

But there is also a conceptual problem built into this "fields of force" figure, insofar as it invites us to reify the situation's influence. It asks us to look for the "source" of behavior in the environment. When we try to adjust the metaphor to everything else the documentary shows and tells us, and to our ordinary ways of making sense of people's actions, we confront its ambiguity, for it begs a key question. What, if any, autonomous causal powers could the environment have that would warrant our regarding it as the source of behavior and that would not ultimately depend on the contribution of the agent's attitudes toward his situation? The figure itself betrays ambivalence about this point when it smuggles agency back into the picture by making proximity's effectiveness contingent on "psychological distance." To say that extra-personal items "have a controlling effect on" subjects only deepens the mystery. Does this locution imply the existence of unobservable, quantifiable, conduct-controlling forces? But this idea defies the rationality heuristic and is not otherwise hinted at by the documentary. Perhaps the phrase merely suggests the correlation of observed behavior with situational structure. Or maybe it is shorthand for a more accessible notion, namely, that the external situation is a causal factor in the production of action, insofar as action is proximally caused or generated by the agent's perceptions of and psychological responses to the situation. Given either of the latter two interpretations, we are hardly warranted in privileging the situation as a "source" of behavior.

Figuration can have intractable epistemic limitations, but even a failed metaphor can have a salutary effect on knowledge production. It might, for instance, contribute to instruction and illustration. The "fields of force" metaphor helps make Milgram's conceptualization of the data comprehensible, warts and all. It also helps him to present to his audience one of the experiment's underlying intuitions, namely, that an individual's conduct is sometimes much less the product and reflection of long-term, stable personality traits and dispositions than of more transitory, situation-relative factors. By prompting users to work out implications and make comparisons, figuration can also be an input to the exploratory phases of inquiry. Here I refer to those heuristic and initial processes of hypothesis development, prior to the emergence of systematic and precise explanatory theories, during which there is a premium on creative thinking, conjecture, conceptual clarification, and troubleshooting. Maybe pondering a metaphor's inadequacies has helped Milgram, and other social psychologists, to focus attention on the internal constraints on action.[27] What does seem certain is that figuration will not ultimately and inevitably thwart truth-seeking.

I must now take up an idea endorsed by Renov, that is, that the documentary "constitutes" its objects. I cannot profess much of an appreciation of the myriad ontological and epistemological connotations that word seems to have for Renov and White, although I have an intuition of the truism concealed in the refrain, popular among film scholars, that documentaries do not merely record reality but in some sense construct it. Such a movie is partially synthesized from its makers' concepts and perceptions. Its emergence depends upon people organizing their ideas about and experiences of the world; and during its reception, spectators might subsequently (re-)organize **their** ideas and experiences. However, as a bold generalization about the ineluctable nature of non-fictions, including those at the far edge of the Type II side of the spectrum, the claim that documentaries constitute their objects strikes me as faulty and untenable.

Although his rhetoric implies a flirtation with some variety of idealism, Renov doesn't otherwise characterize himself as holding that no reality—or only a smoky, chaotic one—exists independent of the transcendent representation's power to bring into being that which it intends. Thus he would probably agree with me that *Don't Look Back* (D. A. Pennebaker, 1966) depicts people and events that are not exclusively the effects or epiphenomena of the movie's existence, production, or reception. On the other hand, I expect we would also concur that documentary filmmaking activities, at the preparation and shooting phases, can themselves enter into the causation of pre-filmic situations. Moreover, who would dispute that the documentary is never merely the objective description of all and only the actual properties of an item, the existence or mode of being of which is entirely unconditional upon that of the representation? Rather, a documentary normally involves elaboration, excision, and error. Where, then, is the schism?

Perhaps it resides at the level of metaphysics and around the either/or logic Renov embraces. Here the reasoning seems to be that documentary cannot mirror the world so it must have autonomous powers to organize extra-cinematic reality and bring novel formations into being; because it is not transparent, because it is not literally re-presentation, because an event represented is never purely and simply the event itself, because the map is not the territory, documentary is best thought of as creation and as representation expressing itself.

Renov arbitrarily resolves a false dilemma. The only available choice is not between endorsing highly idealized norms of representational success, which documentary can only fail to satisfy, and accepting that documentary principally constructs reality. To think in this way is to preclude our saying with confidence and conviction that cinematic representation is equally well, if not better, regarded as conditionally referring truthfully to reality. Renov ignores the pragmatic dimension of filmmaking and thus the possibility that, by taking advantage of natural as well as conditional constraints, agents may adapt cinematic works to the function of indicating, with moderate success, something about how things stand in some part of extra-cinematic reality.

One last time, I stress that this perspective does not efface the documentary's creative, inventive aspects—although it does suppose that these can occasionally be used to produce salutary epistemic results. Agents construct or constitute non-fictions. In the process, they fashion artifacts with external and mental significance, along with formal and structural properties. Hence there are relevant distinctions to be made between that which is true in the non-fiction, true of the non-fiction, and that which the movie truthfully (or falsely) indicates about some real situation. All three are substantially constrained by the filmmaker's plans. With respect to external significance, documentaries may describe imaginary as well as real situations; and descriptions of real situations need not be wholly accurate nor exhaustively complete.

To insist that documentaries constitute reality is to say nothing of the proximal determinants of how such movies succeed or fail, cognitively. Should we want to explain the sources of epistemic achievements, we would do better to allow ourselves to be oriented by a pair of more substantive epistemological projects. Much research in epistemology and the philosophy of science focuses on two distinct but related issues. One pertains to questions of whether and how the scientific, lay, and sensory processes by which we form or acquire our beliefs reliably lead to true, informative beliefs. The other, already introduced to readers, seeks to clarify the criteria of justification; that is, it tries to explain and ratify those conditions that a belief must satisfy, such that there is some secure indication of its likely truth.[28]

In my estimation, then, one of our epistemic projects could be to analyze the gamut of the documentary's truth-seeking and communicative processes in order to judge whether these are indeed generally, or in a given instance, truth-conducive. I have just given some strength to the hypothesis that narrative and figuration potentially comport with conveying facts. Earlier I showed that photographic imagery can be a reliable method of collecting and preserving information. At my study's outset, I detailed the ontology of the representational artifact in terms of its practical application to conveying facts about extra-representational objects, provided certain moderate constraints obtain. And I've made inroads toward explaining how spectators' perceptual and cognitive states and processes can facilitate their access to cinematic as well as extra-cinematic situations. Mine should not be the last word on these topics. Virtually limitless explanatory work and unriddling remains for those who would make realist surveys of the grounds for cinema's capacity for yielding epistemic successes.

Making a concerted, principled assessment of any documentary's epistemic status means setting our investigative sights well beyond the text's rhetorical strategies and gamboling signifiers. In general, that means examining, insofar as it is possible, relevant aspects of a movie's production history and/or truth-seeking procedures. If and when we have a scholarly interest in judging a work's veracity, and to the extent that we can ascertain what, if anything, its makers are committed to asserting or suggesting, we should like to know how they came by the corresponding beliefs or (putative) facts. The documentarian—or interviewee—who bases his claims on tarot card readings may not, after all, have adopted the best method of inquiry. To the degree to which a filmmaker (or we) cares about an assertion's accuracy, it is appropriate to evaluate it according to something along the lines of Richard Boyd's methodological proto-principle.

Boyd contends that the most probing questions we can ask of a representation reflect a very basic, broad norm of inquiry: "Always inquire, in the light of the best available knowledge, in what ways your current beliefs about the world might plausibly be incomplete, inadequate, or false, and design observations or experiments with the aim of detecting and remedying such possible defects."[29] Boyd tenders this principle as a check on scientific theorizing, but with modifications it is, I think, a fitting guideline for any number of nonscientific modes of inquiry, too.

Not all documentarians should be expected to "design observations or experiments" as tests for defects, yet many can be expected to exercise various nonspecialized perceptual, reasoning, and analytic skills in an effort to minimize error, confusion, and internal inconsistencies. To require such caution of some agents—for example, those attempting to produce motion picture confirmatives—need not be to lapse into positivism. It need not commit us to the notion that the only genuine knowledge is knowledge gained by ostensibly scientific methods, that the only right methods are scientific ones. It does not suppose that unorthodox or irrational processes cannot lead to illuminating insights or the discovery of facts. Nor does a moderate requirement of lay epistemic prudence stipulate that there are any absolutely universal rules ("the principle of induction," "inference from the best explanation," "subsumption under general laws") governing and assuring knowledge production. At most, it implies that epistemic rationality consists of an amalgam of general truistic principles and a plurality of imprecise, discretionary, field-specific, topic-relative guidelines, methods, and heuristics that are, at least for some filmmakers, given their explicit as well as implicit knowledge producing and communicating aims, subjectively feasible and appropriate.

There are, no doubt, a great many other particular questions we can ask of a documentarian's methodology. Two slightly more specific yet still rather broad concerns pertain to the filmmaker's plans with respect to objectivity and content. By "objectivity," I mean impartiality and lack of biased thinking. Ideally, we want epistemic agents—scientists, historians, journalists, ethnographic filmmakers, some documentarians—to acquire and hold their beliefs in an objective way. Notice that objectivity is neither the same thing as nor a guarantee of truth and knowledge. The objectivity, for an agent, of holding or defending a belief that **P** should not be conflated with **P**'s being an "objective fact" (a redundant locution for "it is true that **P**"). Nor should objectivity be confused with disinterestedness, effacement of personal engagement and perspective, or absence of desire, emotion, fear, and other non-epistemic motives. If the cognitive and conative dimensions of human agency are manifestly not disjoined, then only a self-defeating or punitive epistemology would insist on that separation for the sake of knowledge. Rather, objectivity is best construed as a norm against letting biases and so on influence judgment in the wrong way. It requires that epistemic agents try to formulate, accept, and defend beliefs not on the basis of what they (or some other entity) presuppose, hope, want, or fear to be the case but on the basis of the available evidence.

One avenue of inquiry, then, is into the personal, professional, and institutional constraints bearing on the filmmaker's capacity to realize a limited and imperfect form of objectivity. Here, the targets of investigation are the policies, plans, strategies, and procedures adopted with a view to achieving impartiality—where these plans may be more or less successful, and where they may be accompanied by a further plan to design the movie so as to give spectators a strong impression of objectivity. The latter may, but need not, have embedded within itself an intention to deceive the audience, since the makers might literally pretend to be unbiased so as to create the illusion of truthfulness.

I therefore strongly disagree with Nichols's a priori rejection of the possibility of objectivity and his equation of the impression of objectivity with the politically pernicious denial of subjectivity and constructedness.[30] Defensible judgments of whether a documentarian's assertions are objective, or whether an appearance of objectivity is being (deceptively) used to persuasive ends, or of whether an audience's perception of objectivity prompted or reinforced their false beliefs, come only after a body of evidence has been established. Sources of evidence would include materials relating biography, professional conduct, the film's production history and proximal social context of emergence, the context of its reception—anything helping to reconstruct the filmmaker's efforts, if any, to promote objectivity, the audience's uptake, and viewers' actual responses.[31]

It occurs to me that reconstructing the filmmaker's plans with respect to content can have a special utility as a conceptual tool for explaining in what sense a movie constitutes its reality. The nightly television news broadcast, Roger Patterson's Sasquatch film, *Obedience*, and *Chronicle of a Summer* (Jean Rouch and Edgar Morin, 1960) all share at least one trait: They contain "staged" events; in each case, pre-filmic scenes are a more or less direct effect of the producers' intentions and/or of interactions between on-screen subjects and the (other) producers. Yet each of these films constructs pre-filmic reality in different ways, toward different ends, depending on the makers' intentions.

For instance, the producers of the nightly news execute a plan to the effect of: Build a set, outfit it with the right kinds of technology, and put an anchor person in the middle of it all in order to represent a certain actual situation—namely, an anchor person sitting in front of cameras on a television set, reading from a TelePrompTer, in order to relay a selection of carefully scripted items deemed news worthy by a hierarchical organization of journalists and corporate executives, where the structure of this organization and its divisions of labor are indicated explicitly at broadcast's end during the credits (often superimposed over a medium-long shot of the anchor amidst the technology).

On the other hand, Patterson's plan is: Fabricate an imaginary situation, film it, and misrepresent it to audiences as real. Now contrast this strategy with Milgram's complex representational scheme, itself a component in an even larger, long-term data-collection and -communication plan. He contrives to deceive participants as to the nature of their painstakingly pre-arranged situation, which is being recorded on film, unbeknownst to them. But he also explicitly describes to his audience details of the bigger picture, that is, his research agenda and results, the nature of the experimental manipulation, how the film footage was recorded, and how the pre-filmic situations are a function of his experimental and documentary plans.

Rouch and Morin—who might also have thought of their urban ethnography of Parisian lifestyles, *Chronicle of a Summer*, as part of an experiment—have yet another kind of plan for constructing reality.[32] One aim of their cinema verité, participant observation method is to create a dynamic between themselves and their subjects, thereby eliciting from their subjects a significant involvement in the practical as well as theoretical problems of filmmaking—this with the further intention of triggering spontaneous, largely unforeseeable moments of intimacy, confrontation, and personal transformation.

I conclude now with a refinement of my thesis that non-fictions, including those of Type II, can be inputs into epistemic justification. There are two ways in which cinematic non-fictions contribute to justification: as sources of evidence for a belief, and as causes of a belief.[33] We can cite all sorts of factors, taken singularly or jointly, in explaining how someone came to (dis)believe that **P**. Other beliefs, perceptual states, memories, wishes, and emotions may all help sustain or inhibit assent to **P**. Strong motivations, especially affect and desire, surely can trigger incontinent beliefs; that fact goes a long way to explaining why different people respond to the Holliday video as they do, and it helps account for any ideological success of the propaganda film's rhetorical appeals to emotions. But there can be no justified belief without causation, either. I believe there's a dog beside me right now because I can see one, and because my current visual experience is effectively linked to some dog-related information I have tucked away in long-term memory. "Evidence" here refers to a narrower range of mental items—knowledge, beliefs, perceptions, memories, introspection—that are cognitively rather than conatively related to their objects. However, justification is not only a matter of having evidence. It also involves one's reflecting on, evaluating, and reasoning about the content of one's evidential states.

The foregoing comments have a couple of important implications for non-fiction film theory. First, they contradict an assumption at large within Winston's diagnosis of the documentary's trouble, namely, that the genre as whole—except those works which self-consciously deny they make truth claims—historically has suffered from a bad case of scientism. Documentaries are allegedly scientistic because they inherit, via their photographic filiation, a presumptive guarantee of yielding scientific data and "objective evidence."[34] There is nothing terribly scientistic about the notion of evidence; we consider and use the stuff in our most unscientific, ordinary thoughts and actions. More to the point, evidence is not synonymous with (actual or putative) fact or bona fide proof. Presumably, some sensory and cognitive states do preserve information about their representata. Yet broadly stated, one's evidence is good or bad, weak or strong. And someone's belief or perception that **P** can be among her evidence that **P** without it being a fact that **P**.

Winston's diagnosis is consonant with Nichols's warning that documentary imagery, even when indexically bound to an actual historical referent, cannot guarantee its own authenticity. Nichols construes justification as a matter of ontological assurance. If the ontology of the documentary image guarantees that **P**, we can be confident in **P**'s truth. What is hereby virtually assured is a skeptical conclusion about documentary's contribution to justified, true belief. The image's existential bond to its object, he reminds us, does not guarantee our knowing or recognizing what it depicts and what that depiction means about reality. Furthermore, our grasp of what a documentary really shows often depends on factors external to the indexical image, like voice-over commentary, captions, and other people's interpretations; or it is a function of how audio-visual tracks have been manipulated by the filmmaker. Thus, "authentication must itself come from elsewhere and it is often subject to doubt."[35] The documentary may use indexical images, may give an impression of transparency and self-evidence, but it is never itself sufficient warrant for belief.

In the account I prefer, justification is incremental, and is not to be identified with assurance, ontological or otherwise, of truth; it is a matter of how good somebody's evidence is for believing **P**; and a movie, or property thereof, enters into an **agent's** justification for (dis)believing **P** as **one** of his or her sources of perceptual experiences and reasons—evidence—for or against **P**. Watching *Nanook of the North*, a belief, P^1, occurs to me, a "naive" viewer: "Inuit live inside freezing cold igloos!" My perceptions of the film do lend some credibility to this idea since, P^2, I can plainly see that the inhabitants' breath hangs in the air. P^3, what I know or believe about how motion pictures are made, and P^4, what little I know or believe about how this particular film was made, throw additional support to P^1. Yet I still wouldn't have all that much justification for assent to this belief. P^1 is not uniquely or conclusively favored by my current evidence because empirically as well as logically speaking, my evidence is consistent with alternative or rival propositions.

What is more, putting aside any support they may get from P^1, not all of my reasons for adopting this belief are independently secure. My perceptual grounds for P^2 are solid, as are the background beliefs about natural meaning that underwrite it. But my assumption that Flaherty filmed inside an igloo is based on nothing more than what I see on screen, plus the false assumption that he crawled inside with lightweight, handheld camera and lights. One could also criticize my evidence for its lack of comprehensiveness. My conclusion is based on a small sliver of experiences and reasons; I have neither tried to seek out nor actively considered much if any of the available, centrally relevant evidence concerning *Nanook*'s production and its maker's attitudes, methods, plans, and objectives. In short, I have little justification for **P¹**, hence little indication of its truth. Note that my belief could pertain to any aspect of *Nanook*'s representational content: to its collateral information about the Inuit, to Flaherty's attitudes and actions, or to the attitudes of his culture. The criteria of justification would remain the same.

Although its function as a label for a grand generic roundup of otherwise diverse films far exceeds its etymological import, the very name "documentary" seems since the 1970s to have provoked scholars to bury the genre below a mountain of hesitations about its goodness as evidence. At this stage of cinema studies' development—with the awakening of interests in analytic, cognitivist, and realist perspectives; and in light of new and highly relevant contributions to post-positivist philosophy of knowledge—we have an opportunity to make well-informed, thorough adjustments to our attitudes and approaches toward the documentary's epistemic dimensions. I have defended one possible framework within which to do such remedial work. It is a moderate, critically minded variety of realism that requires no assurances of truth but, rather, degrees of justification for regarding some representations as true.

Notes

1. Here I follow Richard Boyd, "Metaphor and Theory Change: What Is 'Metaphor' a Metaphor For?", in *Metaphor and Thought*, ed. Andrew Ortony (New York: Cambridge University Press, 1979), 382.

2. Paul K. Moser, *Knowledge and Evidence* (Cambridge: Cambridge University Press, 1989), 26.

3. Garth Hallet, *Language and Truth* (New Haven: Yale University Press, 1988), offers an introduction to various notions of correspondence and the difficulties associated with them. For critiques of traditional correspondence theories, see Hilary Putnam, *Reason, Truth, and History* (Cambridge: Cambridge University Press, 1981), 56–74.

4. Moser, *Knowledge and Evidence*, 31.

5. See Chapter 2, pp. 63–69.

6. However, were you to form the belief, upon gazing at the depiction, that the pre-filmic subject has such an unusual face, you would possess a false belief, i.e., one that misrepresents reality.

7. I do not suppose for a moment either that valid legal, moral, or political judgments can be realized in isolation from epistemically valid judgments or that sundry practical, legal, and ethical-political considerations cannot exert a powerful influence, for better or for worse, over attempts to gain knowledge of natural as well as human psychological and social realities. Nor do I assume either that verifying that **P** is the case necessarily settles all legal, moral, and political ques-

tions or that the pursuit of empirical truth is always a good and proper thing to do, from a legal, moral, or political perspective. Not least of all, within the limitations of the present discussion, I do not try to resolve the daunting problem of whether claims to the truth in matters of morality and justice might be justified on the same grounds as our beliefs in the existence of cows, electrons, trade deficits, and intentions. Readers curious about how one might defend an affirmative response to this question should consult Richard Miller, *Moral Differences: Truth, Justice, and Conscience in a World of Conflict* (Princeton: Princeton University Press, 1992).

8. On the contributions of such informal inferential strategies as "availability" and "representativeness" heuristics to our ordinary understanding of the natural and especially social world—and the errors that arise from their over use—see Richard Nisbett and Lee Ross, *Human Inference: Strategies and Shortcomings of Social Judgment* (Englewood Cliffs, N.J.: Prentice-Hall, 1980).

9. Bill Nichols, *Blurred Boundaries: Questions of Meaning in Contemporary Culture* (Bloomington: Indiana University Press, 1994), 29; Bill Nichols, "'Getting to Know You . . . ': Knowledge, Power, and the Body," in *Theorizing Documentary*, ed. Michael Renov (New York: Routledge University Press, 1993), 190; Mike Mashon, "Losing Control: Popular Reception(s) of the Rodney King Video," *Wide Angle* 15 (1993): 7–18.

10. Nichols, "'Getting to Know You . . . ': Knowledge, Power, and the Body," 190.

11. Susan Haack, *Evidence and Inquiry: Towards Reconstruction in Epistemology* (Oxford: Blackwell, 1995); Moser, *Knowledge and Evidence*.

12. Ibid., 23–25.

13. Frank P. Tomasulo, "I'll See It When I Believe It: Rodney King and the Prison House of Video," in *The Persistence of History: Cinema, Television, and the Modern Event*, ed. Vivian Sobchack (New York: Routledge, 1996), 82. For his part, Mike Mashon, "Losing Control," 15, contends that, guided by the defense attorneys' analysis, jurors in the first trial of the officers charged in King's beating ended up "literally *seeing things that were not there*"—such as King's control of the situation (Mashon's emphasis).

14. Plantinga, *Rhetoric and Representation in Nonfiction Film*, 57.

15. Nichols, *Blurred Boundaries*, 29. Notice that the theorist implies that natural indication isn't really meaningful; two sentences later he calls the indexical sign of the extra-cinematic event "noise" that is rendered intelligible only by an act of interpretation. I think we ought to consider the implications of the theorist's assertions. It is already a contradiction to claim that images naturally refer to reality but have no meaning. It is idealism to claim that an image's intelligibility must be imposed upon it by the mind of the observer, rather than by the constraints on its emergence. What grounds, I wonder, does Nichols, who is skeptical about the possibility of attaining deeply illuminating knowledge, have for preferring to think that, as a matter of fact, intelligibility is a function of observation and not of the world's structure? Has he managed to pull back the curtain of figuration while Hayden White was not looking and sneak a peek at this one naked truth about the nature of reality? What if we can sometimes achieve a partial and approximate epistemic access to the constraints on the image's emergence, of the

sort that Nichols himself seems to endorse insofar as he assumes that Holliday's tape unquestionably refers to the beating of King—would that not constitute a discovery of the image's largely mind-independent intelligibility? Not least of all, it is epistemically question begging to reify the imagery as noise, while ignoring the contributions to confusion and incoherence of the conceptual apparatuses brought to bear upon it.

16. See the essays collected in Hayden White's *Tropics of Discourse: Essays in Cultural Criticism* (Baltimore: Johns Hopkins University Press, 1978).

17. Hayden White, "The Historical Text As Literary Artifact," in *Tropics of Discourse*, 81–100.

18. Michael Renov, "Introduction," in *Theorizing Documentary*, ed. Michael Renov (New York: Routledge, 1993), 7. The embedded quotation is from Hayden White, "Introduction," in *Tropics of Discourse*, 2.

19. Peter Bates, "Truth Not Guaranteed: An Interview with Errol Morris," *Cineaste* 17 (1989): 17.

20. Roger O. Thornhill and Manny Balestrero are, of course, the protagonists of *North by Northwest* and *The Wrong Man*, respectively.

21. Renov, "Introduction," 3.

22. Sun Microsystems Chief Executive Officer Scott McNealy, cited in John Heilemann, "The Sun King: How Scott McNealy Became the Anti-Gates," *The New Yorker*, 16 March 1998, 30.

23. Robert J. Fogelin, *Figuratively Speaking* (New Haven: Yale University Press, 1988), 96.

24. My approach to figuration is indebted to Fogelin's *Figuratively Speaking*. His account of figuration is itself indebted to Grice's theory of conversation, whereas his analysis of figurative comparison derives from Amos Tversky's set-theoretical approach to similarity, in which judgment of similarity is described as a feature-matching process; see Amos Tversky, "Features of Similarity," *Psychological Review* 4 (1977): 327–352. A concise defense of metaphor's epistemic value, also based on Fogelin's research, can be found in Susan Haack's "'Dry Truth and Real Knowledge': Epistemologies of Metaphor and Metaphors of Epistemology," in *Aspects of Metaphor*, ed. Jaakko Hintikka (Dordrecht: Kluwer, 1994), 1–22. A somewhat different, but nonetheless realist, perspective on metaphor can be found in Boyd, "Metaphor and Theory Change." Like Fogelin, I am inclined to treat metaphors as elliptical similes but cannot here defend my preference for this traditional, but embattled, Aristotelian view; those interested in how the rescue effort might proceed should refer to Fogelin, *Figuratively Speaking*, 25–67, as well as to his "Metaphors, Similes, and Similarity," in Hintikka, *Aspects of Metaphor*, 23–39.

25. See especially Stanley Milgram, "Behavioral Study of Obedience," *Journal of Abnormal and Social Psychology* 67 (1963): 371–378 and "Some Conditions of Obedience and Disobedience to Authority," *Human Relations* 18 (1965): 57–76.

26. Milgram, "Some Conditions of Obedience and Disobedience to Authority," 74.

27. When Milgram eventually offered a theoretical analysis and explanations of his findings, and of the phenomenon of obedience to authority, it would be in a mixture of cybernetic, psychoanalytic, and cognitivist concepts. One of his cen-

tral notions is that of the "agentic shift," in which a person, perceiving him or herself as a subordinate within a social hierarchy, comes to believe himself or herself to be an instrument of another's wishes, rather than an autonomous and fully responsible individual. See Stanley Milgram, *Obedience to Authority: An Experimental View* (New York: Harper and Row, 1974). In their analysis of Milgram's classic research, Lee Ross and Richard Nisbett, *The Person in the Situation: Perspectives of Social Psychology* (New York: McGraw-Hill, 1991), 52–58, grant a crucial etiological role to the subject's limited and deficient understanding of a novel situation, the agent's cognitive breakdown producing irresolution, failed disobedience, and a propensity to cede to the desires of a decisive authority figure.

28. On the distinction, see Haack, *Evidence and Inquiry,* 203–205. Haack compares the difference between guidelines for the conduct of inquiry and criteria of justification to the difference between cooking directions and criteria for judging nutritional value. "Don't overcook the broccoli" is a good, albeit imprecise, rule of thumb for making a healthy meal; and knowing that the chef tried to follow that rule is one very conditional indicator that the vegetables could be full of vitamins. But *contra* reliablist theories of justification, Haack argues that it is not rules and processes, be they causally or somehow counterfactually connected to the generation of true statements, that give knowers the type of security (in believing the goal of truth to have been achieved) most closely associated with justification. Their roles in justification are derivative. To advert to a reliable process, **k**, in the production of a true and justified belief **P** is to suppose that there is evidence and reason to believe that **k** produces true beliefs. Moreover, **k** makes no contribution to justification until it becomes part of the evidence and reasoning at our disposal, that is, until we believe it to be truth-conducive. For Haack's criticisms of reliablism, see *Evidence and Inquiry,* 139–157. Moser, *Knowledge and Evidence,* 71–77, expresses similar criticisms. For firsthand accounts in favor of reliablism, see two works by Alvin Goldman: "What Is Justified Belief?" in *Justification and Knowledge,* ed. George Pappas (Dordrecht: Reidel, 1979), 1–23; and *Epistemology and Cognition* (Cambridge, Mass.: Harvard University Press, 1986).

29. Boyd, "Metaphor and Theory Change," 406. This proto-principle extends, of course, to the cinema scholar's own research.

30. The following passage, from *Representing Reality,* 195, presents Nichols's position and tone: "[Documentaries] also share with fiction those very qualities that thoroughly compromise any rigorous objectivity, if they don't make it impossible. This impossibility is also evident in the more standardized and enforced objectivity of journalism.

Objectivity has been under no less siege than realism and for many of the same reasons. It, too, is a way of representing the world that denies its own processes of construction and their formative effect. Any given standard for objectivity will have embedded political assumptions. In broadcast journalism, these might include belief in the legitimacy of capitalism, the state, the nuclear family, and the expert."

31. Plantinga's careful research into the compromised objectivity of *The Twentieth Century*, a documentary television series that ran from 1957 until 1966, is an excellent example of the kind of approach I am endorsing. His attention to his-

torical evidence, measured conclusions, and his adoption of a moderate notion of objectivity make his work the model for future investigations of the successes and failures of documentarians' impartiality; see *Rhetoric and Representation in Nonfiction Film*, 200–213.

32. Morin, in a synopsis written prior to filming, refers to their proposed project as "an experiment lived by its authors and actors." He immediately elaborates on this remark by writing that, by asking people various questions about their lifestyles, level of personal happiness, attitudes, and aspirations, he and Rouch shall produce "an experiment in cinematographic interrogation." For the aforementioned synopsis, and the author's recollections of the filmmaking process, see Edgar Morin, "Chronicle of a Film," trans. Steven Feld and Amy Ewing, in *Chronicle of a Summer*, ed. Steven Feld, special issue of *Studies in Visual Communication* 11 (1985): 4–29.

33. Haack, *Evidence and Inquiry*, 76–77, distinguishes between evidence for and causes of a belief.

34. Brian Winston, *Claiming the Real: The Documentary Film Revisited* (London: British Film Institute, 1995), 127–163.

35. Nichols, *Realism and Representation*, 153.

Works Cited

Allen, Richard. *Projecting Illusion: Film Spectatorship and the Impression of Reality*. New York: Cambridge University Press, 1995.
Allen, Richard, and Murray Smith, eds. *Film Theory and Philosophy*. Oxford: Oxford University Press, 1997.
Ansen, David. "What Does Oliver Stone Owe History?" In *JFK: The Book of the Film*. Edited by Oliver Stone and Zachary Sklar, 294–295. New York: Applause Books, 1992. First published in *Newsweek*, 23 December 1991, 49.
Armes, Roy. *Film and Reality: An Historical Survey*. London: Penguin, 1974.
Atkins, Thomas R., ed. *Frederick Wiseman*. New York: Simon and Schuster, 1976.
Audi, Robert. *The Structure of Justification*. Cambridge: Cambridge University Press, 1993.
Bach, Kent. "Part of What a Picture Is." *British Journal of Aesthetics* 10 (1970): 119–137.
Bach, Kent, and Robert Harnish, *Linguistic Communication and Speech Acts*. Cambridge, Mass.: M.I.T. Press, 1979.
Bain, Alexander. *The Emotions and the Will*. 3d ed. London: Longmans and Green, 1875.
Barnes, Annette. *On Interpretation*. Oxford: Blackwell, 1988.
Barnouw, Erik. *Documentary: A History of the Non-Fiction Film*. 2d rev. ed. New York: Oxford University Press, 1993.
Barry, Iris. *Let's Go to the Movies*. London: Chatto and Windus, 1926.
Barsam, Richard Meran. "American Direct Cinema: The Representation of Reality." *Persistence of Vision* 3/4 (1986): 131–156.
——. *The Vision of Robert Flaherty*. Bloomington: Indiana University Press, 1988.
——. *Nonfiction Film: A Critical History*. Rev. ed. Bloomington: Indiana University Press, 1992.
Barthes, Roland. *Elements of Semiology*. Translated by Annette Lavers and Colin Smith. London: Cape, 1967.
——. *S/Z*. Translated by Richard Miller. New York: Hill and Wang, 1974.
Barwise, Jon, and John Perry. *Situations and Attitudes*. Cambridge, Mass.: M.I.T. Press, 1983.
Bates, Peter. "Truth Not Guaranteed: An Interview with Errol Morris." *Cineaste* 17 (1989): 16–17.
Bateson, Gregory, and Margaret Mead. *Balinese Character: A Photographic Analysis*. New York: New York Academy of Sciences, 1942.
Bazin, André. *What Is Cinema?* 2 vols. Translated by Hugh Grey. Berkeley: University of California Press, 1967–1971.

———. "The Evolution of the Language of Cinema." In *What Is Cinema?* Vol. 1. Berkeley: University of California Press, 1967.

———. "The Ontology of the Photographic Image." In *What Is Cinema?* Vol. 1. Berkeley: University of California Press, 1967.

Benson, Thomas W., and Carolyn Anderson. *Reality Fictions: The Films of Frederick Wiseman.* Carbondale: Southern Illinois University Press, 1989.

Black, Max. "How Do Pictures Represent?" In *Art, Perception, and Reality.* Edited by E. H. Gombrich, Julian Hochberg, and Max Black, 95–129. Baltimore: Johns Hopkins University Press, 1971.

Booth, Wayne C. *The Rhetoric of Fiction.* Chicago: University of Chicago Press, 1961.

Bordwell, David. *Narration in the Fiction Film.* Madison: University of Wisconsin Press, 1985.

Bordwell, David, and Noël Carroll, eds. *Post-Theory: Reconstructing Film Studies.* Madison: University of Wisconsin Press, 1996.

Boyd, Richard. "Metaphor and Theory Change: What Is 'Metaphor' a Metaphor For?" In *Metaphor and Thought.* Edited by Andrew Ortony, 356–408. New York: Cambridge University Press, 1979.

Branigan, Edward. *Narrative Comprehension and Film.* New York, Routledge, 1992.

Bratman, Michael. *Intentions, Plans, and Practical Reason.* Cambridge, Mass.: Harvard University Press, 1987.

Breitbart, Eric. "From the Panorama to the Docudrama: Notes on the Visualization of History." *Radical History Review* 25 (1981): 115–125.

Calder-Marshall, Arthur. *The Innocent Eye: The Life of Robert J. Flaherty.* New York: Harcourt, Brace and World, 1963.

Carroll, Noël. "From Real to Reel: Entangled in the Nonfiction Film." *Philosophical Exchange* 14 (1983): 4–45.

———. "The Power of Movies." *Daedalus* 114 (1985): 79–104.

———. *Mystifying Movies: Fads and Fallacies in Contemporary Film Theory.* New York: Columbia University Press, 1988.

———. *Philosophical Problems of Classical Film Theory.* Princeton: Princeton University Press, 1988.

———. "Fiction, Nonfiction, and the Film of Presumptive Assertion: Conceptual Analyses." In *Film Theory and Philosophy.* Edited by Richard Allen and Murray Smith, 173–202. Oxford: Oxford University Press, 1997.

Champagne, John. "'Stop Reading Films!' Film Studies, Close Analysis, and Gay Pornography." *Cinema Journal* 36 (1997): 76–97.

Cherniak, Christopher. *Minimal Rationality.* Cambridge, Mass.: M.I.T. Press, 1986.

Chisholm, Roger. *Perceiving: A Philosophical Study.* Ithaca: Cornell University Press, 1957.

"Chronology." In *Robert Flaherty, Photographer/Filmmaker: The Inuit, 1910–1922: An Exhibition.* Vancouver, B.C.: Vancouver Art Gallery, 1979.

Ciochon, Russel, John Olsen, and Jamie James, *Other Origins: The Search for the Giant Ape in Human Prehistory.* New York: Bantam, 1990

Clark, Herbert H. "Responding to Indirect Speech Acts." In *Pragmatics: A Reader.* Edited by Steven Davis, 199–230. New York: Oxford University Press, 1991.

Currie, Gregory. *The Nature of Fiction*. Cambridge: Cambridge University Press, 1990.
———. "Visual Fictions." *Philosophical Quarterly* 41 (1991): 129–143.
———. "Photography, Painting, and Perception." *Journal of Aesthetics and Art Criticism* 49 (1991): 23–29.
———. "Impersonal Imaginings: A Reply to Jerrold Levinson." *The Philosophical Quarterly* 43 (1993): 79–82.
———. "The Long Goodbye: The Imaginary Language of Film." *British Journal of Aesthetics* 33 (1993): 207–219.
———. *Image and Mind: Film, Philosophy, and Cognitive Science*. Cambridge: Cambridge University Press, 1995.
Dennett, Daniel. *Brainstorms: Philosophical Essays on Mind and Psychology*. Montgomery, Vt.: Bradford, 1978.
———. *The Intentional Stance*. Cambridge, Mass.: M.I.T. Press, 1989.
Davis, Steven, ed. *Pragmatics: A Reader*. New York: Oxford University Press, 1991.
Dretske, Fred. *Seeing and Knowing*. London: Routledge and Kegan Paul, 1969.
———. "The Percept in Visual Cognition." In *Perception and Cognition: Issues in the Foundations of Psychology. Minnesota Studies in the Philosophy of Science*, vol. 9, edited by C. Wade Savage, 107–127. Minneapolis: University of Minnesota Press, 1978.
———. *Knowledge and the Flow of Information*. Oxford: Blackwell, 1981.
———. *Explaining Behavior: Reasons in a World of Causes*. Cambridge, Mass.: M.I.T. Press, 1988.
———. "Meaningful Perception." In *Visual Cognition*. 2d ed. Edited by Daniel N. Osherson and Stephen M. Kosslyn, 331-352. Cambridge, Mass.: M.I.T. Press, 1995. Vol. 2 of *An Invitation to Cognitive Science*. 4 vols. Gen. ed. Daniel N. Osherson. Cambridge, Mass.: M.I.T. Press, 1990–1998.
Ebert, Roger. "Interview with Oliver Stone." In *JFK: The Book of the Film*. Edited by Oliver Stone and Zachary Sklar, 249–253. New York: Applause Books, 1992.
Eco, Umberto. "Articulations of the Cinematic Code." In *Movies and Methods*. Edited by Bill Nichols, 590–607. Berkeley: University of California Press, 1976.
Eitzen, Dirk. "When Is a Documentary?: Documentary As a Mode of Reception." *Cinema Journal* 35 (1995): 81–102.
Ellis, John. *Visible Fictions*. London: Routledge and Kegan Paul, 1982.
Feagin, Susan. "Incompatible Interpretations of Art." *Philosophy and Literature* 6 (1982): 133–146.
Feld, Steven, ed. *Chronicle of a Summer*. Special issue of *Studies in Visual Communication* 11 (1985): 2–78.
"Filmography." In *Robert Flaherty, Photographer/Filmmaker: The Inuit, 1910–1922: An Exhibition*. Vancouver, B.C.: Vancouver Art Gallery, 1979.
Flaherty, Robert. "Robert Flaherty Talking." In *The Cinema 1950*. Edited by Roger Manvell, 11–29. London: Pelican, 1950.
———. "How I Filmed *Nanook of the North*." In *Film Makers on Film Making: Statements on Their Art by Thirty Directors*. Edited by Harry M. Geduld, 56–64. Bloomington: Indiana University Press, 1969.
Flaherty, Robert, and Francis Hubbard Flaherty. *My Eskimo Friends*. Garden City, N.J.: Doubleday and Page, 1924.

Flaherty, Frances Hubbard. *The Odyssey of a Filmmaker: Robert Flaherty's Story*. New York: Arno Press, 1972.

Fodor, Jerry. *The Language of Thought*. New York: Crowell, 1975.

———. "Précis of *The Modularity of Mind*." *Behavioral and Brain Sciences* 8 (1985): 1–42.

Fodor, Jerry, and Zenon Pylyshyn. "How Direct Is Direct Perception?: Some Reflections on Gibson's 'Ecological Approach.'" *Cognition* 9 (1981): 139–196.

Fogelin, Robert J. *Figuratively Speaking*. New Haven: Yale University Press, 1988.

———. "Metaphors, Similes, and Similarity." In *Aspects of Metaphor*. Edited by Jaakko Hintikka, 23–39. Dordrecht: Kluwer, 1994.

Gaut, Berys. "Film Authorship and Collaboration." In *Film Theory and Philosophy*. Edited by Richard Allen and Murray Smith, 149–172. Oxford: Oxford University Press, 1997.

Geduld, Harry M., ed. *Film Makers on Film Making: Statements on Their Art by Thirty Directors*. Bloomington: Indiana University Press, 1969.

Giannetti, Louis. *Understanding Movies*. 7th ed. Englewood Cliffs, N.J.: Prentice-Hall, 1996.

Gibson, J. J. *The Ecological Approach to Visual Perception*. Boston: Houghton Mifflin, 1979.

———. "The Information Available in Pictures." *Leonardo* 4 (1971): 27–35.

Giles, Dennis. "The Name Documentary: A Preface to Genre Study." *Film Reader* 3 (1978): 18–22.

Goldman, Alvin. *Epistemology and Cognition*. Cambridge, Mass: Harvard University Press, 1986.

———. "What Is Justified Belief?" In *Justification and Knowledge*. Edited by George Pappas, 1–23. Dordrecht: Reidel, 1979.

———. "Perceptual Objects." *Synthese* 35 (1977) 257–284.

Gombrich, E. H. *Art and Illusion*. London: Phaidon, 1960.

Gombrich, E. H., Julian Hochberg, and Max Black, eds. *Art, Perception, and Reality*. Baltimore: Johns Hopkins University Press, 1971.

Goodman, Nelson. *Languages of Art*. Indianapolis: Bobbs-Merrill, 1968.

Gordon, David George. *Field Guide to the Sasquatch*. Seattle: Sasquatch Books, 1992.

Graham, John. "'There Are No Simple Solutions': Wiseman on Filmmaking and Viewing." In *Frederick Wiseman*. Edited by Thomas R. Atkins, 33–46. New York: Simon and Schuster, 1976.

Green, John. *Sasquatch: The Apes Among Us*. Seattle: Hancock House, 1978.

Gregory, Richard L. *Eye and Brain: The Psychology of Seeing*. 3d ed. New York: McGraw-Hill, 1978.

Grice, H. P. "Meaning," *Philosophical Review* 66 (1957): 377–388.

———. "The Causal Theory of Perception." *Proceedings of the Aristotelian Society*. Supplementary Volume 35 (1961): 121–152.

Grierson, John. "Documentary (1)." *Cinema Quarterly* (Winter 1932): 67–72.

———. *Grierson On Documentary*. 2d rev. ed. Edited by Forsyth Hardy. London: Faber and Faber, 1979.

———. "First Principles of Documentary." In *Grierson On Documentary*. Edited by Forsyth Hardy, 35–46. London: Faber and Faber, 1979.

Guynn, William. *A Cinema of Nonfiction*. Rutherford, N.J.: Farleigh Dickenson University Press, 1990.
Haack, Susan. "'Dry Truth and Real Knowledge': Epistemologies of Metaphor and Metaphors of Epistemology." In *Aspects of Metaphor*. Edited by Jaakko Hintikka, 1–22. Dordrecht: Kluwer, 1994.
———. *Evidence and Inquiry: Towards Reconstruction in Epistemology*. Oxford: Blackwell, 1995.
Hallet, Garth. *Language and Truth*. New Haven: Yale University Press, 1988.
Handelman, Janet. "An Interview with Frederick Wiseman." *Film Library Quarterly* 3 (1970): 5–9.
Haugeland, John. "The Nature and Plausibility of Cognitivism." *Behavioral and Brain Sciences* 2 (1978): 215–260.
Heilemann, John. "The Sun King: How Scott McNealy Became the Anti-Gates." *The New Yorker*, 16 March 1998, 30–35.
Hermerén, Göran. *Aspects of Aesthetics*. Lund: LiberVörlag, 1983.
Hintikka, Jaakko, ed. *Aspects of Metaphor*. Dordrecht: Kluwer, 1994.
Hjort, Mette, ed. *Rules and Conventions: Literature, Philosophy, Social Theory*. Baltimore: Johns Hopkins University Press, 1992.
Hochberg, Julian. "The Perception of Pictorial Representations." *Social Research* 51 (1984): 841–862.
Hoffer, Thomas, and Richard Nelson, "Evolution of Docudrama on American Television Networks: Content Analysis, 1966–1978." *The Southern Speech and Communication Journal* 4 (1980): 149–163.
Hoffer, Thomas, Richard Nelson, and Robert Musburger. "Docudrama." In *TV Genres: A Handbook and Reference Guide*. Edited by Bryan Rose. Westport, Conn.: Greenwood Press, 1985. 80–111.
Jackson, Frank. *Perception*. Cambridge: Cambridge University Press, 1977.
Jacobs, Lewis, ed. *The Documentary Tradition*. 2d ed. New York: W. W. Norton, 1979.
Jacobs, Lewis. Introduction to *The Documentary Tradition*, edited by Lewis Jacobs, 2–9. New York: W. W. Norton, 1979.
Jacobson, Harlan. "Michael and Me." *Film Comment* 25 (1989): 16–26.
Jensen, Gorden D., and Luh Ketut Suryani. *The Balinese People: A Reinvestigation of Character*. Oxford: Oxford University Press, 1992.
Johnson-Laird, P. N. *Mental Models: Towards a Cognitive Science of Language, Inference, and Consciousness*. Cambridge, Mass.: Harvard University Press, 1983.
Kemp, G. N. "Pictures and Depictions: A Consideration of Peacocke's Views." *British Journal of Aesthetics* 30 (1990): 332–341.
Kilborn, Richard. "*Drama Over Lockerbie*: A New Look at Television Drama-Documentaries." *Historical Journal of Film, Radio and Television* 14 (1994): 59–76.
Korzybski, Alfred. *Science and Sanity: An Introduction to Non-Aristotelean Systems and General Semantics*. Lakeville, Conn.: International Non-Aristotelean Library, 1933.
Kracauer, Siegfried. *Theory of Film: The Redemption of Physical Reality*. New York: Oxford, 1960.
Krantz, Grover. *Big Footprints: An Inquiry into the Reality of Sasquatch*. Boulder, Colo.: Johnson Books, 1992.

Kuehl, Jerry. "Truth Claims." *Sight and Sound* 50 (1981): 272–274.
Kuhn, Annette. "Theories of the Feminist Documentary." In *New Challenges for Documentary*. Edited by Alan Rosenthal, 79–102. Berkeley: University of California Press, 1988.
Lakoff, George. *Women, Fire, and Dangerous Things: What Categories Reveal About the Mind*. Chicago: University of Chicago Press, 1987.
Lamarque, Peter, and Stein Haugom Olsen. *Truth, Fiction, and Literature*. Oxford: Clarendon, 1994.
Lardner, George, Jr. "On the Set: Dallas in Wonderland." In *JFK: The Book of the Film*. Edited by Oliver Stone and Zachary Sklar, 191–198. New York: Applause Books, 1992. First published in the *Washington Post* 19 May 1991, D1.
Levin, G. Roy. Introduction to *Documentary Explorations: 15 Interviews with Filmmakers*. Edited by G. Roy Levin, 1–5. New York: Doubleday, 1971.
———, ed. *Documentary Explorations: 15 Interviews with Filmmakers*. New York: Doubleday, 1971.
Levinson, Jerrold. "Seeing, Imaginarily, At the Movies." *The Philosophical Quarterly* 43 (1993): 70–78.
Lewis, David K. *Convention*. Cambridge, Mass.: Harvard University Press, 1968.
———. *Philosophical Papers*. 2 vols. New York: Oxford University Press, 1983–1986.
———. "Veridical Hallucinations and Prosthetic Vision." In *Philosophical Papers*. Vol. 2. New York: Oxford University Press, 1986.
Livingston, Paisley. *Literary Knowledge: Humanistic Inquiry and the Philosophy of Science*. Ithaca: Cornell University Press, 1988.
———. *Literature and Rationality: Ideas of Agency in Theory and Fiction*. Cambridge: Cambridge University Press, 1991.
———. "Film and the New Psychology." *Poetics* 21 (1992): 93–116.
———. "Characterization and Fictional Truth in the Cinema." In *Post-Theory: Reconstructing Film Studies*. Edited by David Bordwell and Noël Carroll, 149–174. Madison: University of Wisconsin Press, 1996.
———. "Cinematic Authorship." In *Film Theory and Philosophy*. Edited by Richard Allen and Murray Smith, 132–148. Oxford: Oxford University Press, 1997.
Livingston, Paisley, and Alfred Mele. "Intention and Literature." *Stanford French Review* 16 (1992): 173–196.
Lycan, William G. "Form, Function, and Feel." *Journal of Philosophy* 78 (1981): 24–50.
MacBean, James Roy. "*Two Laws* from Australia, One White, One Black." In *New Challenges for Documentary*. Edited by Alan Rosenthal, 210–226. Berkeley: University of California Press, 1988.
Manvell, Roger, ed. *The Cinema 1950*. London: Pelican, 1950.
Marr, David. *Vision: A Computational Investigation Into the Human Representation and Processing of Visual Information*. San Francisco: W. H. Freeman, 1982.
Mashon, Mike. "Losing Control: Popular Reception(s) of the Rodney King Video." *Wide Angle* 15 (1993): 7–18.
McGinn, Colin. *The Character of Mind: An Introduction to the Philosophy of Mind*. 2d ed. Oxford: Oxford University Press, 1997.
McWilliams, Donald E. "Frederick Wiseman." *Film Quarterly* 24 (1970): 17–26.

Mele, Alfred. *Springs of Action: Understanding Intentional Behavior*. New York: Oxford University Press, 1992.

———. "Motivation: Essentially Motivation-Constituting Attitudes." *The Philosophical Review* 104 (1995): 397–423.

Mele, Alfred, and Paisley Livingston. "Intentions and Interpretations." *MLN* 107 (1992): 931–949.

Metz, Christian. *Language and Cinema*. Translated by Donna Jean Umiker-Sebeok. The Hague: Mouton, 1974.

Minh-ha, Trinh T. "The Totalizing Quest of Meaning." In *Theorizing Documentary*. Edited by Michael Renov, 90–107. New York: Routledge, 1993.

Milgram, Stanley. "Behavioral Study of Obedience." *Journal of Abnormal and Social Psychology* 67 (1963): 371–378.

———. "Some Conditions of Obedience and Disobedience to Authority." *Human Relations* 18 (1965): 57–76.

———. *Obedience to Authority: An Experimental View*. New York: Harper and Row, 1974.

Miller, Richard. *Moral Differences: Truth, Justice, and Conscience in a World of Conflict*. Princeton: Princeton University Press, 1992.

———. *Fact and Method: Explanation, Confirmation, and Reality in the Natural and the Social Sciences*. Princeton: Princeton University Press, 1987.

Morin, Edgar. *Le Cinéma ou l'homme imaginaire: essaie d'anthropologie sociologique*. Paris: Minuit, 1956.

———. "Chronicle of a Film." Translated by Steven Feld and Amy Ewing, 4–29. In *Chronicle of a Summer*. Special issue of *Studies in Visual Communication* 11 (1985), edited by Steven Feld.

Morrow, Lance, and Martha Smilgis. "Plunging Into the Labyrinth." In *JFK: The Book of the Film*. Edited by Oliver Stone and Zachary Sklar, 298–303. New York: Applause Books, 1992. First published in *Time*, 23 December 1991, 74–76.

Moser, Paul K. *Knowledge and Evidence*. Cambridge: Cambridge University Press, 1989.

Nichols, Bill. *Ideology and the Image*. Bloomington: University of Indiana Press, 1981.

———. "The Voice of Documentary." In *New Challenges for Documentary*. Edited by Alan Rosenthal, 48–63. Berkeley: University of California Press, 1988.

———. *Representing Reality: Issues and Concepts in Documentary*. Bloomington: Indiana University Press, 1991.

———. "'Getting to Know You . . .': Knowledge, Power, and the Body." In *Theorizing Documentary*. Edited by Michael Renov, 174–91. New York: Routledge, 1993.

———. *Blurred Boundaries: Questions of Meaning in Contemporary Culture*. Bloomington: Indiana University Press, 1994.

———, ed. *Movies and Methods*. Berkeley: University of California Press, 1976.

Nisbett, Richard, and Lee Ross. *Human Inference: Strategies and Shortcomings of Social Judgment*. Englewood Cliffs, N.J.: Prentice-Hall, 1980.

Novitz, David. *Pictures and Their Use in Communication*. The Hague: N. Nijhoff, 1977.

Ortony, Andrew, ed. *Metaphor and Thought*. New York: Cambridge University Press, 1979.
Osherson, Daniel N., and Stephen M. Kosslyn, eds. *Visual Cognition*. 2d ed. Cambridge, Mass.: M.I.T. Press, 1995. Vol. 2 of *An Invitation to Cognitive Science*. 4 vols. Gen. ed. Daniel N. Osherson. Cambridge, Mass.: M.I.T. Press, 1990–1998.
Paget, Derek. *True Stories?: Documentary Drama on Radio, Screen, and Stage*. New York: St. Martin's Press, 1990.
Pappas, George, ed. *Justification and Knowledge*. Dordrecht: Reidel, 1979.
Peacocke, Christopher. "Depiction." *Philosophical Review* 96 (1987): 383–410.
Peirce, Charles Sanders. *Collected Papers of Charles Sanders Peirce*. 8 vols. Edited by Charles Hartshorne, Paul Weiss, and A. W. Burks. Cambridge, Mass.: Harvard University Press, 1931–1958.
Perkins, Moreland. *Sensing the World*. Indianapolis: Hackett, 1983.
Plantinga, Carl. "Defining Documentary: Fiction, Non-Fiction, and Projected Worlds." *Persistence of Vision* 5 (1987): 44–53.
_____. "The Mirror Framed: A Case for Expression in Documentary." *Wide Angle* 13 (1991): 41–53.
_____. "Blurry Boundaries, Troubling Typologies, and the Unruly Nonfiction Film." Review of *Representing Reality*, by Bill Nichols. *Semiotica* 98 (1994): 387–396.
_____. "Dialogue: Carl Plantinga Responds to Dirk Eitzen's 'When Is a Documentary?: Documentary As a Mode of Reception." *Cinema Journal* 36 (1996): 94–96.
_____. "Moving Pictures and Nonfiction: Two Approaches." In *Post-Theory: Reconstructing Film Studies*. Edited by David Bordwell and Noël Carroll, 307–324. Madison: University of Wisconsin Press, 1996.
_____. *Rhetoric and Representation in Nonfiction Film*. New York: Cambridge University Press, 1997.
Ponech, Trevor. "Visual Perception and Motion Picture Spectatorship." *Cinema Journal* 37 (1997): 85–100.
_____. "What Is Non-fiction Cinema?" In *Film Theory and Philosophy*. Edited by Richard Allen and Murray Smith, 203–220. Oxford: Oxford University Press, 1997.
Prince, Stephen. "The Discourse of Pictures: Iconicity and Film Studies." *Film Quarterly* 47 (1993): 16–28.
Putnam, Hilary. *Reason, Truth, and History*. Cambridge: Cambridge University Press, 1981.
Pylyshyn, Zenon. "Computation and Cognition: Issues in the Foundations of Cognitive Science." *Behavioral and Brain Sciences* 3 (1980): 111–132.
Renov, Michael, ed. *Theorizing Documentary*. New York: Routledge, 1993.
Renov, Michael. Introduction to *Theorizing Documentary*. Edited by Michael Renov, 1–11. New York: Routledge, 1993.
_____. "Towards a Poetics of Documentary." In *Theorizing Documentary*. Edited by Michael Renov, 12–36. New York: Routledge, 1993.
Robert Flaherty, Photographer/Filmmaker: The Inuit, 1910–1922: An Exhibition. Vancouver, B.C.: Vancouver Art Gallery, 1979.

Robinson, J. O. *The Psychology of Visual Illusion*. London: Hutchinson University Library, 1972.

Rock, Irvin. *The Logic of Perception*. Cambridge, Mass.: M.I.T. Press, 1983.

Rose, Bryan, ed. *TV Genres: A Handbook and Reference Guide*. Westport, Conn.: Greenwood Press, 1985.

Rosenthal, Alan. Introduction to *New Challenges for Documentary*. Edited by Alan Rosenthal, 509–516. University of California Press, 1988.

———. *Writing Docudrama: Dramatizing Reality for Film and TV*. New York: Focal Press, 1994.

———, ed. *New Challenges for Documentary*. Berkeley: University of California Press, 1988.

Ross, Lee, and Richard Nisbett. *The Person in the Situation: Perspectives of Social Psychology*. New York: McGraw-Hill, 1991.

Rothman, William. *Documentary Film Classics*. Cambridge: Cambridge University Press, 1997.

Ruby, Jay. "'The Aggie Will Come First': The Demystification of Robert Flaherty." In *Robert Flaherty, Photographer/Filmmaker: The Inuit, 1910–1922: An Exhibition*. Vancouver, B.C.: Vancouver Art Gallery, 1979.

Saladin D'Anglure, Bernard. "Nanook, Super Male: The Polar Bear in the Imaginary Space and Social Time of the Inuit of the Canadian Arctic." In *Signifying Animals: Human Meaning in the Natural World*. Edited by Roy Willis, 178–185. London: Unwin Hyman, 1990.

Savage, C. Wade, ed. *Perception and Cognition: Issues in the Foundations of Psychology*. Minneapolis: University of Minnesota Press, 1978. Vol. 9 of *Minnesota Studies in the Philosophy of Science*. 16 vols. to date. Minneapolis: University of Minnesota Press, 1956–.

Schell, Jonathan. *The Fate of the Earth*. New York: Knopf, 1982.

Schier, Flint. *Deeper Into Pictures: An Essay on Pictorial Representation*. Cambridge: Cambridge University Press, 1986.

Scruton, Roger. *Art and the Imagination: A Study in the Philosophy of Mind*. 2d ed. London: Methuen, 1982.

———. *The Aesthetic Understanding*. New York: Methuen, 1983.

Searle, John. "Indirect Speech Acts." In *Pragmatics: A Reader*. Edited by Steven Davis. New York: Oxford University Press, 1991. 265–277

Sibley, Frank N. "Analyzing Seeing (I)." In *Perception*. Edited by Frank Sibley, 81–132. London: Methuen, 1971.

———, ed. *Perception*. London: Methuen, 1971.

Sklar, Zachary. "Exchange: Jousting After Camelot." In *JFK: The Book of the Film*. Edited by Oliver Stone and Zachary Sklar, 472–473. New York: Applause Books, 1992. First published in *The Nation*, 9 March 1992, 290.

Sobchack, Vivian, ed. *The Persistence of History: Cinema, Television, and the Modern Event*. New York: Routledge, 1996.

Sofsky, Wolfgang. *The Order of Terror: The Concentration Camps*. Translated by William Templer. Princeton: Princeton University Press, 1997.

Stecker, Robert. "Incompatible Interpretations." *Journal of Aesthetics and Art Criticism* 50 (1992): 292–298.

———. "Relativism About Interpretation." *Journal of Aesthetics and Art Criticism* 53 (1995): 14–18.
Stefansson, Vilhjalmur. *The Standardization of Error*. London: Kegan Paul, Trench, and Trubner, 1928.
Stone, Oliver. "Oliver Stone Talks Back." In *JFK: The Book of the Film*. Edited by Oliver Stone and Zachary Sklar, 349–353. New York: Applause Books, 1992. First published in *Premiere*, January 1992, 66–70.
———. "Stone's *JFK*: A Higher Truth?" In *JFK: The Book of the Film*. Edited by Oliver Stone and Zachary Sklar, 198–202. New York: Applause Books, 1992. First published in the *Washington Post*, 2 June 1991, D3.
———. "Who Is Re-Writing History?" In *JFK: The Book of the Film*. Edited by Oliver Stone and Zachary Sklar, 276–278. New York: Applause Books, 1992. First published in the *New York Times*, 20 December 1991, A35.
Stone, Oliver, and Zachary Sklar, eds. *JFK: The Book of the Film*. New York: Applause Books, 1992.
Tomasulo, Frank P. "I'll See It When I Believe It: Rodney King and the Prison House of Video." In *The Persistence of History: Cinema, Television, and the Modern Event*. Edited by Vivian Sobchack, 69–88. New York: Routledge, 1996.
Tversky, Amos. "Features of Similarity." *Psychological Review* 4 (1977): 327–352.
Ullman, Shimon. "Against Direct Perception." *Behavioral and Brain Sciences* 3 (1980): 373–415.
Underwood, Geoffrey, ed. *Implicit Cognition*. Oxford: Oxford University Press, 1996.
van Fraassen, Bas. *The Scientific Image*. Oxford: Oxford University Press, 1980.
Vertov, Dziga. *Kino-Eye: The Writings of Dziga Vertov*. Edited by Annette Michelson and translated by Kevin O'Brien. Berkeley: University of California Press, 1984.
———. "The Essence of Kino-Eye." In *Kino-Eye: The Writings of Dziga Vertov*. Edited by Annette Michelson, 49–50. Berkeley: University of California Press, 1984.
Walton, Kendall. "Pictures and Make-Believe." *Philosophical Review* 82 (1973): 283–319.
———. "Transparent Pictures: On the Nature of Photographic Realism." *Critical Inquiry* 11 (1984): 246–277.
———. *Mimesis As Make-Believe: On the Foundations of the Representational Arts*. Cambridge: Harvard University Press, 1990.
———. "On Pictures and Photographs: Objections Answered." In *Film Theory and Philosophy*. Edited by Richard Allen and Murray Smith, 60–75. Oxford: Oxford University Press, 1997.
Warnock, G. J. "Seeing." *Aristotelian Society Proceedings* 55 (1955): 201–218.
Weitz, Morris. "The Role of Theory in Aesthetics." *Journal of Aesthetics and Art Criticism* 15 (1956): 27–35.
Westin, Alan. "'You Start Off with a Bromide': Wiseman on Film and Civil Liberties." In *Frederick Wiseman*. Edited by Thomas R. Atkins, 47–60. New York: Simon and Schuster, 1976.
White, Hayden. *Tropics of Discourse: Essays in Cultural Criticism*. Baltimore: Johns Hopkins University Press, 1978.

———. Introduction to *Tropics of Discourse: Essays in Cultural Criticism*. Baltimore: Johns Hopkins University Press, 1978.

———. "The Historical Text As Literary Artifact." In *Tropics of Discourse: Essays in Cultural Criticism*. Baltimore: Johns Hopkins University Press, 1978.

Williams, Christopher, ed. *Realism and Cinema*. London: Routledge and Kegan Paul, 1980.

Williams, Linda. "Mirrors Without Memories: Truth, History, and the New Documentary." *Film Quarterly* 3 (1993): 9–21.

Willis, Roy, ed. *Signifying Animals: Human Meaning in the Natural World*. London: Unwin Hyman, 1990.

Wilson, George. *Narration in Light: Studies in Cinematic Point of View*. Baltimore: Johns Hopkins University Press, 1986.

Winston, Brian. *Claiming the Real: The Documentary Film Revisited*. London: British Film Institute, 1995.

Wiseman, Frederick. "Reminiscences of a Filmmaker: Frederick Wiseman on *Law and Order*." *Police Chief* 36 (1969): 32–35.

Wittgenstein, Ludwig. *Philosophical Investigations*. Translated by G. E. M. Anscombe. 3d ed. New York: Macmillan, 1958.

Wollheim, Richard. *Art and Its Objects*. New York: Harper, 1971.

Index

Abdul, Paula, 198
Accuracy, 4, 12, 53, 88–89, 271
Ackerman, Chantal, 191
Adams, Randall, 19–20, 129, 175, 262, 265
Aesthetics, 151
Agee, Arthur, 89
Agency, 7, 27, 66, 88, 112, 128, 144, 220, 258, 261, 268, 272
  agentic shift, 279(n27)
Alien Autopsy: Fact or Fiction (McGough), 64, 81, 182
Allen, Richard, 64, 186–187, 189, 209(n24)
Allen, Woody, 147
Anderson, Carolyn, 110, 221, 222, 245(n31)
Anthropological truisms, 255–256
Apocalypse Now (Coppola), 147
Arguments, 16, 24–25, 38(n29)
Armes, Roy, 125–126
Arnulf Rainer (Kubelka), 33
Asby, Hal, 129
Aspects of Aesthetics (Hermerén), 37(n20)
Assertions, 11, 12, 13, 15, 18–19, 26, 28, 30–31, 52, 143, 153, 154, 161, 166, 171, 173(n30), 214–215, 231, 271
  and fiction, 160, 169. *See also* Nonfiction cinema, hybrid forms
  linguistic versus cinematic, 22–23
Assumptions, 66, 80, 98, 152, 153, 157, 164, 175, 218, 219, 225, 238, 252, 279(n30). *See also* Communicative assumptions; Communicative presumption; *under* Perception
Atomic Café, The (Rafferty, Loader, Rafferty), 123
Audiences, 14, 19, 20, 23, 24, 25, 26, 27, 30, 31, 34, 42, 44, 52, 60, 62, 64, 66, 81, 88, 108, 110, 111, 117, 129, 139, 144, 145, 148, 153–154, 155, 157, 158, 163, 168, 170, 187, 191, 197, 214, 218, 222, 273
Audiovisual features, 85, 92, 122, 123, 236, 275
Authorial intentions, 1, 2, 3, 5, 8, 11, 12, 13, 15, 18, 20, 23, 24, 26, 28, 29, 30–31, 59, 82, 84, 92–93, 96(n4), 98, 139, 145, 153, 154, 213, 218, 219, 220–221, 236, 242, 243(n8), 249
  of artists, 65
  author's consciousness of, 105–106
  and content, 116, 122
  and implied authorship, 110–111
  and multiple authorship, 111–112
  skepticism about, 34–35, 157, 221
  See also Authorship; Meaning(s), dependence on intentions
Authorship, 112–114, 154
  authors versus makers, 112, 113
  implied/multiple, 110–112, 113, 221, 222–223, 243(n8)
  See also Authorial intentions

Bach, Kent, 13, 16, 31
Background knowledge, 54, 88, 93, 168, 179, 181, 182, 200, 205, 228,

293

256. *See also* Beliefs, background beliefs
Bain, Alexander, 197, 211(n34)
Bakker, Jim and Tammy, 106
Barnouw, Erik, 5, 121, 125, 141(n18)
Barry, Iris, 125
Barsam, Richard Meran, 5, 9, 125
Barwise, Jon, 47, 81–82
Bateson, Gregory, 11, 14, 71(n34), 228
Battle of Algiers (Pontecorvo), 169
Battle of San Pietro, The (Huston), 27
Bazin, André, 6, 43, 66, 239
Being There (Kosinski/Asby), 128–129
Beliefs, 3–4, 13, 15, 16–17, 18, 19, 27, 42, 49, 52, 67, 76, 77, 129, 175, 179, 187, 188, 189, 191, 195, 196, 197, 215, 238, 260, 272
  acquiring, 270
  attitude of belief, 11, 20, 23, 138, 149, 159, 161, 164, 165, 232, 233, 252. *See also* Authorial intentions
  background beliefs, 225, 226, 235, 257. *See also* Background knowledge
  circular, 255
  and evaluative judgments, 102
  false, 64, 65, 271, 273
  justification for, 4, 217, 247, 251–260, 270, 274, 275, 276, 279(n28)
  kinds concerning interpretative response, 216
  mutual contextual beliefs (MCBs), 31–32, 38(n43), 62, 156, 214, 229, 232, 233
  perceptual, 201, 204, 205
  See also Knowledge; Truth
Benson, Thomas, 110, 221, 222, 245(n31)
Bigfoot. *See* Sasquatches
Bikel, Ofra, 17
Birds, The (Hitchcock), 148
Blank, Les, 250
Booth, Wayne, 221
Bordwell, David, 207(n7)
Boyd, Richard, 271
Bratman, Michael, 103

Brayne, William, 120, 121
Bullitt (Yates), 148
Burden of Dreams (Blank), 250

Carroll, Noël, 6, 18–19, 71(n28), 77, 209(n14)
Causality, 31, 50, 55, 57, 60, 85, 98, 100, 101, 109, 111, 145, 176, 183, 199, 200, 202, 203, 206(n2), 220, 252, 254, 257, 268
  causes of a belief, 274
  and pre-filmic situations, 269
  and psychological states, 104–105, 107–108, 110
Cavell, Stanley, 239
Cayrol, Jean, 239–242
Champagne, John, 207(n7)
Characterization, 128–129, 135–136, 146, 150, 183
Characters of Shakespeare's Plays, The (Hazlitt), 147
Chronicle of a Summer (Rouch and Morin), 273, 274
Cinema verité, 121, 168, 274
Citron, Michelle, 159, 161, 168
COE. *See* Course of events
Cognition, 54, 189, 240, 254
  cognitive aims, 163
  and language, 207(n7)
  See also Perception, cognitive
Coherentism, 217, 255
Collaborations. *See* Cooperation policy
Communicative action, 144–145, 161, 162, 218, 231, 266
  intrinsically/extrinsically motivated, 164–165
Communicative assumptions, 19, 20, 22, 24, 31, 214, 231. *See also* Assumptions; Communicative presumption
Communicative pragmatics, 2, 12, 26, 144, 161, 173(n30)
Communicative presumption (CP), 32–34. *See also* Communicative assumptions
Comolli, Jean-Louis, 9, 96(n9)

Index
295

Comprehension, 23, 24, 53, 58, 73, 150, 175, 180, 185, 186, 189, 191, 225
Computer-generated imagery, 22, 87
Confirmatives, 17–18, 36(n14), 128, 129, 139, 166, 271
Constatives, , 16, 18, 20, 30, 53, 155, 175, 213, 214, 218, 224, 228, 234, 246, 247, 251, 252, 260
  disputative, 230
  See also Intentions, constative; Speech acts, constative
Constructivism, 78, 177–178, 201
Content, 8, 14, 19, 41, 53, 81, 105, 119, 127, 159, 160, 213, 214, 218, 222, 233, 234, 235, 238, 272
  examples of, 87–95
  of fiction, 145, 148, 149, 190
  intentional basis of, 84, 116–123. See also Authorial intentions
  of intentions, 98–99, 100, 118
  of interpretive response, 215, 216
  and mental significance, 118
  perceptual, 200
  as situations, 73, 82, 119. See also Situations
  as visually determined, 58
  See also under Authorial intentions; Plans
Context, 54, 84, 238, 253. See also Beliefs, mutual contextual beliefs
Continuity policy, 130–131, 136
Conventions, 22, 37(n20), 38(n24), 57, 165, 190. See also Perception, conventions concerning; Representations, representational conventions; Social conventions
Cooperation policy, 131–133
Coppola, Francis Ford, 147
Counterfactual dependence, 56, 57, 59, 60, 61, 73, 85, 91, 117, 192, 198, 199, 201, 225
Course of events (COE), 253, 254, 257, 258, 264, 265. See also Situations
Cowan, Paul, 166
CP. See Communicative presumption

Crumb (Zwigoff), 88–89, 183
Cues, 20, 26
Culture, 27, 151
Currie, Gregory, 21, 38(n24), 58, 146, 149, 150, 172(n8), 210(n31), 222, 243(n8)
  representation thesis of, 198–199, 201–206

Daughter Rite (Citron), 159–160, 161, 162, 165, 168
Day After, The (Meyer), 169
De Bont, Jan, 189
Deceptions, 19, 34, 62, 63, 64, 68–69, 97(n15), 196, 227, 272, 273. See also Hoaxes; Representations, misrepresentations
Definitions, 151, 152. See also Intentions, defined; Non-fiction cinema, defined; Representations, defined/characterized
de Hory, Elmyr, 63
Democracy on Trial: The Morgentaler Affair (Cowan), 166, 171
Dennett, Daniel, 203
Depictions, 41, 52, 55, 56, 60, 80, 86, 91, 93, 94, 171, 188, 191–192, 193, 204, 239, 254
  perceptual approach to, 54
  See also Representations
Desires, 27, 101, 108, 109, 188, 224, 247, 256, 257, 274
Detour (Ulmer), 262
Dietrich, Marlene, 112, 149
Dishonored (von Sternberg), 149
Disputatives, 230, 243(n20)
Distorting lens, 67–68, 249
Docudramas, 158, 166–168
Documentaries, 7(n1), 9, 260, 276. See also Non-fiction cinema
Documentary film theory, 34, 35, 274
Don't Look Back (Pennebaker), 105, 106, 269
Dretske, Fred, 45, 50, 179, 206(n2)
Dylan, Bob, 105, 106

Eco, Umberto, 57
Editing, 22, 131, 136, 190, 235, 236
Eitzen, Dirk,. 25–26
Epistemology, 4, 41, 76, 77, 216, 248, 270, 272
Epistephilia, 108, 114(n14), 261
Eraserhead (Lynch), 27
Essentialism, 23–34, 151, 152, 153, 154
  light, 30
Eternal Jew, The (Hippler), 69, 78
Evaluative judgments, 102–103. *See also* Judgments
Evidence, 274–275, 276
Executive attitude, 100, 117
Expectations, 33, 34, 188, 191, 229. *See also* Communicative presumption
External significance, 59–60, 61, 81, 183, 256. *See also* Natural external significance

Fact and Method: Explanation, Confirmation, and Reality in the Natural and the Social Sciences (Miller), 97(n13)
Fallibilism, 217
Family resemblance terms, 151, 152, 173(n19). *See also* Non-fiction cinema, open concept of
Fellini, Federico, 169
F For Fake (Wells), 62–63
Fiction, 144–150, 160, 163, 165, 170, 171, 172(n8), 173(n30), 190, 192, 210(n31), 233, 262. *See also* Non-fiction cinema, fiction/non-fiction distinction; Non-fiction cinema, hybrid form
Figuration, 266–269, 278(n24)
Film noir, 262
Fitzcarraldo (Herzog), 250
Flaherty, Frances Hubbard, 125
Flaherty, Robert, 40, 124–139, 147
  comments of, 127, 128, 129, 130, 134, 139, 141(nn 22, 28), 181
Fodor, Jerry, 202
Fogelin, Robert, 266, 278(n24)

Force, 143–171, 213, 214, 216, 217, 218, 222. *See also* Illocutionary force
Frakes, Jonathan, 182
Frontline, 17

Gates, William, 89
Ghost channels, 50
Gilbert, Peter, 89
Gimme Shelter (Maysles and Zwerin), 107
Glenn Miller Story, The (Mann), 171
Grierson, John, 9, 75, 77–78

Haack, Susan, 217, 255, 279(n28)
Hand-held camera work, 23
Harnish, Robert, 13, 16, 31
Hazlitt, William, 147
Hermerén, Göran, 37(n20)
Herrmann, Bernard, 113
Herzog, Werner, 250
High School (Wiseman), 25, 26, 110, 235
Hippler, Fritz, 69, 78
Historians, 261
Historicism/ahistoricism, 23, 25, 30, 71(n31)
Hitchcock, Alfred, 113, 148, 262
Hoaxes, 9, 53, 79. *See also* Deceptions
Hoffer, Thomas, 167
Holliday, George, 9, 59, 252–259
Hoop Dreams (James, Marx, Gilbert), 89–90, 96(n12)
"How I Filmed *Nanook of the North*" (Flaherty), 141(n28)
Hughes, Howard, 63
Huston, John, 27
Hybrid form. *See under* Non-fiction cinema
Hypothesis revision, 84

Idealism, 277(n15)
Identity relation, 43, 44, 66, 225, 227, 239–240
Ideology, 5, 6, 9, 25, 34, 42, 108–109, 208(n14), 247, 274
Illocutionary force, 15, 19, 28, 29, 31, 32, 34, 118, 122, 128, 143, 144,

Index

146, 155, 156, 158, 160, 161, 227–233, 263–264
constative versus imaginative, 148
Illocutionary purpose, 164
Illusionism, 203
Images
  as intentional artifacts, 51, 226
  meanings of, 21, 54, 277(n15)
  relation to actual world, 9–10, 24, 41, 43, 57, 181, 275, 277(n15). *See also* Reality, relation to
  subliminal imagery, 96(n10)
  transparency of, 187, 189, 197–200
Imagined seeing, 191–197, 210(n31)
Imagining, 145–146, 149, 150, 159, 164, 167, 168, 169, 194, 232, 233, 260. *See also* Imagined seeing; Pretending; Situations, imaginary
Indexing, 26–29, 38(n36), 153–154
Inference, 206, 222, 228, 229, 232, 233, 235, 237
Information, 41, 47–48, 49, 52, 53, 58, 59, 77, 81, 82, 171, 178, 182, 188, 192, 199, 200, 203, 247, 254, 257, 264
  as by-product, 106, 265
  informational versus causal relations, 50, 51
  and interpretation*, 85
  loss of, 66
Innocence Lost (Bikel), 17
Intentional fallacy, 34
Intentions, 88, 89, 144, 164, 257, 259
  acquisition of, 101–103
  collective, 112
  constative, 143, 154. *See also* Constatives
  content-defining, 127
  coordinative power of, 104
  defined, 99–100
  versus desires, 101
  effective communicative intentions, 117–118, 124, 131–132, 148, 156, 157, 169, 214, 219, 222, 223, 234, 237, 238
  mixed, 136, 157

  motivational/representational aspects of, 99–104
  plans as representational content of, 98–99, 103–104
  See also Authorial intentions; Meaning(s), dependence on intentions; Non-fiction cinema, moderate intentionalist view of
Internalism, 217
Interpretation, 3, 23, 24, 25, 42, 52, 59, 66, 78, 81, 189, 213–242, 246, 253, 260, 264
  constraints on, 218
  first principles of, 217–227
  interpretation*, 73–74, 81, 82, 84, 85, 87, 92, 93, 94, 111, 117, 135, 168, 249, 253, 265. *See also* Interpretation, natural interpretation*
  interpretive success, 235, 237, 253
  kinds of, 215–216
  natural interpretation*, 85, 86, 87, 88, 89, 91, 92, 94, 117, 134, 135, 217, 235, 238, 253, 257
  questions answered by interpretive response, 214–215
Irving, Clifford, 62–63

James, Steve, 89
Jeanne Dielman, 23 Quai Du Commerce, 1080 Bruxelles (Ackerman), 191
JFK (Stone), 152, 228–233, 243(n15), 244(nn 22, 26)
Judgments, 102–103, 215, 218, 234, 236–237, 256
  judgmental heuristic, 252
Jurassic Park (Spielberg), 9

Kemp, G. N., 65
Kilborn, Richard, 167
King, Rodney, 9, 59–60, 252–259, 277(n13)
Knowing/knowledge, 108, 139, 175, 179, 204, 205, 206, 218, 247, 248, 252, 260, 272. *See also* Background knowledge; Epistemology

Korzybski, Alfred, 71(n34)
Kosinski, Jerzy, 128
Kracauer, Siegfried, 125
Kubelka, Peter, 33, 34
Kuehl, Jerry, 167
Kuhn, Annette, 160
Kurosawa, Akira, 150

Lamarque, Peter, 145, 146
Language, 20–23, 32, 33, 81–82, 149, 185
 and cognition, 207(n7)
 language of thought debates, 179
 linguistics, 46, 76, 80
 written, 57–58, 192
 See also Speech acts; *under* Perception
Lasseter, John, 87
Laughter and Tears: The Joan and Melissa Rivers Story (Scott), 169, 170, 171, 174(n38)
Law and Order (Wiseman), 120–121, 140(n2)
Lee, Spike, 25
Le Train arrive à la gare de Ciotat (Lumière), 67
Letter From Siberia (Marker), 151–152
Lewis, David, 21, 37(n20)
Literary Knowledge: Humanistic Inquiry and the Philosophy of Science (Livingston), 96(n8)
Livingston, Paisley, 96(n8), 104, 146, 152, 173(n19)
Loader, Jane, 123
Lumière, Auguste and Louis, 67
Lynch, David, 27

MacBean, James Roy, 126
McGough, Tom, 64, 81
Makavejev, Dusan, 160
Make-believe. *See* Pretending
Manhattan (Allen), 147
Mann, Anthony, 171
Man with a Movie Camera, The (Vertov), 86
Maps, 44, 66, 71(n34)
Marker, Chris, 151

Marlene (Schell), 111–112
Marx, Fred, 89
Mashon, Mike, 277(n13)
Maysles, Albert and David, 107, 236
MCBs. *See* Beliefs, mutual contextual beliefs
Mead, Margaret, 11, 14, 228
Meaning(s), 2, 5, 22, 31, 41, 42, 43, 47, 52, 90, 94, 109, 111, 133, 203, 218, 219, 221–222, 234, 238, 244(n22), 253, 256–257, 258
 counterfactual, 64
 dependence on intentions, 99, 105, 106, 110–111, 116, 120, 124, 126, 139
 figurative, 266–269, 278(n24)
 linguistic versus cinematic, 21–22, 38(n24), 82, 149. *See also* Perception, and language
 natural, 10–11, 25, 48, 49–50, 51, 52, 54, 58, 59–60, 61, 62, 65, 73, 86, 88, 216, 235
 natural pictorial/natural non-pictorial, 54, 58–59, 63
 non-natural/symbolic, 48–49, 52, 53, 61, 62, 63, 64, 65, 73, 90. *See also* Representations, symbolic
 perceptual access to cinematic meaning, 180–186. *See also* Perception
 relational theory of, 46
 and situations, 80. *See also* Situations
 unexpected/undesired, 106–107
 See also Interpretation
Medium awareness, 189, 190, 191
Mele, Al, 99, 100, 101, 102, 104
Méliès, Georges, 83
Memory, short-term, 189, 190, 191
Mental states/significance, 53, 118, 219, 224, 229, 234, 253, 256, 262. *See also* Psychological states
Metaphor. *See* Figuration
Methodology, 271, 272
Meyer, Nicholas, 169
Milgram, Stanley, 90, 216, 267–269, 273, 278(n27)

Index 299

Miller, Glenn, 171
Miller, Richard, 97(n13)
Mimesis, 44, 186. *See also* Resemblance
Minh-ha, Trinh T., 15–16, 43, 247
Models, 83–84, 92, 159, 166, 249
Moderate intentionality. *See* Non-fiction cinema, moderate intentionalist view of
Moore, Michael, 68–69, 105, 223
Morgentaler, Henry, 166
Morin, Edgar, 44, 273, 274, 280(n32)
Morris, Errol, 19, 122, 129, 262–267
Moser, Paul, 248
Motives, 99–100, 101, 102, 108, 109, 164–165, 250, 259, 267, 274
Müller-Lyer figure, 187, 195, 196
Myths, 230–231, 244(n22)

Nanook of the North (Flaherty), 40, 124–139, 146–147, 275–276
  lost footage, 127
  sealing sequence, 125, 135, 141(n22)
  walrus hunt sequence, 137, 138, 139, 141(n28)
Narration in the Fiction Film (Bordwell), 207(n7)
Narrative, 128, 130, 136, 137, 141(n17), 150, 190, 191, 249–250, 260, 262
  erotetic, 214, 242(n1)
  narrative structure, 263
  requirements for veridical documentary narrative, 264–265
Natural counterfactuality, 56
Natural external significance, 64, 65, 86, 90, 94, 95, 106. *See also* External significance
Nelson, Richard, 167
New Journalism, 160
Nichols, Bill, 5, 9, 23–24, 24–25, 38(n29), 77, 108, 120, 165, 167, 221, 247, 253, 257, 275, 277(n15), 279(n30)
Night and Fog (Resnais), 119, 235, 239–242, 245(n34), 264

Night of the Living Dead (Romero), 209(n24)
Nisbett, Richard, 279(n27)
Non-fiction cinema
  and aboutness condition, 9–10, 40–41, 74, 85, 153, 270, 275. *See also* Images, relation to actual world; Reality, relation to
  as constituting its objects, 261, 269–270
  defined, 1, 8, 9, 10, 11, 23, 24, 153, 163
  examples of content, 87–95
  fiction/non-fiction distinction, 1–2, 23, 27, 122, 143, 150, 151, 156, 164, 167, 228. *See also* Fiction
  hybrid form, 143–144, 148, 155, 157–158, 160, 162
  moderate intentionalist view of, 3, 99, 104–114, 116–119
  open concept of, 153. *See also* Family resemblance terms
  poetic, 16
  theory, 34, 35, 274
  typology concerning, 119–120
North by Northwest (Hitchcock), 113

Obedience (Milgram), 90–92, 97(n15), 216, 267–269, 273–274
Objectivity, 4, 8, 12, 272–273, 279(nn 30, 31)
Observational cinema, 120, 123
Olsen, Stein Haugom, 145, 146
Optical illusions, 187. *See also* Müller-Lyer figure

Paintings, 55, 56, 65, 198, 199
Participation Thesis, 149–150
Patterson, Roger, 9, 79, 93, 96(n4), 118, 273
Peacocke, Christopher, 54, 193
Peirce, C. S., 204
Pennebaker, D. A., 105, 106, 269
Perception, 3, 54, 55, 58, 66, 68, 149, 150, 175–206, 216, 217, 218, 254
  assumptions about, 226–227

cognitive, 176–177, 179, 183, 184, 185, 186, 204, 205, 225, 235, 236, 256
conventions concerning, 184–185
errors in, 184, 188, 198
and language, 178–179. *See also* Meaning, linguistic versus cinematic
naturalized mode of, 208(n14)
perceptual heuristics, 225–226, 255
primary/secondary, 179, 195, 205, 206, 225
seeing objects versus seeing facts, 201, 204–205
sensory versus cognitive, 176–177, 184, 195
See also Imagined seeing; Projective illusion
Perry, John, 47, 81–82
Person in the Situation, The: Perspectives of Social Psychology (Ross and Nisbett), 279(n27)
Philosophical Investigations (Wittgenstein), 150–151
PI. *See* Projective illusion
Plans, 92, 98–114, 105, 111, 112–114, 155, 165, 219, 223, 233, 234, 236, 242, 260, 270, 272
complex/mixed, 139, 157, 158–171, 192, 228, 232
and content, 117, 120, 122, 123, 130, 131, 133, 135, 139, 150, 273
incompleteness of, 120
long-term general, 126–127, 133
post-filmic, 121–122, 136
as representational content of intentions, 98–99
Type I/II, 120–123, 134, 234, 235, 252, 253, 257, 262, 266, 269, 274
updating, 133
Plantinga, Carl, 5, 15, 16, 26–29, 38(n36), 77, 79, 92, 150–151, 152, 153–154, 155, 221, 223, 233, 242(n1), 256, 279(n31)
Pleasure, 108
Pontecorvo, Gillo, 169

Portrayals, physical versus nominal, 71(n28)
Positivism, 271–272
Pot-Bouille (Zola), 96(n8)
Presence, 43, 44
Pretending, 194, 210(n29), 232, 265. *See also* Imagining
Problem solving, 178, 257
Projective illusion (PI), 186–191, 197, 209(n24)
Prototype theory, 152, 153, 155
Psychological states, 3, 116, 118, 188, 224, 248, 257, 258, 263. *See also* Mental states/significance; *under* Causality
Puzzle solving, 84

Rafferty, Kevin and Pierce, 123
Rashomon (Kurosawa), 150
Rationality, 7, 66, 98, 139, 187, 203, 225, 272
rationality constraint, 49, 52, 59, 116
rationality heuristic, 19, 218, 219, 223, 226, 258, 268
See also Reasoning
Realism, 6, 35, 108, 203, 204, 216, 223, 260, 261, 271, 276
anti-realists, 78–79, 97(n13), 222, 247
Reality, relation to, 124, 125, 136, 137, 139, 147, 167, 197, 198, 239, 240, 248, 251, 261, 264, 269, 270, 274. *See also* Images, relation to actual world; Non-fiction cinema, and aboutness condition
Reasoning, 3, 7, 98–99, 100, 111, 117, 120, 139, 155, 162, 163, 189, 215, 216, 234. *See also* Rationality
Reassemblage (Minh-ha), 15
Recognition, 201, 202, 203, 204, 205
Reflexive films, 25
Reich, Wilhelm, 160
Reich Propaganda Department, 69
Reiner, Rob, 168
Relativism, 256
Renov, Michael, 247, 261, 262, 269–270

Representations, 9, 24, 51–63, 108, 170, 176, 181, 199, 205, 248, 250, 266, 276
   defined/characterized, 45, 74–79
   misrepresentations, 47, 48, 49, 63–69, 94, 139, 187–188, 191, 195, 247, 249, 253, 261, 273. *See also* Deceptions; Hoaxes
   and natural meaning, 51
   natural versus artificial, 2, 48–49
   non-pictorial, 182
   problematizing, 261
   representational conventions, 13, 21
   representational systems, 22, 40–41, 42–51, 52, 53, 61, 66–67, 85, 217
   representation thesis, 198–199, 201–206
   senses of term "representation," 42–43
   symbolic, 48, 49, 269. *See also* Meaning(s), non-natural/symbolic
   See also Depictions
Reproductive illusion, 64
Resemblance, 44–45, 54, 187, 203, 252
   and perceptual similarity, 55–56
Resnais, Alain, 119, 239–242
Reversal of Fortune (Schroeder), 170
Riefenstahl, Leni, 34
Rivers, Joan, 169, 174(n38)
Roger and Me (Moore), 68–69, 105, 223
Romero, George, 209(n24)
Rosenthal, Alan, 162
Ross, Lee, 279(n27)
Rotha, Paul, 125
Rothman, William, 126, 239
Rouch, Jean, 121, 273, 274, 280(n32)
Ruby, Jay, 141(n18)
Rushes, 131

Salesman (Maysles and Zwerin), 236
Sasquatches, 79, 93, 94, 95, 96(n4), 118, 273
Schell, Maximillian, 111–112
School Daze (Lee), 25, 26
Schroeder, Barbet, 170

Scientism, 274
Scott, Oz, 169
Scruton, Roger, 145
Sculptures, 55
Semiology, 43. *See also* Signs
Sherman, Cindy, 185
Shot-reverse shots, 22, 190
Signs
   indexical, 50–51, 55
   natural, 41–42, 49–50, 50–51, 52
   non-identity with object, 43, 44
Sincerity, 32
Situations, 73, 74, 117, 118, 119, 269
   categories of, 82
   imaginary, 82–84, 92–93, 135, 137, 138, 139, 168, 170–171, 270, 273
   real, 82, 88–89, 139, 270
   static/dynamic, 80
   theory of situation semantics, 81–82
   typical, 82, 89–90
   See also Course of events
Smith, Roger, 105
Social constructions, 145
Social conventions, 27–28
Sofsky, Wolfgang, 241–242
Spectators. *See* Audiences
Speculation, 231
Speech acts
   constative, 13, 17, 20–21
   indirect illocutionary acts, 161–162
   as prohibitives, 16
   theory, 2, 20–21, 155, 161, 173(n30)
Spielberg, Steven, 9
Stefansson, Vilhjalmur, 125, 135
Stone, Oliver, 152, 228–233
   statements about *JFK*, 230–231, 244(nn 22, 26)
Style, 8, 119–120
Substitutions, 43–44, 192
Suggestives, 16
Surname Viet Given Name Nam (Minh-ha), 15
Symbolism, 135. *See also* Meaning(s), non-natural/symbolic; Representations, symbolic

Takes, 85, 96(n10)
Television, 87
  crime fiction, 23
  news, 17, 19, 33, 246, 273
  talk shows, 17, 53
Thin Blue Line, The (Morris), 19–20, 122, 175–176, 259–260, 262–267
This is Spinal Tap (Reiner), 168
Thomas, Anthony, 106
Thy Kingdom Come (Thomas), 106
Titicut Follies (Wiseman), 237–238, 252
Tourou et Bitti (Rouch), 121
Toy Story (Lasseter), 87
Trance and Dance in Bali (Bateson and Mead), 11–12, 13, 14–15, 228
Transparency, 211(n45). *See also under* Images
Trip to the Moon, A (Méliès), 83
Truth, 4, 6, 8, 18, 32, 41, 52, 83, 108, 146, 147, 214, 233–242, 246–276
  consensus theory of, 152
  as correspondence, 247–251, 264–265
  independence of, 250
  and models of reality, 249
  truth claims, 15–16, 25, 114(n14), 139, 153
  truth-seeking, 16, 17, 20, 166, 267, 271
Tversky, Amos, 278(n24)
Twentieth Century, The 279(n31)
Twenty Thousand Leagues under the Sea (Verne), 147
Twister (De Bont), 189–190

Ulmer, Edgar G., 262
Unobservables, 90–92, 97(n13)

Untitled Film Still #54 (Sherman), 185, 186

Van Fraassen, Bas, 97(n13)
Verne, Jules, 147
Vertov, Dziga, 78, 86
Vietnam: A Television History, 151
Visual-field properties, 54
Voice, 221, 223, 224, 242(n1)
Von Bulow, Claus, 170
Von Sternberg, Josef, 149)

Walton, Kendall, 144–145, 147, 149–150, 160, 163, 173(n30), 192–193, 194, 195, 197, 198, 209(n24), 210(n31)
War Game, The (Watkins), 92–93, 165–166, 167–168, 171, 249, 263
Warren Commission, 230, 231, 232
Watkins, Peter, 92, 165, 167, 168
Wells, Orson, 62–63
What is Cinema? (Bazin), 6
White, Hayden, 260–261, 269
Wilson, George, 210(n29)
Winston, Brian, 247, 274, 275
Wiseman, Frederick, 4–5, 25, 110, 120, 121, 123, 140(n2), 237, 245(n31)
Wittgenstein, Ludwig, 150–151, 152
WR: Mysteries of the Organism (Makavejev), 160, 161
Wrong Man, The (Hitchcock), 262

Yates, Peter, 148

Zola, Émile, 96(n8)
Zwerin, Charlotte, 107, 236
Zwigoff, Terry, 88, 89, 183